Time and Identity in *Ulysses* and the *Odyssey*

The Florida James Joyce Series

UNIVERSITY PRESS OF FLORIDA

Florida A&M University, Tallahassee
Florida Atlantic University, Boca Raton
Florida Gulf Coast University, Ft. Myers
Florida International University, Miami
Florida State University, Tallahassee
New College of Florida, Sarasota
University of Central Florida, Orlando
University of Florida, Gainesville
University of North Florida, Jacksonville
University of South Florida, Tampa
University of West Florida, Pensacola

Time and Identity in *Ulysses* and the *Odyssey*

STEPHANIE NELSON

Foreword by Sebastian D. G. Knowles

UNIVERSITY PRESS OF FLORIDA

Gainesville · Tallahassee · Tampa · Boca Raton
Pensacola · Orlando · Miami · Jacksonville · Ft. Myers · Sarasota

Cover: Frank Budgen describes Joyce quizzing him on what Penelope was thinking about, pointing to a picture of the statue he had in his Zurich flat. Joyce's idea was that she was trying to recollect what Odysseus looked like because he had been gone many years and they had no photographs in those days (Budgen, *Making of "Ulysses,"* 188).

27 26 25 24 23 22   6 5 4 3 2 1

Library of Congress Cataloging-in-Publication Data
Names: Nelson, Stephanie A. (Stephanie Anne), 1958– author. | Knowles, Sebastian D. G. (Sebastian David Guy), author of foreword.
Title: Time and identity in Ulysses and the Odyssey / Stephanie Nelson ; foreword by Sebastian D.G. Knowles.
Other titles: Florida James Joyce series.
Description: Gainesville : University Press of Florida, [2022] | Series: The Florida James Joyce series | Includes bibliographical references and index. | Summary: "A unique in-depth comparative study of two classic literary works, this volume examines essential themes in James Joyce's Ulysses and Homer's Odyssey, showing how each work highlights and clarifies aspects of the other"— Provided by publisher.
Identifiers: LCCN 2021052463 (print) | LCCN 2021052464 (ebook) | ISBN 9780813069357 (hardback) | ISBN 9780813070155 (pdf)
Subjects: LCSH: Joyce, James, 1882–1941. Ulysses. | Homer. Odyssey. | Time in literature. | Identity (Philosophical concept) in literature. | BISAC: LITERARY CRITICISM / Modern / 20th Century | LITERARY CRITICISM / Ancient & Classical
Classification: LCC PR6019.O9 U68455 2022 (print) | LCC PR6019.O9 (ebook) | DDC 823/.912—dc23/eng/20211110
LC record available at https://lccn.loc.gov/2021052463
LC ebook record available at https://lccn.loc.gov/2021052464

The University Press of Florida is the scholarly publishing agency for the State University System of Florida, comprising Florida A&M University, Florida Atlantic University, Florida Gulf Coast University, Florida International University, Florida State University, New College of Florida, University of Central Florida, University of Florida, University of North Florida, University of South Florida, and University of West Florida.

University Press of Florida
2046 NE Waldo Road
Suite 2100
Gainesville, FL 32609
http://upress.ufl.edu

For my parents

Contents

Foreword

There are times when Homer sounds astonishingly like Joyce. Take Nausicaa for instance: when the noble Odysseus comes out of the bushes to meet the Phaeacian princess, he covers his genitals with a tree branch. This is perhaps the Homeric equivalent of the "clinging twig" that Kitty removes before Father Conmee as she emerges in "Wandering Rocks": "the young woman abruptly bent and with slow care detached from her light skirt a clinging twig" (*U* 10.201–2). But let us look at Odysseus's branch more closely:

ὣς εἰπὼν θάμνω ὑπεδύσετο δῖος Ὀδυσσεύς,
ἐκ πυκινῆς δ' ὕλης πτόρθον κλάσε χειρὶ παχείη
φύλλων, ὡς ῥύσαιτο περὶ χροῒ μήδεα φωτός. (*Odyssey* 6.126–29)

Thus speaking, noble Odysseus came out of the bushes.
From the dense wood he broke with his fat hand a leafy sapling
So that he might shield his male organs, holding it around his body.

Since Odysseus is appearing before the lovely Nausicaa and her maids, he has to hide his μήδεα, as you generally would in this situation. For clarity's sake, Homer establishes that these are the genitals of a man: μήδεα φωτός. And what is the item, you may ask, with which he shields himself? A leafy sapling from the dense wood (πυκινῆς δ' ὕλης). You cannot tell me that the Greeks around the fire didn't laugh long and hard at that one. Just to make the joke even more Joycean, the Greek word for "wood" is ὕλη, from which we get *Ulysses*. See the wheeze?

Stephanie Nelson shows us the Homer we have been missing. Too often in *Ulysses*, Nelson rightly says, the sight gags and swift allusions serve to undermine Homer's real importance to Joyce, undermining through trivial correspondence what is a deep and shared sense of comedy and character. Again and again, Nelson looks at the three main characters in Homer's epic and the three main characters in Joyce's novel with fresh eyes, making us see things we never saw before. In focusing on the human element in the

Odyssey, we see what was there all along. By turns playful and scholarly, the author takes us through the dense thickets of Homeric scholarship to reveal the ὕλη underneath.

Sebastian D. G. Knowles
Series Editor

Acknowledgments

First and foremost I would like to thank Fritz Senn, who has brought so many, sometimes unexpectedly, to Joyce. Without the welcoming and open atmosphere of the Zurich James Joyce Foundation and his Joyce Workshops, I could never have written this book. It is a rare venue that can bring together so many different people, coming from so many different places (in all senses of the word) and all working toward their own independent understanding, here of Joyce. In the midst of Stephen's "dead breaths I living breathe" Fritz breathes new life into academia, and I have been a great beneficiary.

Thanks also to Fritz, I know many of my wonderful Joycean friends, Sabrina Alonso, Bill Brock, Tim Conley, Sophie Corser, Leah Flack, Frances Ilmberger, Vicki Mahaffey, Jolanta Wawrzycka, and particularly Clive Hart, may he rest in peace. Barry Spence has also been a wonderful fellow sojourner on my Joycean road. I owe an inestimable debt to you all and to the whole Joycean community for so kindly welcoming in a stranger. Ruth Frehner, Ursula Zeller, and everyone I have encountered at the Zurich James Joyce Foundation have exemplified this welcome.

I would also like to single out for thanks the University Press of Florida: the series editor, Sebastian Knowles; my acquisitions editor, Stephanye Hunter; my copyeditor, Beth Detwiler; and the quite wonderful readers who reviewed the manuscript. I have seldom encountered such attention, diligence, and generosity. They have all made what can be a painful process a complete pleasure. The series editor and the readers will also note many, many occasions where I have benefitted from their suggestions and borrowed their ideas. These rapidly became too numerous to footnote, so I would like to acknowledge here this particular resort to "stolentelling" and express my deep-felt thanks for their care and attention.

My thanks go as well to my friends and colleagues at Boston University who, as I pressed Joyce upon them, have practiced the lesson of the *Wake*'s Anna Livia Plurabelle: "patience; and remember patience is the great thing, and above all things else we must avoid anything like being or becoming out of patience." These include Herb Golder, Brandon Jones, Brian Jorgensen, Jay Samons, Steve Scully, David Roochnik, Ann Vasaly and Rich Young, Diana Wylie, and in addition and as always, my great friends Mark Wielga, Louis Petrich, and Jon Tuck.

Finally, I would like to thank my family, my stepmother Dirane Kelekyan, my brother James, sister-in-law Lisa, and nieces and nephews (my niblings) Ellie (and family), Nathaniel, Jonathan, and Abbey. In particular, as in my dedication, this seemed, of all books, the one to dedicate to my parents. I am very grateful for what you all have made me.

Abbreviations

CW	James Joyce, *Critical Writings,* edited by Ellsworth Mason and Richard Ellmann (Ithaca, NY: Cornell University Press, 1989)
FW	James Joyce, *Finnegans Wake* (New York: Penguin, 1999)
JJ	Richard Ellmann, *James Joyce.* New edition (New York: Oxford University Press, 1982)
LI, LII, LIII	James Joyce, *The Letters of James Joyce,* edited by Stuart Gilbert (vol. 1) and Richard Ellmann (vols. 2–3) (New York: Viking, 1957–66)
OCPW	James Joyce, *Occasional, Critical, and Political Writing,* edited by Kevin Barry (Oxford: Oxford World's Classics, 2000)
P	James Joyce, *A Portrait of the Artist as a Young Man,* edited by Chester Anderson (New York: Viking, 1968)
SH	James Joyce, *Stephen Hero,* edited by Theodore Spencer. Revised with foreword by John J. Slocum and Herbert Cahoon. Expanded edition (New York: New Directions, 1963)
SL	James Joyce, *The Selected Letters of James Joyce,* edited by Richard Ellmann (London: Faber and Faber, 1975)
U	James Joyce, *Ulysses,* edited by Hans Walter Gabler et al. (New York: Random House, 1986)

Introduction

Joyce and Homer

When Penelope sets her test, saying that she will marry the man who can draw Odysseus's bow (19.571–81), it is a real test. Whether Penelope has recognized Odysseus or not, neither know if the man of, say, forty-five, after many hardships, can still perform the feat that was his trademark twenty years before. For the suitors (and Telemachus) the challenge is to see if they can match up to Odysseus. But a similar challenge exists for Odysseus himself: is he the man he once was? In what sense is the worn veteran the same as the young warrior who set out for Troy, leaving a young wife and infant son behind?[1]

It is not an abstruse question, and James Joyce did not need to be a scholar of Classical Greek to see it. He had already explored the constant change of an emerging self in *A Portrait of the Artist as a Young Man* and the *Odyssey*'s depiction of Odysseus as himself a kind of artist would only encourage the interest. In any case, Leopold Bloom has a concern very like Odysseus's:

> I was happier then. Or was that I? Or am I now I? Twentyeight I was. She twentythree. When we left Lombard street west something changed. Could never like it again after Rudy. Can't bring back time. Like holding water in your hand. Would you go back to then? (*U* 8.608–11)

Similarly for Telemachus and Stephen Dedalus, for Penelope and Molly Bloom, and even for the gods of the *Odyssey* and the various narrative styles of *Ulysses*, the prime question will be how to reconcile change and identity.

Since the need for a book on the relation of the *Odyssey* and *Ulysses* might not be obvious, I should explain. This book is a comparison of the *Odyssey* and *Ulysses,* not a study of how Joyce used Homer, which has been examined by numerous scholars.[2] I do not believe there is any one way in which Joyce used Homer; rather, *Ulysses* uses the *Odyssey* in as many ways as *Finnegans Wake* uses Tim Finnegan.[3] More importantly, however, I intend a thematic comparison, a study of a specific concern that, I believe, lies at the heart of both works: the challenge of identity within the constant flux of time. Many links between the works, often superficial, have been duly noted. But while it is fun to hunt out where Nausicaa's laundry shows up in *Ulysses* (and Joyce was most certainly not beyond fun), that is not all there is.

Scholars have looked extensively at both *Ulysses*'s and the *Odyssey*'s interest in time, memory, and identity. That there has been no full-length study of the two together seems due to a number of factors, some incidental, some intrinsic to scholarship. In the first place, scholars necessarily hesitate to step outside of their area of expertise, a step that is inevitable when treating two authors as different (and with as fully developed scholarly industries) as Homer and Joyce. Moreover, and perhaps surprisingly, Joyce's deliberate allusions can serve more to undercut than to reinforce the connection between the works. This is true both of the humorous references scattered throughout and of the Homeric correspondences that Joyce drew up for Carlo Linati and Stuart Gilbert (the Linati and Gilbert "schemas"[4]). The differences between the schemas suggest that neither is definitive, and while the allusions create both humor and an important leitmotif, a critic can track down only so many laundry baskets before feeling an urge to turn to more substantial matters.[5]

Even more insidiously, Joyce's superficial play with Homer seems, with some important exceptions, to have blinded scholars to the thematic relationship between the works.[6] This is not entirely the scholars' fault. Joyce was as fond of red herrings as he was of riddles and puns, all of which simultaneously invite readers in and keep them at arm's length.[7] So, for example, Joyce used Homeric names for his episodes, both in his notes and with friends, but did not include the titles "Telemachus," "Nestor," etcetera, in the published text.[8] In some ways he even had this relation to Homer himself, in that, while he supplemented his excellent Latin, Italian, and French with Modern Greek and Dano-Norwegian (to read Henrik Ibsen), he remained content with only deciphering the classical language.[9]

This book, then, compares two works concerned with similar themes. As Percy Bysshe Shelley put it in his *Defense of Poetry*—a work cited by both Joyce and Stephen Dedalus—"The plant must spring from its seed or it will bear no flower."[10] The comparison brings out numerous places where *Ulysses* reflects, plays with, opposes, or rewrites Homer, and, as Fritz Senn has often pointed out, vice versa. Just as the *Odyssey* helps us think through *Ulysses*, so *Ulysses* brings out aspects of the *Odyssey* that many layers of interpretive varnish have obscured.[11] *Ulysses* clearly is not about the reunion of a brave hero, a stalwart son, and a chaste and patient wife. With its help, we can see that neither is the *Odyssey*, which is probably why Joyce was drawn to it.[12]

Finally, a comparison of *Ulysses* and the *Odyssey* sheds additional light on both epic poetry and the modernist novel. Modernist writers, it seems, were not the first to pay attention to the banal incidents of everyday life or to track the individual, subjective sense of time passing. And on the other side, Joyce's intense concern with the interaction of text and reader recalls something too easily forgotten: Homer's direct oral interaction with his audience, both in light of what is commonly termed "reader-response theory" and in making us remember that Homer's audience were not readers.

HOMERIC ISSUES AND JOYCEAN CONCERNS

Throughout this book I use "Homer" simply as shorthand for the poet of the *Odyssey*, not unlike Stephen's "Rutlandbaconsouthamptonshakespeare or another poet of the same name" (*U* 9.866). I do not know if the poet of the *Odyssey* also composed the *Iliad*, nor do I know that there was a single defining poet. I certainly know nothing else about him (or her, according to Samuel Butler). For my purposes here, I do not believe it matters. What does seem clear, as will be explored in chapter 1, is that both the *Iliad* and *Odyssey* emerged from a long oral tradition. This tradition stretched from the fall of the Mycenaean civilization (and possible fall of Troy) in the thirteenth century, through the loss of literacy and contraction of society that followed, to the regaining of literacy and the beginnings of the polis in the Archaic Age, around the eighth century.[13] The tradition gave rise to a *kunstsprache* (or artificial language) composed of a variety of Greek dialects, whose formulae allowed for spontaneous oral composition.[14] Thus, the *Iliad* and the *Odyssey*, Hesiod's (or the Hesiodic) *Theogony* and *Works and Days* and the Homeric Hymns, as well as the poems of the lost epic cycle, share a common diction, including epithets, set scenes, similes, and given characters. The poet is perfectly capable of crafting the poem, but what he shapes is an epic tradition with its own independent reality.

Although the developing interest in oral tradition, not only in the case of Greek epic but also contemporary and worldwide, has somewhat stilled the controversy, Unitarian Homeric critics, who look to a single poet (either of both the *Iliad* and *Odyssey* or a single poet for each) still argue with Ana lytic critics, who believe that the poems grew out of the tradition without the need for a single shaping voice.[15] While Joyce did not have access to Milman Parry's work on orality, the same issues were open to him, beginning from Friedrich Wolf's 1795 claim that, lacking writing, the Homeric poems must have grown out of a loose collection of rhapsodes' songs.[16] Butler, a favorite of Joyce's, saw this "Wolfian heresy" as responsible for the questioning of Shakespeare's identity as well—and responded by "proving" that the *Odyssey* was composed by a young Sicilian princess who included herself as Nausicaa.[17] As it happens, the question of authorship, though in a rather different form, goes to the heart of this book, which suggests that not only Homer, but all of us, are in some sense both one and many. James Joyce, after all, was an actual person, and yet he changed radically over time and contained multitudes.

Just as we do not know if there was a Homer, we do not know how or why the *Odyssey* was written down or where its book divisions came from. Since the twenty-four books of the poem correspond to the twenty-four-letter version of the Greek alphabet, the division seems connected to writing, but more than that we cannot say. The poem as we have it falls into two distinct halves, with Odysseus's return to Ithaca occurring at exactly the midpoint, and each of the halves falling into three clear divisions:

Bks. 1–4: the Telemachia   Bks. 13–16: Eumaeus's hut
Bks. 5–8: Calypso to Phaeacia   Bks. 17–20: from Eumaeus to the palace
Bks. 9–12: the Wanderings   Bks. 21–24: the palace and Penelope

Tempting as it can be to attribute significance to the very neat divisions, for our purposes the arrangement matters mostly because Joyce played with this structure in putting together *Ulysses*.

Finally, in regard to terminology, I refer to "Calypso's island" rather than "Ogygia," and "Phaeacia" rather than "Scheria" (which is Homer's term), purely for the sake of simplicity. In a more significant case, I also periodically substitute "mythic/heroic world" for "mythic/heroic time," and similarly, "human/ordinary world" for "human/ordinary time." Apart from simply varying the phrases, the substitution points out that the sorts of time Homer deals with are what Mikhail Bakhtin termed "chronotopes" or, in Einsteinian relativity, "spacetime": time as formulating a distinct order of the cosmos rather than as an arbitrary measure.[18] Much the same is true of Joyce's use of inner, experiential, and outer clocktime (although references to an "inner" and "outer" world have not generally seemed necessary).

Like the *Odyssey*, *Ulysses* has its own language, including the use of dashes in place of quotation marks and Joyce's refusal to allow periods at the end of "Mr" etcetera. I refer to chapters (or "episodes") by the Homeric names that Joyce used with friends and mark these with quotation marks, so that "Cyclops," for example, is the twelfth episode in *Ulysses*, not the giant blinded by Odysseus. I similarly use quotation marks for the three major divisions of the novel, the "Telemachia," "Wanderings," and "Nostos" (or homecoming), as Joyce called them (*LI* 113, 145).

In many cases I have adopted what has become conventional terminology among Joyceans, hence "initial style"[19] for the narrative mode of the first part (chaps. 1–9), and "gigantisms" for the interludes in the "Cyclops" episode. As I wish to emphasize the multiplicity of the styles that Joyce uses in the second part of the novel, I largely avoid referring to a singular "Arranger" responsible for the variations, although I do use this terminology in the final chapter for reasons that will be obvious there.[20] In other cases, where the nomenclature can be misleading, as with the "headlines" that punctuate "Aeolus," I try to use more neutral terms, such as "headers." Just as Ithaca appeared strange to Odysseus after twenty years away, *Ulysses* makes us see the familiar with new eyes. In this light I try not to inadvertently decide what something is in the process of naming it.

Ulysses, like the *Odyssey*, has a very deliberate structure, which I have summarized in the appendix for convenience. However the twenty-four-book division of the *Iliad* and *Odyssey* came about, it soon entered the tradition, so that Virgil composed the *Aeneid* in twelve books, followed by John Milton, who rearranged the original ten books of *Paradise Lost* into twelve. Never to be outdone, Joyce split the difference and composed *Ulysses* in eighteen episodes. As in the *Odyssey*, there is a distinct break half-way through, here after the ninth episode, "Scylla and Charybdis." Joyce marked this location on a fair copy of one of the manuscripts by writing: "New Year's Eve, 1918 / End of First Part of *Ulysses*" (*JJ* 442n) and on the Linati schema with "Central point—umbilicus" (or "Punto Centrale—

Ombelico," since Joyce wrote the schema in Italian).[21] It is at this point that what Joyce termed the "initial style," a combination of third-person narration and interior monologue, definitively gives way to the widely different narrative styles of the second part. Here also the episodes get progressively longer.[22] The "first" and "second parts" of the novel refer, accordingly, to episodes 1–9 and 10–18, not to a page count.

Joyce picked Odysseus as his "favorite hero" while still a schoolboy (*JJ* 46; *U* 17.644) and studied the *Aeneid* as a key part of his Latin course.[23] Since his aim was to compose the great English epic, he also could not ignore Milton. His true love, however, was Dante, to the extent of choosing the "feminine" study of Italian at university over the properly masculine study of Classics.[24] And so, as *The Divine Comedy* is organized in threes (though the three poems of, respectively, 34, 33, and 33 cantos also make a perfect 100), *Ulysses* has a tripartite structure, along with its binary division. Here, however, the structure forms a tryptic like a medieval altar painting: marked in the original edition with roman numerals, the "Telemachia" (episodes 1–3), the "Wanderings" (4–15), and the "Nostos" (16–18) make a neat 3–12–3 pattern. Dante would be proud.[25]

As we will see throughout, Joyce makes extensive use of the structure of *Ulysses* and not least as a way of organizing the novel's narrative time. As he spelled out on the schemas, each episode represents one hour of June 16, 1904, the day on which the novel is set and which is now traditionally referred to as Bloomsday.[26] The three episodes of the "Telemachia" thus cover 8:00 a.m., 10:00 a.m., and 11:00 a.m. in Stephen Dedalus's day (in the Gilbert schema), at which point the novel doubles back to cover Bloom's day in "Calypso" (8:00 a.m.), "Lotus Eaters" (10:00 a.m.), and "Hades" (11:00 a.m.). With some gaps, the episodes progress continually, hour by hour from there, just as Homeric time always progresses. The structure enables Joyce to reinforce the tryptic arrangement by repeating the morning hours and also to place the transition from the second to the third section, "Wandering" to "Nostos," at midnight. It also allows him to put the midpoint of the novel at 4:00 p.m.: the time when Bloom's wife, Molly, will start an affair with Blazes Boylan. The hour, critical to Bloom, thus marks a major shift in everything else in the novel as well.

Despite the publicity generated over the various editions of *Ulysses*, the question is not crucial for the nonspecialist. Any reputable edition will work for the purposes of this book, although references are to the Hans Gabler edition (1986), primarily because of the convenience of the marginal line numbers.[27] Using episode-line number format then, "11.950" refers to line 950 in the eleventh episode, "Sirens"; and when ambiguous, the reference to *Ulysses* appears as "*U* 11.950." In an ideal world, a reader would approach *Ulysses* as we all approach life: we come to see the patterns and the importance of things through experience and wonder, not because they come to us pre-labeled. But this is not always an ideal world, so one of the many helps available—such as this outline for example—may be useful.[28]

Finally, I should note here that since I hope this book will be useful to both Classicists with an interest in reception but with no expertise in Joyce and to Joyceans with an interest in Homer but without a background in Classics, I have been liberal in including text references to both works. My endnotes, also, include references for Homer that may seem very basic to Classicists, and references for *Ulysses* that may seem the same to Joyceans. Moreover, as a Classicist by profession, I have no problems with citing older scholarship, although I apologize that the sheer bulk of critical works on Homer and Joyce has limited my citations largely to works in English. I hope these will supply further places to look for readers intrigued by, but perhaps unfamiliar with, any given topic touched on here.

THE EPIC TRADITION

"Scylla and Charybdis," where Stephen performs his Shakespeare piece, includes the remark that "our national epic has yet to be written" (9.309). The observation is suggestive, particularly since the episode also contains *Ulysses*'s only explicit references to Homer, in Russell's "The rarefied air of the academy and the arena produce the sixshilling novel, the musichall song . . . but the desirable life is revealed only to the poor of heart, the life of Homer's Phaeacians" (9.107–10) and Mulligan's spoof of William Butler Yeats on Lady Gregory: "The most beautiful book that has come out of our country in my time. One thinks of Homer" (9.1164–65). As we will see in chapter 2, the episode is also studded with hints that Stephen will grow up to become Joyce, and so the author of the scene.

The point seems pretty clear. Like Homer (who both founded and defined Greek culture), Shakespeare (who largely created modern English), Virgil (9.454, 1124), Dante (9.34, 86–88, 285–86, 831), and Milton (9.18–19, 32–33, 873, 954), Joyce is writing his nation's epic.[29] Like Milton, Dante, and Virgil's Aeneas, he will do so in defeat and apparent exile. And like William Shakespeare (and Homer), by joining an epic tradition, he will become "the father of all his race" (9.868–89), achieving what he aspired to in the last lines of *Portrait*: "to forge in the smithy of my soul the uncreated conscience of my race" (253).

As with everything in Joyce, things prove rather more complicated. Joyce tempts us to see Stephen as his young self, just as he tempts us, through his inclusion of actual people and events, to see the Dublin of Bloomsday as purely historical. Neither is simply the case, and the same holds for *Ulysses* and the epic tradition. This is not so much because *Ulysses* is not an epic, as because there is really no such tradition.[30] As we will see, Milton refers back to Dante, and Dante to Virgil, and Virgil to Homer, and *Ulysses* (like Shakespeare) to them all. But the literary world Joyce enters into has many other facets as well, Ovid, Ossian, a bevy of medieval theologians and heretics, *Titbits*, Friedrich Nietzsche, Aristotle, music hall artists, and advertising jingles. Joyce is nothing if not eclectic. The "epic tradition" we consider here is thus merely a particular line that Joyce and many others absorbed as schoolboys. As far as *Ulysses* is concerned, the tradition, like Martello Tower or Trinity College or Joyce's bad eyesight, is just there. What Joyce does with it is what is interesting.

I

Time in Joyce and Homer

Very early in *Ulysses*, Stephen considers the problem of how identity persists over time: "So I carried the boat of incense then at Clongowes. I am another now and yet the same" (*U* 310–12). As we have seen, Bloom contemplates the same question: "Or was that I? Or am I now I?" (*U* 8.608). He, however, has a less positive spin:[1]

> Wildly I lay on her, kissed her: eyes, her lips, her stretched neck beating, woman's breasts full in her blouse of nun's veiling, fat nipples upright. Hot I tongued her. She kissed me. I was kissed. All yielding she tossed my hair. Kissed, she kissed me.
> Me. And me now.
> Stuck, the flies buzzed. (8.913–18)

In a very simple sense, this is also the issue of the *Odyssey*: how can you return to the past? How is the person who returns after twenty years the same as the person who left?[2] Homeric characters are not as prone to philosophic musings as Joycean ones, but in the *Odyssey*, as in *Ulysses*, the question of identity centers on the problem of time.[3]

François Hartog's exploration of different modes of viewing time opens with Odysseus weeping at Demodocus's songs of Troy. Hartog, who describes "historicity" as "this primary experience of *estrangement*, of distance between self and self, to which the categories of past, present and future give order and meaning, enabling it to be grasped and expressed," argues that what lies behind Odysseus's tears is the disconnect between the self he was and the self he is now. He is "suddenly confronted with his inability to link his previous identity as the glorious victor of Troy to his present one as a shipwrecked and destitute castaway who has lost everything, right down to his own name. What he lacks is precisely the category of the past through which he could recognize himself in that other who is nonetheless himself."[4]

The complete break between past and present that Odysseus experiences also marks the distinction between mythic and ordinary time.[5] This division is common in epic: between the heroes who are the objects of song,—who lived in the distant and unfamiliar world of the Mycenaean kings,—and the real men and women of the audience who listen to that song.[6] As Hartog puts it, "for the epic to function as such, one essential condition must be fulfilled: the "others" must change into "men of former times," that is, a gap must open up between "past" and "future." "The contract underlying the epic poem is that as soon as a bard starts singing, a break occurs, and the *klea andron* [famous deeds of men] are transformed into the glorious deeds of "men of former times," those who came before (*proteroi*)."[7] Thus, in Phaeacia, as Demodocus sings the famous deeds of Odysseus (8.75, 499–520), he creates a division in Odysseus himself between the hero of mythic time and the man hearing the stories.[8]

The paradox of the *Odyssey* is that Homer not only reinforces the division between the mythic and the ordinary, he also breaks it. As a man of former time, "Odysseus should be dead—yet there he stands."[9] In fact, Odysseus's task, in many ways, will be precisely to breach the distinction between mythic and ordinary time. His movement from Calypso's island to Ithaca, from an offer of unaging immortality to a wife and child who have, in his absence, been through twenty years of change, is in this sense a movement from myth into real life. Phrased in those terms, it is perhaps not surprising that he desires the move.

*   *   *

Ulysses moves in the opposite direction, not from the mythic to the ordinary, but from being an intensely realistic Modernist novel whose focus is precisely the ordinary, to a verbal mythologizing that makes the first part of the novel seem almost mundane. As the novel moves from realism into its varied narrative styles a division it has established, between internal and external time, begins to dissolve, most obviously in what Joyce called (in his Linati schema) a "fusion" of Bloom and Stephen.[10] The initial distinction, common in Modernism, between time as it is experienced and "clocktime," encouraged us to seek identity in the inner experience of the characters.[11] As the various styles of the second part take over, and the experience of one character begins to appear in the thoughts of another, identity becomes more complicated.[12] But although no longer expressed in the contrast of inner and outer, the issue of identity persists. It is just that while Homer moved into a world unusual for epic, the ordinary, Joyce moves into one at least as unusual for the novel—a realm outside of ordinary time.

Joyce emphasizes his particular use of time both by reversing the movement of the *Odyssey* and by having the second part of *Ulysses* repeat the first. Here, too, he reflects Homer. Just as Odysseus's Wanderings are essentially episodic, *Ulysses's* second part moves outside of ordinary narrative time and into vignettes, most vividly in elements like the interpolations of "Cyclops" or the question-answer format of "Ithaca." And as the Wanderings are structured in rings and doublings, Circe and Calypso, the Cyclops and the Lestrygonians, the departing from and returning to Circe's island, so also episodes such as "Oxen of the Sun," "Circe," "Ithaca," and "Penelope" recapitulate the events of the novel's first half, as, in the novel's pet phrase, a "retrospective sort of arrangement."[13] As in the *Odyssey*, the change shows us identity under a very different aspect of time.

In both cases the move also further complicates the distinction between kinds of time. In Joyce this happens as the various narrative styles break down the division between the inner and the outer. A similar thing happens in the *Odyssey*, and not only in Odysseus's breach of the barrier between mythic and ordinary time. Odysseus's return to Ithaca has generally been seen as a rejection of a life without *kleos*, or "fame." This answer can only be partial, since a hero seeks *kleos* exactly because he cannot have immortality.[14] Nonetheless, the point reminds us of the irony of the poem. In fighting his way out of the fixed world of myth, Odysseus gains *kleos*, and so becomes once more the subject of song. The poem thus returns back upon itself, just as *Ulysses's* move outside of narrative time will return us, in "Penelope," to a different sort of timelessness.

HOMER'S KINDS OF TIME: MYTHIC AND ORDINARY

It is not surprising that the *Odyssey* does not share Joyce's concern with the difference between clocktime and time as it is experienced. Homer, after all, had no clocks. The distinctions he employs, however, are as complex as Joyce's. Homeric time, for example, always moves forward. There are no flashbacks (the Wanderings being told completely within narrative time) and, although Homer plays with the possibility, extremely few simultaneous events.[15] Alongside this, however, the convention of Homeric similes allows the poet to frame mini-narratives that exist completely outside of the world of the poem. "Reverse similes" allow the poet to identify one character's experience with another, just as Joyce does in "fusing" Stephen and Bloom. Similes of the natural world introduce a timeless element: lions will always seek prey (4.335–40; 6.130–35) although Odysseus will encounter the suitors and Nausicaa only once.[16] And, as we will see, objects in Homer also carry their past history along with them, setting them against the steady stream of Homeric narrative.

The most important of Homer's time distinctions, however, divides the epic heroes of old from the audience of Homer's poem. As in the persistent refrain of Iliadic heroes, hurling a rock "such that it would take two men, as men are now, to carry" (*Iliad* 20.286 etc.; *Odyssey* 8.221–24), the time of the Homeric heroes is not "our" time—even back when "our" time was that of archaic Greece. In the *Odyssey* Homer takes this one step further, by associating Ithaca with his own time and the epic world of the heroes with the magic, fairy-tale world of the Wanderings. He is aided by the gap of five hundred years between the historical events the tradition describes and his own time. During this time, between the great Mycenaean kings and the Archaic Age, trade shrank, culture declined, writing was lost. Homer thus lived in a world very different, and much smaller, than the one he sang of. The resulting discontinuity, which runs throughout Greek epic, becomes thematic in the *Odyssey*.

The first half of the *Odyssey* is peopled by nymphs, witches, and giants, while the second half features an old nursemaid and a pig-keeper. The contrast is a stark one. In the world of Odysseus's adventures, gods involve themselves in human affairs. Ithaca is rather less glorious. Here, as in the limited communities of Hesiod's *Works and Days,* composed in the same tradition and not long after the Homeric poems, men cope with theft and laziness, not the fall of civilizations. Like Hesiod's "hero," a farmer, not a warrior, Odysseus, once returned, suggests challenging the nobles in Ithaca to a plowing contest (18.366), while the king's father has retired to become a gardener, hoeing his plants in a grimy tunic (24.227).

In this way, Homer uses the gap between the heroic "old days" of the Trojan War and his own time to create a sense of two different worlds. The difference reveals the challenge of peace to one whose manhood was spent in war, a side of Odysseus that Joyce was very interested in. It also serves as a critique of heroism. The great and ancient times of the heroes involve monumental culture, Cretan palaces, extensive trade, war chariots, and piles of gold and silver. But in the *Odyssey,* that ancient time can also seem static and purely self-referential, while Ithaca, where a mangy dog lies on a heap of dung in the courtyard of the palace, becomes the goal Odysseus struggles to reach. As Joyce put it in his early essay, "Drama and Life": "It is a sinful foolishness to sigh back for the good old times, to feed the hunger of us with the cold stones they afford. Life we must accept as we see it before our eyes, men and women as we meet them in the real world, not as we apprehend them in the world of faery" (*OCPW* 28).

The Heroic and Magical versus Ithaca, the Ordinary

Telemachus's journey in the first four books of the *Odyssey* mirrors Odysseus's wanderings, not least in that both introduce their protagonist to a very different world: Odysseus to the magic world of adventures and Telemachus to the world of heroes. The comparison also links these two different kinds of mythic time. As their tales of Troy make clear, Nestor, Menelaus, and Helen are of the Iliadic world of the heroes, while the magical adventures seem to have been constructed out of folktale.[17] As one scholar has put it, Odysseus during his adventures seems less like the great warrior Achilles than like Sinbad the Sailor.[18] Homer, however, goes out of his way to connect the two, and in so doing further emphasizes the ordinariness of Ithaca.

A link between the heroic and the magical first becomes evident in Telemachus's visit to Menelaus, where we learn of Helen acquiring magical drugs in exotic Egypt, Menelaus's future existence in Elysium, his tale of struggling with Proteus, and Odysseus's entrapment by Calypso. Telemachus thus becomes the vehicle for two kinds of linking: as he encounters the heroes of old, the audience sees the heroic world through the eyes of the ordinary, while at the same time a connection is made between heroic time and the magical time that Odysseus inhabits. This is then reinforced in Book 11 when, in the midst of the adventures, Odysseus describes encountering Helen's mother, Leda, in Hades (11.295), and we hear another account of Agamemnon's death (3.255 ff.; 4.517 ff.; 11.405 ff.), and yet more reminiscences of Troy.[19] Most significantly, however, Odysseus's stay in Phaeacia, a halfway house between the adventures and ordinary life, reinforces the connection between the magical and the heroic.[20]

Phaeacia conflates the heroic and the world of the adventures largely through its indeterminacy. Zeus declares that Odysseus will be conveyed home by "neither gods nor mortal men" (5.32) but rather by the Phaeacians (5.31–42, 286–90, 345), a people both magical and human. The princess shyly avoids talking about marriage and takes a mule-cart to do the laundry (6.56–70), but the ships also steer themselves, achieving the longest of journeys in a few hours (7.34; 8.555 ff.). As part of the magical world, the Phaeacians once neighbored the Cyclopes (6.2 ff.); Alcinous marries his niece just as Aeolus marries his sons to his daughters (10.5 ff.; 7.63 ff.); and the gardens, whose fruits ripen year-round, resemble Calypso's (5.63 ff.; 7.114 ff.). But Odysseus's stay also emphasizes the heroic. Two of Demodocus's songs are of Troy, and the other displays a comic side to the gods that recalls Hera's seduction of Zeus in the *Iliad* (8.266 ff.; *Iliad* 14.153 ff.). Odysseus's honor is challenged at games reminiscent of those in *Iliad* 23, and gifts complete the scene, as commonly in the *Iliad* (8.400 ff.; *Iliad* 6.230–36; 7.299–305; 23.555–65, 586–623, 795–97). Alcinous asks about Odysseus's heroic companions (11.371–72), and, as we have seen, it is here that Odysseus experiences most vividly the disjunction between his past heroic self and the ragged beggar he is about to become in Ithaca.

Ithaca, in contrast, shares neither the magic of Odysseus's adventures nor the Bronze-Age splendor of the heroic. As Robin Osborne points out, "The palaces, the silver bath tubs, the chariots of war, the exotic armour, the treatment of iron as a precious metal, the existence of bride-price as well as dowry, the domination of the labour force by slaves: all of these will have served to distance the world described in the poems from that experienced by an eighth- or early seventh-century audience."[21] In the *Odyssey*, silver bathtubs appear in Sparta (4.128), not in Ithaca. Pirates and Phoenician traders, part of Homer's world, are regularly mentioned, but not the elaborate armor of the *Iliad*'s Achaians (*Iliad* 1.17; 2.331 etc.): the only "greaves" of the *Odyssey* are the patched oxhide leggings Laertes wears for gardening (24.229). The poem's references to a "bride-price" only emphasize how far Penelope's suitors are from any standard heroic code (2.51 ff.; 15.18 etc.),[22] and as to horses, the great symbol of aristocracy, of the *Iliad*'s war chariots, and of Hector, the "breaker of horses" (*Iliad* 24.804 etc.; also of Nestor 3.17, and Diomedes 3.181), as Telemachus points out, they do not suit tiny, rocky Ithaca (4.600–619).

In fact, the heroic world that Telemachus encounters in visiting Nestor and Menelaus serves as a stark contrast to the world he is used to in Ithaca. Telemachus finds Nestor engaged in the sacrifice of no less than eighty-one jet-black bulls (3.5 ff.), to which he will add a heifer with horns covered in gold (3.425). This splendor is then eclipsed by Menelaus's palace, which Telemachus thinks must resemble that of Zeus (4.71 ff.). The difference goes beyond mere grandeur. Nestor's antiquity (Odysseus describes his grandmother, and her union with Poseidon, among the ancient heroines he saw in Hades, 11.235 ff.; 3.408 ff.) is matched by Menelaus's position as the son-in-law of Zeus himself (4.561 ff.). Other than Odysseus, Nestor is the only human in the *Odyssey* able to recognize a specific god in disguise (3.371 ff.), while Menelaus recounts his physical struggle with one. Even the type-scenes of bathing distinguish Ithaca from the heroic: in Pylos, Nestor's own daughter bathes Telemachus (3.464 ff.), just as Helen bathed Odysseus in Troy (4.252), and as Circe and Calypso bathe their guests (5.264; 10.361, 450). In Ithaca, and strikingly so in the case of Odysseus (19.317–475), the task is left to the servants (17.88; 23.154; 24.366).[23] Pylos and Sparta, like Troy and the world of Odysseus's adventures, are of an order of things quite different from Ithaca. It is no wonder that Telemachus finds himself speechless (3.21 ff; 4.88).[24]

* * *

Since Homer himself existed in the mythic shadows of the past (from a twenty-first century point of view), it can be difficult for us to see his Ithaca as an ordinary world. Nonetheless, the gap between Ithaca and the world of the heroes is emphatic. Some differences amount to little more than a change of tone, such as the infrequency in Ithaca of patronymics or accounts of a character's ancestry.[25] To the suitors, the women Odysseus sees in the Underworld are purely creatures of legend (2.118; 11.235, 266). In contrast to "Mentes"'s account of Odysseus seeking poison, the suitors, who know nothing of drugs, mock the very idea (1.261; 2.328). We are still in the world of Odysseus, and so of a particular tie to Athena, but here when the goddess provides a boat, she simply borrows one (2.386; 4.634). Ithacans are aware of the gods, but expect them to come in disguise (17.483–87). Homer can even seem uncannily like Joyce in juxtaposing the ordinary and heroic to comic effect: pigkeepers dine with nobles; the aristocracy prepare their own dinner; and Homer calls out Eumaeus as the "divine swineherd" (*dion huphorbon*; 14.3 etc.) and "the swineherd, leader of men" (14.22, etc.).[26]

The contrast also rather undermines Telemachus. That Odysseus is trapped with an immortal nymph who wants to make him undying and ageless makes Telemachus's obstacle, a mother who won't let him grow up, rather less remarkable. The problem of being eaten out of house and home pales against the threat of being eaten outright, and unruly maids seem less a threat than magical goddesses.[27] Odysseus single-handedly builds a raft and ventures from the navel of the sea (1.50) to Phaeacia, a twenty-day journey on the open ocean; Telemachus travels overnight from Ithaca to Pylos in a borrowed boat (2.434; 3.1–4). Odysseus has Calypso swear on Styx, the unshakable oath of the gods, not to interfere with his journey

(5.175 ff.); Telemachus takes a simpler route: he doesn't tell his mother he is leaving (2.373).

Above all, however, the difference between a past heroic time and a present ordinary one matters for the discontinuity it creates in regard to Odysseus. In the past world, Odysseus was king, warrior, and hero. In the present ordinary world, there seems to be little place for him. The Assembly has not met for twenty years, and the absence of the king seems to have affected only his own household. When speaking of him, Penelope and Telemachus interject the formulaic "if he ever was" (15.26; 19.315; 24.289 etc.; *Iliad* 3.180; 11.762; 24.426). Mentor laments that no one remembers him (2.230 ff.), and Penelope rebukes Mentor and Antinous for not recalling the past (4.685; 16.424 ff.). Characters continuously remark that there is no one now like Odysseus (2.60; 10.313; 17.537 ff.); even Antinous says so, although hypocritically (21.91–97). The suitors—like the young mockers of "Oxen of the Sun"—ridicule inheritance, prophecy, heroism, and even the idea that Odysseus could save anything by returning (1.384; 2.177 ff.; 2.242 ff.).[28] They convey a sense that the past is dead, and they are the future.

But although Homer portrays Ithaca as ordinary, he does not glorify the alternative. If anything, the depictions of Pylos and Sparta seem to confirm the suitors' view of things. Homer's Nestor, who speaks and speaks until "the sun set and darkness came on" (3.329), does not dispel an impression that the world of the heroes is static and antiquated. Nor do Menelaus and Helen, reliving the good old days of the Trojan War while Helen drugs the wine. Even if we see their stories as a way of negotiating their present relationship, they seem caught in a static cycle of recrimination, as they apparently neglect the marriage of their only child (4.3 ff.). There is no evident way forward.

Although Telemachus has been sent to Pylos and Sparta to become acquainted with his father's heroic world, his most important contact is with Nestor's son, Pisistratus, who is, it is stressed, his own age (3.49; 15.197) and who has his own problems with the older generation. Pisistratus would rather not weep about Troy (where his own brother died, though he never knew him; 4.200) and immediately understands Telemachus's desire to avoid Nestor on his way home (15.195 ff.). He has all the advantages that Telemachus lacks: brothers, a settled position, and a revered father safely returned from the war. Nonetheless, we get a sense that the great heroes of Troy can be difficult to deal with, even for him.

In short, Odysseus's fellow heroes, and not only the ones killed in Troy, have not been able to leave the world of myth. In Homer's humanized and slightly comic picture, Nestor and Menelaus sit and tell their stories like any old war heroes and are politely tolerated (or not) by the young.[29] In this context, Odysseus's return from the heroic world of war to the mundane revalues the mundane, just as *Ulysses* will. The golden age of heroes was, of course, a far more splendid time than our own but, as Telemachus replies when Odysseus promises the help of Zeus and Athena, they are great and powerful, but also a long way away (16.262–65).

Divine and Human Time

The *Odyssey*'s distinction between heroic and ordinary time divides a time in which humans dealt directly with the gods from time "now," when we encounter the divine only in mediated ways and where Athena is always in disguise. The difference reflects as well the break between the sacred and cyclical time of the gods, Mircea Eliade's *illo tempore,* and linear human time.[30] In Genesis, for example, extraordinary longevity distinguishes the people of the primeval age—a time when God could speak to Adam face to face—from the following ages, creating two orders of time divided by the Flood. In Hindu myth, the cycle of four ages, or *yugas* consists essentially of three prior times in contrast to the *kali yuga,* the time we live in now. Similarly, Hesiod gives us a myth of five ages (each a *genos,* or race), but marks off the present Iron Age with a sudden personal irruption that introduces our own time as the worst. The heroes who preceded the poet and his audience, many of whom descended directly from the gods, are seen as a distinct race, completely divided from the present.[31]

While later Classical historians often saw the break between mythic and historical times primarily in terms of what was recoverable, the difference remained critical. Herodotus carefully separates what is said of ancient times from what he knows himself and mocks Hecataeus's claim to be descended from the gods.[32] Rather more sardonically, Thucydides, who reasons his way back to early history, rejects accounts that "for the most part, through [the length of] time, have battled their way into the untrustworthiness of myth."[33] The background to all this, however, appears most explicitly in the division between a Golden and an Iron Age. As Denis Feeney points out in his seminal *Caesar's Calendar,* this marks "a traumatic fault line in experience":

> This is a moment when the human race enters a historical space, not just in terms of coming over a horizon of historically ascertainable time, but in larger terms—this is when humans enter upon patterns

of life that are still current, and begin living a knowable and familiar life, continuous with ours. The terms of this currently lived experience are radically different from those imagined before the tipping point.

The distinction also radically changes the relations of gods and humans:

> once the beginning of history takes the gods away from mating with mortals, the gods are stuck in a timeless zone, one that throws into relief by contrast the new entrapment of humans in time. After the chronological divorce between humans and gods, it is now only human narratives that go on, forward-moving, deriving meaning from death: the gods, without death and without progeny, are by comparison fixed in an undynamic temporal zone. To be in human history is to be in narrative, and the only way out of this forward progression is through death.[34]

This separation between the gods, who are outside of time, and humans, who are inescapably involved with it, is fundamental to the Homeric vision. So is a radical shift in the relation of human beings and the gods. In mythic time, humans encounter the gods directly; in ordinary time, access to the gods is mediated, most importantly through song. This contrast, which lies in the background of the *Iliad*, becomes essential in the *Odyssey*, where storytelling and perception are fundamental themes. A possible factor in the difference, and one that struck Joyce as well, is that the *Odyssey* is by its very nature a post-Troy poem (if only by ten years), and it was often precisely the fall of Troy that set the dividing line between mythic and ordinary time.[35]

* * *

The importance of the fall of Troy (or "Ilium") is already apparent in the *Iliad*, as expressed, perhaps most movingly, by Hector:[36]

> For well I know this in my heart and my mind,
> that the day will come when sacred Ilium perishes
> and Priam of the strong ash spear, and Priam's people
> (*Iliad* 6.447–49)

We cannot know to what extent the poems respond to the tradition they grew out of, which saw the fall of Troy as marking a fundamental break in time, or to what extent they influenced that tradition. Nor do we know how the *Iliad* influenced the *Odyssey*, which is generally recognized as the later poem. All we know is that much of the Classical tradition located a division between the time of myth and ordinary time at just the moment of Odysseus's wanderings, and that the poet of the *Odyssey* seems to have taken advantage of this fact. As we will see at the end of this chapter, World War I, about which Stefan Zweig wrote "all the bridges are broken between today, yesterday and the day before yesterday," was to mark a similar shift in the twentieth century.[37]

JOYCE'S KINDS OF TIME: INTERNAL AND EXTERNAL

Clocktime and Internal Monologue

In one of Stephen Dedalus's first lines in *Ulysses*, he tells his rival, Mulligan, "I'm not a hero, however" (1.62). Much the same could be said of Bloom. If Joyce is not as interested in the question of heroism as Homer, one reason is his very different approach to time. While Homer explores the nature of identity by contrasting the time of the heroes to ordinary time, Joyce, like Modernists generally, explores identity through a contrast of external and internal time, clocktime and time as it is experienced, Henri Bergson's *durée*.[38]

Clocktime is central to *Ulysses* in its most ordinary sense. Reminders of the time appear, as it were, like clockwork: the milkwoman after eight (1.339), hockey at ten (2.92), the funeral at eleven (4.320; 5.94), meeting at The Ship at half twelve (1.733; 3.58), and, of course, Molly's meeting with Boylan: "At four she said" (11.188, 307, 309, 342, 392).[39] Nosey Flynn describes Bloom as having to check his watch before he takes a drink (8.980) and in fact so he has (8.735). Watches and clocks, church bells ringing the hour, the time-ball on the Ballast Office, even Ponchielli's "Dance of the Hours," punctuate the novel, all underlined by the discovery in "Nausicaa" that Bloom's watch has stopped, significantly, just around 4:30: "because that was about the time he." (13.985).

Joyce also uses time as a dominant organizing feature of *Ulysses*, having each episode take up one hour of a single day. But the regularity also points to a complication. Although the episodes remain an hour long in narrative time, the hour begins to take up more and more pages until, at the extreme, the hour from 11 a.m. to noon ("Hades") occupies 27 pages (in the original

1922 edition) and the hour from 11 p.m. to midnight ("Circe") takes 157. As in M'Coy's response to Lenehan, time in *Ulysses* is not always as definite as it might seem:

> —What's the time by your gold watch and chain?
> M'Coy peered into Marcus Tertius Moses' sombre office, then at O'Neill's clock.
> —After three, he said. (10.507 ff.)

The most immediate reason for the tension in *Ulysses* between the hour-long duration of the episodes and their length in pages is the difference between external and internal time. The first three episodes, as they expand in size, also expand the amount of interior monologue they contain: the 20 pages of "Telemachus" (in the 1922 version) contain roughly 120 lines of Stephen's thoughts; the 22 pages of "Nestor" contain 140 lines of thoughts; while "Proteus," at 13 pages, is nearly all interior monologue, to the despair of many first-time readers.[40] The pattern is then repeated as we restart the morning with Bloom. The 14 pages of "Calypso" contain about 310 lines of interior monologue; "Lotus Eaters'" 15 pages have 385, while the 27 pages of "Hades" contain 480 lines of internal monologue, as well as a significant amount of dialogue. Later, in "Lestrygonians," Bloom has around 800 lines of interior monologue in 33 pages. The result is a sense of internal time gradually expanding, in tension with the regular progression of the hours. This is also, in a sense, what actually happened, as most of Joyce's extensive additions, many made in proofs, were to the internal monologues.

In contrast to the regularity of clocktime, internal time varies radically.[41] Overall, the growing length of the episodes reflects, on the one hand, Bloom's acute awareness of the passage of time as he awaits Molly's 4:00 assignation with Boylan—and then, on the other, his lassitude, delay, and wandering after 4:00 has passed. The same variations occur in particular scenes. Stephen moves from the corridor outside his classroom to Mr Deasy's study instantaneously and, literally, without a thought (2.198–99), while between Zoe's consecutive: "Go ahead, make a stump speech out of it," "Talk away until you're blue in the face" (15.1352, 1958), Bloom experiences the seventeen-page fantasy of the "New Bloomusalem."[42] Even when clocktime has largely ceased to be relevant, it continues to be marked, as in Haines's injunction to meet at 11:10 (14.1027) or Molly's noting the bells of St. George's church: "3 quarters the hour 1 wait 2" (18.1231), at least in part as a contrast to the radical expansion of the episodes.[43]

In fact, a distinction between internal and external time is, in many ways, the material from which the first part of *Ulysses* is constructed. Joyce creates his initial style by combining an almost obsessive realism with the distinct interior voices of Bloom and Stephen. His insistence on using the actual Dublin of June 16, 1904, reinforces the sense of regular external time, while the striking contrast between Bloom and Stephen's ways of thinking emphasizes the interiority. Joyce also brings this out through three brief scenes in "Hades" and "Lestrygonians" in which we suddenly see Bloom from the outside (*U* 6.526–34, 690–706; 8.937–1027). The noticeable jar makes us realize that the experience we have grown accustomed to, which can feel like a direct experience of a real Dublin in real time, is in fact Dublin as mirrored in Bloom's (or Stephen's) consciousness.

Time as Connecting and Isolating

Just as the *Odyssey* brings out Odysseus's separation from Ithaca by trapping him in mythic time, the first part of *Ulysses* explores the isolation and possible coming together of its characters through the contrast of clocktime and internal time. It is a paradox of *Ulysses* that while we expect the inner experience of time to be solipsistic and the public time of clocks and schedules to be shared, external time in Joyce's novel becomes associated with the divisions between people, while the inner experiences of Bloom and Stephen will supply the materials for a coming together through the various narrative styles.[44]

As Norbert Elias argues, time, from a sociological point of view, exists to provide a common measure.[45] The introduction of such things as railroads, the telegraph, or the necessity of coordinating massive numbers of men in World War I created the need for innovations like time zones and wristwatches.[46] The theme is basic to *Ulysses*. Bloom, Martin Cunningham, Simon Dedalus, and Jack Power all learned, from the newspaper or elsewhere, that the funeral was at 11:00. The characters scattered throughout Dublin in "Wandering Rocks" are united by the hour of the day. Gerty McDowell and Bloom have very different views of their encounter, but it occurs for both "after eight because the sun was set" (13.547). And it is because Stephen shares a common measure of time with Haines and Mulligan that he can ensure that he is not at The Ship at half twelve precisely (1.733; 9.545 ff.).

Nonetheless, the uniformity of clocktime in *Ulysses* often brings out the isolation of characters rather than bringing them together.[47] A primary reason is the inner access that Joyce gives us to Stephen and Bloom. In "Nestor," for example, Stephen follows two different lines of thought: first, the lessons he is supposed to be giving and second, and more seriously, his own interests. Later, while being paid by Mr Deasy, he carries on a double conversation, with Deasy and with himself:

> —No thanks at all, Mr Deasy said. You have earned it.
> Stephen's hand, free again, went back to the hollow shells. Symbols too of beauty and of power. A lump in my pocket: symbols soiled by greed and misery.
> —Don't carry it like that, Mr Deasy said. You'll pull it out somewhere and lose it. You just buy one of these machines. You'll find them very handy.
> Answer something.
> —Mine would be often empty, Stephen said.
> The same room and hour, the same wisdom: and I the same. Three times now. Three nooses round me here. Well? I can break them in this instant if I will. (2.225–35)

The case is the same with Bloom, who responds to Dlugacz in "Calypso" while following a quite different train of thought (4.171–90) and speaks to M'Coy about Paddy Dignam while concentrating on the woman across the street (5.91–137). Most emphatically in "Hades," as we will see, the opposition between Bloom's inner thoughts and his outer clock-centric experience becomes thematic, and so emphasizes both his emotional and social isolation.

*   *   *

Joyce further emphasizes the isolation implied by a division between internal and external time by gradually separating the characters' thoughts from the external narrative. In the first three episodes, as we saw in the ever-increasing line counts, interior monologue gradually frees itself and takes over from external description, until, with "Proteus," the novel comes to be located almost entirely in Stephen's head. Stephen's first extended interior monologue in "Telemachus" is occasioned by Mulligan happening to sing a verse from the song Stephen had sung to his dying mother: "And no more turn aside and brood / Upon love's bitter mystery" (1.239). Here Stephen's musings are set firmly within narrative time, as we see when Mulligan calls up to Stephen to (implicitly) stop brooding and (explicitly) come down for breakfast (1.280–88, 235–36).

In "Telemachus," the disjunction between himself, Mulligan, and Haines that occurs in Stephen's thoughts parallels his testiness with them in the narrative. Gradually, however, the thoughts float away from the external action. The pattern continues through "Nestor," where the riddle that Stephen tells the schoolboys (2.101 ff.) is intelligible only within his own private world. And while his response to Sargent (Pisistratus in Joyce's schema) is unexpectedly direct and personal, it also sets off the noncommunication of his conversation with Deasy. Finally, in "Proteus," inner experience has taken over entirely: the reminders of clocktime that punctuated the first two episodes are gone, and even Stephen's destination, which seemed perfectly clear at the end of "Telemachus," is now a mystery both to Stephen and the reader (3.61, 158).

This pattern of increasing both internal monologue and isolation continues despite the characters' interaction with others. Stephen becomes more physically isolated in his first three episodes, moving from Haines and Mulligan to the schoolboys, to Deasy, and finally to his solitary walk on Sandymount Strand. In contrast, Bloom speaks with more and more people: Larry O'Rourke (very briefly), Dlugacz, and Molly in "Calypso"; the postmistress, M'Coy, Sweny, and Bantom Lyons in "Lotus Eaters"; and the whole array of mourners in "Hades." The company, however, only serves to emphasize his isolation.

Nor does it matter that Bloom, unlike Stephen, is attuned to the people he meets. Stephen responds to the external world by re-creating it to fit his thoughts, transforming the old women into midwives (3.29 ff.), the stones into a giant's playthings (3.290 ff.), the cocklepickers into gypsies (3.331 ff.), and the drowned man into the many forms of *Hamlet* and *The Tempest* (3.470 ff.).[48] Bloom's thoughts, in contrast, are generally directed outward. Stephen dwells on obscure heresies and mystic poets; Bloom thinks about kidneys, the breakfast-tray, the cat, the bed, his hat, his missing latchkey, Boland's breadvan, and Larry O'Rourke's. Even in the outhouse, that paradigmatic location of Arius's last thoughts (3.52 ff.), Bloom thinks about the paper he has brought with him (3.500 ff.). But despite all this, his isolation remains. To the extent that the problem of *Ulysses*, like the problem of the *Odyssey*, is not only establishing identity but also escaping from the isolation that identity can impose, it appears that neither clocktime, nor, simply, the time of inner experience, can do the job.

FLUID AND FIXED IDENTITIES

Neither Joyce nor Homer explores various forms of time for their own sake. Both address a more basic question: what it means to be the "same" person despite the changes we experience in time. Why, in the *Odyssey*'s most vivid example, is Proteus Proteus, since he can also be anything else? The question introduces another double view, perhaps best expressed through Plato's Being and Becoming. Both Homer's gods and Joyce's God exist outside of time, and so have what we might term an absolute identity. In contrast, mortals, in ancient epic as in Augustine, live in a world of constant change. The distinction appears in many guises: form against formlessness, determinism against freedom, even the Apollonian against the Dionysian. I will refer to it here as a contrast of fixity and flux, as seen in the fixed mythic identities of gods and heroes in contrast to the change of ordinary time, and in the regular, mechanical ordering of clocks and watches against the flux of inner time. The contrast also implies two opposite threats to human identity: to be fixed, self-contained, and unchanging, and consequently, dead, or to be subsumed and absorbed by change, and so to lose individual identity altogether.[49]

Before we go on, however, it is worth saying explicitly that both flux and fixity inevitably involve their opposite. In a relation that runs through *Ulysses,* and that nearly constitutes *Finnegans Wake,* Joyce adopts an idea he attributes to Giambattista Vico and Giordano Bruno (of Nolan), that any pair of opposites generate one another, and in so doing, form a whole. As he described Bruno's philosophy, it "is a kind of dualism—every power in nature must evolve an opposite in order to realize itself and opposition brings reunion" (*LI* 226).[50] Nor is the goal to steer a course between them. Odysseus, despite the proverbial saying, does not find a way between Scylla and Charybdis, but rather, in a characteristic Homeric doubling, fully encounters the dangers of both, in Stephen's terms, experiencing both "The devil and the deep sea" (9.139).[51]

Rocks and the Sea: Flux and Fixity in the *Odyssey*

If Joyce was devoted to binaries, Homer came from the culture that gave us nature and nurture, land and sea, mortal and immortal, and comedy and tragedy.[52] The contrast between flux and fixity runs throughout the *Odyssey,* as in the opposition of being stranded or being drowned; or of asserting identity, as Odysseus does with the Cyclops; or having it absorbed, as by the

Lotus Eaters or Sirens. The first, watery, half of the *Odyssey* is heralded by Proteus (4.351–587) and associated with transformation and a loss of identity. The second half of the poem, set on rocky Ithaca, concerns the opposite problem: not of maintaining identity, but of re-creating it.

The underlying tension that John Rickard finds in *Ulysses* between form and formlessness, fixity and chaos, thus also underlies the *Odyssey*; and in Homer, as in Joyce, the opposition is summed up in a contrast between rocks or towers and the sea.[53] It is an opposition, paradigmatically, between Scylla and Charybdis. While the whirlpool, Charybdis, is an obvious figure for flux and absorption, Circe's description of Scylla emphasizes, in contrast, the rock, its fixity, and its inapproachability:

> On the other side two cliffs, of which one reaches up to high heaven
> with its sharp peak, and cloud covers it round,
> a dark cloud. That never fails it, nor ever does clear sky
> hold its peak, not in summer nor ever in harvest-time.
> Nor could any man climb it, or get a foothold upon it,
> not if he had twenty hands, and so many feet,
> for the rock is smooth, as if it were polished all over.
>   (12.73–79)

The threats of fixity and flux, paired as rocks and the sea, also appear in the *Odyssey* in the opposition between a death in war, memorialized by a fixed grave mound, and the reabsorption of a death at sea, which recalls in turn the pairing of Athena, goddess of war, and Poseidon. It is such a mound—like the ones raised for Agamemnon and Achilles (4.584; 24.32, 80 ff.), or the one in which Odysseus fixes Elpenor's oar (11.75 ff.; 12.13 ff.)— that Athena urges Telemachus to raise for Odysseus, should he discover that his father is dead (1.285).[54] In contrast, Telemachus sees Odysseus as dissolved by the elements. As he says, unconsciously echoing his father's moment of despair (5.305–12):

> [the gods] have made him unseen above all
> human beings, since I would not grieve thus for his death
> had he been conquered amidst his companions in Troy's land,
> or amidst his friends, when he had wound off the skein of war.
> Then the Achaeans would have made him a burial mound
> and for his son too he would have carried off great fame (*kleos*) for
>   the future.

> But now, with no fame, the storm-spirits have snatched him.
> He is gone, unseen, unheard of, and for me is left grief and sorrow.
>   (1.235–43)

For Telemachus, as for any grieving family, a body, a funeral, and a grave marker means closure, while the uncertainty of not knowing means being unable to move on. In the overall context of the poem, however, the closure, certainty, and *kleos* that Telemachus seeks is also of the realm of mythic time. The certainty of the grave marker may allow Telemachus to move on, but only by fixing Odysseus forever in the past.

*   *   *

While in one aspect, Odysseus's adventures present a danger of being frozen into myth, in another the danger is that of flux: being swallowed up, both figuratively and literally. Athena, a goddess of order, absents herself and Poseidon dominates. Circe threatens to transform Odysseus into an animal, and both the Lestrygonians and the Cyclops threaten him with the ultimate absorption, of becoming food. With the Lotus Eaters, the threat is of being absorbed by forgetfulness, and with the Sirens, of being absorbed by the past. Even Odysseus's salvation, the contrivance of becoming "No-man," is an erasure of his identity. As in the song that floats through Stephen's mind (3.470): "Nothing of him that doth fade, / But doth suffer a sea-change / Into something rich and strange" (*Tempest* 1.2.400–402) what the sea threatens is a fluidity that steals our identity away.

Flux, however, is not the only threat. Homer juxtaposes Circe's island and Hades by having Odysseus encounter Circe (10.203–574); then Hades (11.13–640); then Circe again (12.1–150), just as he faces Scylla (12.234–59); then the island of Helios (12.260–425); then Charybdis (12.426–46). The flux that Circe represents thus sets off Hades, a realm incapable of change, and one whose threat is underlined by Odysseus's account of his own fear (11.43, 633), the only time in the poem when he describes himself as afraid. Here the souls that Odysseus encounters are frozen in the past, each recounting a fixed story. Rather than being the people they were, as they might be in a Christian tradition, these *psuchae* (souls or shades) are only shadows, as Odysseus discovers when he tries to embrace his mother (11.204–24). They cannot even speak without the physical animation of drinking blood (11.147–48). Homer reinforces the distance by referring not to "Achilles," for example, but to "the soul of Achilles," creating a further remove when Odysseus moves from heroines to heroes, since the word *psuche* is feminine.

Odysseus's experience in the Underworld is one of fixity. Agamemnon, fixed in his own experience, may be aware that Penelope is virtuous (11.444 ff.; 11.194 ff.), but for him all women are Clytemnestra (11.427 ff., 456; 24.96–97, 199 ff.). Although the Achilles who prefers the lowest servitude on earth to being lord of all the dead (11.489) seems a long way from the *Iliad,* his enquiries about his father and son, and his assertion of what he would do were he there (11.491 ff.), simply continue his concerns in *Iliad* 24. He is no more fit now to be a *thes,* a hired man without even the place of a slave (*Works and Days* 600–603), than he ever was.[55] Ajax, fixed in his anger against Odysseus, thus only caps the experience of Hades as a realm without change, as does the return to the Underworld in Book 24, where Agamemnon and Achilles are still telling the stories they were fixated on in Book 11.[56]

The two parts of Odysseus's description of Hades, the first apparently directed to Arete and the second to Alcinous, also bring out a curious feature of Homer's Underworld: its sterility. As in Hamlet's Christian afterlife (or *U* 9.1046–52), there appears to be no marrying.[57] Other than Elpenor, who is outside the reaches of Hades, Odysseus first encounters only women (including his mother) and then, after Alcinous's request, only men. The one exception, Teiresias, is a figure notorious for having been both male and female (as in *Metamorphoses* 3.316–38). Nor, for that matter, does Odysseus's meeting with Oedipus's mother (11.271 ff.) provide a comfortable undertone for an epic about return and marriage.

The fixity that Odysseus experiences in Hades also speaks to the primary paradox of the poem: that Odysseus, who has just heard that the worst life on earth is preferable to the best in the Underworld, refuses Calypso's offer, and with it the ability to stay out of the Underworld for good. Homer emphasizes the anomaly through Odysseus's meeting with Heracles. Or rather, Odysseus meets with Heracles's image (*eidolon*) since "he himself rejoiced among the immortal gods" (11.602–3). But while Heracles points to his similarity to Odysseus (11.617–26), the audience knows that there is a critical difference. Heracles now lives, immortal and unaging, with his divine wife, Hebe ("Youth" 11.604); Odysseus will choose instead to return to his usual wife, Penelope, the world of flux, and mortality.[58]

"Hades" and "Circe": Fixity and Flux in *Ulysses*

Ulysses, like the *Odyssey* (and like *Finnegans Wake*), pairs towers and rocks against the sea. The Gilbert schema cites as correspondences for "Scylla and Charybdis," "The Rock—Aristotle, Dogma," and "The Whirlpool—Plato,

Mysticism." These are Stephen's challenges: fixed definition on the one side and absorption on the other.[59] Like Telemachus, Stephen occupies a tower on a cliff that "beetles o'er his base into the sea" (*Odyssey* 1.425-26; *U* 1.567–68; 9.487). He fears water and drowning (1.472–76; 3.20–30; 17.237) and yet lives with "Mercurial Malachi" (1.519), who ends the episode conversing with a young man clinging to a "spur of rock" in the sea (1.680). Most of all, however, as Joyce's "Proteus" amply illustrates, the flux of the sea is associated in *Ulysses* with the flux of inner experience; the greatest danger of absorption that Stephen faces will be absorption in himself.

The contrast runs throughout *Ulysses*.[60] On Sandymount Strand, a name that implies a contrast of sea and cliff, Stephen sets both the Martello Tower and an Aristotelian definition of soul as the "form of forms" against the "suck" of the sea:

> He lifted his feet up from the suck and turned back by the mole of boulders. Take all, keep all. My soul walks with me, form of forms. So in the moon's midwatches I pace the path above the rocks, in sable silvered, hearing Elsinore's tempting flood. (3.278–81)

Bloom's episode on the same strand opens with a similar contrast of fixed rock and tower to the flux of the sea, although in a rather different style:

> the last glow of all too fleeting day lingered lovingly on sea and strand, on the proud promontory of dear old Howth guarding as ever the waters of the bay, on the weedgrown rocks along Sandymount shore and, last but not least, on the quiet church whence there streamed forth at times upon the stillness the voice of prayer to her who is in her pure radiance a beacon ever to the stormtossed heart of man, Mary, star of the sea. (13.2–8)

And finally, Molly's "rocks," in response to another kind of flux, evokes the same opposition:

> —Met him what? He asked.
> —Here, she said. What does that mean?
> He leaned downward and read near her polished thumbnail.
> —Metempsychosis?
> —Yes. Who's he when he's at home?
> —Metempsychosis, he said, frowning. It's Greek: from the Greek. That means the transmigration of souls.
> —O, rocks! She said. Tell us in plain words. (4.336 ff.)

This is appropriate for one who, like Penelope, holds out the (here somewhat uncertain) promise of a fixed home and who hails from no less a rock in the sea than Gibraltar.

As in the *Odyssey*, *Ulysses*'s basic opposition of flux and fixity is brought out through doubling. "Lotus Eaters" and "Sirens," two "female" episodes that threaten absorption through seduction, are set against "Lestrygonians" and "Cyclops," two "male" episodes that replace seduction with violence—a pairing also brought out in the "Love and War" sequence of "Sirens" (11.459 ff.). Stephen's Aristotelian "Rock" and Platonic "Whirlpool" in "Scylla and Charybdis" parallel, philosophically, Bloom's Lestrygonian opposition of the "Dreamy, cloudy, symbolistic" (8.543) vegetarianism of AE against the "Eat or be eaten. Kill! Kill!" (8.703) carnivores of the Burton Hotel. Here, as well, the equivalence of the threats becomes clear. Whether with the cannibals, who (as with the reverend Mr MacTrigger; 8.748, 782) digest you, or the Lotus Eaters, who cause you to forget yourself, what is lost is individual identity.[61]

Above all, however, the themes of flux and fixity, clocktime and time as it is experienced, and the interplay of both with the problem of isolation, emerge in the pairing Joyce takes over from Homer, of Hades and Circe.[62] "Hades," which occurs between 11 and 12 noon, emphasizes clocktime, fixity, and Bloom's social isolation in the midst of "citizens of all classes" (16.1252). "Circe," which occurs from 11 to 12 midnight, involves, even hallucinogenically, time as experienced, flux, and the strange fusion of Stephen and Bloom that we will examine in chapter 6. And, like "Hades," "Circe" is about visiting the dead. Stephen, like Odysseus, encounters the shade of his mother, while Bloom meets both parents (15.248 ff.), his dead son (15.4956 ff.), and even, like Dante encountering Cacciaguida, his grandfather and namesake, Lipoti Virag (15.2304 ff.).[63] Paddy Dignam, who, despite some concern (6.421 ff.), remained quietly in his coffin in "Hades," also appears (15.1228), as does M'Intosh, the spirit conjured by Joe Hynes's misunderstanding (6.891 ff.; 15.1560). Stephen, present in "Hades" by newspaper error (16.1259), is present in "Circe" in fact,[64] and the episode's ending with Rudy, now "a fairy boy of eleven" (15.4957), reflects both the Underworld's location in *Odyssey* 11 and its focus on fathers and sons (11.457 ff.).

Joyce used not only the *Odyssey* but also an entire epic tradition in creating *Ulysses*. Within this tradition, the descent into Hades is a critical element. As Odysseus's final encounter with his heroic comrades, it provides a crucial transition in the *Odyssey* and so is situated nearly at the midpoint of the poem. Virgil then places his hero's visit to the Underworld precisely in the center, using it as a transition from Troy to Italy, from past to future, and from the *Odyssey* to the *Iliad* half of the poem. Dante not only opens *The Divine Comedy* with the descent to Hell, he makes the journey to the afterlife occupy the entire epic, while Milton rings his changes on Dante by beginning in Hell, taking a (literally) chaotic path to earth, and then zooming up to Heaven in Book 3.[65] Given this, it seems odd that Joyce's "Hades" is not more striking—a question that remains unresolved until we encounter "Circe."

* * *

The two episodes are specifically opposite. In "Circe" clocktime becomes absurd as "Old Gummy Granny" tells Stephen: "At 8:35 a.m. you will be in heaven and Ireland will be free" (15.4738), and the End of the World sings in a Scotch accent (15.2180–82). "Hades," in contrast, is an episode of clocktime. "What time is the funeral?" (4.319) is our first mention of clocktime with Bloom; the fateful newspaper of "Lotus Eaters" is purchased to check on its time (5.91 ff., 520 ff.); "Are we late?" (6.85) is one of the episode's first questions, and Martin Cunningham periodically checks his watch to see (6.86, 336). Tom Kernan feels that the service was read rather quickly (6.659), and it is pointed out that time is pressing: "Must be twenty or thirty funerals every day. Then Mount Jerome for the protestants. Funerals all over the world everywhere every minute" (6.513–14); "—How many have you for tomorrow? the caretaker asked. /—Two, Corny Kelleher said. Half ten and eleven" (6.797–98). Even the seduction that Bloom imagines: "It was a pitchdark night. The clock was on the stroke of twelve" (6.755–56) and the joke he recalls: "The one about the bulletin. Spurgeon went to heaven 4 a.m. this morning. 11 p.m. (closing time). Not arrived yet. Peter" (6.787–89) are clock-centered.

Similarly, while "Circe" brings out a blending of characters, "Hades'" focus on the external emphasizes the divisions between them. As Bloom's thoughts, like those concerning his father's suicide, increasingly veer away from what is happening around him, the narrative simultaneously brings out his isolation.[66] The episode opens with the wonderful, if painful: "Are we all here now? Martin Cunningham asked. . . . Come along, Bloom" (6.8). Bloom's conversation with his coworker Joe Hynes (who also owes him three shillings; 7.119) makes a similar point:

—I am just taking the names, Hynes said below his breath. What is your christian [!] name? I'm not sure.

—L, Mr Bloom said. Leopold. And you might put down M'Coy's name too. He asked me to.

—Charley, Hynes said writing. I know. He was on the *Freeman* once. (6.880 ff.)

The unusual scenes in which we see Bloom from outside, as well as his final rebuff by John Henry Menton (6.1019), make it equally clear, in different ways, that he is not one of the crowd.

This sense is underlined by the fact that "the crowd" is now also introduced for the first time. Aside from M'Coy and Bantam Lyons in "Lotus Eaters," the only figure so far that Joyce has brought in from his other works is Stephen Dedalus.[67] In "Hades," in contrast, the shared time is reinforced by a whole host of familiar characters: from "Counterparts" (Paddy Leonard, 6.142); "A Painful Case" (Mrs Sinico, 6.997); "Ivy Day in the Committee Room" (Joe Hynes, Crofton, 6.247); and "Grace" (Cunningham, Kernan, Jack Power, M'Coy, Fogarty, 6.454); from *Portrait* (Simon Dedalus, Mrs Riordan, 6.378); and from real life (John Henry Menton, Father Coffey, John O'Connell, Reuben J. Dodd, Dan Dawson, Collis and Ward, even Peter Paul M'Swiney).[68] As nearly the only character who does not appear somewhere else, Bloom is the odd man out.

Above all, however, the contrast of "Hades" and "Circe" illustrates the opposition of flux and fixity. As "Circe" emphasizes flux, "Hades" tends to fixity. The statues that stud the episode stand in contrast to the living Botanical Gardens, "just over there" (6.770) and to Bloom's "Of course the cells or whatever they are go on living. Changing about" (*U* 6.780–81).[69] Parnell, whose half-built memorial Bloom sees on the way to the cemetery (6.320), and Daniel O'Connell, all of whom is buried in Glasnevin except his heart (6.641 ff.), are turning into fixtures like Nelson's pillar (6.293) in what Joyce described as "the most efficient and courteous way yet discovered of ensuring a lasting oblivion of the deceased" (*OCPW* 127).[70] The shades seeking to cross into the Underworld in the *Odyssey* and *Aeneid* are thus, in *Ulysses*, "Fragments of shapes, hewn. In white silence: appealing. The best obtainable. Thos. H. Dennany, monumental builder and sculptor" and "white shapes thronged amid the trees, white forms and fragments streaming by mutely, sustaining vain gestures on the air" (6.461 ff., 487 ff.). Even our Savior—whose statue adorns the drunk's grave in O'Connell's joke: "*Not a bloody bit like the man*, says he. *That's not Mulcahy*, says he, *whoever done it*" (6.731 ff.)—has no connection to the poor sinner he died for.

The fixity seen in the statues of "Hades" appears in the stories as well. Like the stories told by Nestor, Menelaus, and the heroes in Odysseus's Underworld, Joyce's "Hades" shows us not only Parnell and O'Connell but also ordinary Dublin figures rapidly calcifying into legend. Tom Kernan from "Grace" has reverted to form, drinking, in debt to Fogarty, and intent on his "retrospective sort of arrangement" (6.142, 454 ff.). Reuben J. Dodd Jr. and Sr. (6.251–95), Martin Cunningham's dissolute wife (6.349–57), the barmaid kept by Jack Power (6.242–48), and soon, one suspects, the suicide of Bloom's father, all point to Dublin's ability to freeze her citizens into anecdote. Padraic Colum recalled the young Joyce, with his white tennis shoes, cap, and ashplant, companioning Gogarty on his way to becoming a true Dublin "artist." In Dublin parlance, Ulick O'Connor explained, this had nothing to do with Michelangelo or Shakespeare, but rather meant being a regular character—like those rapidly becoming fossilized in *Ulysses*. One sees why Joyce felt the need to leave.[71]

*   *   *

The dead, like the past, are fixed in "Hades." Bloom's thoughts on the memorials: "Rusty wreaths hung on knobs, garlands of bronzefoil. Better value that for the money. Still, the flowers are more poetical. The other gets rather tiresome, never withering. Expresses nothing. Immortelles" (6.945) are like his idea that a gramophone would preserve the voices of the dead (6.963 ff.), at the price of their saying the same thing over and over. In contrast, the departed in "Circe," like the past events that re-create themselves, are in constant flux: there is no predicting what these dead will say or transform into. From the relatively tame, stereotyped vision of Bloom's mother and father, we move to Paddy Dignam's continual metamorphoses (15.1210–60) and Virag, with his multiplicity of forms (15.2304 ff.). These dead are very active indeed. Even Rudy, whose death Bloom dwells on in "Hades," has grown in "Circe" to the age he would have been had he lived (4.420; 15.4957).

But while the *Odyssey* and *Ulysses* are both grounded in a tension between flux and fixity, this does not mean that the balance is equal. In choosing to return to Ithaca, Odysseus chooses ordinary time over mythic and flux over fixity. Similarly, just as the coming together of Bloom and Stephen in "Circe" will, in some sense, counter Bloom's isolation in "Hades," *Ulysses* privileges inner over external time and the Arranger over the initial style. Plato saw the opposed views of Heraclitus (for whom all was flux) and Parmenides (for whom Being implied the impossibility of change) as fundamental, and felt that Homer leaned toward the Heraclitean (*Theatetus* 152d-e). It could well be argued that, as the end of *Finnegans Wake* flows into its beginning, so did Joyce. Water and rock may be in constant dialectic, but water eventually wears down stone.[72]

THE EPIC TRADITION AND THE USE OF TIME

An epic is thought to embody, or even generate, the collective memory of a culture.[73] Culture, however, like time, is continually changing. Joyce joined a particular and often monumentalized tradition when he titled his novel *Ulysses* (and not least by choosing the Roman version of Odysseus's name), but this tradition was also established through a questioning of its own nature and continuity.[74] Joyce felt he was up to the task. In the *Inferno,* Virgil personally invites Dante to join Homer, Horace, Ovid, Lucan, and himself (4.97–102).[75] Like Dante, Joyce was never known for his modesty.[76]

What Joyce brings to a tradition already concerned with time and change is a new sense of relativity, prefigured in Nietzsche's paradoxical announcement that God is dead. This appears most vividly in contrast to the absolute time that runs, in various ways, from Homer to Virgil to Dante to Milton. Unlike internal time or even clocktime, which is itself finally relative, this is a kind of time completely removed from human experience, and one that runs through the epic tradition.

By introducing Odysseus through his rejection of Calypso's offer, Homer contrasts time as the gods experience it to human time, in which we grow old and perish.[77] Virgil then models the *Aeneid* on Homer, not least to bring out their differences. Here, the absolute view of the gods (and of Jupiter in particular) is fixed not in an Olympus devoid of wind, rain, or snow (*Odyssey* 6.41–46), but in the Roman *imperium sine fine* (authority without end, 1.279), that Jupiter describes to Venus in *Aeneid* 1. The difference is the focus on history, but with a qualification.[78] Within the absolute span of history that the *Aeneid* reaches toward, the fall of Troy, Dido, and Aeneas's wars in Italy are crucial elements in a greater pattern. To Aeneas, trapped within the flux of human time, they are, like the storm that (from his point of view) overwhelms him by chance (1.84 ff.), just one damn thing after another. Like Mr Deasy ("All human history moves towards one great goal, the manifestation of God" 2.380), Virgil portrays an absolute divine will underlying human history. Unlike Mr Deasy, however (and like Joyce), Virgil remains constantly aware that to the human actor, "the manifestation of God" is often nothing but meaningless suffering.

Like Virgil, Dante weaves history into epic, here by including Roman, biblical, and contemporary figures alongside characters such as Aeneas (*Inferno* 4.122) or Ulysses (*Inferno* 26.55–142), and by making Virgil himself Dante's guide.[79] In so doing, however, he also introduces the absolute break in time that the birth of Christ implies for a Christian.[80] Virgil's time is thus "*sub Julio*," that of "the false and lying gods" (*Inferno* 1.70–72; Mandelbaum translation). The "absolute" aspect of time thus brought out is no longer history, but time as it exists for God, time as it will prevail after the Last Judgment, when time as we know it has ceased (as *Inferno* 10.94–108). Within this whole, Virgil's vision can reach only, almost, to the top of Purgatory, the last realm still influenced by human time.

For Dante, as for Virgil, what appears as mere chance in the human realm has a far deeper significance from a divine perspective. Within Dante's Christian understanding, however, very much in contrast to Virgil, God's absolute pattern is centered in the human individual. Details that seem purely personal and coincidental, such as that Dante (actually) turned thirty-five in the year 1300, midway in our three-score years and ten (*Inferno* 1.1; Psalm 90.10), or that this was the first Jubilee year, or that Dante's friend Guido Cavalcante died that year (played with in *Inferno* 10.54 ff.), are as important as the fall of nations. Just as Joyce delighted in incorporating into his novel an actual Zionist office on "Bleibtreustrasse" (Stay-true-street, 4.199) or Marcus Tertius Moses ["from Moses (of Egypt) to Moses (Mendelssohn) there arose none like Moses (Maimonides)," 17.713], Dante delights in all the coincidental detail of his own world. But for him, the detail is also an image of the divine.[81]

Milton's *Paradise Lost,* perhaps the great English epic that Joyce sought to supplant, has left fewer traces than its predecessors on *Ulysses,* which highlights instead *Lycidas* and its themes of drowning and memory (2.56 ff.).[82] Nonetheless, as we will see in chapter 2, the Miltonic Latin and Old Testament ring of Stephen's *non serviam* (I will not serve) recalls *Paradise Lost* and, with it, Milton's take on the contrast between human and divine experiences of time. The tension is now between God's foreknowledge and human freedom.[83] Fixity, now seen as fate, and flux, seen as contingency and free will, once more underlie two radically different senses of time. It is a very different contrast than Homer's unchanging gods and ever-changing men, but it has grown from that root.

Joyce and the Absolute: Natural and Conventional Time

Ulysses sets itself against all of these views of the absolute, appealing instead to Joyce's fellow trickster and questioner of epic, Ovid, whose *Metamorphoses* runs through *Ulysses* as "metempsychosis."[84] Joyce references the culmination of the *Paradiso,* as Dante Pilgrim and Dante Poet become one. Here, as Dante sees how the human and the divine may be the same, the comparison is to a geometer comprehending how the circle might be squared (*Paradiso* 33.133–35). Bloom has also tried his hand at squaring the circle. He, however, failed (15.2400–2402; 17.1696–97).[85]

In a sense this view simply reflects epic's role as a holder of culture. One thing that had happened since Milton is Albert Einstein and with him a prevailing prejudice against the absolute.[86] Joyce contrasts time as it is experienced to clocktime, but in a setting where clocks are subject to relativity, and the time they measure no more absolute than the flux of individual experience. Mr Deasy's view that history is a manifestation of God is set, almost programmatically, against Stephen's that God is a shout in the street (2.380–83). We are inclined to side with Stephen. As with Rip Van Winkle's emerging (in Joyce's version) from Sleepy Hollow, all has changed (13.1115; 15.3153 ff.).

An anecdote that Cornelius Weygandt (the "yankee interviewer" of *U* 7.785; 9.54) heard from George Moore is telling, although, in retrospect, also amusing. Weygandt reports that, having indignantly denied an interest in George Russell's mysticism (Russell's pseudonym was "AE")

> Finally the boy [Joyce] turned questioner and found that "A.E." was seeking the Absolute. Having found this out, he again sighed, this time regretfully, and said decidedly that "A.E." could not be his Messiah, as he abhorred the Absolute above everything else. He was infected with Pater's Relative, said Mr. Russell, "which has fallen like a blight on all English literature." So the boy—he was not yet twenty one—went out into the night with, I suppose, another of his idols fallen.[87]

Although Joyce may not have appreciated Weygandt's recollection, the Absolute, and its absence, continued to matter to him. He was, after all, steeped in scholasticism, and had, as it has been described, a medieval mind: all characteristics that he carefully attributes to Stephen.[88] In *Stephen Hero,* Joyce has his proto-Stephen assailed by the temptations not of the Devil, but of the Church, which demands whether "his own aristocratic intelligence and passion for a supremely satisfying order in all the fervours of artistic creation were not purely Catholic qualities" (205). In *Ulysses,* although Mulligan urges Stephen to read the Greeks "in the original," it is Aquinas that Stephen prefers (1.79; 9.778).[89] As Mulligan puts it: "you have the cursed jesuit strain in you, only it's injected the wrong way" (1.209).

The undermining of the absolute thus means something much more radical in *Ulysses* than just, in Bloom's idiom, moving with the times (16.1403). As an admirer of Dante, Joyce certainly appreciated that taking the *Odyssey* as his model ignored the radical break in time that, for a Christian, occurred with Christ. As Stephen's description of God reminds us (2.386), he also knew that eliminating the divine tended to remove any sense, Virgilian or Christian, of a meaning to history. And to return to the *Odyssey,* removing the background of Being alters the nature of Becoming as well. Each of the epics Joyce followed had shifted the relation of human to absolute time. By calling the absolute itself into question, Joyce went even further. He was seeing what it was like to work without a net.[90]

*   *   *

The three poems of Dante's *The Divine Comedy,* the *Inferno, Purgatorio,* and *Paradiso,* all end with the same word: "stars" (*stelle*). Throughout the *Comedy,* time is carefully (if subtly) marked by the stars, the sole indication that Dante finds himself in his "dark wood" on the evening of Christ's suffering, Holy Thursday, 1300, the spring equinox, and March 25 of the Julian, April 2 (proleptically) of the Gregorian calendar. Like 1904, it was also a leap year (the idea was originated by Julius Caesar). Dante, however, does not say so. The indications of time that he uses are not of human convention (such as days of the week or numbers on a calendar) but rather, on the one hand, liturgical, and on the other the same indications that Homer used in measuring time by "rosy-fingered dawns" and sunsets.[91] His measures expand out, in the *Purgatorio* in particular, but they remain of the same order. Christ's crucifixion, descent into Hell, and resurrection, alongside the sun, stars, and planets, mark time here. He does bring in Pope Boniface's Jubilee year (*Inferno* 18.28; *Purgatorio* 2.98), but then the Jubilee year, enjoined in Leviticus 25, was for him as natural as spring or summer, or as the progress from Lent to Easter.

Homer, who had no conventional panhellenic measure, marks time in natural units. Both Virgil and Milton set their epics in a past whose time-measurements were very different from their own. Dante, like Joyce, writes an epic of contemporary time and so has both natural and conventional ways to mark time, but he uses only the natural. *Ulysses,* in contrast, mingles the natural and conventional indiscriminately.[92] Although we have focused on the hours of the day, perhaps the unit of time most immediately experienced, other conventional gauges pervade the novel—to the extent that figuring out the date becomes something of a game. In "Nestor" we learn that it is half day, Thursday (2.93), in "Calypso" that Milly Bloom turned fifteen yesterday, on the 15th (4.415), and finally in "Wandering Rocks," Miss Dunne clicks 16 June 1904 on her typewriter (10.376). But we are given natural indications of time as well, such as the heat (4.78; 6.134; 11.524 etc.) or the new moon (8.245, 587) or that next Tuesday "will be the longest day" (3.491). Bloom's watch having stopped, he concludes in the old-fashioned way that "it must be after eight because the sun was set" (13.547). We are also reminded of the discrepancies in human measurements of time, like the gap between Greenwich Mean Time and Dublin time (8.571; 17.1674). This is a world, newly, of telegraphs, telephones, and international time divisions. Dublin was just encountering the phenomenon that we know only too well, of talking to others, say, at 12 noon, when it is five in the morning for them.[93]

By conflating the natural and the conventional, Joyce, in contrast to Homer or Dante, calls into question the idea that time may be a natural or inescapable measure.[94] Bloom and Molly both link Molly and Boylan's attraction to the "young May moon" (8.587; 18.80), and it is important to a number of characters that Thursday is payday in Dublin (1.292; 7.113).[95] There is no distinction between the natural time of the one and the purely arbitrary determination of the other. That *Ulysses* is set on June 16, is as important as that this is one of the longest days of the year. Despite "Circe's" Elijah: "God's time is 12.25. Tell mother you'll be there" (15.2191), there is no "God's time" in *Ulysses.* There is only when human beings happen to do things. Whether there is any sort of absolute is not a background, but a question for the novel.

*   *   *

For all of the undermining of "natural" time in *Ulysses,* it would be a mistake to see the novel (as Wyndham Lewis did) as merely preaching the new religion of relativity. Perhaps paradoxically, Joyce was kept from this by no less a force than his own deeply rooted superstition. Dates had an enormous significance for him, so that, for example, it was necessary that *Ulysses* be published on February 2, 1922, his fortieth birthday. We have every reason to believe that June 16, 1904, was not an arbitrary choice; and as Joyce himself pointed out, Molly's birthday is significantly the same as the Virgin Mary's.[96] Milly Bloom's turning fifteen on the 15th of the month (4.15) is noted with as much, if not more, emphasis than the very salient fact of her puberty.[97] As a result, the conflation of natural and conventional markers of time does not so much undermine the natural, as create a deliberate ambiguity in regard to what does and does not have significance. The issue is the same as that between flux and fixity, but with the stakes considerably raised.

Time, according to Aristotle, is number (*Physics* 219b ff.), and as Joyce plays with the idea of absolute time so also with number. Although he parodies his interest in number, the belief was there. As he told Adolph Hoffmeister:

> Number is an enigma that God deciphers. Along with Beckett . . . I have discovered the importance of numbers in life and history. Dante was obsessed by the number three. He divided his poem into three parts. Each with thirty-three cantos, written in terza-rima. And why always the arrangement of four—four legs of a table, four legs of a horse, four seasons of the year, four provinces of Ireland? Why are there twelve tables of the law, twelve Apostles, twelve months, and twelve Napoleon's marshals?[98]

Number is as important to *Ulysses* (and *Finnegans Wake*) as it is to *The Divine Comedy*. But again, there is a crucial difference. For Dante, number had an absolute meaning. For Joyce, it both did and did not. The number three, upon which Dante's poem rests, is the Trinity, the essential *logos* of the universe. In putting the four provinces of Ireland on a level with a horse's four legs, and equating Napoleon's twelve marshals and the apostles, Joyce suggests something rather different.

Joyce includes in *Ulysses* the essential Pythagorean and scientific truth that the universe is number, but he does so in a parodic, Bloomian fashion:

> Because the weight of the water, no, the weight of the body in the water is equal to the weight of the what? Or is it the volume is equal to the weight? It's a law something like that. . . . What is weight really when you say the weight? Thirtytwo feet per second per second. Law of falling bodies: per second per second. They all fall to the ground. The earth. It's the force of gravity of the earth is the weight. (5.39 ff.)

> Numbers it is. All music when you come to think. Two multiplied by two divided by half is twice one. Vibrations: chords those are. One

plus two plus six is seven. Do anything you like with figures juggling. Always find out this equal to that. . . . And you think you're listening to the etherial. But suppose you said it like: Martha, seven times nine minus x is thirtyfive thousand. Fall quite flat. It's on account of the sounds it is. (11.830 ff.)

Much like his Dantesque attempt to square the circle, Bloom's fumblings point us to, but also undermine, any sense of the absolute reality of number.

Ulysses's ambivalence about number also extends beyond Bloom. On the one hand, eleven, the beginning of a new decade, signifies both death and renewal: hence in Stephen's riddle of the fox burying his grandmother, the clock is striking eleven (2.102 ff.); Paddy Dignam's funeral is at 11:00; Rudy Bloom died aged eleven days; and Hamnet Shakespeare, born on February 2 under Aquarius, the eleventh sign of the zodiac, died (in fact) at the age of eleven: the age, as Bloom thinks, that Rudy would be now if he had lived (4.420).[99] On the other hand, however, Joyce also provides a contrast to these "serious" inclusions of number:

if the proportion existing in 1883 had continued immutable, conceiving that to be possible, till then 1904 when Stephen was 22 Bloom would be 374 and in 1920 when Stephen would be 38, as Bloom then was, Bloom would be 646 while in 1952 when Stephen would have attained the maximum postdiluvian age of 70 Bloom, being 1190 years alive having been born in the year 714, would have surpassed by 221 years the maximum antediluvian age, that of Methusalah, 969 years, while, if Stephen would continue to live until he would attain that age in the year 3072 A.D., Bloom would have been obliged to have been alive 83,300 years, having been obliged to have been born in the year 81,396 B.C. (17.452–61)

The number play reflects Bloom's preoccupation with growing old; Joyce's suggestions that Stephen is the younger and Bloom the older version of himself; and even Molly's rather vague sense of her own, Bloom's, and Stephen's ages (18.51, 474, 1326). Given the absurd lengths that Joyce goes to, however, it is not surprising that most readers fail to notice that he has miscalculated.[100]

Joyce's parody does not imply that either time or number is unimportant. As Philip Kitcher has beautifully shown, not only *Ulysses* but also Joyce's entire corpus, is informed by the human paradox of aging, which both deepens our experience and divorces us from our past selves.[101] Time and number may have the ties to a deeper reality that they possess for Virgil and Dante. But it is no longer clear how that deeper reality connects to the lives that we ordinary human beings live day to day.

World War I: Ignoring a Shift in Time

Just as Joyce refuses to either anchor time and identity in an absolute or to view them as merely relative, he also chooses to ignore (and display that he is ignoring) obvious shifts in time. One such is apparent to anyone who remembers 1999: there are no mentions of the new century. In fact, the word "century" appears only three times in the novel: of Crotthers, the Scots student, in the style of Sterne: "a whole century of polite breeding had not achieved so nice a gesture" (14.743); of "the nifty shimmy dancers, La Aurora and Karini, musical act, the hit of the century" (15.3247); and in Bloom's aspirational "fumed oak sectional bookcase containing the Encyclopaedia Britannica and New Century Dictionary" (17.1523). What is missing is any reference to which century is meant. As one would expect of someone aged eighteen in 1899, Joyce's early writings are full of "fin de siècle" references (e.g., *OCPW* 32)—but neither the phrase nor the idea appears in *Ulysses*.[102] Four years into the twentieth century, the characters of *Ulysses* do not seem very interested in the change.

The more important marker of time that Joyce ignores, however, is available only to Joyce's audience, not his characters. This is World War I. A number of studies have considered the mirror game that Joyce plays by setting what is, in many ways, a novel about 1922, in 1904.[103] Many of these are concerned with his attitudes toward history and politics, particularly Irish nationalism and the war, both of which deeply involved Joyce.[104] His brother Stanislaus had been interned, and neutral Zurich, where Joyce was writing *Ulysses*, talked constantly of the war.[105] The deaths of Joyce's friends and acquaintances, Tom Kettle at the Somme and Francis Sheehy-Skeffington and Patrick Pearse (Joyce's classmate and former Irish teacher), in the 1916 Easter Rising, touched him personally (*JJ* 399–400).[106] As Robert Spoo has elegantly shown, the history lesson of "Nestor," along with the entire "Telemachia," contains a running reference to World War I, and to the graveyards that await the eight-year-olds that Stephen teaches in 1904.[107] Joyce's final words in *Ulysses*: "Trieste-Zurich-Paris / 1914–1921," spanning the war, the Easter Rising, and Irish independence, ensure that we notice the relation.

Joyce himself would later dramatize his relation to World War I, telling Jan Paradowski:

I wrote the greater part of the book during the war. There was fighting on all fronts, empires fell, kings went into exile, the old order was collapsing with a crash; and I had, as I sat down to work, the conviction that in the midst of all these ruins I was building something for the most distant future.[108]

Joyce's involvement with the immense political changes of the twentieth century, as seen in this romantic retrospective, is important. It is equally important, however, that by setting his novel as he does, Joyce obscures the changes. The anachronism is deliberate, even though the novel was begun before the war. As Joyce told Arthur Power soon after finishing *Ulysses*: "A book, in my opinion, should not be planned out beforehand, but as one writes it will form itself, subject, as I say, to the constant emotional promptings of one's personality."[109] Joyce's "genetic" approach to his novel, constantly adding and revising as he wrote, allowed for the inclusion of the political changes occurring all around him.[110] He chose to focus elsewhere.[111]

*   *   *

The sense that the war created a definitive break in time makes Joyce's lack of reference all the more pointed. As a "great" war, World War I, like the Trojan War or the war of the *Mahabharata,* was world-historical. In myth, rather grimly, this meant a war designed as a divine check on human overpopulation. In a more contemporary view, the war ended the idea that tradition had any relevance to modern life:

So it was that as the leaves fell, and the ground turned to mud and the German howitzers, with their twelve horse teams plodded patiently up to the line, the British Army was poised over an abyss. It could be saved only by a reckless squandering of the virtues which, like its delusions, sprang from a background of peace and a stable, ordered society. Bravery, perfect discipline, absolute conviction of right and wrong and the existence of God; a whole code of behavior that is now little more than an object of derision—these were to be pitted against the largest and the most highly trained army in the world.[112]

The same sense of a radical shift appears in contemporary remarks on the war and the Irish rebellion: "The lamps are going out all over Europe, we shall not see them lit again in our life-time" (Sir Edward Grey, August 3, 1914); "All changed, changed utterly: / A terrible beauty is born" (Yeats, "Easter 1916"); "Things fall apart; the center cannot hold; / Mere anarchy is loosed upon the world" (Yeats, "The Second Coming"; written 1919, published 1921).[113] In a novel largely about time, change, and identity, it is thus striking that "the war" in *Ulysses* is primarily the Boer War of 1899–1902 (14.909; 15.795; 18.388).[114]

Joyce's attitude toward history comes out as well in his reference to the *Odyssey*, whose hero prefers his rocky island to the greatest of divinely engineered wars. In choosing this as his model, Joyce took on a theme of human aging that the epic tradition set against Achilles's choice of a short and glorious life.[115] He also chose a focus on life after war. As Declan Kiberd put it: "Joyce chose for a hero not the militarist Cuchulain but the draft-dodger Ulysses, for he believed that the ordinary was the domain of the artist, adding the ironic observation that the extraordinary could safely be left to journalists."[116] Joyce's own comments go even further:

> Why was I always returning to this theme? Now *nel mezzo del cammin* [in the middle of the journey, *Inferno* 1.1] I find the subject of Ulysses the most human in world literature. Ulysses didn't want to go off to Troy; he knew that the official reason for the war, the dissemination of the culture of Hellas, was only a pretext for the Greek merchants, who were seeking new markets. When the recruiting officers arrived, he happened to be plowing. He pretended to be mad. Thereupon they placed his little two-year-old son in the furrow. Observe the beauty of the motifs: the only man in Hellas who is against the war, and the father. Before Troy the heroes shed their lifeblood in vain. They want to raise the siege. Ulysses opposes the idea. [He thinks up] the stratagem of the wooden horse. After Troy there is no further talk of Achilles, Menelaus, Agamemnon. Only one man is not done with; his heroic career has hardly begun: Ulysses. (*JJ* 416–17)[117]

As Joyce explains, he was not interested in Odysseus as a hero of war; he was interested in him as a hero whose story went beyond mere war. To the generation slaughtered between 1914 and 1918, the Edwardians of 1904 mattered about as much as the dodo bird. Even after it turned out not to be the war to end all wars, the Great War seemed to mark a seismic shift in history. By setting his own epic as he does, Joyce implicitly denies that such a fundamental shift in history occurred.[118]

Nor is Joyce interested in making a myth of the past, whether Celtic Twilight, antebellum, or Classical.[119] As Joyce's various comments make clear, Odysseus, Penelope, and Telemachus were for him ordinary human beings.

Like Samuel Butler, who remarked skeptically about Penelope's putting off the suitors:

> Did she find errands for them to run, and then scold them, and say she did not want them? or make them do commissions for her and forget to pay them, or keep on sending them back to the shop to change things, and they had given ever so much too much money and she wished she had gone and done it herself? Did she insist on their attending family worship?

Joyce insisted on seeing the mythic world in completely human terms.[120] His subject was not world cataclysm but how a young man finds a way to his future self and how an older one deals with losing his youth. In this way his point of view was not that different from Homer's.[121]

Stephen and Telemachus

The Case of the Displaced Son

If Odysseus's challenge is to move from the world of myth back into the ordinary, Telemachus's lies in just trying to keep the ordinary together. He is firmly fixed in the world of Ithaca. But while his main difficulty seems to be the suitors, the greater challenge to his finding his proper place may be Odysseus himself. As the poem opens, Telemachus is daydreaming that his father might "scatter the suitors through the house / and hold his own place (*timē*) and be lord of his own possessions" (1.114–17), an apparent solution to his problems. Once Odysseus has arrived, however, the problem is not only that the place he takes is the one that Telemachus aspired to but also how anyone could be son to such a father.

In David Pierce's notable image, *Ulysses*'s Homeric correspondences are not meant to reproduce, but to strike a chord with the *Odyssey*—and a chord, whether consonant or dissonant, exists only through difference.[1] The differences between Stephen and Telemachus are as notable as the similarities. In many ways, in fact, Joyce has reversed Homer. Telemachus is no poet, as Stephen Dedalus and Odysseus are. He is rather the practical one, careful of his property, like Bloom, but very unlike Stephen. Nonetheless, the two face similar challenges. Both want to leave the past behind, but are also reliant on it. Both are stymied in their attempts to become their future selves. And both need to measure up to their fathers. For Stephen, however, this means proving himself worthy of the "old father, old artificer" with whom he ended *Portrait* (253). In this respect, he faces the most extreme stretch in identity, and the greatest existential challenge of *Ulysses*, which is growing up to write the novel he is part of.

PROBLEMS WITH PROPERTY

Telemachus and the Household Goods

Telemachus's firm location in the ordinary world is grounded in his appreciation of property. The *Odyssey* is very much a poem about things, and Odysseus is a hero very aware of the need to acquire them. Telemachus shares this appreciation, but with a focus on maintenance and stability. From his first speech to "Mentes" (1.159–62), to his complaints in the Assembly (2.48–79), to his discussion with Menelaus (4.316–21), Telemachus's prime concern is, as he says, not to rule, but just to be master of his possessions (1.394–98). Like Penelope, he is appalled at the suitors' unseemly riot (18.227–32). Unlike Penelope, who barely mentions the consumption of goods, his worries are consistently about keeping his things together.[2] As Penelope sums up the situation to the disguised Odysseus:

> Now I cannot escape from this marriage, nor can I discover
> any other device. My parents are eager to have me marry
> and my son is angry that they eat away our livelihood,
> now that he knows it.
>   (19.157–60)

Telemachus is "centred in the sphere / Of common duties" as Tennyson's *Ulysses* has it (39–40). His conservative tendencies also form a strong contrast not only to Stephen Dedalus but also to Odysseus.[3] For while Odysseus may be more interested in possessions than most Homeric heroes, like most Homeric heroes his primary interest is the status that goods confer (11.355–61). Of course, he takes care to keep his goods safe (see 8.443–48; 13.203–21), but his persistent interest, with the Cyclops (9.266–68), with the Phaeacians (13.40–41), in his lying tales in Ithaca (13.262 ff.; 14.222 ff., 285–86; 17.419 ff.), in his plans after the suitors' deaths (23.255 ff.), and in his own accounts of Odysseus (14.321 ff.; 19.280 ff.) is in acquiring goods, rather than preserving them.

In this regard, Odysseus, in contrast to his son, remains linked to the heroic. In the world of the *Iliad*, goods are important because they bring *timē* (honor or status). Achilles's concern when he is stripped of his prize is *timē*, not possessions, as is clear when he refuses Agamemnon's immense restitution in Book 9.[4] In contrast, Telemachus worries about the practical, as does the world he belongs to. The attention of the swineherd, Eumaeus, and the cattleherd, Philoitius, to tending their animals, the description of Argus's mettle in hunting, the concern that the weapons on display in the hall are being fouled with smoke (16.282–90; 19.1–25), even Noëmon's need to use his boat (4.634–37), all point to a world where things exist for use more than for status.[5]

The *Odyssey*'s themes of flux and fixity, and of human isolation, also clarify why a concern with property matters. As we will see in chapter 6, the persistence of objects is a critical factor in the poem, not least because their pasts are embedded within them. Nestor thus takes his seat on white, polished stones "on which, before him, / Neleus had sat, in council like the gods, / but he, already conquered by his doom, had gone to the house of Hades" (3.408–10), while Odysseus settles on his own threshold "which the carpenter had once / planed expertly and made straight by the chalkline" (17.340–41). Similarly, in regard to others, Helen uses a workbasket "which Alcandre, Polybus' wife / gave her, who dwelt in Thebes / in Egypt, where most possessions are stored in the houses" (4.125–27). Menelaus offers Telemachus a silver bowl, "the work of Hephaestus; the hero Phaidimos gave it to me / king of the Sidonians, when his house sheltered me / there, as I returned home" (4.617–19).[6] Even the wine jars Telemachus takes on his voyage are lined up in the storeroom "for whenever Odysseus / should return home, even after suffering many hardships" (2.342–43). And as the examples make clear, in embodying their own pasts, objects also embody the connections between individuals. For Telemachus to be master of the household, then, implies a good deal more than just having a lot of stuff.

Similarly, although implying a rather different relation between people, Telemachus is regularly associated with weapons, which are also holders of the past. Here, however, the balance between conservation and use becomes rather more fraught. The spear rack on which Telemachus first places "Mentes"'s spear "where indeed other / spears stood of steadfast-minded Odysseus, many of them" (1.128–29) reappears as he and Odysseus store the weapons (16.281–98; 19.16–46) that he later goes to retrieve (22.101–15), a task that he botches (22.153–57). We see the importance when Penelope retrieves Odysseus's bow, given him by Iphitus, "which once great Eurytus had carried, but to his son / he left it, when he had died in his lofty house" (21.32–33). Even this is only part of a thirty-line account of the bow's history and the complex, and heroic, human interrelations it embodies (21.11–41). It will thus be an important moment, as we will see below, when Telemachus tries to use the bow.

Objects in this way are also the roots of identity—one reason why it matters that Odysseus brings nothing back from either Troy or his Wanderings. The world he has to rejoin is the world he left, which is now not his, but Telemachus's. The world of objects is not simply persistent; Laertes's shield, for example, "which he used to bear in his youth" is fouled with mildew, and the stitches of the handles all rotted (22.183–86). And while Odysseus's bow has not suffered rot (21.10–41, 393–95), even the continuity, given that he himself has changed, can be alienating. The bow is the same, but Odysseus may no longer be able to draw it. He knows his courtyard immediately (17.264–71), but the change in Argus points also to the changes in himself (17.290–327). Despite its continuity, this world is as alien to him as it is normal to Telemachus. It is this continuity that Telemachus strives to maintain, since it involves the link to the past that, despite himself, he relies upon. The continuity was threatened first by the arrival of the suitors. It is now challenged by the return of Odysseus.

Stephen and Debt

For Stephen, too, property is linked to identity. His problem, however, is not maintaining his possessions, but coping with debt. As pointed out in his opening refusal to borrow more "secondhand breeks" from Mulligan (1.113), Stephen is plagued by debt, and of all sorts: "My two feet in his boots are at the end of hismy legs" (3.17); "That is Kevin Egan's movement I made" (3.439); "Smile, Smile Cranly's smile" (9.21); "Walk like Haines now" (9.1114); "*Stephanos*, my crown. My sword. His boots are spoiling the shape of my feet" (9.947 ff.). He resists his indebtedness to Ireland, to the British Empire, to "the man with my voice and my eyes," and to God, who willed his parents' coupling (3.45). Significantly, a particularly charged reflection on identity is occasioned by debt, as he realizes that one of the (nearly) four pounds he has in his pocket would repay George Russell (whose pseudonym was "AE"):

I paid my way. I paid my way.

Steady on. He's from beyant Boyne water. The northeast corner. You owe it.

Wait. Five months. Molecules all change. I am other I now. Other I got pound.

Buzz. Buzz.

But I, entelechy, form of forms, am I by memory because under everchanging forms.

I that sinned and prayed and fasted.

> A child Conmee saved from pandies.
> I, I and I. I.
> A.E.I.O.U. (9.203–12)

As different as Stephen is from Telemachus, he too is striving for stability within a world of change, a quality that stands out in "Proteus" in his fear of "seachange" (3.482) and here in his insistence on a stable self that underlies "everchanging forms." Like Menelaus, and in a way like Telemachus, Stephen attempts to force meaning out of change by making it be still. The difficulty is that stability, for Stephen, also means debt.

If Stephen is unlike Telemachus in his profligacy, he is like him in facing the threat of dispossession. His final thought in "Telemachus," as he watches Mulligan, is thus "Usurper" (1.744), part of his self-conscious paralleling his situation to that of Hamlet. Stephen's "me she slights" (1.419) casts Mulligan as his rival with the milkwoman who suggests to him Ireland ("silk of the kine" 1.403), while his comment in the Library: "I am tired of my voice. The voice of Esau" (9.981) reflects Mulligan's supplanting him (as Jacob supplanted Esau) both at Moore's literary party (9.305–6) and in creation (9.875–77).[7] Even the style of the episode seems to follow Mulligan's "the play's the thing!" (9.876–77) as it moves dutifully into play format (9.893–934).

For Stephen, however, as for Hamlet, dispossession is a double-sided sword. To reclaim his heritage means also reclaiming the burden it imposes, the nightmare that he is so famously attempting to escape (2.377). Identity, when it is seen as soul, the "form of forms" (2.75–76; 3.280) that Stephen and Aristotle oppose to the flux of the material world, has the stability Stephen desires.[8] But flux offers the promise of escape ("I am other I now. Other I got pound"). In addition, by casting the contrast as "I, I and I. I.," Stephen brings in the issue that pursues him throughout *Ulysses,* the extent to which the self he now is is continuous (I, I) or discontinuous (I. I) with his past in *Portrait,* the "child Conmee saved from pandies" (55–58). Again, the sword is double-edged. A continuous self implies debt, a discontinuous one the loss of identity.

* * *

The theme of debt emerges in *Ulysses* not only in a literal but also in a literary sense, the sense critical to Stephen's identity as an artist. Stephen resents debt, which he sees as his bondage to the past, as in his view of Ireland as a pawnshop (3.46–47). Nonetheless he constantly incurs it.[9] He also seems surprisingly resigned to the impossibility of repaying what he owes:[10]

> Mulligan, nine pounds, three pairs of socks, one pair brogues, ties. Curran, ten guineas. McCann, one guinea. Fred Ryan, two shillings. Temple, two lunches. Russell, one guinea, Cousins, ten shillings, Bob Reynolds, half a guinea, Koehler, three guineas, Mrs MacKernan, five weeks' board. The lump I have is useless. (2.255–59)

How far he really faces up to these debts, however, is left ambiguous. In his inner discourse in "Telemachus": "He wants that key. It is mine. I paid the rent. Now I eat his salt bread" (1.630), Joyce does not clarify whether "I paid the rent" is Stephen's direct thought, or his idea of what Mulligan will say, which has led generations of Joyceans to ponder whether Stephen is or is not the landlord here.[11]

The problem of acknowledgment becomes critical in the case of Stephen's literary debts. His telegram to Mulligan and Haines is about the need to acknowledge debt: "*The sentimentalist is he who would enjoy without incurring the immense debtorship for a thing done*" (9.550), but is itself "cribbed out of Meredith" (14.1486), an acknowledgment that Stephen never makes. And similarly with most of his literary borrowings, which also comprise almost all of his compositions. Mulligan, early in "Telemachus," cites Oscar Wilde: "The rage of Caliban at not seeing his face in a mirror . . . If Wilde were only alive to see you!" (1.143–44). Stephen does not mention that his "cracked lookingglass" (appropriately) also comes from Wilde (1.146).[12] Stephen's fox riddle (2.102) is taken from P. W. Joyce, and when Haines locates Douglas Hyde's *Love Songs of Connacht* (9.93–95) he will find in it the stanza of verse that Stephen composes in "Proteus" (3.397 ff.; 7.522 ff).[13] Even Stephen's portrait of Shakespeare: "a man who holds so tightly to what he calls his rights over what he calls his debts" (9.788), stems from Mr Deasy's association of the bard with "the proudest word you will ever hear from an Englishman's mouth . . . *I paid my way*" (2.244 ff.; italics in the original).[14]

It is unclear how far Stephen acknowledges these debts. He is not above misrepresentation, as when he claims that he is spending money earned from his poetry (11.264; 15.3533), but he also openly derives his "Pisgah Sight of Palestine" from the conversation in the newspaper office, as MacHugh recognizes (7.1062). In the Library he repeats MacHugh's reference to Antisthenes on Penelope without attribution (7.1035; 9.621), but acknowledges

Brunetto Latini, if only to himself (9.374). He may expect that the telegram taken from Meredith will be recognized, and he may not know that his comment about the lookingglass was made before. It is hard, however, to imagine that he does not see the "Proteus" stanza, which he repeats only to himself, as original, just as it is hard to see Joyce as not deliberately copying it. Like Gilbert and Sullivan's Wandering Minstrel, who adopts and adapts Hamlet's "king of shreds and patches" (*Mikado* 1.2; *Hamlet* 3.4.103), Stephen's world, it seems, is made up of what was said before—sometimes, perhaps, more than he knows.[15]

* * *

Stephen's literary debts are also directly tied to his debts to the past. In the most obvious connection, we have already seen the tendency in *Portrait*, in his copying the Count of Monte Cristo's "Madam, I never eat muscatel grapes" (63) and with Byron:[16]

> On the first line of the page appeared the title of the verses he was trying to write: To E--C--. He knew it was right to begin so for he had seen similar titles in the collected poems of Lord Byron. (*P* 70)

Stephen's description of the artist as an impersonal God standing outside his creation (*P* 215) repeats Flaubert, and, most critically, even his rejection of servitude is borrowed:[17]

> —I will not serve, answered Stephen.
> —That remark was made before, Cranly said calmly.
> —It is made behind now, said Stephen hotly. (*P* 239)

Despite his resistance, the Stephen of *Ulysses* carries the Stephen of *Portrait* with him, from bon mots such as Ireland, the old sow who eats her farrow (*P* 203; *U* 15.4581), to his rebellion, to memories of being pandied at Clongowes.[18] Stephen had once seen his past as faded out of existence:

> He had not died but he had faded out like a film in the sun. He had been lost or had wandered out of existence for he no longer existed. How strange to think of him passing out of existence in such a way, not by death but by fading out in the sun or by being lost and forgotten somewhere in the universe! It was strange to see his small body appear again for a moment: a little boy in a grey belted suit. (*P* 93)

The past, however, has not disappeared. It is instead frozen into the pages of *Portrait*. Stephen enters into the new novel laden with the debts of the old.[19]

* * *

The theme of debt becomes most crucial when we consider what it is that Stephen is dispossessed of. Paradoxically, what seems most likely is that it is the writing of *Ulysses*. Joyce teases us throughout with the card already played in the title of *A Portrait of the Artist as a Young Man*, now suggesting that Stephen is the future author of *Ulysses*. Thus, Mulligan's mocking declaration (in 1904) that Stephen will "write something in ten years" (10.1089–92) seems to point to the novel's final "Trieste-Zurich-Paris / 1914–1921."[20] In the Library, where it may be Stephen manipulating the page layout in a way that prefigures the Arranger, he seems to record the scene for a future work ("See this. Remember" 9.294; "Listen" 9.300), notably just as the remark surfaces that "Our national epic has yet to be written" (9.309).[21] As he says: "in the future, the sister of the past, I may see myself as I sit here now" (9.383–84); that is, the future Joyce may re-create the scene that the Joyce of 1904 played. As Telemachus should inherit his father's estate so, it seems, Stephen should "forge in the smithy of my soul the uncreated conscience of my race" under the auspices of his true father, Daedalus (*P* 253), or even Joyce.[22]

Here again, at least in Stephen's eyes, the problem is debt. As Perry Meisel has pointed out, Stephen's sense in "Proteus" of the "dead breaths I living breathe" reflects the fear that it is impossible to say anything new.[23] As Stephen knows only too well, even one's language is the creation of others.[24] He thinks in looking at the English dean of studies in *Portrait*: "His language, so familiar and so foreign, will always be for me an acquired speech. I have not made or accepted its words. My voice holds them at bay. My soul frets in the shadow of his language" (*P* 189). Tortured by what Meisel calls "the sense that one's life or one's art is the echo or repetition of another's,"[25] Stephen wants both to inherit what is his own and to be free from his debts to the past. The two are not compatible.

A particular example, however, reveals how borrowings may take on a life of their own, and in so doing address Stephen's difficulty. In *Portrait*, Stephen's "I will not serve," echoes Lucifer's *non serviam*, referred to in the hell-fire sermon (117). In *Ulysses*, Stephen's repetition of the idea, "The intellectual imagination! With me all or not at all. *Non serviam!*" (15.4227–28; italics in the original), becomes a much fuller paradigm. It reflects his opening role as "servant" (1.312, 638–44), Joyce's addition of the pre-fallen Satan: "Allbright he falls, proud lightning of the intellect, *Lucifer, dico, qui nescit occasum*" ("Lucifer, I say. Who does not know fall / setting"

3.486–87; italics in the original) and, in the new, epic setting, the specific Satan of Milton's *Paradise Lost,* who also attempts to repudiate his debts (4.49–53), claims to be self-created (5.853–69), refuses to repent (15.4212–19, 4.79 ff.) and is trapped in his own thoughts (4.73–113; 9.118–34; and see 3.486–87).[26]

In contrast to the ever-changing Odysseus, Stephen, like Telemachus, aims at stability. As Joyce said, he "has a shape that can't be changed" (*JJ* 459).[27] This also reflects Milton's Satan, who, possessed by "A mind not to be changed by Place or Time" (*Paradise Lost* 1.253), refuses any acknowledgment of his debt to God. Milton, however, also suggests another option, as Satan realizes that in his determination to "quit / The debt immense of endless gratitude" he "understood not that a grateful mind / By owing owes not, but still pays, at once / Indebted and discharg'd" (4.551–57).[28] The element that Stephen has not factored in is change. He may be the same, but also different in the future, hence the last phrase of: "in the future, the sister of the past, I may see myself as I sit here now *but by reflection from that which then I shall be*" (9.383–85; italics added). That new self may see that there is an advantage to acknowledging one's debts, for example, by entitling a novel "*Ulysses.*"[29]

PROBLEMS WITH FAMILY

Nor is dispossession the only thing that Stephen and Telemachus have in common. They are both trapped on an island from which they have made one minor (and not particularly successful) excursion. They both have absent fathers that they closely resemble and complicated relations with their mothers. And for both, as for most people, problems with their parents involve issues with the past, their identity, change, and being unable to move on.[30]

Telemachus and His Mother / Telemachus, His Father's Son

Like Odysseus, Telemachus's issue with identity stems from what is essentially a stoppage in time. In his case, however, his mother is behind the problem. Like Odysseus, he is held on an island by a female who, out of love, will not let him leave. And just as Calypso's hospitality amounts to a kind of hiding, as her name implies, Penelope's need to keep Telemachus safe results in a concealment that his visit to his father's comrades is meant to break through. Telemachus needs to move into the future. As Athena frames it, he must either find out that his father is alive or, learning that he is dead, raise a funeral mound and get on with business (1.287 ff.).

The problem appears in Penelope's reenactment of Odysseus's parting words:

> "I do not know whether the god will spare me, or if I will be taken,
> right there in Troy; here let all things be cared for by you.
> Remember my father and mother in our halls
> as now, or even more, with my being far off.
> But when you should see our son growing his beard
> marry whomever you wish, forsaking your home."
> That man spoke thus; now all this is being accomplished.
>   (18.265 ff.)

Penelope can hold open a space for Odysseus's return only until Telemachus becomes a man. When he does, it will be time for him to take over the household and for her to marry again. Telemachus will occupy the space once held by Odysseus, and there will no longer be either a household or a wife for Odysseus to return to. As a result, for Penelope waiting for Odysseus means keeping Telemachus a child. For Telemachus it means being trapped by a mother who cannot allow him his independence.[31]

An implicit and growing tension between Penelope and Telemachus underlies his attempts to assert his authority. Homer makes it clear that the self-assertion is a new element in his relation with his mother, as it is, explicitly, with the suitors (2.310–15), by using the same formulaic phrase to describe both the suitors (1.381; 18.410; 20.268) and Penelope (1.360; 22.354) as surprised by it.[32] The tension appears even more vividly in Telemachus's insistence that his mother not be told of his voyage, and her response to the news:

> For if I had learned he was planning this journey,
> then either he would have remained, keen though he was on the
>   voyage,
> or he would have left me dead in the halls.
>   (4.732–34)

It would seem that time is on Telemachus's side. Penelope knows that Telemachus wants her to marry again (19.530 ff.), although, as he tells the Ithacan Assembly, he cannot force her (2.130 ff.). His readiness to believe that she is planning a marriage (15.15 ff.; 16.73 ff.) and his nonchalance in telling her what he has learned of his father (17.101 ff.), also signal a coming change.[33] But by the time Penelope has acknowledged that Telemachus is an adult, and that she can no longer continue to wait for Odysseus's return, the person she declares this to is Odysseus himself.

*   *   *

The relation of Telemachus and Penelope is, in this way, as difficult as the one between Stephen and his mother, between Stephen and "Mother Ireland" or, in Stephen's favorite model, between Hamlet and Gertrude. In addition, just as Hamlet's father may do even more to stifle him than Claudius, Penelope's need to maintain Odysseus as a real presence sets Telemachus not only against his mother in his struggle for independence but also, implicitly, against his father. This is not an unusual relation. Epic heroes tend to be individualists; they seldom maintain an equal partnership with their fathers or sons.[34] One does not picture a time, for example, when Odysseus and Laertes happily shared the rule of the kingdom.

If Telemachus's problem with Penelope lies in the fixity of their relation, with Odysseus, he has the opposite problem, of competing with a cipher. Odysseus is notoriously "of many turns" and for no one more than for his son. The primary issue is the one that Telemachus poses in his first appearance in the poem:

> Indeed my mother says I am his. But I myself,
> I do not know. No one actually ever knows his father.
> But for me, I wish I had been son to some fortunate man,
> someone that old age overtook, among his possessions.
> But now the man who, of all mortal men, is the most ill-fated,
> that one's son they say I am, since you ask me about it.
> (1.215–20)

Is Telemachus his father's son? He cannot know. No child can know his father (just as, as is brought up not infrequently in *Ulysses*, no father can know his child). Telemachus, unlike Odysseus, is almost never called by his patronymic, a form of address more characteristic of the heroic than the ordinary world. His father has also been absent since he was an infant, so that, although "Mentes," Nestor, Menelaus, and Helen all make a point of his resemblance to his father (1.208; 3.123 ff.; 4.140 ff.), he has no way to judge for himself. In those days, as Joyce remarked to Frank Budgen and Paul Suter, there were no photographs (*JJ* 430).[35]

But of course, what the question "Are you your father's son?" really asks is whether Telemachus can measure up. In a sense the poem itself asks this question, as Telemachus's challenge and journey appear as miniature versions of the tests his father endures.[36] Though more subtly than Simon Dedalus, who tells his old Cork buddies: "There's that son of mine there not half my age and I'm a better man than he is any day of the week" (*P* 95), "Mentes," Nestor, and Menelaus, with varying degrees of indirection, all compare Telemachus's inaction to what Odysseus would have done (1.253 ff.; 3.216 ff.; 4.332 ff.; and see 2.270 ff.).[37] And each of them brings up Orestes (1.298 ff.; 3.196, 304 ff.; 4.546 ff.).[38] Even without having heard (as the audience has) Zeus's opening description of how Orestes overcame his mother's paramour, took revenge for his father, and gained control of his rightful kingdom (1.28 ff.), Telemachus gets it: Orestes, only a child when Agamemnon left for Troy, has measured up to his father. Telemachus has done nothing. His name, "fighting from afar" may reflect his father's skill as an archer (as Eurysaces's name, "he of the broad shield," reflects his father, Ajax)—or, as "far from the battle," it may simply imply that he, in contrast to his father, is no warrior.[39] Whoever his father was.

There is, however, another side to the question. As we saw in chapter 1, the *Odyssey* can take a somewhat skeptical view of heroism. While Telemachus may wonder whether he can match the stories told about his father, he may also wonder whether his father ever matched them. Telemachus never meets Orestes, and no mention is made of the tradition that Menelaus, disastrously, promised his daughter, Hermione, to both Orestes and to Achilles's son, Neoptolemus (whom she is marrying when Telemachus visits, 4.1 ff.). As we have seen, however, both Menelaus and Nestor could well strike the younger generation as long on stories but rather short on action. No one appears to be volunteering to help drive out the suitors. The great deeds of the olden days are wonderful to hear, but, as the suitors seem to feel, not necessarily relevant to how people operate today.

Homer makes it clear that Telemachus has grown up among people, his mother, his grandmother (while she was alive), Eurycleia, and Mentor, who are steeped in the legends of his father's greatness. We never learn what Telemachus thinks of these stories. In *Portrait* Stephen feels himself beset by voices urging him to be a gentleman and a good catholic, strong and manly and healthy and true to his country, to raise up his father's state and be a decent fellow (83–84)—voices that he sees as calling him away from his own identity. Homer's tendency to present his characters through their actions rather than their thoughts means that Telemachus has no such reflections. Nonetheless, there is a suggestion of something similar.

Allowing ourselves (for now) one final venture into Telemachus's psyche, it is worth looking at his self-assertion when the leader of the suitors, Antinous, urges him to eat and drink with them as he used to (2.305):

> Antinous, there is no way that among all of you in your insolence
> I can dine, unwilling as I am, and enjoy myself at my ease.
> Is it not enough that earlier you wore down many excellent
> possessions of mine, you suitors, and I still a child?
> But now, when I am grown, and hearing the stories of others
> I understand, and the heart has grown great within me.
>   (2.310–15)

Telemachus is about twenty years old, and the suitors, as Homer goes out of his way to tell us, have been at the palace for the past three years (2.89). In other words, Telemachus, a seventeen-year-old only child, raised by his doting (or smothering) mother, grandparents, and household on stories of the (probably unmatchable) greatness of his father, suddenly encounters the most celebrated young nobles from the islands all around, who flatter him and welcome him into their company. Like Stephen and Buck Mulligan (or Joyce and Gogarty), while the present resentment may be understandable, so is the past attraction. This is the final twist on the question of whether Telemachus is his father's son: not only whether he can be but also whether, in his heart of hearts, he wants to be.[40]

The *Odyssey* does not explicitly position Telemachus between flux and fixity in the way that Joyce positions Stephen. Nonetheless, his relations to his father, who is unknown, and his mother, who needs to keep him fixed in childhood, contain elements of that divide. Both sides of the opposition also exist in his relation to his father. On the one hand, as one whose fame goes from Ithaca to Pylos to Sparta to Phaeacia (beyond the reach of Telemachus's knowledge) and as high as heaven (9.20), Odysseus, the great warrior of Troy, has taken his place among the fixed figures of legend. On the other hand, Odysseus, the father Telemachus never knew, in the different accounts of Nestor, Menelaus, Mentor, the suitors, Penelope, Helen, and (undoubtedly) both Eurycleia and his grandparents, must also be to Telemachus an ever-changing figure. In the heroic world, where one is defined by one's patronymic, this is a problem. One can see why Telemachus might prefer a world where identity is located in property.[41]

Stephen's Parents: "Proteus" and "Scylla and Charybdis"

Stephen's opposite relations to his father and mother pull him between poles of flux and fixity in a far more intellectual fashion than Telemachus experiences. In Stephen's intense scholasticism, flux is the primary characteristic of the physical realm, the realm of Becoming, in contrast to unchanging Being, or, in Stephen's terms, that "eternity of which this vegetable world is but a shadow" (9.88). Hence, he answers the possibility that "I am other I now" with the Aristotelian (and Augustinian) response: "I, entelechy, form of forms, am I by memory" (9.205, 208–9). And, in scholasticism, form is the masculine principle and matter the feminine. Stephen carries these associations over to his father, whose "form" he is growing into, and his mother, whom he associates with the flux of the sea.[42] Correspondingly, his thoughts about paternity tend to the abstract, while recollections of his mother bring on an immediate, visceral fear of absorption. In "Scylla and Charybdis" paternity appears as a theological puzzle; in "Telemachus" and "Circe" May Dedalus appears as a nightmare and hallucination (1.270–79; 15.4181–242). Stephen, of course, is caught between the two.

Stephen's relation to his mother and father as flux and fixity appears as well in the connection of motherhood to food and of paternity to God the Father. The association also reflects Homer, where ever-changing humans, who live for a day, eat bread (*Iliad* 21.464–66) while the immortal, unchanging gods eat ambrosia, a word which, etymologically, means "immortality."[43] Thus different meals are placed before Odysseus and Calypso (4.196 ff.), and therefore Odysseus, who is very mortal indeed, is also very alive to the demands of the "shameless belly" (7.216; 15.344; 18.53 ff. etc.). In this light, Stephen's rejection of food suits his fear of change, just as his vision of the artist as God (*P* 233; *U* 9.862–71, 1028) aspires to eternity. In contrast to the physicality of "stately, plump" Buck Mulligan (who opens the novel parodying the transformations of "body and soul," 1.21), Stephen sees only a "dogsbody to rid of vermin" (1.136). He follows his discourse on soul as a "simple substance," which is incorruptible (16.756), by saying he cannot eat (16.785–89).[44] Spirit, the realm of the Father, is eternal and unchanging, while the material, maternal world of the body is continually in flux—and nowhere more so than in digestion.

*   *   *

As in his description of history as a nightmare (2.376), Stephen feels that the past controls him, not least by shaping his subconscious self, the realm of dreams. The nightmare, however, is not only history but also the "night mère" who haunts his dreams in her grave clothes (1.102–5; 15.4156–243). And "*mare*" is also, of course, Latin for "sea."[45] Mulligan's opening description of the sea as a mother (1.77, 80, 108, 196) thus points, for Stephen, to the attempt of both to absorb him (1.278), with the green of the Irish Sea connecting his mother's "green sluggish bile" (1.109) to Mother Ireland as well.[46] As "Proteus" makes clear, Stephen's escape to Paris has accomplished nothing. He can no more escape his mother than a fish can escape the water.

The connection of Stephen's mother with the sea, prepared in "Telemachus," comes to a head in "Proteus," the quintessential episode of flux. Having circled around thoughts of his mother throughout the episode (3.31–47, 61–69, 184–85, 197–204, 359–61, 395–96) the relation of Stephen's isolation to his guilt over his mother's death becomes clear:

> The man that was drowned nine days ago off Maiden's rock. They are waiting for him now. The truth, spit it out. I would want to [save him]. I would try. I am not a strong swimmer. Water cold soft. When I put my face into it in the basin at Clongowes. Can't see! Who's behind me? Out quickly, quickly! . . . If I had land under my feet. I want his life still to be his, mine to be mine. A drowning man. His human eyes scream to me out of horror of his death. I . . . With him together down . . . I could not save her. Waters: bitter death: lost. (3.322–30; last two sets of ellipses in the original)[47]

The guilt ("I could not save her") that he cannot escape also connects absorption and transformation in Stephen's mind, and associates both with drowning, as appears in his new version of *The Tempest*'s "sea-change" (1.2.397 ff; U 3.482): "God becomes man becomes fish becomes barnacle goose becomes featherbed mountain" (3.476–80).[48] But while he substitutes "Old Father Ocean" (3.483) for Mulligan's "great sweet mother" (1.77–78; 3.31–32), just as he links drowning to the masculine world of *Lycidas* (3.474), a series of women still enter in: Helen, the "*Prix de Paris*" (3.483); Queen Victoria, "the old hag with the yellow teeth" (3.493); and even, in "barnacle goose," Nora Joyce. In an apparently random recollection of a Tennyson poem: "Of all the glad new year, mother, the rum tum tiddledy tum" (3.491–92), Stephen's mother also returns.

*   *   *

Stephen's relation to his father is in many ways the opposite of his relation to his mother. While his mother appears to him unbidden, he declines to see his father (16.251–59), and although their paths cross repeatedly (6.39–44; 7.351–511; 10.800–883; 11.253–70), they never meet.[49] This is not least because he prefers a purely conceptual approach to paternity. As his discourse in the library makes clear, the father that Stephen chooses to engage with is not Simon Dedalus, but his original creator, the unchanging and eternal God the Father:

> Wombed in sin darkness I was too, made not begotten. By them, the man with my voice and my eyes and a ghostwoman with ashes on her breath. They clasped and sundered, did the coupler's will. From before the ages He willed me and now may not will me away or ever. A *lex eterna* stays about Him. (3.44 ff.)

Mulligan's mockery, however, points to the reason for the abstraction:

> It's quite simple. He proves by algebra that Hamlet's grandson is Shakespeare's grandfather and that he himself is the ghost of his own father.
> —What? Haines said, beginning to point at Stephen. He himself?
>   Buck Mulligan slung his towel stolewise round his neck and, bending in loose laughter, said to Stephen's ear:
> —O, shade of Kinch the elder! Japhet in search of a father! (1.555–60; 2.152)

It is precisely being "the ghost of his own father," a "shade of Kinch the elder" that poses the danger.[50] Unlike Telemachus, who cannot know if, as everyone says, he resembles his father, Stephen can see only too well that he is rapidly becoming the "chip of the old block" (7.899) that everyone in Dublin recognizes, the Dublin character that Colum and O'Connor recalled and that Joyce himself fled.[51]

Against the fluidity implied by Plato and Russell's mysticism ("Streams of tendency and eons they worship" 9.85) Stephen opposes the stability of Aristotelian definition: "Horseness is the whatness of allhorse" (9.84). He resists "Mercurial Malachi" (1.518), in many ways the ultimate shapeshifter, and his temptation to "play them as I do" (1.506), just as he resists Mulligan's invitation to the sea (1.471–77).[52] Like Odysseus, he clings to the tree (*Odyssey* 12.430–41) as the whirlpool threatens to suck him down: "Hold to the now, the here, through which all future plunges to the past"

(9.89).[53] The problem is that his particular Aristotelian telos threatens to turn him into his father.

Hamlet: Being One's Own Father

Stephen's way out of the impasse appears primarily in "Scylla and Charybdis," an episode that all but explicitly opposes flux and fixity. As it concerns Stephen, the aspiring author, it is appropriately set in the National Library, the home for old books. Here Stephen attempts a new solution, not to switch one kind of indebtedness for another by changing fathers, but to avoid the son's indebtedness altogether by becoming his own father. Having jettisoned Simon for the original Daedalus, he aims to be not the son of Daedalus, who (like Satan) aspires too high and falls, but Daedalus himself. The same scenario plays out in his discourse on Shakespeare.

The shift is particularly significant since *Hamlet* also encapsulates Stephen's relations to his mother and father. Stephen identifies with *Hamlet* self-consciously, from his "customary suits of solemn black" (*Hamlet* 1.2.78) and "Hamlet hat" (*U* 3.395) to the dispossession of "hismy sandal shoon" (3.492; *Hamlet* 4.5.26). The reference also operates on a level beyond the characters' awareness, in the line that Stephen and Bloom identically misquote: "*Hamlet, I am thy father's spirit*" (7.67; 9.170; and see 15.3655) and in the blending of the two in the cuckolded Shakespeare of "Circe" (15.3820 ff.).[54] And most importantly, *Hamlet* tells once more the story of the *Odyssey*, of an absent father, a mother courted by a usurper, and a dispossessed son, although, despite Stephen, from the perspective of the son rather than that of the father.[55]

Other uncomfortable elements of the play also emerge. There is, for example, the competition between father and son that appears as early as Hamlet's "but no more like my father / Than I to Hercules" (1.2.151–53). Whatever Joyce might have thought of Oedipal interpretations of the play, Stephen has a decided interest in the meeting of the younger Hamlet with his father, and so in the lines: "and in the porches of mine ears did pour" (7.750, 881; 9.465) and "List," conveniently close to the actual name of the librarian, Thomas Lyster (9.144, 171, 890; 15.1216). The scene suggests the destruction of the younger Hamlet through the demands of his father.[56] It also resembles the danger incurred by Telemachus's foil, Orestes, who, in Aeschylus's *Oresteia*, claims an inheritance he may well be destroyed by. The father who demands his child as a sacrifice also appears in *Stephen Hero* in Stephen's resentment that his father expects him to redeem the family fortunes (111); in *Portrait* in the voice that bids him "raise up his father's fallen state by his labours" (84); and in *Ulysses* transferred onto Stephen's vision of his sister, Dilly, as Ophelia: "She is drowning. . . . She will drown me with her, eyes and hair. Lank coils of seaweed hair around me, my heart, my soul. Salt green death" (10.875 ff.).[57]

As with God the Father and God the Son, or Daedalus and Daedalus's son, Icarus, or Hamlet *père* and *fils*, Stephen as son seems doomed to subordination and destruction. Stephen's response is to refuse Hamlet's supposed quest, "The Son striving to be atoned with the Father" (1.578). Rather than accepting the role of the son, he casts himself as the father. Rather than looking for a father-substitute, he associates Shakespeare, "the father of all his race" (9.868), with Hamlet the father, and himself, also a "bard" (1.73, 134, 475; 2.431; 7.528 etc.), with them both. Similarly, he replaces the Holy Family, of father, mother, and child, with the Holy Trinity of father, son, and holy spirit, allowing him to eliminate the mother and make father and son one substance. The result, for Stephen, is not that the Father is Himself his Own Son, but rather that the Son is Himself His Own Father (9.863–71). The son, then, need not serve as a sacrifice for the father, because he *is* the father.[58] Phrased in this way, however, and in light of traditional Christianity, this clearly is not going to be a way out.

THE DISPLACED SON

Like Telemachus, Stephen resembles his father, but is not quite sure who his father is. In Stephen's case we share the perplexity: the actuality to which Stephen is the potential might be Simon, or Daedalus, or Joyce himself. In some ways the question remains a mystery. Although the relation remains ambivalent, Telemachus does develop a connection to his father, culminating in Book 24 of the *Odyssey*, where father, son, and grandson fight together. In contrast, *Ulysses* ends with Bloom and Molly in bed. There is no Book 24.

Telemachus, Odysseus, and Penelope

Despite the novel's interest in the Holy Family, the Royal family, and even the conifer family (12.1266 ff.), *Ulysses*, like the *Odyssey*, focuses most of all on the nuclear family. In a correspondence less often noted, Joyce also echoes Homer in the scarcity of scenes that bring mother, father, and child together. In *Ulysses* this is built into the situation. Bloom is deliberately keeping away from Molly, his son is dead, and his daughter is in Mullingar. Stephen's mother is dead, he never meets his father, and he hardly ever thinks of his father and mother together. Even Bloom's thoughts of Stephen and his parents tend to be either of Stephen and his father (6.74; 17.470 ff.) or of Stephen and his mother (14.1362; 17.466 ff.)—and not of all three together. Nor are Bloom, Molly, and Stephen ever in the same room together.

For most of the *Odyssey* as well, Odysseus, Penelope, and Telemachus are simply in different locations. Gradually, however, their separation begins to seem pointed. When Odysseus first reaches the palace, Penelope's separation of herself from the men's feasting makes it natural that Odysseus should have separate conversations with Telemachus and with Penelope, while his insistence that Penelope not know of his return ensures that his relation with Telemachus develops independently from his relation to her.[59] The poet also brings this out in the few scenes where Penelope appears among the men by giving us, alternatively, Odysseus's and Telemachus's perspective, showing us, for example, Telemachus seeking control when Penelope rebukes the suitors (18.226 ff.) and then Odysseus's amusement when she cadges presents from them (18.281 ff.). Similarly, Odysseus does not speak to Penelope in her chambers, as she suggests (17.507, 529, 544), but defers the conversation until the suitors, and Telemachus, are gone (17.569 ff.; 19.47, 53). Whatever light this casts on his feelings about seeing her, the result is that, underlined by identical lines describing her entrance into the hall (17.36–37 = 19.53–54), we picture either Telemachus or Odysseus speaking to Penelope in the great hall, but not both together.

It is, however, with the recognition scene that Homer's reluctance to bring Telemachus, Odysseus, and Penelope together becomes most obvious. As seems natural, once Telemachus and Odysseus have taken their revenge on the suitors, Penelope joins them. At this point, Telemachus's outrage at her refusal to acknowledge Odysseus (23.97 ff.) calls attention to the distance between father, mother, and son. Her response, however, is unexpected: "If in truth it is indeed / Odysseus, and he has come home, we two will know one another, and better, for we have signs / hidden from others, that only we two know about" (23.109–11). Odysseus then promptly sends Telemachus away to feign a wedding party.[60] Penelope's unusual use of "*noi*," the first person dual, "we two," reinforces a feeling that her "hidden from others" includes Telemachus as one of the "others." This will also be the only scene where Telemachus, Odysseus, and Penelope speak together.

As I will argue in chapter 4, the many anomalies of *Odyssey* 24 point to an important open-endedness in the epic. One more definite effect of the book should, however, be mentioned here. This is its effective separation of Odysseus's *nostos* into a female and a male component. When Telemachus leaves in Book 23 (accompanied by Eumaeus and Philoitius), Odysseus is the only male to remain, so that his reuniting with Penelope takes place in an entirely female atmosphere (including the unseen Athena). In contrast, Book 24 provides an almost entirely male setting for the coming together of father, son, and grandson, from the masculine heroic dead who open the book to the final description of Athena "likening herself to Mentor in shape and in voice" (24.548). Whatever reunion Odysseus has with Telemachus, it is sharply distinguished from his reunion with Penelope.

*   *   *

The ambivalence of Book 24 that we will examine in chapter 4 gives Odysseus's joining together with Telemachus a rather curious feeling of uncertainty. A similar tone characterizes other occasions when Telemachus tries to establish his identity. When we first see him, his hopes that his father might return and resolve the situation are presented as daydreams (1.114 ff.). When Athena (disguised as "Mentes") compliments him on being like his father, his response, as we have seen, is that no one knows who his father is. Both Penelope and the suitors are surprised by his attempts to take control, and his appeal to the Assembly ends with his throwing down the scepter and breaking into tears (2.80), an ineffectuality repeated in his unwillingness to speak to Nestor or Menelaus.[61] It is only well after Telemachus has escaped from Ithaca and Athena has left him on his own, that confidence emerges, particularly as his success in gaining a suitable gift from Menelaus (4.594) shows him, as Menelaus notes, as the master of his father's (and mother's) craft.

Once Odysseus has reclaimed mastery of his household, however, Telemachus's role is again uncertain. Although he joins his father in fighting, he also reverts to simply taking orders, and fails in the one task he is given, of fetching armor (22.101, 153 ff.). As Odysseus and Penelope reunite, he is doing what his father told him to, staging a wedding, which, whatever others might think (23.148 ff.), celebrates his mother and father's union—before his own birth. His one independent decision, to hang the maidservants rather than put them to the sword (22.461), echoes the added cruelty of Eumaeus and Philoitius in dealing with Melanthius (23.174, 192) and is undermined by the pathos of the poet's description (22.465 ff.).[62] Rather than a conquering warrior, or the master of his own household,

Telemachus looks like a resentful, and somewhat brutal, adolescent. The son may, in this way, be as much displaced by the return of the father as he was by the usurpation of the suitors.

None of this means, simply, that Telemachus's pursuit of adulthood is blocked by Odysseus's return. It suggests rather that the poet has left the question open. The ambiguity appears most dramatically in the test of the bow, the weapon that may have given Telemachus ("fighting from afar") his name. Telemachus's unexpected attempt to string the bow points to a desire to test himself against his father (and in front of his mother), and as clearly shows a lack of foresight. If he fails, he achieves only his own humiliation, while if he succeeds, he ruins the effect of Odysseus's surpassing the suitors. Unable to communicate directly, Odysseus tenses up, the only way he has of warning his son off. Telemachus's response: "Shame! I will then be of no account [*kakos*] and a weakling / or I am too young, and cannot trust in my hands / to ward off another when someone has first started a quarrel" (21.131–33), may not point to the failure that the suitors (and Penelope) presumably see it as, but it nonetheless implies that he will never succeed in matching himself against his father.

There is, however, another, equally valid way to read the scene. Telemachus's public failure may also be a success in precisely the way that Odysseus (and Penelope) are uniquely able to succeed, by apparently submitting. The true test may be not the feat of strength but Odysseus's all but imperceptible signal; Telemachus's victory may lie in his ability to see the sign and repress his desire to prove his strength.[63] The poem does not tell us which interpretation is right. As with the ambivalence of Book 24, or that of Stephen's footsteps as he leaves *Ulysses* (17.1243), the question remains open. It may be, however, that Telemachus truly inherits not in dominating but in yielding.

Stephen the Would-Be Author

Stephen's reflection on "the man with my voice and my eyes and a ghost-woman with ashes on her breath" is, interestingly, one of the few places in *Ulysses* where he thinks of his father and mother together. Just as Telemachus develops separate relations with his mother and father, when Stephen thinks, for example, of his mother's deathbed, his father does not appear, while his long and convoluted exploration of art and paternity in the Library casts Shakespeare as a father, but Anne Hathaway as an adulterous wife rather than a mother. Instead of joining father and mother, Stephen uses the claims of each against the other.[64] His thought of the reciprocal

love of mother and child ("subjective and objective genitive" 2.165),[65] becomes in "Scylla and Charybdis" a desperate attempt to undo the bond of
paternity:

> *Amor matris*, subjective and objective genitive, may be the only true
> thing in life. Paternity may be a legal fiction. Who is the father of any
> son that any son should love him or he any son?
>   What the hell are you driving at?
>   I know. Shut up. Blast you. I have reasons. (9.842–46)

Just as he transforms Mulligan's "green sweet mother" into "Father Ocean"
in "Proteus," in the Library Stephen uses the emotional tie he feels to his
mother to undo his sense of indebtedness to his father, while simultaneously using his mental gymnastics regarding paternity to escape from his
feelings about his mother. Neither attempt is any more successful than his
effort to take the role of parenthood completely for himself.

Stephen's role in *Ulysses* is, if anything, even more ambivalent than
Telemachus's in the *Odyssey*. The novel ends on the note struck in *Odyssey*
23, with Telemachus dismissed and Odysseus and Penelope in bed. Nor
have Stephen and Bloom bonded—not surprisingly, since another father
figure is the last thing that Stephen needs. Most importantly, and in contrast to *Portrait*, Stephen is like Telemachus in being only a secondary character. Telemachus regains Odysseus by also giving up the barely glimpsed
possibility of being master in his own house (1.359, 397 etc.).[66] While Stephen never recognizes the full implications of his: "I'm not a [read "the"]
hero, however" (*U* 1.62), the statement comes close to defining him.[67] The
one hope for Stephen seems to lie in his being not the hero, but rather the
author of the novel. Before that is possible, however, he will have to escape
a bondage that is less to his past than to himself.

*   *   *

Stephen's search for independence rather than for a father figure may simply mark a difference between *Ulysses* and the *Odyssey*. It may also, as I have
argued, point to a deeper level in Telemachus's relation to his father. But
however the reference is taken, it is clear that both works bring out a deep
ambivalence in independence. While this theme will emerge most vividly
when we examine Odysseus and Bloom, it also appears in *Ulysses*'s intense
sense, however fiercely he seeks the condition, that Stephen is alone. The
passage we looked at in chapter 1, where Stephen thinks: "My soul walks
with me, form of forms. So in the moon's midwatches I pace the path above

the rocks, in sable silvered, hearing Elsinore's tempting flood" (3.279–81), reflects the scene where Horatio and Marcellus warn Hamlet against the ghost's tempting him to the flood or the cliff "that beetles o'er his base into the sea" (1.4.69–79). Like Hamlet, Stephen is between rocks and the "suck" of the sea (3.278). In his case, however, there is no one to keep him back, since only his soul walks with him.[68]

Stephen's attempt to escape his past by becoming, like Shakespeare, father to his race, only creates another kind of bondage, a bondage to himself. The end of his discourse in the Library reveals the futility of the attempt:

> He laughed to free his mind from his mind's bondage.
> Judge Eglinton summed up.
> —The truth is midway, he affirmed. He [Shakespeare] is the ghost and the prince. He is all in all.
> —He is, Stephen said. The boy of act one is the mature man of act five. All in all. (9.1016–21)

> —And what a character is Iago! undaunted John Eglinton exclaimed. When all is said Dumas *fils* (or is it Dumas *père?*) is right. After God Shakespeare has created most. (9.1027–29)

> —You are a delusion, said roundly John Eglinton to Stephen. You have brought us all this way to show us a French triangle. Do you believe your own theory?
> —No, Stephen said promptly.
> —Are you going to write it? Mr Best asked. You ought to make it a dialogue, don't you know, like the Platonic dialogues Wilde wrote. (9.1064–68)

Just as Best's question: "Are you going to write it?" divides belief and art, his suggestion that any work derives from another (as Dumas *fils* derives from Dumas *père*) deflates the possibility of creation. Stephen's solution is artistic self-creation ("He found in the world without as actual what was in his world within as possible" 9.1041). The difficulty is that this implies the impossibility of escaping oneself: "Every life is many days, day after day. We walk through ourselves, meeting robbers, ghosts, giants, old men, young men, wives, widows, brothers-in-love, but always meeting ourselves" (9.1044–46). In Stephen's world of black and white either we exist only as derivatives of others, or we, as self-created, are trapped within ourselves. His laughter will not be enough "to free his mind from his mind's bondage."

Stephen's lack of connection emerges as well in a homoerotic and autoerotic subtext to the Library scene, brought out in references to Plato's *Phaedo* (9.1139) and, more particularly, to Brunetto Latini. The references suggest a view of art as self-involved, solipsistic, and consequently sterile—the opposite of that which allows us to connect. Combined with his explicit references to the *Inferno* (9.34, 831), Stephen's quotation from "Messer Brunetto" himself (9.374) suggests *Inferno* 15 and Dante's association of Brunetto and the sin of sodomy with the danger that art may involve laying up a sterile "*Tresor*" on earth rather than an eternal one in heaven (15.119).[69] Mulligan delightedly picks up on the theme that Stephen introduced: "in the economy of heaven, foretold by Hamlet, there are no more marriages, glorified man, an androgynous angel, being a wife unto himself" (9.1052–53) with his scurrilous rhyme: "*Being afraid to marry on earth / They masturbated for all they were worth*" (9.1151–52) and his playlet: "*Everyman His Own Wife or A Honeymoon in the Hand (a national immorality in three orgasms)*" (9.1171).

Mulligan's play, the only literary creation of the Library scene (aside from the Library itself), also puts the final nail in the coffin of artistic self-creation. Mulligan uses his spontaneous, parthenogenic, Athena-inspired creation to upstage Stephen's Hamlet argument (9.1025, 1053), taking over, in the process, not only the *Hamlet* reference but also Stephen's appropriation of Mulligan's wordplay on fathers and sons (1.554 ff.; 9.862 ff.):

> Himself his own father, Sonmulligan told himself. Wait. I am big with child. I have an unborn child in my brain. Pallas Athena! A play! The play's the thing! [see *Hamlet* 2.2.616] Let me parturiate! (9.875 ff.)

The playlet, which we are eventually shown (9.1171–89), solves Stephen's problem by eliminating the mother, like Zeus giving birth to Athena from his own head (as Aeschylus, *Oresteia, Eumenides* 734–41). In being not about birth, however, but about masturbation, it also suggests that the muse involved may not be a productive one.

*   *   *

In Joyce's tripartite structure, Stephen's "Telemachia" is set against the last "Nostos," section, which largely concerns Molly. Similarly "Proteus," the only episode (with its companion piece, "Nausicaa") set entirely outside, balances "Penelope," the only episode set entirely inside, the one as Monologue (male) and the other as Monologue (female).[70] This opposition and pairing of Stephen and Molly, which we will explore further in chapter 5, points to both Stephen's isolation and his relation to Joyce.[71] In some ways Stephen fears flux exactly as he fears the female, because he is tempted by it ("Seadeath, mildest of all deaths known to man" 3.483), and he is tempted by it as it implies a connection to others. In the Library, as he describes Anne Hathaway's seduction of Shakespeare he thinks: "And my turn? When?" (9.261). "Ithaca" later connects his hydrophobia to his "disliking the aqueous substances of glass and crystal, distrusting aquacities of thought and language" (17.239–40).[72] While Joyce's "aquacity" does not exactly clarify things, the example of glass or crystal suggests transparency, that is, the ability of an aqueous substance to join with that which appears through it.

Stephen's disappearance from *Ulysses* parallels the *Odyssey* in suggesting that the reconciliation of husband and wife, male and female, may also displace the son, as in Stephen's Oedipal "The son unborn mars beauty: born, he brings pain, divides affection, increases care" (9.854). In terms of *Ulysses*'s self-reference, if we accept June 16 as the day of Joyce's first coming together with Nora, Stephen's disappearance may also signal a movement from the male world of *Portrait* to the more female focus of *Ulysses* and *Finnegans Wake*. As Fritz Senn has pointed out, despite Richard Ellmann's conjecture that June 16 was the day Nora and Joyce first walked out together, and had their first sexual encounter, we know for certain only that Joyce met Nora around then.[73] It is also true that, within the novel, nothing equivalent happens to Stephen.[74] This however, may be the point. Stephen remains the author *in posse*, not *in esse*, that is, not Joyce, but Joyce before Nora.

While Joyce deliberately suggests that Stephen is the future author of *Ulysses*, he also augments Stephen's "actuality of the possible as possible" (3.67) with a number of "possibilities of the possible as possible" (9.349). Stephen, as author in potential, both is and is not the future author. There is, for example, some promise to his role as Satan, as in William Blake's claim that "The reason Milton wrote in fetters when he wrote of Angels & God, and at liberty when he wrote of Devils & Hell, is because he was a true Poet and of the Devil's party without knowing it."[75] In *Ulysses*, however, "I will not serve" suggests not only Milton but also *Don Giovanni*. As we will see in chapter 3, Bloom's (mistaken) *Voglio e non verrei* reflects Leporello's "I want to be a gentleman / and I want not to serve any longer" (*Voglio far il gentiluomo, / e non voglio più servir*)—before he reverts, in terror, to "I don't want to be heard" (*Non mi voglio far sentir*).[76] In modern parlance, the allusion makes of Stephen not a Don Giovanni (see U 9.458–59), but a Don Giovanni wannabe.

While Joyce associates Stephen with *Paradise Lost*, he also links him to *Lycidas*. It is the great poem of Milton's youth (2.56–91), but also a poem about the threat of never fulfilling one's promise ("For Lycidas is dead, dead ere his prime"). The most promising composition that Stephen comes up with in *Ulysses* may be the story of Anne Kearns and Florence MacCabe, told first to Professor MacHugh and then to Bloom (7.917; 17.639–41). It is drawn from a coupling of his experience in "Proteus" with his imagination, and significantly opens with "Dubliners" (7.922). Here too, however, Joyce is ambiguous. The title MacHugh suggests, from Virgil's first Eclogue, again links Stephen to a great writer's early work (7.1053–56). In contrast, Stephen's title, "A Pisgah Sight of Palestine," suggests that he may glimpse the promised land, but never enter it. "With," as Lenehan puts it, "a great future behind him" (7.875–76, and see 871–76).[77]

Ulysses's turn from the male to the female may be traced in the movement from the "Telemachia," with its focus on Stephen, to the "Nostos," and its focus on Molly. The change also occurs in the move suggested by Philip Kitcher, from Joyce as Stephen, the artist "as a young man," to Joyce as Bloom, a middle-aged husband and father.[78] In this light, Stephen can become himself only by giving up himself. He can be the author of *Ulysses* only by no longer being the hero of *Portrait*. Like Dante, Joyce introduces into his novel a suggestion that the author is transformed through his authorship. Like Milton, he does so by taking the problem of debt in a different direction. Stephen rejects his father. Joyce wrote Harriet Weaver after his father's death that "Hundreds of pages and scores of characters in my books came from him" (*LI* 312). In contrast to Stephen, Joyce conquers by yielding. His stories are other people's.[79]

Odysseus and Bloom

Names and Stories

Field shepherds, wretched disgraces, mere bellies,
we [the Muses] know how to speak many false things that are like real ones,
and we know, when we are willing, to utter truth.
So spoke the daughters of great Zeus, ready-worded,
and they gave me a staff, a branch of flourishing laurel,
they had plucked, a wonder, and breathed into me a voice
divine, so I might give fame to what will come and what was before,
and bid me hymn the race of the blessed who are forever,
but always to sing themselves, first and last.

(Hesiod, *Theogony* 26–34)

As George Dimock eloquently put it, Odysseus's task is to live up to his name, and his name is "Trouble."[1] To regain his identity he must reenter the world of time, change, and danger, and he will do so largely through words: both names and stories. Leopold Bloom is no poet, but he too negotiates a world of words, and for him, as for Odysseus, they are double-edged. Stories and names anchor meaning, as in the fame (or *kleos*) that the Muses enable Hesiod to give, but meanings can also change, be adapted, and falsified. As the Muses told Hesiod, they are as much the masters of falsehood as they are of truth, and as their interest in what is, what was, and what will be shows, they are as much about time as about either.

Human beings deal with change over time through stories and names and both are ambiguous.[2] Names are both fixed and fluid, reifying "Rudy" but also creating a range of identities from "Baby Tuckoo" to "Kinch the Knifeblade." Stories create connection and meaning, primarily by having a plot, the thread that changes Stephen's "I. I" to "I, I," or the difference, as E. M. Forster puts it, between "The king died and then the queen died" and "The king died and then the queen died of grief."[3] But they can also be dangerous. Stories inevitably leave gaps. They can also be false, and in many different ways. And most importantly, their permanence is a threat. Just as Herodotus writes his *History* so that events "should not become faded through time, and the deeds shown forth both by Greeks and by foreigners, great and worthy of wonder, not lose their *kleos*" (1.1), narrative can make *kleos* permanent, but it does so by ending change. The epithet for *kleos*, after all, is *aphthiton* (imperishable).[4]

NAMES AND IDENTITIES

While both Bloom and Odysseus are storytellers, Bloom's successful stories are told to himself rather than to others. His attempt to tell Stephen the story of "Cyclops" (16.1078–148) goes as badly as his earlier attempt to tell Stephen's father the story of Reuben J. Dodd (6.264–76). The story of his day, told to Molly, reminds even him of the cessation of "mental intercourse between himself and the listener" (17.2285–86). Nor are Bloom's the only stories to miss their mark. It is by no means clear that either McHugh or Bloom sees the point of Stephen's "parable," any more than the schoolboys understand his riddle (7.1053–62; 17.639–59; 2.101–17). As with his discourse in the library, stories in *Ulysses* often seem to say more to the teller than to the listener. In this way, like clocktime, while they are intended to bring people together, they may rather mark their isolation. This is particularly notable in *Ulysses*, where even the overall narrator is unstable, but the *Odyssey* shares the same tendencies.

A more basic use of words should circumvent the problem. This is the use of words as names, a use inherently directed toward others and without any intrinsic truth or falsehood. A name, after all, is a name purely because it is agreed upon, and what is agreed upon is an identity. The issue is fundamental to both *Ulysses* and the *Odyssey*. Bloom's name (and not Bloom the dentist, 10.1114; 15.4351) is a continuing subject of inquiry, while the meaning of Odysseus's name both opens his story (1.62) and gets an entire scene to itself (19.405 ff.). Nor, as Bloom transforms into "Henry Flower" and Odysseus into *Outis* or "Noman," is the question a simple one.[5]

Names, since they exist simply to label things, should be the essence of language.[6] This is, however, the problem. In the first place, they do not change, while people do. According to the name, the same "Stephen Dedalus," hides under the table in *Portrait* (8) and is knocked unconscious in *Ulysses*. The same "James Joyce" (with various additions) appears on a birth certificate, a register at Clongowes, examination papers, a (somewhat delayed) marriage license, and a death certificate.[7] And, of course, on the cover of *Ulysses*. This problem with names is even greater in Homer, where characters have only one of them. Unlike, say, Martin Cunningham, who can be Martin Cunningham, Mr Cunningham, Cunningham, or Martin, Menelaus is "Menelaus" whether he is a castaway or a king, and to his guests, his wife, his daughter, his servants, his peers, or the gods.

Names are given, and so inherently relate to others—hence Stephen's "the name that we are told is ours" (9.927).[8] With people, however, this means that we acquire our names before we are actually ourselves. As a result, names, necessarily, are arbitrary markers, a fancy version of the Cat in the Hat's assistants, Thing 1 and Thing 2. And yet we take them as part of our identity.[9] It is a rare person who does not know the "meaning" of their name. Joyce was responsible for Stephen Dedalus's "speaking name," but his play in *Finnegans Wake* makes it clear that he saw "James Joyce" as equally significant, whoever chose it for him. But then "Homer" too, at least according to Gregory Nagy, may be the creation of his name: "he who fits [the song] together."[10]

One solution, of course, is modifications. To the question (inevitable in works of wandering) "Who are you?" the answer can be Father Conmee S.J., Sweny, the druggist (15.340), *fidus Achates* (6.49; 16.54), or "Mentes, son of skillful Anchialus . . . , / lord over the oar-loving Taphians" (1.180). Achilles is thus "swift-footed," Agamemnon: "king of men," Penelope: "resourceful," and Athena: "gray-eyed." Moreover, like the distinction between Stephen's sister, "Dilly," "Councilor Nannetti," and "Lenehan" (whom only Terry the barman or Miss Dunne would call Mr, 12.1218; 10.395), epithets, formulaic as they are, can reflect nuances in a relation. Only the most mechanical of critics would claim that purely metrical considerations make Odysseus "sacker of cities" with the Cyclops (9.504, as 1.2) and *polutropos*, "of many turns," with Circe (10.330)—the only time other than the poem's first line that the epithet appears.[11]

But once names are modified, we return to the problem of flux. Stories give fixity at the risk of trapping us in our own narrative. One alternative is ever-varying stories, like Odysseus's in Ithaca, but at the cost of losing identity. So also with names. An unvarying name may belie the changing person, but an epithet, while flexible, reminds us that the name is simply invented by whoever happens to give it.

And most importantly, as problematic as they may be, names inevitably tease us with the suggestion of meaning. Although opaque to most readers now, the opposition between Anticleia (Anti-fame) and Eurycleia (Wide-fame), signaled when the nurse is introduced (2.429–33), continues as Eurycleia celebrates a revenge that Odysseus's mother never mentioned might be needed (11.180–96; 23.407–18). Joyce takes full advantage. *Ulysses* is not the only one of his works to hide its meaning in the title. "The Sisters" reorients the narrative; "Clay" provides the key to the story; and "The Dead," in many ways, is made by the title. The self-reflexivity of *The Portrait of the Artist as a Young Man* comes essentially from the title. It is thus no surprise that Joyce would be every bit as interested in naming as Homer was.

Odysseus: Being Noman and Being Trouble

The difficulty of using names to fix identity may explain why names are so problematic in the *Odyssey*. Odysseus, famous for calling himself Noman, actually names himself very infrequently. In Phaeacia he reveals his name, after three books and two days, only as the introduction and *sphragis* of his story. In the five versions of himself that he creates on Ithaca, he names himself only twice, as Aithon (Gleaming, 19.183) to Penelope and as Eperitus ("Quarrelman" or also possibly "Picked Man" 24.306) to his father.[12] Nor does he call himself "Odysseus" when he discloses his identity to Telemachus, Eumaeus and Philoitius, the suitors, or his father.[13] The hesitancy is characteristic. Achilles's name occupies half of the first line of the *Iliad*; the *Odyssey* opens simply with "man" (*andra*). The hero is unnamed until the very last line of the prologue (1.21).[14]

As we hear first with Athena (1.62) and as is made explicit in the story of his scar (19.406 ff.), Odysseus's name means "man of wrath," or "the one who is hated" (1.62), or, as above, "trouble."[15] This speaks to his tendency not to own it. Concealment is safest, whether in Troy, as in Helen's story (4.244 ff.), in Phaeacia, dedicated to Odysseus's enemy, Poseidon, or in Ithaca.[16] To have a name is to be a target, as quite literally when the blinded Cyclops hurls his boulder toward the voice of "Odysseus, sacker of cities, / son of Laertes, whose home is on Ithaca" (9.504–5). Tellingly, it is this declaration that also occasions Odysseus's future trouble, as the Cyclops precisely repeats his words: "Poseidon, . . . grant that Odysseus, sacker of cities, / son of Laertes, whose home is on Ithaca, may never reach home" (9.530–31). Odysseus is no fool, and his outburst here is very unlike, for example, the cautious explorer described by Helen. The scene makes clear the danger of naming oneself. But it also makes clear the unbearable tension built up in being "Noman," a tension we will see again in Odysseus's dealings with the suitors.

For while there is danger in a name, it is also a connection to one's past self. Odysseus's assertion of himself to the Cyclops, adorned with all his heroic epithets, is juxtaposed with the Cyclops's lament that he had expected an "Odysseus" who was great, strong, and handsome, not a "little man, of no account and feeble" who conquers by craft (9.510–17). For all the trouble the assertion creates, when Odysseus names himself in Phaeacia, he is again: "Odysseus, son of Laertes, known to all men / for cunning designs, and my fame (*kleos*) reaches heaven. / I dwell on sunny Ithaca" (9.19–21). He takes ownership of his Wanderings and as a hero, albeit as a hero of craft. He may be moving from epic to ordinary time, but to regain his identity requires a connection to his former name, with all its warrior trappings.

*   *   *

Just as there is little point in having a name if no one knows it, naming is completed in the response of others. When Athena greets Odysseus on Ithaca, she, like his comrades in the Underworld (11.92, 405, 473, 617) addresses him as a hero: "Zeus-sprung, son of Laertes, resourceful Odysseus" (13.375; and see 16.167; 24.542).[17] To Telemachus he is "Odysseus, my father" (16.194), to Eurymachus "Odysseus of Ithaca" (22.45), to Laertes "Odysseus, my son" (24.328), to Calypso "fate-ridden man" (5.160), and to the Sirens "much-praised Odysseus, great glory of the Achaeans" (12.184). Two others respond even more simply. Eurycleia, who nursed him, says only "you are indeed Odysseus" (19.474), and in a scene remarkably bare of epithets, Penelope, finally, calls her husband just by his unadorned name (23.209).[18]

In the Greek tradition the fixity of names has its tragic aspect. Helen, whose name means "destruction," Pentheus, whose name means "grief," and Ajax, whose name means "alas," are epitomized by a terrible identity beyond their choosing. But the bare, unadorned name can also allow for an openness that comes from only marking an individual. It is just after she calls him "Odysseus" that Penelope declares that the gods took from the two of them a going together from youth to old age (23.210–12). The statement comprehends the young, the middle-aged, and the old Odysseus. Unlike "Zeus-sprung, son of Laertes, resourceful Odysseus" or "Odysseus, my father" or "Odysseus of Ithaca" or even "Odysseus of many turns," the name alone, trouble though it may be, can point not to some absolute identity, but just to the singular person who holds it, throughout all his changes.

Ulysses and What's in a Name

Stephen's reflection on names in "Eumaeus" calls forth a curious response from Bloom:

> —Sounds are impostures, Stephen said after a pause of some little time, like names. Cicero, Podmore. Napoleon, Mr Goodbody. Jesus, Mr Doyle. Shakespeares were as common as Murphies. What's in a name?
> —Yes, to be sure, Mr Bloom unaffectedly concurred. Of course. Our name was changed too, he added, pushing the socalled roll across. (16.362–66)[19]

Bloom's "our name was changed too" could reflect the strangeness of Stephen's name (as 1.34; 9.949–50) or even, more whimsically, the change from "Joyce" to "Dedalus." It also reflects Bloom's nonchalance. He is as comfortable with renaming as he is with the "socalled roll" (which in fact must be pushed). Stephen, in contrast, despite his protestations, is as resistant to being renamed as he is to any other sort of change.

Stephen plays with other people's names, but resists changes to his own. He does not respond when Mulligan calls him "Kinch" and the "fearful jesuit" (1.8) even before he has been identified as "Stephen Dedalus" (1.11). In the Library his play with others' names: "A.E.I.O.U." (9.213), "Socratididion's Epipsychidion" (9.237), "Hughie Wills? Mr William Himself. W. H.: who am I?" (9.526) matches the narrator's "littlejohn Eglinton" (9.365), "Sonmulligan" (9.875), and "Quakerlyster" (9.918), while "Mageeglinjohn" (9.900) reminds us that the actual William Magee renamed himself John Eglinton.[20] Stephen, however, plays with his own name only once. Otherwise, he invents a name for himself only by ventriloquizing the renaming: "Mulligan will dub me a new name: the bullockbefriending bard" (3.430).

Telemachus, like his father, withholds his name at a feast, but unlike Odysseus with the Phaeacians, it takes Menelaus and Helen barely a hundred lines to guess it (4.116–18, 140–41)—and even then it is Pisistratus who acknowledges the name (4.156–61). Stephen, similarly, has a problem controlling his name, despite his desire to keep it fixed. He is torn between a devotion to its significance, carried over from *Portrait,* and a sense of the mere arbitrariness of words, as in, say, "Rutlandbaconsouthamptonshakespeare or another poet of the same name" (9.866). The one time Stephen plays with his name: "*Bous Stephanoumenos.* Where's your configuration?

Stephen, Stephen, cut the bread even. S. D: *sua donna. Già: di lui. Gelindo risolve di non amare S. D*" rejects the possibility of a female counterpart (*sua donna;* his woman) to himself, and leads first to "*Stephanos,* my crown. My sword. His boots are spoiling the shape of my feet" and then to his own failure to live up to his name: "Fabulous artificer. The hawklike man. You flew. Whereto? Newhaven-Dieppe, steerage passenger. Paris and back. Lapwing. Icarus. *Pater, ait.* Seabedabbled, fallen, weltering. Lapwing you are. Lapwing be" (9.939–41, 947–48, 952–54).

As with "Odysseus" as "Trouble," the reason for Stephen's ambivalence appears in his name. Just as he has to be "Stephen" because his father has already taken "Mr Dedalus," he may be not Dedalus, but Dedalus's son.[21] His "given" name is equally double-edged. Just as "Telemachus" could be "one who fights from afar," an archer, or "one far from battle," "*Stephanos,* my crown," suggests the poet "crowned" with laurel, while "*Bous Stephanoumenos*" suggests rather the ox garlanded for slaughter, a reference made particularly pointed in the cattle-laden "Oxen of the Sun" (*U* 14.1115; *P* 168). And it is the name of the first martyr (*P* 159).

Stephen's problem, as always, is with the absolute. He wants words to be his own creation, but he also wants them to have an inherent meaning. It is a problem he has been struggling with for some time, particularly as it appears in the welter of languages:[22]

> God was God's name just as his name was Stephen. *Dieu* was the French for God and that was God's name too; and when anyone prayed to God and said *Dieu* then God knew at once that it was a French person that was praying. But, though there were different names for God in all the different languages in the world and God understood what all the people who prayed said in their different languages, still God remained always the same God and God's real name was God.
>
> It made him very tired to think that way. (*P* 16)

*   *   *

In respect to names, Bloom is the opposite of Stephen: he changes his own name, but not that of others. The only liberty he takes with another's name, in fact, occurs as he tries to revive the unconscious young man before him at the end of "Circe" by calling him "Stephen" (15.4924 ff.).

Unlike Stephen, Bloom simply accepts that names, like identities, are fluid. In this way he is like Mulligan, who, surprisingly, gets to decide even what the narrator calls him, and who renames himself ("the buck himself," "Mercurial Malachi," "Ballocky Mulligan" 1.42, 518; 9.1176) and others with equal abandon. Bloom accordingly renames himself, most emphatically as "Henry Flower," and has played with his various names since his youth, as in his epistolary poem, anagrams, and acrostic (17.399 ff.). Unlike Mulligan, however, Bloom does not use the fluidity of names as a means of control. He gladly accepts names from others, such as "Mackerel" (8.404–5; 15.3331), "Leopoldleben" (15.274), "Poldy," or "Papli." Nor is he, like Mulligan, simply a relativist, as we see when he is "nettled not a little" by "L. Boom" in the newspaper (16.1262, noted by Molly at 18.1264).

Fluidity, for Bloom, is in fact a sort of identity. Family is where he seeks belonging, and a fluidity of name runs throughout his family. Rather than merely arbitrary changes, however (as Bloom's mother went from Higgins to Bloom), the fluidity is of variations on a theme, from "Virag" (Hungarian for flower) to "Bloom" to "Henry Flower" to Bloom's anagrams and acrostics, to even Molly's proleptic "Don Miguel de la Flora" (18.771). Unlike Hamlet, or Dumas, *père* and *fils,* the Jewish custom of naming a boy after his grandfather, together with changes of nationality (and an implicit desire to pass), have meant that Lipoti Virag, Rudolph Virag/Bloom, Leopold Bloom, and young Rudy Bloom have names that are both different and the same, just as Marion and Millicent Bloom have become Molly and Milly.[23] Stephen resists changes to his name; for Bloom this is just who he is.

The names that others attempt to give Stephen, Bous Stephanoumenos, Kinch, Wandering Aengus, are intended to characterize him. Bloom's different names, Papli, Poldy, Leopoldleben, are about his relations to others. It is an aspect of naming that he is very aware of. In his childhood poem for the newspaper he is (properly) "L. Bloom" (17.392–401) and in his poem for Molly, "Poldy" (17. 410–16); the acrostic that includes "Old Ollebo, M.P." is made on "Leopold Bloom" (17.404–9), like "Mr David Sheehy M.P. (10.17). Martha Clifford responds to "Henry Flower" as intended: "I often think of the beautiful name you have" (5.248) and, adopting the "language of flowers" that Bloom has initiated (5.261), reifies the name with a dried flower (4.239). And as the mystery man of "Nausicaa," Bloom's "I. . . . AM. A." (13.1256–71) is appropriately never completed.[24]

In contrast to Stephen's attempt to find some absolute identity, Bloom accepts that if names are about who we are, they are even more about who we are in relation to others. And as that is multiple, so are our names. The sudden slowing of Bloom's heart when he sees the letter addressed not to "Mrs Leopold" but to "Mrs Marion Bloom," indicates how important something so relative can be. In this light it is encouraging, if to the reader rather than to Bloom, that the text's "Mrs Marion" is followed by *Ulysses*'s very first "Poldy" (4.245).[25]

*　*　*

No one is surprised to find a character in fiction addressed by multiple names, though non-native readers of Russian novels (like me) may sometimes chafe at the practice. But we do not expect the narrator to take that liberty. After they are introduced, and however others address them, "Raskolnikov" is "Raskolnikov" to the narrator just as Oliver Twist is "Oliver." Homer, of course, with his established epithets, is a somewhat different case. *Ulysses* goes to extremes. In the second half of the novel in particular names, like identities, are up for grabs. Bloom may predominate with "Siopold" (11.752), "Herr Professor Luitpold Blumenduft" (12.468), "childe Leopold" (14.160), "Leopold the first" (15.1473), "Mr B." (16.394) etcetera, but in "Oxen of the Sun" change of names is the norm, while in "Circe," anyone from Reuben J Antichrist (15.2145) to Rumbold, Demon Barber (15.4536) is fair play. A much quieter change, however, that occurs near the end of the novel, is most notable, as the narrator suddenly begins to refer to the famously introduced "Mr Leopold Bloom" as the rest of us do: as "Bloom." Like Penelope's bare "Odysseus," Bloom seems to have broken out of his many roles to become merely himself.

One thing that the change alerts us to is the implications of naming throughout. In the first ("realistic") part of *Ulysses*, the narrator's use of names follows the social conventions that Joyce himself insisted upon.[26] A person's given name is used by family and close friends: Stephen is thus "Stephen," as he was in *Portrait*, because we have known him from childhood. "Mr" is used on formal occasions, by strangers, and as a term of respect, hence "Mr Power," "Mr Cunningham," or "Mr [not Stephen] Dedalus" (6.6; 7.239; 10.654; 11.192 etc.). One man addresses another by his surname; women address each other by their given names; and members of the opposite sex address each other by title, hence "Josie" to Molly (18.203 etc.) is "Mrs Breen" to Bloom (8.203, 211 etc.). Social class also enters in. In contrast to barflies such as Lenehan or M'Coy, or Stephen's coevals such as Lynch or Dixon, the narrator gives "John Henry Menton" or "John Howard Parnell" their full name. And similarly with nicknames. Just as the other characters exhibit their feelings about "Doughy" Dan Dawson through the name (7.336–40), the narrator's "Buck" Mulligan, "Blazes" Boylan (a nickname he apparently dislikes), "Long John" Fanning, "Nosey" Flynn, or "Gerty" express rather different degrees of familiarity.[27]

Naming thus implies a relationship between narrator and character just as it does between the characters. Just as Jane Austen's heroine is "Elizabeth" and her hero "Mr. Darcy" because the viewpoint is female, the narrator of *Ulysses* is clearly male, since he refers to Josie as "Mrs Breen." We also know something about his levels of intimacy and social position from the fact that he speaks of "Martin Cunningham" and "Mr Power" in contrast to "Corny Kelleher" or "Lenehan." All of which makes it only more surprising that the character the narrator seems to know best is regularly "Mr Bloom."

After all the pyrotechnics with names in the "Wanderings," Bloom emphatically regains his "Mr" at the opening of "Eumaeus" only to lose it after "L. Boom," his *"new* misnomer" (16.1275; italics added). From this point on he will be simply "Bloom (properly so dubbed)" (16.1307).[28] The change is subtle, but pointed. However used we are to changing epithets, when the narrator of the *Odyssey* addresses Eumaeus in the vocative, we take notice.[29] Similarly here, as familiar as we are with "Bloom" (and this is how Joyce spoke of him to friends), we remark that a change has been made.[30]

The result is that we do not know, after all, how even the narrator regards Bloom. Stephen, except when the Arranger becomes extreme, is "Stephen." Since Molly never appears with another woman, the narrator can refer to her simply as "she." Although "Bloom" should be how one male addresses another with whom he is intimate, the other characters that the narrator calls by their surnames are those like "Hynes," "Lenehan," or "Corley" who do not have the social status to be called anything else. "Bloom," in contrast, is both a *tutoyer* and a distancing. His father can call him simply "Leopold" (5.206; 6.126, 364; 15.260–61; 17.1881–85). No one else does.[31] Not even the novel, it seems, knows him that well.

THE ROLE OF STORYTELLING

Given the Muses' warning to Hesiod that they, like Odysseus, "know how to speak many false things that are like real ones" (*Theogony* 27 = *Odyssey* 19.203) one might expect that the critical question about language would be if it is true. Despite the inquiries of many of the poem's characters, the *Odyssey* is surprisingly uninterested in the issue.[32] What will matter most to Penelope is not that Odysseus knows the true construction of their bed, but that he cares about it. Similarly, Homer's decision to have Odysseus narrate the Wanderings should be an either/or proposition: either Odysseus is reliving actual events or Homer means us to wonder about their veracity. As we will see, both are true. One reason is that stories here, as in *Ulysses,* are often less about re-creating the past than they are about connecting to the future.

Words are elusive. They can both imprison and release, as the Sirens threaten to trap Odysseus in the song of Troy (12.189–90) while the tale of his Wanderings releases him from Phaeacia.[33] His own stories both disguise and reveal him in Ithaca. Words also tend to double back on themselves, the inevitable recycling that was a problem for Stephen. Here too, however, the dilemma can become a solution, as we will see when Bloom rewrites the stories of Rip Van Winkle, Don Giovanni, and Parnell. The ability not to invent, but to retell, is, of course, inherent in epic. Just as Odysseus ends the first half of the *Odyssey* by telling Alcinous that "It is hateful to me / to again tell a tale [*muthologein*] plainly told" (12.352–53), and in a poem particularly notable for its doublings,[34] Bloom's way of using stories is not to invent new ones (as Odysseus often does), but to rearrange old ones. One might say he was simply, in the Modernist creed, "making it new."[35]

As was noted in chapter 1, unlike actual people who grow and change, epic heroes in epic time are fixed in their stories. There is, however, a qualification, and it comes through retelling. Ordinary time is linear: we are born, grow old, and die. Mythic time, in contrast, returns upon itself, like the cycle of the seasons. The same story is told over and so becomes new, as Telemachus describes the story of the heroes returning from Troy as "the song that comes round newest to the listeners" (1.325–27, 351).[36] An actual person, or a person in a novel, has only one life; Elizabeth Bennet or Pierre Bezukhov exist only in the works their authors created for them. Odysseus, however, like Sinbad or Paul Bunyan, has as many incarnations as there are versions of his story.[37] Words may take deeds out of time, as Herodotus intended, but a story may also repeat, and with changes. Odysseus, the son of Laertes, can become in Euripides's *Cyclops* or Sophocles's *Philoctetes,* the lying son of Sisyphus (*Cyclops* 104; *Philoctetes* 416–18, 1311–13). Similarly Bloom, in re-creating stories for himself, can also re-create himself in them.

Odysseus: Telling Himself the Wanderings

Kleos, or fame, is inherently linked to narrative, as in its verbal form, *kleo* (to sing, celebrate, make famous), but, as we have seen, that narrative can be a trap.[38] In this regard, it may matter that Odysseus gives distinctly different accounts of himself to the disguised Athena (13.253–86), Eumaeus

(14.192–359), Antinous (17.415–44), Penelope (19.165–202, 221–48, 268–99), and his father (24.244–79, 303–14).[39] This is strange, since good liars are usually simple and consistent. It is even unhomeric, since epic happily repeats stories, even verbatim, such as that of Penelope's web (2.94–107 = 19.139–52 = 24.129–42). But while Odysseus's changing story is problematic, not least in terms of identity, it has its advantages.

As has often been noted, Odysseus's lies are also, in many ways, experiments in alternative truth.[40] With his father—for whom he is "Quarrelsome" from "Wandertown," son of "Unsparing," the son of "Muchwoe"—the approach of the false to the true is through names.[41] Another common feature, later seized on by Dante and Tennyson, is explicit in the story he tells Eumaeus:

> Work never was dear to me,
> nor care for my house, though that raises goodly children,
> but for me always ships driven by oars were dear
> and wars, and well-polished spears, and arrows . . .
>   (14.222–25 and see 244–46)

The self that Odysseus creates here is drawn on to explore, like the hero who, "striving for his *psuche* and homecoming for his companions" (1.3), seeks identity for himself, but associates homecoming rather with others.[42] It does not take a psychologist to think that Odysseus, now returned, may himself be wondering why it took him so long to get home.

Odysseus's role as a hero of words and craft itself implies an issue with identity. It is notable that the two who recognize Odysseus unassisted in Ithaca are the goddess Athena and the dog Argus, neither of whom needs words to communicate. But anyone who can so easily re-create himself through words must also at some point wonder what "real" identity he has, a question compounded as much for the audience as for the hero, when Homer hands over the Wanderings to Odysseus himself to narrate.

The greatest of Odysseus's tales occupies Books 9–12 of the *Odyssey* and gives the English word "odyssey" its meaning. The account has been so influential that it can be difficult to remember how strange the conflation of poet and hero actually is. In epic the hero provides the deeds, the poet the words that make those deeds immortal; the two are generally not confused.[43] Here, however, the switch in narration matches the poem: both are on multiple levels.

One reason to give Odysseus the story of the Wanderings must be the necessary undermining of certainty that results. Homer does not make us question the third-person narrator, as Joyce does, but he does introduce a narrator known for duplicity. When the third-person narrator says that Aegyptus's son was eaten by the Cyclops (2.15–20), or describes what Hermes said to Calypso (5.97–115), it is true. Most of Odysseus's story, however, is not vouched for in this way.[44] The doubling that occurs throughout the Wanderings, together with the common folktale motifs, remind us that Odysseus's stories exist in many versions other than this one. As a result, we cannot know if Odysseus has experienced, invented, or recycled the stories. Perhaps he too, like Homer, understands the use of Stephen's "dead breaths I living breathe." Homer does not say. But he does open up grounds for the questions.

There is another reason as well why Homer might give his best stories to Odysseus. As Joyce pointed out in his lectures in Trieste, describing how England took over Ireland's story (*OCPW* 108–26), there is a critical distinction between telling your own story and having it told by others.[45] That Odysseus cares about stories is clear. He weeps both times that Demodocus sings about Troy and is described the second time as like a woman who weeps over the body of her husband killed in war (8.523–30)—that is, as if he felt what it was to be the conquered and not the conqueror. But as moved as he is by hearing his own story, he may be even more affected by telling it.

When we first meet Odysseus in Book 5, we learn, quite possibly to the audience's surprise, of Calypso's offer to make him immortal and unaging (4.135 and contrast 1.55 ff.). What is not explained is why anyone would refuse a life without old age, sickness, or loss, quite literally the life of the gods. And even more so, since, as we will learn, Odysseus knows what it is to be dead, with no *noos*, or intellect, twittering like bats, unable to recognize even a dearly loved son (11.141 ff.). But then again, as we have also seen in looking at Odysseus's voyage to the Underworld, being immortal and unchanging with Calypso is not all that different from being dead, a factor that may well have influenced Odysseus.[46] This, however, we can understand not in Book 5, but only six books later, when we have heard the backstory to Odysseus's decision.

The reflection is an important reminder of the embeddedness of the oral epic in time.[47] Readers of the *Odyssey*, like readers of *Ulysses*, can choose to look at any portion of the story in any order they wish. On the page the narrative is, in this sense, synchronous. Not so with oral poetry, where one can hear the story only as the poet speaks it, however well known it may be. A reader jumps easily from Calypso to Hades and back again. When Homer sang his song, as Oliver Taplin has calculated, his audience heard about the Underworld six hours after hearing of Odysseus's decision to return.[48]

Just as the reason for Odysseus leaving Calypso becomes clearer when we have heard about his visit to Hades, his long concealment of his identity on Phaeacia becomes more understandable when we know that asserting his identity with the Cyclops earned him the anger of Poseidon, the patron god of Phaeacia.[49] When Athena sheds sleep on Odysseus, as he lies exhausted and battered by twenty days at sea, we appreciate her care. After we learn what he has gone through to get here, we see why he wonders about her earlier absence (6.328–31; 13.316–23).

Perhaps even more importantly, however, just as Homer understands us to be an oral audience, he understands Odysseus to be an oral poet. When in Book 21 Odysseus strings his bow "as when a man, knowing in the lyre and song / easily pulls a cord over a new peg" (21.406–7), the simile, suggestive as it is, still assigns the hero to his proper role of providing deeds for the poet to sing.[50] In telling the Wanderings, in contrast, Odysseus is the speaker of the deeds, and as such must listen to them as well. It is possible that, as we understand Odysseus's refusal of immortality only after hearing his story, it is only in retelling his story that Odysseus completely absorbs it. After all, this is the way in which Homer moves both us and Odysseus from the first to the second half of the poem, a transition that in *Aeneid* 6 is accomplished by the move from souls of the past to souls of the future.

Homer's characters do not think about how time is like a river or wonder, explicitly, if they are still their past selves. Instead, we have Odysseus's Wanderings, which say as much about Odysseus as about what happened to him. Nor is this because they are an allegory for the soul, as they became in an extensive later tradition.[51] The poet could give us an allegory without making Odysseus the narrator. Rather, it seems critical that Odysseus, in telling his story, to some extent controls and to some extent relives it.[52] As Joyce might have put it, it is not so much the experience as the retrospective arrangement of it that allows Odysseus to reenter Ithaca.

Bloom: Other Perspectives and Other Roles

The single most obvious difference between Bloom and Odysseus is that Bloom is no storyteller: his field is rather advertising, the art of the modern age (17.581).[53] Despite Lenehan's "There's a touch of the artist about old Bloom" (10.582), it would be hard to beat Bloom's spontaneous composition: "*The hungry famished gull / Flaps o'er the waters dull*" (8.62) for bad poetry. Similarly, his flatfooted attempt at storytelling: "They were both on the way to the boat and he tried to drown. . . . ." (6.272; ellipsis in the original) is immediately eclipsed by Cunningham: "Reuben and the son were piking it down the quay next the river on their way to the Isle of Man boat and the young chiseller suddenly got loose and over the wall with him into the Liffey" (6.278 ff.). Joyce, however, gives Bloom another register as well.[54] When he thinks of a dead child, like Rudy, it is of a "dwarf's face, mauve and wrinkled" (6.326). The detail is vivid, as in his thoughts of the arsenic stains on his father's face (6.359 ff.), a scene he never saw ("Poor papa! Poor man! I'm glad I didn't go into the room to look at his face" 6.207–8). While he has no skill in telling a story, Bloom does have, it seems, a rather remarkable ability to think one. Like Odysseus's relation to words, this may be both a trap and a solution.

What Bloom shares with Odysseus is something that storytelling depends on. Like the man who "saw the cities of many men and knew their mind" (*Odyssey* 1.3), Bloom, remarkably, can see the world from a point of view other than his own, and can even understand how others see him, a gift almost nonexistent among Dublin males.[55] This ability makes him singularly attractive, particularly to modern readers, but it is not without its cost. Bloom tries to understand even those who challenge him, such as Jack Power ("Only politeness perhaps. Nice fellow. Who knows is that true about the woman he keeps?" 6.243), John Henry Menton ("Fellow always like that, mortified if women are by" 6.1013), and even the Citizen ("Suppose he hit me. Look at it other way round. Not so bad then. Perhaps not to hurt he meant. Three cheers for Israel" 13.1219). In a way this is admirable. The problem is that such a susceptibility to others' points of view can make it difficult to maintain one's own.[56]

Bloom does not understand parallax, the apparent shift of position created by different points of view (8.110–12, 578–79; 17.1052), but unlike anyone else in *Ulysses*, he wonders about it. His tendency to think about what others are thinking, even when he himself is not directly concerned, is particularly striking after Stephen's complete self-involvement in "Proteus." It is also, in many ways, the point of advertising.[57] As we meet Bloom, he is considering what Molly likes for breakfast (4.11 ff.), what Larry O'Rourke is up to (4.111 ff.), and what the butcher Dlugacz intends (4.186). Later he speculates that Martha Clifford might be having her period (5.285), decides not to ask Nannetti about *voglio*: "if he didn't know only make it awkward for him" (7.152), and considers the feelings of streetwalkers: "If you don't answer when they solicit must be horrible for them till they harden" (13.870).

As Bloom considers other perspectives, he also thinks about how he looks to others. We meet him, accordingly, talking to the cat: "Wonder what I look like to her. Height of a tower? No, she can jump me" (4.28). Similarly with the pigeons: "Their little frolic after meals. Who will we do it on? I pick the fellow in black" (8.368 ff.).[58] It is often only later that we find out how much Bloom actually saw, just as we learn only much later that Odysseus recognized Athena in Phaeacia (*Odyssey* 13.321 ff.).[59] In "Ithaca" we find that Bloom, unlike most first-time readers, understands the "Throwaway" mystery (17.323 ff.), and in "Nausicaa" we learn that he knows of a scene that, at the time, seemed to be conducted entirely behind his back (7.440 ff.):

> Walk after him now make him awkward like those newsboys me today. Still you learn something. See ourselves as others see us. So long as women don't mock what matter? That's the way to find out. (13.1056 ff.)

If Odysseus is a shapeshifter through words, then Bloom is one in his ability to switch perspectives. Nor is this just the result of our seeing his inner thoughts. While Stephen's inner world is abstruse, abstract, and self-involved, it also reveals him as striving (if with limited success) to "be" rather than "seem."[60] Bloom, in contrast, simply accepts that most of life means playing a role. When Mrs Breen notes his black suit ("Going to crop up all day, I foresee. Who's dead, when and what did he die of?" 8.215), he plays along ("May as well get her sympathy" 8.218) and with an excellent sense of timing ("Now that's quite enough about that. Just: quietly: husband" 8.226). In fact, the perspective becomes so real for him that he is annoyed later when Goulding fails to notice: "He doesn't see my mourning. Callous: all for his own gut" (11.833; and see 8.942–48).

Bloom's tendency to see other points of view even affects his purely internal monologue. In the little scene we see him play in "Lotus Eaters," designed so that he can take his "Henry Flower" card from his hatband, his thoughts follow not his actual intention, but the appearance he is aiming to create:

> While his eyes still read blandly he took off his hat quietly inhaling his hairoil and sent his right hand with slow grace over his brow and hair. *Very warm morning.* Under their dropped lids his eyes found

the tiny bow of the leather headband inside his high grade ha. Just there. His right hand came down into the bowl of his hat. His fingers found quickly a card behind the headband and transferred it to his waistcoat pocket.

So warm. His right hand once more more slowly went over his brow and hair. (5.20–48; italics added)

Similarly, in avoiding Boylan, Bloom's internal monologues follow the show he is putting on: "Mr Bloom reviewed the nails of his left hand, then those of his right hand. The nails, yes. Is there anything more in him that they she sees?" (6.200); "I am looking for that. Yes, that. Try all pockets. Handker. *Freeman.* Where did I? Ah, yes. Trousers. Potato. Purse. Where?" (8.1188–89).[61] Here, however, the fact that Bloom's show is meant as much to distract himself as to distract others points to another side of his role-playing. If the ability to take on many roles is a challenge to identity, it may also be a way out of being locked into one's own story.

Parnell, Don Giovanni, and Rip Van Winkle

Unlike Odysseus, at least when he is in Ithaca, Bloom tends to borrow his stories from others. The significance to Bloom of a book by Leopold von Sacher Masoch [*sic*] (10.591), the eponymous hero of masochism, will appear later in "Circe" (15.2770 ff.). A passage from *Sweets of Sin* that he reads in the same central episode haunts him throughout the day (10.606–23; 12.88, 189, 301, 1188; 13.1261; 15.3770). Similarly, the stories of Don Giovanni, Rip Van Winkle, and Parnell reappear regularly in his thoughts and, as with any story that moves into the mythic, in multiple versions.

Don Giovanni and the Parnell story both concern men brought to grief by courting women who should be off limits to them. Just as *Hamlet* tells the story of the *Odyssey* but from the viewpoint of the son, these tell the story again, but from the viewpoint of the suitors. Molly, who plays Penelope, is also both Zerlina and Kitty O'Shea, "as she also was Spanish or half so, types that wouldn't do things by halves, passionate abandon of the south, casting every shred of decency to the winds" (16.1408). But astonishingly, bit by bit (and apparently unconsciously), Bloom takes for himself the role not of the cuckold, Masetto and Captain O'Shea, but rather of the handsome seducer.[62]

The first use that Bloom makes of the Parnell story is to reject the possibility of return, the topic that introduces Parnell into the conversation in the Cabman's Shelter:[63]

Looking back now in a retrospective kind of arrangement all seemed a kind of dream. And then coming back was the worst thing you ever did because it went without saying you would feel out of place as things always moved with the times. Why, as he reflected, Irishtown strand, a locality he had not been in for quite a number of years looked different somehow since, as it happened, he went to reside on the north side. (16.1400–1406)

The reflection is important for Bloom, not least for the recognition that neither the home nor the "you" that one tries to return to remains the same.[64] Bloom cannot return to his youth, or to Lombard Street West, or, for that matter, to the same home he left this morning. In some respects that will prove to be a good thing.

Bloom, however, goes further in thinking about Parnell, twice recalling how he returned Parnell's hat during the violence in the *United Ireland* offices (16.1333–39, 1495–528). The connection to John Henry Menton's hat (6.1007 ff.; 16.1524) brings in as well Bloom's surprising victory, cutting out Menton at bowls in front of Molly. Perhaps as a result, Bloom thinks, extraordinarily:

the simple fact of the case was it was simply a case of the husband not being up to the scratch, with nothing in common between them beyond the name, and then a real man arriving on the scene, strong to the verge of weakness, falling a victim to her siren charms and forgetting home ties, the usual sequel, to bask in the loved one's smiles. The eternal question of the life connubial, needless to say, cropped up. Can real love, supposing there happens to be another chap in the case, exist between married folk? (16.1379 ff.)

Bloom can question the possibility of love "between married folk" here because he is clearly identifying himself not with the inadequate husband, but with the "real man" "strong to the verge of weakness." His next act is to bring out his photograph of Molly, another "Spanish type" (16.1426), leading to his second, now elaborated account of how "He, B, enjoyed the distinction of being close to Erin's uncrowned king in the flesh" (16.1495–96, and compare 16.1333–39).[65]

Perhaps even more significant than Bloom's appropriation of Parnell may be the story that he takes as its archetype, *Don Giovanni*. Bloom's focus on "*La ci darem*," the seduction duet that Molly will sing that afternoon with Boylan (18.149), begins with Zerlina's *vorrei e non vorrei* (I would like to and I wouldn't like to) misremembered as *voglio e non vorrei* (I want to and I wouldn't like to) (4.327). As we saw in looking at Stephen, the mistake recalls Leporello's slapstick *voglio*, desiring first not to serve and then not to be seen—and relevant to Bloom as well, who serves Molly her breakfast and avoids being seen by Boylan (6.200 ff.; 8.1168 ff.).[66] There is, however, an unusual twist. On a conscious level, even when he finally follows Boylan rather than avoiding him, Bloom chooses to "See, not be seen" (11.357). But on an unconscious level, rather than correcting the mistake, he switches roles. He returns to *voglio* (I want to), even after he has recognized the mistake (6.221, 237–40; 7.155; 15.355; 16.347), but also after he has taken the main role for himself. Beginning by humming the Don's part in *La ci darem* (5.225), now with the letter from Martha in hand, he will complete the duet by having Mrs Breen sing *voglio* (15.469–73) to his Don in "Circe," as further accusations of his being a Don Juan await (15.1064).[67]

Bloom's identification with Don Giovanni has a mirror in the *Odyssey's* story of Aphrodite and Ares (8.266–366). Odysseus's enjoyment here is in stark contrast to his weeping at the surrounding stories about Troy (8.86, 367–69, 521). Since he has just described himself as worn down by years and toil (8.182–83), we do not expect him to enjoy the story of a beautiful wife betraying an older, crippled husband with her handsome seducer, even when the husband gets compensation through entrapment.[68] It seems, however, that when gods are the actors, Odysseus can appreciate the humor. Similarly with Bloom and his reorientation of *Don Giovanni*. His memory may increase Zerlina's eagerness to be seduced, and Molly, at the end of the novel, may still think of him as the hapless Masetto (18.1507), but by taking Don Giovanni's perspective, he can enjoy the tale. And, as the unconscious can, he is able to have it both ways—identifying with the handsome seducer and also, as Bloom switches to the "*a cenar teco*" that signals the Commendatore's revenge (8.1039 ff.; 15.1886), enjoying a story where the seducer gets his just deserts.

* * *

In replaying the stories of Parnell and Don Giovanni, Bloom takes advantage of the paradoxical human ability to take on contradictory roles. With Rip Van Winkle, Joyce is interested in the ability of the story itself to have contradictory meanings. One side of this lies in the interaction of myth and history. Parnell is a purely historical person, then mythologized, and *Don Giovanni* one version of a traditional figure. Rip Van Winkle provides a third alternative, a character invented by Washington Irving, based on a

German folktale, who then becomes a folk-figure in his own right. Joyce's interest in how Bloom processes the story, however, goes even further, as the story itself introduces a circularity opposite to Bloom's understanding of it.

For Bloom, the story of Rip Van Winkle is simply a negative *Odyssey*: Rip sleeps, returns after twenty years, and finds not a waiting household, but his past eliminated and himself forgotten. He has done some editing to achieve this result. Washington Irving's story ends with Rip, freed from his wife's nagging by her death, settling down to a happy and honored life with his daughter. In Bloom's version this disappears, as does Rip Van Winkle's son, and with him any reference to his own son, Rudy. *Argumentum ex silentio* does not make for a strong case, but since Irving's version incorporates many themes that we will look at in chapter 4, and since the Rip Van Winkle fantasy in "Circe" follows the suggestion that Boylan might impregnate Molly (15.3141–45, 3152–213), it is worth looking at the passage:

> [H]e had no courage to ask after any more friends, but cried out in despair, "Does nobody here know Rip Van Winkle?"
>
> "Oh, Rip Van Winkle!" exclaimed two or three. "Oh, to be sure! that's Rip Van Winkle yonder, leaning against the tree."
>
> Rip looked, and beheld a precise counterpart of himself as he went up the mountain; apparently as lazy, and certainly as ragged. The poor fellow was now completely confounded. He doubted his own identity, and whether he was himself or another man. In the midst of his bewilderment, the man in the cocked hat demanded who he was, and what was his name?
>
> "God knows!" exclaimed he at his wit's end; "I'm not myself—I'm somebody else—that's me yonder—no—that's somebody else, got into my shoes—I was myself last night, but I fell asleep on the mountain, and they've changed my gun, and everything's changed, and I'm changed, and I can't tell what's my name, or who I am!"[69]

Just as Bloom connects questions of identity with his son: "I was happier then. Or was that I? Or am I now I? . . . Could never like it again after Rudy. Can't bring back time" (8.608–10), young Rip, as a repetition of his father, brings on his father's crisis of identity. This part of the story Bloom suppresses.

What Bloom sees in the story of Rip Van Winkle is the purely linear time that makes return impossible: "Quite a number of stories there were on that particular Alice Ben Bolt topic, Enoch Arden and Rip Van Winkle and does anybody hereabouts remember Caoc O'Leary . . ." (16.424–27).[70] Nonetheless, a theme of circularity emerges purely from the story's focus on sleep. In contrast to the idea of death (the twin of sleep, see *Theogony* 755–57; 13.80) that Bella brings up just after this (15.3204–12), the Rip Van Winkle reference emphasizes sleep as return: "all is changed by woman's will since you slept horizontal in Sleepy Hollow your night of twenty years. Return and see" (15.3153–55). The theme is reinforced by Joyce's transferring the story to "Sleepy Hollow," a location that gets in its own comment at 15.3156–58, and by Bloom thinking of it again as he falls asleep in "Nausicaa":

> young eyes Mulvey plump bubs me breadvan Winkle red slippers she rusty sleep wander years of dreams return tail end Agendath swoony lovey showed me her next year in drawers return next in her next her next. (13.1282–85)

There is a theme not only of sleep but also of circularity here. In Bloom's drowsy thoughts, "Agendath" recalls "next year in Jerusalem" (7.207), and "return" and "next" jostle one another. At first this seems the opposite of the lesson that Bloom took from Rip Van Winkle earlier:

> Rip van Winkle we played. Rip: tear in Henny Doyle's overcoat. Van: breadvan delivering. Winkle: cockles and periwinkles. Then I did Rip van Winkle coming back. She leaned on the sideboard watching. Moorish eyes. Twenty years asleep in Sleepy Hollow. All changed. Forgotten. The young are old. His gun rusty from the dew. (13.1112–16)

Bloom sees the story as showing that the past is simply over, as is the event he associates with it, the day he first met Molly, playing charades at Dolphin's Barn (4.344–45; 8.273). In fact, however, what we see is how the recollection of the past is shaped by the present. Just as the "breadvan" of fifteen years before is now colored by the Boland (recalling Boylan) breadvan that Bloom saw in "Calypso" (4.82),[71] the memory altogether has been triggered by Bloom's correspondence with Martha Clifford, who also lives at Dolphin's Barn (11.897–900):

> She kissed me. Never again. My youth. Only once it comes. Or hers. Take the train there tomorrow. No. Returning not the same. Like kids your second visit to a house. The new I want. Nothing new under the sun. Care of P. O. Dolphin's Barn. Are you not happy in your? Naughty darling. At Dolphin's barn charades in Luke Doyle's house.

> Mat Dillon and his bevy of daughters: Tiny, Atty, Floey, Maimy, Louy,
> Hetty. Molly too. (13.1102–6)

Bloom's contradictory "The new I want. Nothing new under the sun" then
leads into further ideas of circularity, and from there to Rip Van Winkle:[72]

> Eightyseven that was. Year before we. And the old major, partial to
> his drop of spirits. Curious she an only child, I an only child. So it
> returns. Think you're escaping and run into yourself. Longest way
> round is the shortest way home. And just when he and she. Circus
> horse walking in a ring. Rip van Winkle we played. (13.1108–12)

The impossibility of return merges here with an idea that events are cyclical: "Think you're escaping and run into yourself." Just as Bloom leaves his
"I. . . . AM. A." (13.1256–70) open-ended as he drops off to sleep, he points
to an end that is also a new beginning: "Chance. We'll never meet again. But
it was lovely. Goodbye, dear. Thanks. Made me feel so young" (13.1271–73).

Rip Van Winkle brings together linear and cyclical time simply in being
about sleep. The cycle of day and night, sleep and waking, is, after all, how
humans experience linear time.[73] This reflection runs throughout *Ulysses,*
for example, in Joyce's references to Ponchielli's "Dance of the Hours"
(4.526; 13.1012; 15.4054–84). Thus also, as Irene de Jong notes, Homer shapes
his narrative with the beginnings and ends of the day.[74] Sleep also has a
critical role in the *Odyssey,* where Homer plays the continuity of day following night against the discontinuity that Odysseus experiences on waking
on Phaeacia (5.486 ff.), with Aeolus's winds (10.31 ff.), Helios's cattle (12.335
ff.), or on Ithaca (13.187 ff.).[75] As the examples make clear, sleep can be both
restorative and destructive, but it always marks a new beginning.[76]

*   *   *

Significantly, Bloom's sleep comes at the end of a chapter, which provides
another kind of break, and another reflection upon completion. As Clive
Hart has pointed out, *Ulysses* is full of gaps.[77] The gaps point out the inherent incompletion of narrative: as Tristram points out in *Tristram Shandy,* if
he included everything his story would take as much time as his life.[78] Like
sleep, however, the gaps can also be restorative. After his sleep at the end of
"Nausicaa," we will next see Bloom in the episode of birth, at the maternity
hospital, the beginning of his time together with Stephen.

Bloom's sleep also marks a major change in the narrative time of the novel—and one that makes its own comment on the need for gaps. Ever since the initial transition from "Telemachus" to "Nestor," Joyce has left abrupt gaps between the episodes, most emphatically between "Cyclops" and "Nausicaa," where the gap is pronounced enough to appear as "a blank period of time including a cardrive, a visit to a house of mourning, a leave-taking" (17.2051–52) in the liturgical summary of Bloom's day.[79] From "Oxen of the Sun" onward, however, these breaks cease, and, as Homer's narrative proceeds forward without breaks, we follow Bloom and Stephen from the maternity hospital, to Burke's pub, to Nighttown, to the Cabman's Shelter, and back to Bloom's house on Eccles St.[80] The narrative continuity also brings out the increasingly radical difference in narrative styles. In other words, the continuity only emphasizes the gaps. No matter how complete the narrative is, its meaning will always be open to change.

4

Odysseus and Bloom

Ambiguity and Doing the Deed

Ulysses, at first, does not seem to contain a parallel to Odysseus's move from the mythic to the ordinary. The bedroom that Leopold Bloom leaves in "Calypso" he reenters in "Ithaca." Nonetheless, just as Bloom has to recognize how that bedroom has changed, he must also, like Odysseus, move back into uncertainty and trouble. As Bloom realizes in contemplating his proposal to Molly: "Me. And me now. / Stuck, the flies buzzed" (8.912 ff.), he is caught. Bloom, of course, fails to notice that two flies, not one, are stuck, a point that will resonate as we learn more about Molly and about Bloom's response to the death of his son. Nonetheless, it seems that he is just as trapped as Stephen, although the trap emerges not in trying to escape the past, but in wanting to return to it.[1] The question will be what he can do about that.

THE PASSIVE HERO

Even more than words and stories, the characters of the *Odyssey* and *Ulysses* focus on action or inaction as the key to overcoming their isolation. To put it metaphorically, while Stephen and Telemachus are associated with the fixity of rocks and towers, Bloom and Odysseus are sailors, clinging to rafts in the midst of a storm, yielding and resisting simultaneously. Or, less poetically, both are faced, in the ever-changing flux that is time, with the challenge of preserving identity but not becoming trapped within it. The situation implies a form of activity that is paradoxically passive. It also means that Bloom, at any rate, will have to reevaluate what it means to be stuck.

Like Bloom's "unconquered hero" to Boylan's "conquering hero" (11.340–42), Odysseus prevails by enduring. His initial heroism in Ithaca is, accordingly, passive. He gains entrance to Eumaeus's hut by not fighting the dogs that guard it (14.29 ff.), reaches the palace by not fighting Melanthius (17.235–38), and yields to the missiles hurled at him in the great hall (18.394–97; 20.299–305).[2] Just as the story of Penelope's weaving is told three times in the course of the *Odyssey*, so is the story of Odysseus and the wooden horse, the ultimate tale of infiltration (Menelaus's story: 4.271–89; Demodocus's song: 8.500–520; Odysseus's account: 11.523–32).[3] The story characterizes him, as the weaving and unweaving characterizes her. It also applies to the "dark horse" of *Ulysses*, Bloom, associated with the outsider, Throwaway, the unexpected winner of the Gold Cup.[4] Bloom too reenters his house through a "stratagem" (17.83), not through the front entrance used trangressively by Boylan, but through the female space of the scullery and kitchen (marked by the presence of "four smallsized square handercheifs . . . and one pair of ladies' grey hose" (17.152–53; 18.1094–99), just as he reenters his bed with "circumspection" as well as "solicitude" (17.2115–21).

Bloom's infiltration is also a feature in his marriage (13.1241; 15.3706). In the few depictions of marriage we have in *Ulysses*, Ritchie Goulding rules the household from his bed, "sirred" by his son (3.61–98); Simon Dedalus ("Our father who art not in heaven" 10.291, 654–716) shows up most places in Dublin except his home; and Paddy Dignam is liminal ("The last night pa was boosed he was standing on the landing there bawling out for his boots to go out to Tunney's for to boose more" 10.1067–69).[5] In contrast, Bloom achieves his place exactly by not demanding it: as Molly recalls, one reason she accepted his proposal was "I knew I could always get round him" (18.1579).[6]

Odysseus and Bloom also share a link to the feminine, a quality associated with passivity. Bloom, "the new womanly man" (15.1798) with "his firm full masculine feminine passive active hand" (17.289), thus recalls Erwin Cook's argument that Odysseus is as much a passive as an active hero, with all the feminine and masculine connotations that implies.[7] Tongue in cheek though it may be, Samuel Butler's claim that the *Odyssey* must be the work of a woman has something to it.

The opposition of the passive, the feminine, and endurance to the masculine, the active, and striking out, connects as well to an overall opposition of cunning to force. As Gregory Nagy has pointed out, this opposition underlies Odysseus's identity as a hero of *metis* (cunning), paired against Achilles, the paradigmatic hero of force.[8] Similarly, Hesiod's *Theogony* associates deeds, activity, and violence with the masculine (as in Cronus's castration of Uranus or Zeus's thunderbolt), and words and cunning with the feminine (as in Earth's wise counsel or Metis, "cunning intelligence," the wife that Zeus is able to absorb). *Ulysses* takes on these associations as well, for example in John Wise Nolan's challenge to Bloom, the "nice pattern of a Romeo and Juliet" (12.1492): "Right, says John Wyse. Stand up to it then with force like men" (12.1475).

*   *   *

Bloom is unique in *Ulysses* as a man who actually speaks to a woman (Josie Breen) neither related to him nor in a service role. Odysseus is also characterized by his relation to females, an association that may be most clearly expressed in Phaeacia.[9] With the help of Athena, Odysseus enters the great hall of Arete and Alcinous unseen and clothed in mist (7.14–17, 37–42). But while Athena can set the stage, Odysseus must play the role. His antagonist, beneath the surface of the action, is Arete. Nausicaa's insistence on the impropriety of being seen with a stranger (like her embarrassment at mentioning marriage, 6.66–67, 273–89) prepares us for conventional gender roles, a situation that Odysseus negotiates masterfully. A rather different order of things emerges when Nausicaa and Athena tell Odysseus to supplicate not Alcinous but Arete (6.310–15; 7.53–77).[10] A quiet, underlying drama follows, from Arete's initial silence in Book 6, to her questioning Odysseus about the clothes given him by Nausicaa (7.233–40), to her telling him to safeguard the gifts suggested by Alcinous (8.423–45) to, finally, her praise after Odysseus describes the heroines of the Underworld (11.335–41).[11]

When Odysseus tells Alcinous his name in Book 9, he is in fact answering the question posed in Book 7 by Arete (7.237–38), the question he never got back to. Odysseus generally addresses Alcinous, not Arete. His explicit proof of himself occurs in the games, where she is not present. Alcinous responds to Arete's announcement that "the guest-friend (*xenos*) is mine, though each has a share in honor" (11.338) with the tried and true "the conveyance will be a care for men / for all, but most for me, since mine is the power in the household" (11.352–53, and see 1.358–59; 21.352–53; *Iliad* 6.492–93). Nonetheless, Odysseus, in making Arete the last person he celebrates in Phaeacia (13.56–62), seems to understand where the true contest lay. Not his overt assertion of himself at the purely masculine games (8.104–10, 140–240, and see 321–24) but the unspoken contest with Arete has finally led to his homecoming.

Ambiguity and Change

The passive and feminine sides of Bloom and Odysseus also bring out their ambiguity. In both cases the ambiguity is inherent. For Odysseus this is, at least in part, because he has a double source in both folklore and epic.[12] For Bloom it is associated with being Jewish, a mysterious and feminine race.[13] Even more importantly though, when Joyce created an Odysseus who cannot tell stories and has hardly ever left Dublin ("not to say that he had ever travelled extensively to any great extent but he was at heart a born adventurer though by a trick of fate he had consistently remained a land-lubber except you call going to Holyhead which was his longest" 17.501–4), he merely reflected the paradox of an epic hero who is fighting his way out of epic, a sailor who, like Joyce's Murphy ("tired of all them rocks in the sea . . . and boats and ships" 16.622) is trying to escape the sea.

The ambiguity that characterizes both Bloom and Odysseus emerges most vividly in the many different appearances they take on. Bloom himself suggests the issue in confusing "metempsychosis" (change of soul, or *psuche,* into a new body) and "metamorphosis" (change of shape): "Metempsychosis, he said, is what the ancient Greeks called it. They used to believe you could be changed into an animal or a tree, for instance. What they called nymphs, for example" (4.375–77). The distinction, of course, raises the essential question of both *Ulysses* and the *Odyssey:* is a change of form (metamorphosis) also a change of *psuche* or not?[14]

Shapeshifting also underlies the relation of *Ulysses* to the *Odyssey.* Despite the correspondence used here for the sake of convenience—of Stephen as Telemachus, Bloom as Odysseus, and Molly as Penelope—there are no simple equivalences between the works. Rather, Joyce's characters are, like Ovid's, always multiple and always transforming. As Fritz Senn points out, while Molly is Calypso (and also Penelope), so is the (very Ovidian) Nymph whose picture is over the bed (4.369 ff.). Bloom is Odysseus, but so is the "versatile [or 'many-turning'] allround man," Mulligan (16.288), and so is Murphy, the *soi-disant* returned sailor of "Eumaeus," who is equally "Morpheus," Sleep, the transformer. And Mulligan, of course, is also Mercury ("Mercurial Malachi" 1.518) and, as Stephen's *fidus Achates,* another double for Bloom (6.49; 16.55).[15]

The overall transformations of both works, however, are epitomized in their heroes, for whom shapeshifting is practically the norm. Bloom's multiple incarnations in "Circe" reflect a chameleon-like ability to take his coloring from those around him, a result of his ability to adopt their perspectives. Odysseus too, as the grandson of the master trickster, Autolycus, is by nature *polutropos* and opposite to both Achilles and Ajax, the quintessential heroes of fixed identity.[16] Both are, inherently, many different things to many people, with the natural result that it is hard to pin down just who they are in themselves.

*　*　*

Ulysses and the *Odyssey* explore the nature of shapeshifting under opposite circumstances, but in doing so both call into question the nature of action. As we saw in chapter 1, the *Odyssey* begins episodically and shifts to a strong narrative, while *Ulysses* reverses the *Odyssey* in beginning with a strong narrative drive that then shifts to an episodic approach removed from narrative time. In both cases, however, when narrative time dominates, the characters deliberately take on their transformations, and when they are removed from narrative time, those transformations tend to be imposed upon them.

Odysseus in Ithaca is like Bloom in the first part of *Ulysses* in deliberately adapting himself to those around him. He becomes an old beggar (13.429–37), a transformed father (16.172–78), the victor over Irus (18.69–71), and finally the restored hero (23.156–65). Although the outer transformations are Athena's, Odysseus very much creates the roles.[17] In the fantastic world of the Wanderings, in contrast, where Odysseus is threatened with transformations that range from the Lotus Eaters to Circe, his challenge is primarily to persist despite the transformations that threaten to absorb him. The effect is not unlike our view of Bloom under Joyce's ever-changing narrative styles.

Bloom's transformations in the second part of *Ulysses* resemble Odysseus's Wanderings both in being shared with others and, more particularly, in being not something he does but something done to him. In fact, aside from the loss of his button (15.1339–41; 16.35–39) and a certain awareness of Gerty's appreciation (13.833–36), it is unclear that he knows how many forms he has taken on. The shapeshifting is nonetheless remarkable, from the "Bloowho," "greasabloom," "Siopold," "Bloo mur" etcetera (11.86, 180, 752, 860) of "Sirens" to the mysterious stranger in "Nausicaa," to the many guises of "Cyclops" and "Oxen of the Sun." In "Circe" alone Bloom undergoes almost thirty transformations, far more than any other character in the episode.[18]

There is, however, less difference between the two parts of *Ulysses* in this regard than between the two halves of the *Odyssey*. Bloom has spent the first half of *Ulysses* adopting roles, but, like Odysseus's unpromising appearance as a speaker (*Iliad* 3.204 ff.), the shapeshifting is easily missed, particularly in contrast to the flamboyance of Mulligan. The second part of *Ulysses*, which repeats in technicolor the themes of the first, simply makes the shapeshifting unmistakable. Unlike Odysseus, who spends the first half of the *Odyssey* attempting to maintain his identity, Bloom does not resist the changes. Both experience a shapeshifting they choose and a shapeshifting that is imposed upon them. Bloom, unlike Odysseus, accepts either.

But while Bloom seems willing to accept passivity, as he accepts his feminine side, inaction remains as problematic for him as it is for Odysseus. This is largely because inaction is tied up with the inevitability of change, as in his regular association of change and water:

Seaside girls. Torn envelope. Hands stuck in his trousers' pockets, jarvey off for the day, singing. Friend of the family. Swurls, he says. Pier with lamps, summer evening, band.

> Those girls, those girls,
> Those lovely seaside girls.

Milly too. Young kisses: the first. Far away now past. Mrs Marion. Reading, lying back now, counting the strands of her hair, smiling, braiding.

A soft qualm, regret, flowed down his backbone, increasing. Will happen, yes. Prevent. Useless: can't move. Girl's sweet light lips. Will happen too. He felt the flowing qualm spread over him. (4.439–52)

Won't last. Always passing, the stream of life, which in the stream of life we trace is dearer thaaan them all. (5.563–64)

How can you own water really? It's always flowing in a stream, never the same, which in the stream of life we trace. Because life is a stream. (8.93–95)

And, definitively,

I was happier then. Or was that I? Or am I now I? Twentyeight I was. She twentythree. When we left Lombard street west something changed. Could never like it again after Rudy. Can't bring back time. Like holding water in your hand. (8.608–11)

Even the rocks Bloom thinks of, which are usually the emblems of fixity, are "drifting around" (8.583 and see 17.1052 ff.), like Joyce's "Wandering Rocks" or the moon, symbol of change and so of women (17.1157–70).[19]

But while Bloom's awareness of change is all-pervasive, it is ambivalent as well. Given the melancholy of these reflections, it may seem surprising that Bloom is also, in contrast to Stephen's hydrophobia (17.237), a "waterlover, drawer of water, watercarrier" (17.183). In what has been dubbed the "Water Hymn," we are told what Bloom admires in water: some 104 detailed variations in its use, properties, and forms (17.216 ff.).[20] In other words, what appeals to Bloom about water is precisely what he also fears in it: its ability to change.

As Bloom's thoughts of the "seaside girls" and of Rudy make clear, he fears change because he fears losing his relation to others. The association also brings out another side to Bloom and Odysseus's shapeshifting. As Joyce told Frank Budgen, Hamlet is only a son, while Odysseus is son to Laertes, father to Telemachus, husband to Penelope, lover of Calypso, companion in arms of the Greek warriors around Troy, and king of Ithaca (JJ 435). The poem illustrates all these roles, showing us not only Odysseus's transformations after his return but also Odysseus in infancy (19.395 ff.), childhood (24.336 ff.), youth (19.412 ff.), as a young husband (18.259 ff.), a son (11.150 ff.), a fellow-warrior (11.385 ff.), and even, transformed and proleptically, as old and decrepit (14.429 ff.; 19.358–60).[21] We also see, beginning with Helen's description (4.240 ff.), how he changes depending on who he is with: Nausicaa, Eumaeus, Telemachus, Irus, the suitors, the maids, or Penelope. Similarly, as we have seen, Bloom's transformations reflect his many roles and relations. The fact of these different selves is not a problem for him as it is for Stephen. His problem is rather the transience of relation that they imply.

The shift from the first to the second part of Ulysses not only brings out Bloom's shapeshifting but also reveals how closely it follows Bloom's relations to others. Thus, Bloom's transformations, as "greaseabloom" (11.180), as "ben Bloom Elijah" (12.1916), as "Mr Canvasser Bloom" (14.1004), or as "Leopoldeben" (15.275), reflect the multiple roles expressed more quietly by the initial style, of Poldy, Papli, advertising canvasser, and "My Dear Son Leopold" (17.1881; 5.206).[22] Similarly our sense of the shapeshifting that Odysseus deliberately undertakes in Ithaca is colored by the transformations he has had to face in his Wanderings. Having seen him resisting an absorption by others, from the Lotus Eaters to the Cyclops to Circe, we now see him using his ability to adapt to others as a means of establishing himself. The attempt will make the interaction of active and passive heroism only the more complicated.

Isolation and Being Stuck

Odysseus's relations to others are as ambiguous as Bloom's. While Achilles is the supreme individual hero of the *Iliad,* one who, like Aristotle's great-souled man, cannot live in reference to others except, perhaps, to a friend (*Ethics* 1124a1), Odysseus is the most social of heroes—so much so that he will end up condemned by Greek tragedy as the yes-man of the Atreidae.[23] He is the only hero to identify himself through his son (*Iliad* 2.260; 4.354), and the only one to be primarily focused on his wife.[24] He is also, and concomitantly, a particularly human hero. At his most intense, Achilles refuses sleep (*Iliad* 19.1–6; 24.1–13), in contrast to the regular theme of sleep in the *Odyssey.* He also refuses food, receiving nectar and ambrosia instead (*Iliad* 19.344–56). Odysseus, in the *Iliad,* as in his own epic, insists on the necessity of eating (19.225–33), a quintessentially social activity.[25]

Nonetheless, Odysseus is surprisingly alone. For all his sociability, he seems a hero who keeps his own council, one who, like Bloom, is "Assumed by any or known to none" (17.2008). Unlike Achilles and Patroclus, Sarpedon and Glaucon, Agamemnon and Menelaus, or Nestor and his son Antilochus, Odysseus has no close companion at Troy, an absence only underlined by his (perhaps spurious) expedition with Diomedes in *Iliad* 10.[26] Nor does he have a companion at sea, like Aeneas and his famously faithful Achates, or, in another respect, like Dante and Virgil. The only companions of Odysseus that are named more than once (and only four are named at all) are Elpenor and Eurylochus. The first is rather sweet but pathetic, and Odysseus's relation with the second, who opposes him over both Circe and the cattle of the sun, is, to put it mildly, fraught.[27] In fact, the history of Odysseus's Wanderings, seen from another point of view, describes his gradually causing the death of all his companions. Polyphemus, Teiresias, and Circe all predict (formulaically) his return "in evil case, with the loss of all his company" (9.533–35; 11.110–15; 12.139–41), an outcome we are continually reminded of (1.6; 2.17–20; 4.558–60; 5.14–17, 133; 24.427–28). It is no surprise then that Odysseus returns home alone—or that he wishes to reshape his story. It is equally understandable that the narrator feels a need to explain that the situation is not (entirely) his fault (1.5–9). What may come as a surprise, perhaps also to himself, is that Odysseus's final challenge will be not to regain his power and position but rather to reconnect with others.

* * *

Bloom is like Odysseus both in being anomalous and in his isolation. As we have seen in looking at "Hades," Bloom's isolation, in its outward aspect, is of a very different kind than Stephen's. Unlike Stephen (or Joyce) who is, in Stephen's description of his father, "All Irish . . . All too Irish" (16.382 ff.), Bloom is a Jew who is not really a Jew (16.1082 ff.), Hungarian and Irish, baptized both Protestant (twice) and Catholic (17.740 ff.), of multiple professions and abodes, perhaps a Freemason, perhaps a Zionist, perhaps even a radical nationalist (12.1635 ff.).[28] He, however, takes the social isolation that results surprisingly well.[29] His response to Crawford's "He can kiss my royal Irish arse" (7.991), is simply cautious: "A bit nervy. Look out for squalls. All off for a drink. Arm in arm. . . . Usual blarney" (7.983–84). Society is not that crucial to him. The promise and threat of Zionism and the east (4.84–98, 191–228) give way to thoughts of Molly: "To smell the gentle smoke of tea, fume of the pan, sizzling butter. Be near her ample bedwarmed flesh. Yes, yes" (4.237–39).

Bloom is like Odysseus, and unlike the other men of *Ulysses,* in that the relations that are most complicated for him, and that touch most closely on his identity, are to his family. Although the impulses play out differently, he is also like Stephen in both yearning for and fearing a connection with others. But while with Stephen the avoidance is most obvious, and the yearning only gradually becomes clear, the opposite is true of Bloom. Unlike Odysseus, who gives no indication for most of the poem that his return is directed toward his wife and son, Bloom's attachment is clear from the first. Nor does it bother him that others think of him in connection with Molly (5.131; 6.693–94; 8.763; 10.546–83; 11.476–515; even 11.1256–57) and ridicule the attachment (8.949–52; 12.1650–52; 15.3706). His concern, in this case, is with Rudy, Milly and Molly, not with how he seems to others.[30] The difficulty is that with each of them the preoccupation is over what he can no longer have.

* * *

Finally, Bloom is like Odysseus in that his sense of family splits into a male and a female component, with Rudy and his father linked on the one side, and Milly and Molly on the other. Both sides involve loss. Just as Stephen links the female to matter and flux and the male to unchanging form, Bloom thinks of Milly and Molly in relation to flow, change, and succession and of Rudy and his father along with the fixity of death. This also creates a crucial difference between Bloom's situation and that of Odysseus. On the male side, as we saw in chapter 2, Odysseus's reconnection culminates in Book 24 with grandfather, father, and son fighting together (with Odysseus as both father and son).[31] Bloom has no equivalent. His living child is not a son, but a daughter: "There is none now to be for Leopold, what Leopold was for Rudolph" (14.1076).[32]

On the female side, Milly, as a young version of Molly, recalls the inevitability of change, as in the "lovely seaside girls" passage above, "Molly. Milly. Same thing watered down" 6.87; 15.540), or Bloom's mistaking Milly for Molly in the Rip van Winkle passage (15.3162–66). It is also in associating Milly and Molly with flow (or, for those interested in the cyclical nature of time, with their "periods," 13.781–85, 1031–232) that *Ulysses* reveals that Bloom cannot divide the male and female sides of his family as Odysseus does. Bloom's losses of Molly and Rudy are connected.[33] While Bloom describes his day to Molly, the narrator of "Ithaca" asks:

> What limitations of activity and inhibitions of conjugal rights were perceived by listener and narrator concerning themselves during the course of this intermittent and increasingly more laconic narration? (17.2271 ff.)

The answer for Bloom is

> By the narrator [Bloom] a limitation of activity, mental and corporal, inasmuch as complete mental intercourse between himself and the listener [Molly] had not taken place since the consummation of puberty, indicated by catamenic hemorrhage, of the female issue of narrator and listener [Milly], 15 September 1903 (17. 2284 ff.)

But for Molly the answer is:

> By the listener [Molly] a limitation of fertility[,] . . . complete carnal intercourse, with ejaculation of semen within the natural female organ, having last taken place 5 weeks previous, viz. 27 November 1893, to the birth on 29 December 1893 of second (and only male) issue, deceased 9 January 1894, aged 11 days (17.2271 ff.)

That Bloom and Molly have not had "complete carnal intercourse" since Rudy's birth and death says a lot about their lack of "complete mental intercourse" as well. Bloom, it turns out, is as haunted by Rudy's death as Stephen is trapped by memories of his mother.[34] We learn this, however, only gradually. Bloom thinks of Rudy in "Calypso" when he reflects on his daughter's birthday ("He would be eleven now if he had lived" 4.420) and in "Hades," along with thoughts of his father's suicide. His passing thought in "Lestrygonians": "Could never like it again after Rudy" (8.610 and see 8.24) does not specify whether he means himself or Molly and is cryptic about the "it."[35]

At the same time as we realize how Bloom is haunted by Rudy we also come to see his sense of guilt: "Meant nothing. Mistake of nature. If it's healthy it's from the mother. If not from the man. Better luck next time" (6.325 ff.; 14.1239–50; and see 18.1445–46). Bloom has abandoned his father's traditions ("Are you not my son Leopold, the grandson of Leopold? Are you not my dear son Leopold who left the house of his father and left the god of his fathers Abraham and Jacob?" 15.260–62; 5.200 ff.; 17.1893 ff.), just as Stephen has abandoned his mother's. He sees Rudy's death as due to his own failure. Like Stephen, he is hemmed in not only by the past but also by his sense of responsibility for it.[36]

*　*　*

Bloom's resistance to "ejaculation of semen within the natural female organ" points, in the "baldest, coldest way" (*LI* 164), to his fear of the future and its threat of loss. Another pregnancy might mean only another death. The fear, however, also robs him of identity. Unlike Stephen, who rejects paternity ("The images of other males of his blood will repel him. He will see in them grotesque attempts of nature to foretell or to repeat himself" 9.434 ff.), Bloom links his identity to that of his son: "If little Rudy had lived. See him grow up. Hear his voice in the house. Walking beside Molly in an Eton suit. My son. Me in his eyes" (6.75).[37] The Siren song of the Croppy Boy, for Bloom, thus means Rudy:

> All gone. All fallen. At the siege of Ross his father, at Gorey all his brothers fell. To Wexford, we are the boys of Wexford, he would. Last of his name and race.
> I too. Last of my race. Milly young student. Well, my fault perhaps. No son. Rudy. Too late now. Or if not? If not? If still?
> He bore no hate.
> Hate. Love. Those are names. Rudy. Soon I am old. (11.1063–69)

According to "Ithaca," if Bloom is "mutable (aliorelative)" because (like Stephen) from "maturity to senility he would increasingly resemble his paternal procreator" (17.1354–56), he is "solitary (ipsorelative)" because

> *Brothers and sisters had he none.*
> *Yet that man's father was his grandfather's son.*
> (17.1351–53, italics in the original)

Both his son and father are dead, and Bloom's is (like Odysseus's), a family of only sons (*Odyssey* 16.117 ff.; *U* 13.1109).[38] Seen as particular to him (ipsorelative), the riddle implies he is alone. Seen, however, as the state of human beings within time, the condition, like the riddle, applies to everyone: everyone's father was his grandfather's son. It depends, as Molly will show us, on the "his."

We do not know if Bloom will be able to escape from the trap he has created for himself. The narrator of "Ithaca" points out that for Bloom and Molly "to form by reunion the original couple of uniting parties"—to simply remake the past—is impossible. In contrast, that they could "reunite for increase and multiplication," an idea that both Molly (18.166 ff.) and Bloom (11.1066) consider, is only "absurd" (17.1963 ff.). One possible example of this absurdity occurs in the apparition of Rudy that ends the "Wandering" section, the part of the story where Odysseus, at any rate, began his transition from mythic to ever-changing human time. The fantasy is characterized by the number eleven, the start of a new decade, and so the number of death and renewal.[39] As part Bloom's son, part Stephen's Hamnet Shakespeare, and also, as Virgil's Marcellus, an element of a world that might have been, the apparition brings to a head the growing "fusion" (as Joyce termed it) of Stephen and Bloom that has been developing within the narrative styles.[40] Unlike Bloom's son, however, who died at eleven days, this Rudy is "a fairy boy of eleven, a changeling" (15.4957), the age Hamnet Shakespeare was when he died, and the age Rudy would have been had he lived.

It is tempting to take the apparition as a sign that Bloom can now break out of his past. Bloom here addresses Stephen as "Stephen" for the only time (15.4929), as Dante is called "Dante" only by Beatrice, and only as, with his past sins washed from him, he is about to move from the *Purgatorio* to the *Paradiso* (*Purgatorio* 30.55).[41] In a more conventional work, arrangements such as this, which are made by the narrator, are decisive: when Telemachus sneezes in Homer it is a good omen, not the sign of an oncoming cold (17.541); when Elizabeth Bennet happens upon Darcy at Pemberley more than a social call will ensue.[42] In *Ulysses*, however, where each narrative style is only one of many, this is not necessarily the case. Molly, for example, who is doubtful (18.474–76), is right about the year of her birth, while the hyper-objective scientific narrator of "Ithaca" is wrong (17.2275–76;

18.474–75).[43] Similarly, the apparition of Rudy may imply, on one level of the novel, a breaking free from the past. This does not necessarily mean that Bloom, who never consciously registers the vision, can move on.

DEEDS AND IMPOSING IDENTITY

Killing the Suitors in the *Odyssey*: A Warrior's Outburst

The first half of the *Odyssey* is episodic and characterized by doublings, breaking into three distinct sections: Telemachus, Calypso and Phaeacia, and the Wanderings. Odysseus here is more often passive than active, maintaining rather than imposing his identity.[44] In the second half of the *Odyssey*, in contrast, a continuous narrative takes over, broken only by Book 15, which brings Telemachus back from Sparta. Here, after a self-constraint that has continued from the coast of Ithaca to Eumaeus's hut to the palace and even to Penelope's bedroom, Odysseus will burst into action, though not with the effect we are expecting.

Like Stephen's desire to establish himself by eliminating the competition, the honor that a Homeric warrior gains, he takes from another in battle, making the pursuit of *timē* (honor) a zero-sum game.[45] The *Odyssey*, accordingly, seems to be heading to a climax in which Odysseus regains his identity by killing the suitors, which is precisely how Aristotle read the poem (*Poetics* 1455b17). This narrative arc begins with Zeus's mention of Orestes's vengeance, leading Athena to bring up Odysseus and then the suitors (1.35–43, 88–92), and continues with Telemachus's daydreams about how Odysseus might "scatter the suitors through his house" (1.116), an idea continually repeated from this point on (1.244 ff., 250 ff.; 3.205 ff.; 4.164, 317 ff.). Odysseus's conversations with Teiresias (11.115 ff.), Athena (13.375 ff.), and Eumaeus (14.80 ff.), point to the suitors, as does most of his time in Ithaca. And the revenge does make for a dramatic climax, as Odysseus masters the bow, kills Antinous, and triumphantly reveals his identity before getting down to business.

As we will see in chapter 5, the great surprise of the *Odyssey* is that this is not the climax of the poem.[46] Odysseus's real contest turns out to be not with the suitors but with his wife. To descend to speculation, it is easy to imagine an earlier version of the story in which Odysseus slays the suitors, Penelope falls into his arms, and all live happily ever after.[47] Homer's audience would expect the death of the suitors to reestablish Odysseus's identity—highlighting Penelope's refusal to acknowledge him by making it a surprise. Homer's version, however, does more than give us a new twist on the story. In the complex of associations that the *Odyssey* and *Ulysses* share, opposing the active to the passive, the masculine to the feminine, and deeds to words, it shifts the emphasis from the former to the latter. Rather than imposing his identity on others by force, Odysseus will be tricked into revealing who he is through a woman's words. Just as he regains his formulaic, epithet-laden name from Athena, but the simple "Odysseus" from Penelope, his deeds yield to her words.

Odysseus's revenge is prepared by a pattern of silent endurance and then outburst that runs throughout the poem.[48] We begin with endurance. As Achilles is the hero of force and deeds, and Odysseus of words and endurance (as his epithet, "much-enduring" [*polutlas*], implies), the *Iliad* opens with Achilles's rage and what it did, the *Odyssey* with what its hero learned and suffered. The opening comes, however, with a backstory—"after he sacked Troy's holy citadel" (1.2)—that reminds us of the traditional hero of war. It also points to a critical difference between the *Iliad* and the *Odyssey*: here, as in Hesiod's five ages, the time before ours was the time of war, heroism, and Troy; ours is a time of guile (*Works and Days* 156–201).[49]

Unlike battle, the sea requires adaptation and endurance rather than aggression. Particularly during his Wanderings, where the challenge is to maintain his identity, Odysseus conquers by simply holding on: clinging to the Cyclops's ram (9.431 ff.), to the fig tree above Charybdis (12.433 ff.), (enforcedly) to the mast when listening to the Sirens (12.177 ff.), to the wreckage that carried him through the sea (5.324 ff.; 12.420 ff.), or to the cliffs of Phaeacia (5.426 ff.).[50] He has been able to take an active warrior's role only twice, in his outburst against the Cyclops, and in arming himself against Scylla (12.111–26, 225–59). The second was useless, and the first much worse than that. In Ithaca as well, with Melanthius (17.235 ff.), Antinous (17.463 ff.), Irus (18.90 ff.), Penelope (19.209 ff.), and the serving maids (20.5 ff.), the temptation to act must be resisted. The strain of this "holding on" and the internal division it causes appears when he "addresses his heart" "and his heart was persuaded and remained greatly enduring / without flinching, but he himself (*autos*) rolled this way and that" (20.23–24).[51] Given the tension thus created, it is no surprise that action, when it finally bursts forth, is brutal. For the poem, the move from the Wanderings to Ithaca has been a move from the mythic to the ordinary. For Odysseus, however, as we saw in chapter 1, the move is from being a hero to being a beggar. He wants the slaughter to reestablish his identity.[52]

Although the death of the suitors will turn out not to conclude Odysseus's return, it is nonetheless emphatic. It is also considerably more ambivalent than might at first appear.[53] Odysseus's position becomes far less morally ironclad after Eurymachus acknowledges guilt and offers compensation (22.45 ff.).[54] Similarly, the poet's focus on the feast is telling, as the dying Antinous ("he kicked the table back from him sharply / striking with his foot; food spilled to the ground, / bread and meat and cooked foods were spoiled" 22.19–21 ff.) recalls Agamemnon's murder at a feast (11.409), the Centaurs and Lapiths (21.295–304), and even the Cyclops's murder of his guests. Odysseus has returned to his warrior role, as "Mentor" points out (22.226 ff.), or as in the Iliadic similes that appear throughout the episode. But that role is now colored by his account of senselessly plundering the Cicones, replayed in his "Cretan lies" (9.40 ff.; 15.259–75; 17.425–39), by his disastrous assertion of identity with the Cyclops, and by his tears, as a woman weeps over a husband slain while defending family and city (8.523–30).[55] Odysseus will later refuse to glory in the deaths (22.409 ff.; echoed, unknowingly, by Penelope at 23.59).

Ambivalent as it is, the slaughter plays a crucial role in Odysseus's return. In this poem, however, it cannot be the final step.[56] The slaughter attempts to return Odysseus to his past by undoing the break between the self who left for Troy and the self who returned. In this light, once more, Penelope's first words after she has acknowledged her husband's identity are crucial. The gods have not allowed them to spend the time from youth to old age together (23.210–12). Odysseus cannot connect future and past by eliminating what has come between. There needs to be more.

Killing the Suitors in *Ulysses:* One on a List

At first glance Bloom, in contrast to Odysseus, appears to take a completely passive role in regard to Boylan. The impression is reinforced by *Ulysses*'s move not away from but into the episodic. The first half of the novel is all about going somewhere: Mulligan going for a swim, Haines going to the library (1.469–71), Stephen going to school and the newspaper office (and not The Ship), Bloom going to the pork butcher, the Post Office, the funeral, to meet Keyes etcetera. Then, with the wandering of "Wandering Rocks," this all stops, as Joyce recapitulates the events of the first half. The fugal structure of "Sirens" makes its beginning prefigure its end; the interpolations of "Cyclops" break into the narrative; and above all, the-question-and-answer format of "Ithaca," which Joyce described as the end of the novel proper, emphasize both the staccato feeling of the second half and its abstraction from narrative time.

Joyce, however, who never includes one opposite without the other, also joins the episodic and the linear, and so, implicitly, also the passive and active. "Aeolus" signals its overall ring-structure in nearly its first sentence:

> Grossbooted draymen rolled barrels dullthudding out of Prince's stores and bumped them up on the brewery float. On the brewery float bumped dullthudding barrels rolled by grossbooted draymen out of Prince's stores (7.21–24)

Nonetheless, the episode's headers move in a linear progression from the staid to the sensational.[57] In "Oxen of the Sun," Joyce's juxtapositions, of Bunyan and Pepys, for example (14.470 ff.), give us a series of snapshots more like the interpolations of "Cyclops" or the individual fantasies of "Circe" than like the ever-forward movement of the initial style. These, however, are embedded in the temporal progression of gestation, just as "Circe," "Eumaeus," "Ithaca," and "Penelope," despite their staccato feel, make up a continuous narrative.

Joyce has similarly complicated the issue of Bloom's passivity. Molly's elusive thought in "Penelope" about Bloom sending Milly to Mullingar "only hed do a thing like that all the same on account of me and Boylan thats why he did it Im certain the way he plots and plans everything out" (18.1007–9) chimes with Corley's surprising mention of having seen Bloom and Boylan together, which Bloom appears to recall (16.197–241). A number of commentators have suggested accordingly that Bloom has been complicit in the affair, perhaps related to his fantasy of voyeurism in "Circe" (15.3726–820), perhaps because he has on some level felt a need to end the stalemate in which he and Molly have landed.[58] Joyce, however, has chosen to leave this unclear, even, one suspects, to himself. The relation of being active to being passive is again more complicated than it might seem.

Whether Bloom actively furthers Molly's affair or passively accepts it, his approach is very much in contrast to Odysseus's. In one of the major differences between them, Bloom tries neither to eliminate the past nor to impose his own identity on the future. As we will see, Odysseus's approach, of assertion by elimination, leaves the ongoing problem of the suitors' relatives to be dealt with. Even more important is what lies behind that: the impossibility of making what has happened go away. Accepting this, Bloom regards Molly's affair with "more abnegation than jealousy, less envy than equanimity" (17.2195). He eliminates not the doer, but the offense: "From outrage (matrimony) to outrage (adultery) there arose nought but outrage (copulation) yet the matrimonial violator of the matrimonially violated had not been outraged by the adulterous violator of the adulterously violated" (17.2196–99). Bloom's problem is not the impossibility of eliminating of the past. Rather, as he fades into Molly's universal "he," it will be seeing that he has established any identity at all.

Bloom, like Odysseus, has his moment of outburst and, like Odysseus's, it occurs with a Cyclops. For Bloom, however, the outburst is primarily a means of avoidance.[59] His well-known protest against his Cyclops, the Citizen, is a distraction from what is in fact occurring "now. This very moment. This very instant," which is Molly's adultery:

—And I belong to a race too, says Bloom, that is hated and persecuted. Also now. This very moment. This very instant.
    Gob, he near burnt his fingers with the butt of his old cigar.
—Robbed, says he. Plundered. Insulted. Persecuted. Taking what belongs to us by right. At this very moment, says he, putting up his fist, sold by auction in Morocco like slaves or cattle.
—Are you talking about the new Jerusalem? says the citizen.
—I'm talking about injustice, says Bloom.
—Right, says John Wyse. Stand up to it then with force like men.
    That's an almanac picture for you. Mark for a softnosed bullet. Old lardyface standing up to the business end of a gun. Gob, he'd adorn a sweepingbrush, so he would, if he only had a nurse's apron on him. And then he collapses all of a sudden, twisting around all the opposite, as limp as a wet rag.
—But it's no use, says he. Force, hatred, history, all that. That's not life for men and women, insult and hatred. (12.1467–75)

Bloom has reverted almost immediately from his one manly outburst to his usual passive and feminine role, "twisting around all the opposite, as limp as a wet rag." Deeds, as such, are not a temptation for him.

Leopold Bloom, a very civilized man, slays his wife's suitors (as Joyce's Gilbert schema informs us) with the bow of reason, and does so the more easily since they are identified not as Blazes Boylan and his ilk, but as "scruples." His preferred approach to revenge, rejecting even Hephaestus's "automatic bed," is not violent but monetary:

Assassination, never, as two wrongs did not make one right. Duel by combat, no. Divorce, not now. Exposure by mechanical artifice (automatic bed) or individual testimony (concealed ocular witnesses), not yet. Suit for damages by legal influence or simulation of assault with evidence of injuries sustained (selfinflicted), not impossibly. Hushmoney by moral influence, possibly. (17.2201 ff.)

But even more, he is inclined to just accept the situation, aware as he is of "the futility of triumph or protest or vindication: the inanity of extolled virtue: the lethargy of nescient matter: the apathy of the stars" (17.2224 ff.). Like the trickster, Autolycus, of Shakespeare's tragic comedy, he is no fighter (*Winter's Tale* 4.3.107).

In Bloom's case, however, a disinclination to fight is also a disinclination to assert his particularity at all. He already understands the lesson that Odysseus will have to learn, that identity is determined by the thoughts of others. His problem will be the difficulty of fixing what anyone else thinks. Unlike Odysseus, Bloom reenters his bed (whatever its original provenience) accepting that he is only one of an ongoing series:

If he had smiled why would he have smiled?

To reflect that each one who enters imagines himself to be the first to enter whereas he is always the last term of a preceding series even if the first term of a succeeding one, each imagining himself to be first, last, only and alone whereas he is neither first nor last nor only nor alone in a series originating in and repeated to infinity. (17.2126–31)

Bloom's self-abnegation in being just one of a series is complicated by the fact, recognized only gradually by Joyceans, that it is far from clear what the series is of.[60] If the list is of men that Bloom has been jealous of, he has noticed a good deal more than Molly realized, for example, "that gentleman of fashion staring down at me with his glasses and him the other side of me talking about Spinoza and his soul thats dead I suppose millions of years ago" (18.1113; 17.2138; 11.1059). If it is men who have admired Molly, it both allows for a great deal of gradation, from (presumably the glance of) "a bootblack at the General Post Office" to Molly's intercourse with Boylan (17.2141), and curiously excludes Gardner, Molly's only other lover since Mulvey. Nor does Molly have anything but contempt for most of the men on the list.[61] The "equanimity" (17.2177) that "Ithaca" attributes to Bloom thus equalizes quite a bit. The difficulty is that it does not leave any individuating place for Bloom.

THE PLACE OF WAR AND THE OPEN-ENDED

Although Homer does not simply reject violence as Joyce does, the *Odyssey*, like *Ulysses*, links an open ending to a questioning of its role.[62] In the case of the *Odyssey*, this occurs in the curious fairy-tale tone of the poem's ending. *Ulysses* has no equivalent, but achieves something of the same tone in its displacement in time. In contrast to the more general view of the war, the old world, for *Ulysses*, did not end in 1914. It remains open.

The problem with war, like the problem with eliminating the competition generally, is that time does not conveniently end with the denouement, as it does in a tragedy. There is always more. When he wrote *Ulysses*, Joyce could have seen this in any story of continuing violence. Later on, he might have noticed it in the reclassification of the "Great War," or "the war to end all wars" into World War I (or, as Joyce put it in *Finnegans Wake*, "alls war that ends war" 279.5–6). In contrast to Joyce's, Homer's age de-escalated, away from the great civilization of the Mycenaeans toward small settlements, and away from the great war at Troy toward small raids and piracy. The difference, however, did not induce a glorification of war. Book 24 of the *Odyssey* is, as we have seen, the poem's masculine resolution in arms. It is also, like Joyce's Edwardian setting, a curiously irresolute resolution.

War, Epic, and *Odyssey* 24

To be a Homeric hero is to be "a speaker of words and a doer of deeds" (*Iliad* 9.443 etc.) and the deeds concerned are those of war.[63] Accordingly, epic is often seen as the genre of war and of the political. Although the *Iliad* was composed before or during the development of the Greek city-state, and depicts no cultural difference between Trojans and Greeks (who are for Homer not "Greeks" or "Hellenes" but Achaeans, Danaans, and Argives), it also counterpoints the fall of the hero and the fall of the city and so is named for Ilium (or Troy), not Achilles. Virgil, of course, makes war—including the Roman Civil Wars—central to the *Aeneid*, just as *The Divine Comedy* and *Paradise Lost* deeply involve or reference the civil wars and politics of Florence and England. Those who would term *War and Peace* an epic, do so largely on these grounds, while their very different concerns make sprawling works such as *Don Quixote, Tristram Shandy,* or the *Metamorphoses* seem anti-epic.

The *Odyssey*, here, is an outlier, as is *Ulysses*.[64] Both works have an important reference to war, but also keep the reference at arm's length. Just as Joyce sets his work before the war, Homer sets his afterward, and both privilege ordinary time over a heroic time of war. Modern commentators have, accordingly, used the *Odyssey* to discuss the readjustment faced by veterans returning from battle.[65] The application reminds us that Odysseus remains a warrior even in Ithaca. The slaughter of the suitors vividly recalls Odysseus's need to connect to his former identity. This is also why Book 24 is so crucial.

Book 24 is sufficiently odd that Homeric scholars have doubted its authenticity pretty much since there have been Homeric scholars.[66] The book opens unexpectedly, to say the least, with the souls of the suitors suddenly appearing in Hades, and for no apparent reason. The third retelling of Penelope's weaving and unweaving seems to add little to the poem; Odysseus's final lie to his father accomplishes nothing and is, if anything, cruel; and many scholars do not see why Telemachus requires yet another warlike bonding experience with his father. Nor, according to any version of the myth, will Laertes do anything after his heroic revival except fade again into the background of Odysseus's story. Most significantly, however, Book 24 is anomalous in having a fairy-tale ending unlike anything else in the poem. But then, like the other objections, this can appear more a strength than a flaw.

As we noted above, the difficulty of eliminating the competition is that there is always more to eliminate. The problem is inherent in stories of revenge, which, in this sense are open-ended in a negative way. From the story of Orestes, which Homer uses as a foil throughout the *Odyssey,* Aeschylus was to create the *Oresteia,* one of the world's great accounts of self-generating vengeance. A similar situation pertains in the *Odyssey.* Having caused the death of the most promising young men of one generation, Odysseus has now returned to slaughter another (23.117–22; 24.426–71). The response of the fathers and brothers of the suitors is as inevitable as that of the Hatfields and McCoys, or of Mark Twain's Grangerfords and Shepherdsons.[67] Whoever wins, there will always be someone left to avenge the slain, until there isn't.

Luckily, however, Homer has Athena, and with her a resolution that, by putting the *dea* into deus ex machina, creates a more positive open ending.[68] One more visit by Athena to her father, paralleling the comic effect of doubling Books 1 and 5, solves the problem. After some surprise: "My child, why do you ask these things and question me? / Was not this what you yourself planned out in your mind?" (24.478–79 ~ 5.22–23), Zeus decides that everyone should forget their quarrels and live happily ever after

(24.482–86).[69] The message is delivered just as our three heroes—father, son, and grandfather, particularly granddad—prove their mettle (24.506 ff.). Peace, then, is broken out all over, and the *Odyssey* ends in a mist of well-being.

The fairy-tale quality of the scene is also set off by its contrast to one of the most human in the poem. Despite the caviling of critics, it is not difficult to see why Odysseus, whose heroic world is one of patronymics, needs his father's recognition. Homer underlines the emotion by paralleling the scene, in the last book of the poem, with Odysseus's meeting his mother at the end of the poem's first half. There, in the midst of the souls of the Underworld, his mother, who died of longing for him (11.197–203), gazed at him without recognition (11.140–44). Here, his father, self-exiled in his grief (11.187–96), does the same, although Odysseus is no longer in disguise, and after another Underworld scene where the dead immediately know one other. What Odysseus gains is not immediate recognition but a sense of the deep grief of a father for his lost son, a sense that brings about a nearly physical response: "his spirit (*thumos*) was stirred, and through his nostrils / a sharp force pressed forth, gazing on his own father" (24.318–19). Not merely his scar, as with Eurycleia, Eumaeus, and Philoitius (21.217–25), or the account of his hunting (24.331–35), but another story, of his father's gift, when he was a child, of fifty vines and thirteen pear, ten apple, and forty fig trees, brings them together (24.330–44). The memory seems as rooted as the trees, a motif throughout the poem, from the wild and domestic olives that sheltered Odysseus on Phaeacia, to the fig tree he clings to over Charybdis, to his bedpost.

Odysseus's reconnection to his father and his childhood completes the reconstruction of his identity.[70] The passage, with all its purely human pathos, also sets off the very different scenes that surround it. The return to the Underworld and the souls of the dead, continuing their everlasting discussion of *kleos* and burials (24.33, 94, 194), reminds us of the world of myth that Odysseus has escaped. The return to battle, now on the poor farm of old Dolios, his sons, and "the old Sicilian woman, who raised them and looked after the old man with care" (24.389–90), almost parodies that world. The heroic reappears as Athena performs another beautification, this time on Laertes (24.367–74), and Laertes echoes Nestor as the aged warrior recalling his glory days (24.376–82). It is there as Rumor, personified, goes through the city (24.413–16), in the report of a god urging Odysseus on (24.442–49), in the prophet "who alone saw before and behind" (24.452) and, finally, in the threat of making the (purely local) enemy "without homecoming" (24.528). The discrepancy of these Iliadic motifs in this setting brings out the fairy-tale feel of the ending and (perhaps) the equally fairy-tale world in which the conflict of fathers and sons has only positive consequences (24.504–15).

The open-endedness implied in this conclusion was prepared by the first news that Odysseus shared with Penelope, that their trials are not over (23.248 ff.). The uncertainty of the journeying to come is reinforced by Teiresias's predicting a death for Odysseus in old age and "from the sea" (11.134, 23.281). Or the Greek (*ex halos*) might mean "far from the sea."[71] The ambiguity is a mark of the poem. Accordingly, its final line returns us to Athena formulaically "likening herself to Mentor, both in body and voice."[72] The ending is as subtle and extraordinary as the *Iliad*'s "And so they buried Hector, tamer of horses" (24.804). Nothing in the *Odyssey* is all it seems, no matter how many identities are restored. However definitive Odysseus's return appears to be, Homer's fade-out leaves us, as it left Dante and Tennyson, wondering.[73]

Ulysses: Force, Hatred, History

Although war and violence may be ambivalent in Homer, and this is as true of the *Iliad* as the *Odyssey*, they are not simply negative.[74] In *Ulysses* they are.[75] However it is occasioned, Bloom's protest informs the novel: "Force, hatred, history, all that. That's not life for men and women" (12.1481), and not least because he thinks to include women, an element we will return to in chapter 5. *Ulysses* privileges the passive over the active, acceptance of others over the attempt to impose one's identity on them, and the private over the public.[76] The real nightmare haunting Stephen is not history, but the ghost of his mother. The radical break in time is not the death of prewar Europe, but the death of little Rudy. It divides not one epoch from another, but two people: Molly and Bloom.

As Joyce would be the first to admit, what is extraordinary about *Ulysses* is not what it says but how it says it. That war and violence are bad things is not earth-shaking news. Nor is it a revelation that war and violence connect to the public, the political, and a masculine (we might now say toxically masculine) vision of action. What is remarkable is rather how this truth appears when it is refracted through the novel's various styles.

The particular snapshot form of *Ulysses*'s second part turns the political in particular into a matter of labels. In "Sirens," Siren songs of seduction and violence intertwine, heralded by *Love and War* (with even Simon Dedalus's *Martha* blending with "'Twas rank and fame that tempted thee, /*

'*Twas empire charmed thy heart*" 7.471–72; 11.778–88; italics in the original).
From this point on the narrative styles highlight a variety of categories
imposed by the political. The "gigantisms" of "Cyclops" encapsulate nationalism, imperialism, and even boxing in vignettes reminiscent of newspaper items. In "Oxen of the Sun," political views are determined by literary
style. The rise and fall of the new Bloomusalem in "Circe" (15.1354–956)
parodies Bloom's "arrest" and "trial" (676–1264) and the romantic gauze of
"Nausicaa" is informed by a distinct political and economic agenda. Even
Robert Emmet's last, apparently open-ended speech closes with a definitive
"*Done.*" (11.1294, 62). Against these, Bloom's revolution "on the due install-
ment plan" (16.1101) begins to look better and better.

Ulysses does in fact develop a political identity for Bloom, but only to
reveal how little Bloom actually cares about it. Bloom's real identity is discussed and apparently settled not long into the second half of the novel:

> —And after all, says John Wyse, why can't a jew love his country like
> the next fellow?
> —Why not? says J. J., when he's quite sure which country it is.
> —Is he a jew or a gentile or a holy Roman or a swaddler or what the
> hell is he? says Ned. Or who is he? No offence, Crofton.
> —Who is Junius? says J. J.
> —We don't want him, says Crofter the Orangeman or presbyterian.
> —He's a perverted jew, says Martin, from a place in Hungary and it
> was he drew up all the plans according to the Hungarian system. We
> know that in the castle.
> —Isn't he a cousin of Bloom the dentist? says Jack Power.
> —Not at all, says Martin. Only namesakes. His name was Virag, the
> father's name that poisoned himself. He changed it by deedpoll, the
> father did.
> —That's the new Messiah for Ireland! says the citizen. Island of saints
> and sages! (12.1628 ff.; and see 12.1573)

As often, the passage provides a technicolor version of themes developed
in the first part of the novel, where Bloom is also linked to Zionism and
nationalism. The Zionist appeal from "Bleibtreustrasse" (Stay-true-street,
4.156, 186–87) suggests that Bloom, the "Wandering Jew" (9.1209; 12.1667;
14.72), should "return home" to Jerusalem (7.207; 12.1473; 17.1880, 1982).[77] At
the same time, innuendos of "home rule" and the Manx Parliament (4.100–
104; 7.149–50) connect to Bloom's interest in Arthur Griffith, Sinn Fein,
and radicalism in general (4.101; 5.70–73; 8.423–36; 17.1634–46; 18.383–86).[78]

Joyce cements the connection to Griffith's nationalist *The Resurrection of Hungary* by having the Bloom/Virags come from the revolutionary center, Szombathely (15.1910, 2370; 17.550, 1920, 1960), and in the names Leopold and Rudolph (as also Stephen), which have an important reference to Hungarian history. He even introduces Sinn Fein anachronistically.[79] The novel will go on to confirm much of this, as we learn not only (and surprisingly) that Bloom is rather well off (17.1855–65) but also that he is in fact a Freemason (15.759; 18.381, 1227; 8.184, 960; 12.300) and involved, as the narrator of "Cyclops" reports, in the sale of Royal and Privileged Hungarian Lottery tickets.[80]

Nonetheless, Bloom, unlike Martin Cunningham, is finally uninterested.[81] As captured in his wonderful misremembering: "All that long business about that brought us out of the land of Egypt and *into* the house of bondage" (7.208; 13.1158, italics added), the Promised Land is not, to his mind, all that promising. His "New Bloomusalem" is thoroughly Irish (15.1354 ff.). When he does think about the Freemasons it is only because he went from their meeting to Molly (8.184–85). He is also quite clear on his nationality. When asked he says, "Ireland, says Bloom. I was born here. Ireland" (12.1430). When not asked, the question of home rule arises for him in regard to Griffith's crack about the *Freeman's Journal* and an advertisement he hopes to land (4.101–4; 7.149–51).

In fact, the confirmation of Bloom's political identity stems less from Bloom than from the fact that we are no longer in the initial style. As Hugh Kenner has pointed out, the initial style ignores anything the character himself would not think of—so that, for example, since Bloom has no reason to think of his height, it goes unmentioned until the "mathematico-astronomico-physico-mechanico-geometrico-chemico" (*LI* 164) approach of "Ithaca" chooses to reveal it.[82] Nor does Bloom think about being a Freemason or having sold the lottery tickets or what they think of him in the Castle. It takes the second part of *Ulysses*, which views Bloom from outside, to do that.

Ulysses is finally more interested in the inner, private man than in the outer public one. Just as Bloom's reflections on "home rule" lead us finally back to Molly (4.100–239; 13.1079–116), the attack in "Cyclops" comes not from his politics, which are in fact nationalist, but because he is not standing a drink (12.1574–75, 1759 ff.). As Bloom reflects: "Peace and war depend on some fellow's digestion" (8.754). *Ulysses* is perfectly clear that the world of violence, war, and heroism is out there. The fixed and clear-cut distinctions it invites, however, of right and wrong, good and bad, friend and enemy ("*Sinn Fein! . . . Sinn fein amhain!* The friends we love are by our side and the foes we hate before us" 12.523–24) are, in *Ulysses,* just more attempts to freeze identity. The big words that Stephen says make us so unhappy are not what can denote Bloom truly. That will be up to Molly.

* * *

Stephen and Molly also have little time for the bombast of war. Stephen, in response to Mr Deasy, proleptically reflects the cynicism of a generation destined for World War I:[83]

> —The ways of the Creator are not our ways, Mr Deasy said. All human history moves towards one great goal, the manifestation of God.
> Stephen jerked his thumb towards the window, saying:
> —That is God.
> Hooray! Ay! Whrrwhee!
> —What? Mr Deasy asked.
> —A shout in the street, Stephen answered, shrugging his shoulders.
> (2.380–86)

While Molly has a greater taste for the British and military panoply (18.97 ff.), her view of war is not that different from either Stephen's or Bloom's:

> they could have made their peace in the beginning or old oom Paul and the rest of the other old Krugers go and fight it out between them instead of dragging on for years killing any finelooking men there were (18.394 ff.)

It may be the only issue where all three of them agree.[84]

By setting *Ulysses* in 1904, Joyce not only denies that World War I marked a break in history, he also undercuts the reality of war altogether. Although the Boer War deeply influenced ideas of Irish independence and ended only two years before the dramatic date of *Ulysses,* Joyce sets it in a deliberate haze. When Stephen thinks of the Boers, it is in terms of Kipling's "The Absent Minded Beggar" (9.125; and see 15.795, 4594; 17.1836 ff.; 18.377).[85] Bloom's perusal of an anachronistic regimental poster confuses the regiments (5.567 ff.), while his pro-Boer protest (8.423–40; 15.810), although it occurred only four years before, seems a moment of youthful enthusiasm far in the past.[86] In "Circe," Bloom couples the great battle of Spion Kop with Bloemfontein, a city occupied without opposition, and one that looks like a play on Bloom's name (15.793–98). The central battle of *Ulysses,* Major Tweedy's Battle of Plevna, linked throughout to misremembering and boasting, occurred not in the Boer War, but in the Russo-Turkish War of 1877–78. England was neutral. Tweedy, whose rank is left fuzzy, may have owned a book about it (17.1385 ff.), but he was never there (4.63).[87]

Appropriately enough, since it replaces *Odyssey* Book 24, Joyce uses Molly's monologue to further blur the reality of war. The primary place for the army in *Ulysses* is Gibraltar, but like Molly's half-remembered Spanish (4.60; 18.1471 ff.), Gibraltar is a distant time and place seeded with undetermined details, such as Tweedy's rank, the identity of Molly's mother, or when the Tweedys left and why. Perhaps significantly, it is also one of the few places Joyce wrote about but never visited. The military figures in Molly's life, such as Tweedy's friend, Captain Groves (18.690, 1583), remain vague.[88] As important as Lieutenant Mulvey may have been to her, she remembers his first name, and whether he had a mustache, only with difficulty (18.818–21, 872–73). Lieutenant Gardner is an even less distinct figure, whose death Molly recalls only in the words of a newspaper account (18.389).

Like the bed that does not actually come from Lord Napier (1.60 ff.; 18.1212 ff.), war in *Ulysses* belongs to a world of display, the old world of Empire and Tommies, the world of Bloom's charade in "Circe" ("Dash it all. It's a way we gallants have in the navy. Uniform that does it. *(he turns gravely to the first watch)* Still, of course, you do get your Waterloo sometimes" 15.743–45, italics in the original). Other than Percy Apjohn, whose cause of death: "killed in action, Modder River" is listed alongside "phthisis, Jervis Street hospital," "accidental drowning, Dublin Bay," "pyemia, Heytesbury street," "phthisis, Mater Misericordiae hospital," and "apoplexy, Sandymount" (17.1249–55), the only casualty of war in *Ulysses* is Lieutenant Gardner, who died not of wounds, but of enteric fever, and at Bloemfontein, which was taken without a battle (18.388).[89]

*　*　*

In repositioning war, Joyce does make a political point: he deliberately sets his Irish "national epic" against a Britain that had co-opted Irish language, literature, and identity. By recalling the Boer War and making Molly a "daughter of the regiment" (11.507), he associates war with Britain. He connects Britain's militarism to her colonization of Ireland through the Englishman Haines, who is linked to the appropriation of Irish culture as a commodity (1.424 ff.; 4.480; 9.91 ff.; 10.1055 ff.; 14.1018 ff.), to violence, and perhaps, with his guncase and black panther, to the colonial sport of big-game hunting (1.49–58). Haines also originates the idea that "history is to blame" for Stephen's servitude (1.650), an idea that will haunt him throughout the day.

The exaggerated styles of *Ulysses*'s second part reflect the concerns of the first in a contrast very like Homer's contrast of the heroic and the ordinary, as the gigantisms of "Cyclops" reflect the newspaper world of "Aeolus," and the antediluvian proportions of Bloom and Stephen's ages reflect the contrast, throughout, of old and young (17.447 ff.). Against the violence implicit in Haines's—or epic's—view of history, Joyce thus gives us, on the one hand, Gummy Granny, the Citizen, and Major Tweedy (15.4578–752), and on the other the distinctly unepic Private Carr (15.48 ff., 604 ff., 3995 ff., 4370 ff.) knocking Stephen down in the street.[90]

Joyce's response to history is thus like Stephen's or Bloom's, not to contest Britain's dominance, but to contest the importance of the competition. Looking at the schoolboys who will be just past eighteen when the war breaks out, Stephen thinks of history as "a tale like any other too often heard, their land a pawnshop" (2.48). The suggestion is that the ticket may not be worth redeeming. The best answer to deeds may be not more deeds, but words. Asked what he had done during World War I, Joyce might well have replied, as Tom Stoppard has it: "I wrote *Ulysses*. What did you do?"[91]

5

Molly and Penelope, Weavers of the Wind

Ulysses and the *Odyssey* bring out the connections between isolated characters through their central female characters, Molly and Penelope. This does not, however, work in the way we might expect. While both Odysseus and Bloom find their essential anchor in another person, in both cases the "anchor" is an uncertain one, perhaps surprisingly in the case of the *Odyssey*. As we will see below, the *Odyssey* underlines the uncertainty of return by making an enigma of Penelope. In *Ulysses* we have known Bloom for only six pages when he sees the signs of Molly's coming adultery.

Molly and Penelope lie at the center of their respective works, but the center is largely silent.[1] Both women appear primarily in glimpses and as described by others.[2] They are, in this way, ambiguous—not, like Bloom or Odysseus, because they are shapeshifters, but because *Ulysses* and the *Odyssey* center on them precisely as "other" and unknown.[3] As in the romantic version of "Nausicaa" ("Why have women such eyes of witchery?" *U* 13.107), the essence of a woman lies in her mystery:[4]

> Should a girl tell? No, a thousand times no. That was their secret, only theirs, alone in the hiding twilight and there was none to know or tell save the little bat that flew so softly through the evening to and fro and little bats don't tell. (13.748–53)

The otherness of Molly and Penelope is also, in the case of both works, deeply culturally conditioned. The Dublin of 1904 resembled Archaic Greece in its gendering of space. Even inside the palace, Penelope emerges from and returns to a private chamber located, indeterminately, somewhere away and above, while the suitors (and men in general) occupy the *megaron* (great hall). The more general identification of men with outside public space and women with inside, private space goes back as far as the seventh-century vases that depict male figures in black (as tanned) and females in white (as remaining indoors) and continues through Pericles's admonition that the less public presence a woman has, the better (Thucydides, 2.45). Similarly, men in Dublin occupy public space (and quintessentially the "public houses"), leaving domestic space to the women.[5] Hence the need for infiltration.

In this setting, as the perspective of both works is generally male, and in the case of *Ulysses* explicitly so, women easily become the mysterious other. Luckily, since both works also make a point, as Joyce put it, of being located *sub specie temporis nostri* (under the aspect of our time), this does not have to imply any absolute view. In both the *Odyssey* and *Ulysses,* the central female characters perform the critical function of holding past, present, and future together, and do this, at least in part, by making it necessary to accept the unknown. In both cases, however, it is enough that they do this for Bloom and Odysseus. They do not need to be universal.[6]

Weaving and Unweaving

As we saw in chapter 3, humans (at least in *Ulysses* and the *Odyssey*) create meaning through stories. Storytelling is also associated with weaving, and as weaving is associated with women, and in particular with Penelope, it is another way in which Stephen and Molly Bloom are paired. Stephen's thoughts of the Muses, the "daughters of memory" (2.7), lead through thoughts of Blake (2.8–9) to his "weavers of the wind" (1.662; 2.52) and to weaving and unweaving as an image of art in time (9.376–85). Penelope's weaving connects her with poetry as well, and just as Calypso or Circe sing while they weave, Penelope proves to be an adept storyteller.[7] And while our exploration of Stephen may have led mostly to ways in which he is not suited to author *Ulysses,* that is only because we left out the crucial way in which he is: an uncanny ability with language. *Ulysses* goes out of its way to show us that it is a world created of words. To be a "lord of language" (9.454) is thus something indeed.[8]

But while both Stephen and Molly are associated with weaving, Stephen's discourse in the library also points to a critical difference between them:

—As we, or mother Dana, weave and unweave our bodies, Stephen said, from day to day, their molecules shuttled to and fro, so does the artist weave and unweave his image. And as the mole on my right breast is where it was when I was born, though all my body has been woven of new stuff time after time, so through the ghost of the unquiet father the image of the unliving son looks forth. In the intense instant of imagination, when the mind, Shelley says, is a fading coal, that which I was is that which I am and that which in possibility I may come to be. So in the future, the sister of the past, I may see myself as I sit here now but by reflection from that which then I shall be. (9.376–85)

As we have seen, Stephen's "in the future, the sister of the past, I may see myself" suggests his role as the future author of *Ulysses*. He is, however, unwilling to accept the change necessary for that role. His "that which I was is that which I am and that which in possibility I may come to be" sees change as teleological development: just as the *telos* (end) and true being of an acorn is to develop into an oak tree, what the future holds is simply that Stephen will become himself. As in his Aristotelian idea of soul: "Thought is the thought of thought. Tranquil brightness. The soul is in a manner all that is: the soul is the form of forms. Tranquility sudden, vast, candescent: form of forms" (2.74 ff.), there is no real change, only different stages of a single entity with a given form.

Through this idea of soul as Aristotle's "entelechy, form of forms" (9.208) change promises to become for Stephen what it appeared to be for Penelope, a weaving and unweaving, a change that is not a change. The same tendency appears also, although more comically, in his refusal to wear grey trousers (1.120). Echoing Hamlet's refusal to "cast thy nighted color off" (1.2.68), Stephen rejects grey just as he rejects any kind of gradation: "As I am. As I am. All or not at all" (3.452; 15.4227). The trousers, however, also involve an implicit rejection of time. In contrast to Bloom's regular thoughts about the coming anniversary of his father's death (on June 27, 6.215–16; 8.558–60; 13.1276; and see 18.349–50), Stephen's refusal ignores the fact that the anniversary of his mother's death, and so the end of his period of total mourning, is also only a week away (17.951–53). Like Hamlet's "and my father died within's two hours" (3.2.127), time, for Stephen, is set not by the calendar, but by his experience, and for him that froze when his mother died.[9] In this light, and very much in contrast to Molly, Stephen seems indeed "a most finished artist" (15.2508).

*   *   *

In the context of epic, weaving recalls the singer's putting together the traditional formulae of oral poetry. Similarly, a rhapsode, originally a composer of song, etymologically "stitches" his songs together, a mode of composition particularly suited to Joyce, who described himself as a "scissors and paste man" (*LI* 297).[10] Always quick to see a sign, he even noted that his patron, Harriet Weaver, had a name that reflected his "Penelope" episode (*SL* 289).

To weave is to create a whole from opposites. As such it recalls Giordano Bruno's idea, so important to Joyce, that opposites are also joined and Heraclitus's (very odyssean) "pulling apart from itself it comes together, like the harmony of the bow and the lyre" (Plato, *Symposium* 187a5). Just as a bow or lyre is constituted by opposites pulling apart but also joined, weaving creates from the opposition of warp and woof a whole that is impossible for either on its own. The motif not only suits reflections on time and memory but also echoes through the *Odyssey*, particularly in the structure of the ancient upright loom, whose vertical and horizontal elements, accommodating warp and woof, resemble the mast and yard of Odysseus's ship.[11] Joyce adds yet another layer by referring to the yards of the "threemaster" Rosevean as "crosstrees" (3.504), a term he insisted on even after Budgen pointed out the mistake.[12] Homer matches him with Odysseus's bed, constructed from horizontal beams attached to a vertical, and still rooted, tree.

Like weaving, storytelling is a combining of opposites, now in a number of different ways. Storytelling puts together past and present, as Homer, for example, weaves the story of Odysseus's name and scar into the story of his footbath (19.392 ff.). It creates one story out of a number of distinct experiences and out of the different, even opposed, perspectives of various characters. And it can bring people together. When Odysseus in Book 24 recalls his father giving him the trees, he reconnects them through a story they share. When he tells Alcinous and Arete his story, he makes them (particularly Arete) his allies. And when he retells that story to Penelope (23.300 ff.), he reconnects the world of the adventures to Ithaca, bridging the gap between his past and present. The same is true as Penelope tells her story to him (23.302–5). He may well know already most of what she has to say. That only points to the real need, that Penelope should also reconnect past and present, and share the connection with Odysseus.

Despite all of this, however, the connections made by storytelling are problematic. The image of a web, or a text, also recalls the nets that Stephen tries to fly by in *Portrait* (203).[13] And, as we have seen, stories are untrustworthy. As the image of the net suggests, and as we have seen, stories always have gaps. In other words, they are inevitably edited. When they are finally in bed together, Penelope tells Odysseus about the suitors wasting the household property, which was generally Telemachus's concern, not about her negotiations with them (2.89–92; 23.302–5). Odysseus's adventures now include the Wandering Rocks (23.327), which he did not encounter, but not Nausicaa or the more intimate side of his time with Circe.[14] Most importantly, the summaries make us wonder how complete even the "complete" versions are. The effect is rendered beautifully as Bloom tells Molly the story of his day in "Ithaca":

> With what modifications did the narrator reply to this interrogation?
>
> Negative: he omitted to mention the clandestine correspondence between Martha Clifford and Henry Flower, the public altercation at, in and in the vicinity of the licensed premises of Bernard Kiernan and Co, Limited, 8, 9 and 10 Little Britain street, the erotic provocation and response thereto caused by the exhibitionism of Gertrude (Gerty), surname unknown. Positive: he included mention of a performance by Mrs Bandmann Palmer of *Leah* at the Gaiety Theatre, 46, 47, 48, 49 South King street, an invitation to supper at Wynn's (Murphy's) Hotel, 35, 36 and 37 Lower Abbey street, a volume of peccaminous pornographical tendency entituled [*sic*] *Sweets of Sin*, anonymous author a gentleman of fashion, a temporary concussion caused by a falsely calculated movement in the course of a postcenal gymnastic display, the victim (since completely recovered) being Stephen Dedalus, professor and author, eldest surviving son of Simon Dedalus, of no fixed occupation, an aeronautical feat executed by him (narrator) in the presence of a witness, the professor and author aforesaid, with promptitude of decision and gymnastic flexibility.
>
> Was the narration otherwise unaltered by modifications?
>
> Absolutely. (17.2250–68)

The account raises the problem of gaps, which is also the problem we have seen with lists: since they are never complete, we are never sure what they are listing. Here the mention of *Leah* seems clear enough, but not why *Sweets of Sin* or Bloom's "aeronautical feat" are "modifications," nor do we know how Stephen hurt his hand, if this is what is being modified in regard to "Stephen Dedalus, professor and author." Most of what happened during the day does not appear at all. Nor are *Ulysses*'s other summaries complete. "Ithaca" attempts to sum up *Ulysses* just as the litany of the Daughters of Erin (15.1940–62), Bloom's biblical exegesis (17.2042–58), "Oxen of the Sun," and "Circe" have done earlier, and as "Penelope" will do finally. As more details are added, the gaps become only more apparent, and most vividly in the white space created by the page layout in "Ithaca." If a story is a web, it is one with wide interstices. In this light, Molly's response is telling:

> yes he came somewhere Im sure by his appetite anyway love its not or hed be off his feed thinking of her so either it was one of those night women if it was down there he was really and the hotel story he made up a pack of lies to hide it planning it Hynes kept me who did I meet ah yes I met do you remember Menton and who else who let me see . . . (18.34–39)

As we see in Molly's re-creation of Bloom creating his story, the stories that Odysseus and Penelope, and Molly and Bloom, tell each other connect disparate individuals by creating common ground, but they also leave plenty of room for individual interpretation.

Penelope and Molly: Past, Present, Future

If weaving is connected to poetry, it seems odd that we first meet Penelope asking Phemius to leave off his song. As we have seen, however, another problem with stories is that they can divide a finished past from an ongoing present. Penelope does not weep because Phemius has reminded her of Odysseus. She is "always remembering / my husband whose fame (*kleos*) is wide through Hellas and amidst Argos" (1.343–44). She weeps because the song threatens to freeze him and his *kleos* into a past that is not recoverable.

Penelope herself, however, makes clear that this is not the only way that stories may relate to time. Like her weaving and unweaving, or her messages to the suitors (1.249–51; 2.89–92; 13.379–81), Penelope's stories may seem to the suitors, Telemachus, and the audience, to simply hold off the future.[15] But in fact, they will be a way to hold future and past together. As she tells the story of Odysseus leaving for Troy to the suitors, presumably to win gifts, the past (possibly a construct of her own) becomes a way of influencing present and future (18.259 ff.). Similarly, and in a far more ambiguous way, her accounts of Odysseus's kindness as king (4.686 ff; 16.424 ff.), and her problematic dream of the geese (19.535–58), interact with the growing inevitability of a future marriage (19.535 ff.). Unlike the shades in the Underworld, who seem trapped in the stories they tell, Penelope tells her stories as a way to address change, because, as she says, things cannot simply remain as they are (18.272–73; 19.157 ff.).[16]

Storytelling may be an attempt to freeze the past, but it can also allow a fluid past to live into, and so shape, the present. In this light, as in

Penelope's "if he ever was" of Odysseus (19.315; and see *Odyssey* 24.289; *Iliad* 3.180; 11.761; 24.246), the past can be as fluid as the future. This dynamic appears in the story of Penelope's weaving and unweaving. Like the story of Odysseus and the Trojan horse, it is told three times. Unlike the Trojan horse stories, however, which use different events and different viewpoints (Demodocus's version being told from the Trojan point of view), the three accounts are virtually identical and told in largely identical words. This does not change the fact that the story says very different things when told by the suitors before and after the slaughter (2.94–110; 24.129–58), and by Penelope to the disguised Odysseus (19.138–56). Just as the shroud that Penelope weaves and unweaves is and is not always the same shroud, so with the story.[17] In contrast to Stephen, who sees weaving and unweaving as a way to resist change, for Penelope stories are a way to interact with time. As the story of being stymied in her weaving shapes her present, the next story she tells the stranger, about how Odysseus used to set up axes to test his archery (19.570–80), will, as it is reenacted, shape her future. The weaving and unweaving, after all, leads to a reweaving.

* * *

Although Molly is not a great producer of textiles (even the darning of Bloom's socks is left to Mrs Fleming, 6.106), a point is made of her knitting the little wooly jacket that Rudy was buried in (14.266 ff.; 18.1448). She is also true to her name, "Tweedy," in her monologue, which enacts the interlocking of opposites, particularly past and future, with the present thrown in for good measure:

> **he annoyed** me so much **I couldnt put** him into a temper still **he knows** a lot of mixedup things especially about the body and the inside **I often wanted** to study up that myself what **we have** inside us in that family physician **I could always hear** his voice talking when the room was crowded and watch him after that **I pretended I had** a coolness on with her over him because **he used to be** a bit on the jealous side **whenever he asked** who are you going to and **I said** over to Floey and **he made** me the present of Byron's poems and the three pairs of gloves so **that finished** that **I could quite easily get** him to make it up any time **I know how Id** even supposing **he got in** with her again and **was going out** to see her somewhere **Id know** if he refused to eat the onions **I know** plenty of ways **ask him** to tuck down the collar of my blouse or **touch him** with my veil and gloves on going out

1 kiss then **would send them all spinning** however alright **well see** then **let him go** to her she of course **would only be too delighted** to pretend **shes mad in love** with him that **I wouldnt so much** mind **Id just go** to her and **ask her do you love** him and **look her** square in the eyes **she couldnt fool** me but **he might imagine** he was (18.178–95; emphasis added)

It is not a removal from time, but rather a weaving of different times together—an actualization of Stephen's "that which I was is that which I am and that which in possibility I may come to be" (9.380), or Bloom's "But tomorrow is a new day will be. Past was is today. What now is will then morrow as now was be past yester" (15.2409–10).[18]

Molly's blending of opposites, on one level, occurs simply in her fluid, half-awake, unpunctuated stream of consciousness. On another, it occurs in her slipping seamlessly from one possibility and time frame to another, and by holding together, in a series of undifferentiated "him"s: Boylan, Bloom, Stephen, her past lovers, and most of the male characters of the novel.[19] Joyce does not specify whether the tendency is particular to Molly, to women, or just to being between sleep and waking—although Bloom also blurs past, present, and future, and runs multiple "she"s together as he nods off at the end of "Nausicaa."[20] But for Molly, "Penelope" is all we know. Whatever other perspectives she might have, for us it is all the weaving.

Molly's blending of past, present, and future particularly resonates since "Penelope" largely recapitulates *Ulysses*. The almost encyclopedic view of events and characters, beginning with Stephen's "Dante" Riordan (18.2 ff), extends to her father's stamps (18.130), the thunderstorm (18.134 ff.), Mina Purefoy (18.159 ff.), Josie Breen (18.169 ff.), "U. p: up" (8.258; 18.229), Professor Goodwin (18.335 ff.), Mastiansky (18.417), Lenehan after the Glencree dinner (18.426), Ben Dollard's trousers (18.561, 1285 ff.), Penrose (18.572 ff.), Martin Harvey (18.1054 ff.), *Aristotle's Masterpiece* (18.1238 ff.), and Jack Power and his barmaid (18.1272 ff.). Even more critically, "Penelope" gives us a new view of the events from which Bloom constructs his past: the choir party where Bloom sprained his foot (18.25 ff.), Mary Driscoll (18.56 ff.), the dispute at Cuffe's (18.510 ff.), the bee sting (18.953), the statue of Narcissus (18.1013 ff., 1349), the stray dog that Bloom brought home (18.1086–87), seeing Stephen at Mat Dillon's (18.1327), the lovemaking when Rudy was conceived (18.1446), Bloom's proposal on Howth (18.1570 ff.).[21] As such, the episode recapitulates the novel's themes of loss, displacement, entrapment, and escape, but now woven in a new way.

Molly's world is constituted from the same elements as Bloom's, and she is as aware as he is of change and loss. For Molly, however, the past is not a lost world. "Either/or" is not in her vocabulary.[22] The past is perfectly free to blend with present and future, just as "Love's Old Sweet Song" stretches from "the dear dead days beyond recall" to "even today," "forevermore," and "till the end" (4.314).[23] Time has become indefinite. As Molly says, she "never know[s] the time even that watch he gave me never seems to go properly" (18.344–45).[24]

In presenting a flux of events in indeterminate time, "Penelope" also definitively collapses the distinction between internal and external time. What comes from "outside" in "Penelope," like the train whistle (18.596 ff., 874 ff.), or the bells of St. George's (heard now for the third and fourth time, 4.44; 17.1232; 18.1231, 1540), or even her period (18.1104–8), are also inner thoughts. Clocktime (or bell-time), Molly's girlhood in Gibraltar, her menstruation, and her coming tryst with Boylan in Belfast all exist simply as they are perceived, in a complex whole that recapitulates *Ulysses* just as Penelope and Odysseus, in bed together, recapitulated their poem.

As we have seen, the second part of *Ulysses* often reflects back the first, but time-stopped and as vignettes. In place of the ongoing time of the initial style, we have gaps and discontinuities. "Penelope" reintegrates what has been broken up, but now as a web rather than as a linear narrative. The episode thus simply refuses to acknowledge the problem that plagues both Stephen and Bloom: the need to identify which of a multiplicity of selves is the "real" one. The monologue, which is pointedly self-contradictory, portrays the self as Protean and memory as fluid and creative.[25] It is thus Molly, and not God, whose indefinite time is described by Joyce's Linati schema as also infinite.[26]

Memory as Creative

The contrast of inner and outer time in *Ulysses,* like the contrast of mythic and ordinary time in the *Odyssey,* brings out the complex relationship of time and identity. Underlying all of this, however, is another factor that subverts these distinctions and introduces a further opposition between Molly and Stephen Dedalus. This is memory.[27] As Augustine points out in his *Confessions,* it is memory that creates time: the past, which is over, exists only as we recall it, and the future, which has not yet occurred, exists only in the expectations built up from memories of the past.[28] And as has been proverbial since Hesiod first learned that her daughters both lie and tell the truth, Memory is a goddess, but not always a reliable one.[29]

The problem of memory as untrustworthy runs throughout *Ulysses,* particularly in Bloom's constant attempts to remember. It appears as early as Stephen's history class, both in the boys' inability to remember their lesson and in the association that leads to Stephen's image of "weavers of the wind": "Fabled by the daughters of memory. And yet it was in some way if not as memory fabled it. A phrase, then, of impatience, thud of Blake's wings of excess" (2.7–9). For Stephen, who is in many ways Molly's opposite, time is linear and the past very much a matter of either/or. His image of weaving is, accordingly, often a negative one. The thought of the first episode: "Idle mockery. The void awaits surely all them that weave the wind" (1.662–63) describes, in the second, the attempt to escape an inescapable past:

> Had Pyrrhus not fallen by a beldam's hand in Argos or Julius Caesar not been knifed to death. They are not to be thought away. Time has branded them and fettered they are lodged in the room of the infinite possibilities they have ousted. But can those have been possible seeing that they never were? Or was that only possible which came to pass? Weave, weaver of the wind.

It is an idea that the boys' interjection links to narrative:

> —Tell us a story, sir.
> —O, do, sir. A ghoststory (2.48–55)

The negative implications are evident, as "weaver of the wind" recalls Blake's Daughters of Memory (or of Albion) who merely "Weave the Web / Of Ages and Generations," in contrast to the daughters of Inspiration who have the true vision.[30]

Weaving, for Stephen, recalls "Old Ireland's windingsheet" (15.4641–42; 2.355–56; 6.18), the nets he must escape (*P 203*), and the world of entrapment in *Hamlet*.[31] The image of nets reappears in "Proteus" as Stephen associates "Elsinore's flood" (3.281; 9.478–79) with "a maze of dark cunning nets; farther away chalkscrawled backdoors and on the higher beach a dryingline with two crucified shirts" (3.154–56). Memory is a shroud he would like to unweave, but cannot. His visits to his uncle (3.61–103), his schooldays (3.105–108), his vocation and rejection of the church (3.109–134), his ambitions as a writer (3.136–46), his failed escape to Paris (3.161–264), and above all, his mother's death (3.329–30) accompany him. Weaving and reweaving is a way to resist change (9.376–78), but as such it is also an entrapment.

* * *

Molly represents the other possibility: of memory as creative. As John Rickard points out, Joyce, like other Modernist writers, saw memory as a force that shapes the past, rather than merely recording it.[32] Even the novel's interest in gramophones and photographs suggests this, since behind even an exact recording of the past lies the choice of what to record.[33] Joyce's interest in the involuntary movements of the mind, like Proust's focus on involuntary memory, points in the same direction—to memory as active rather than passive.[34] Just as Bloom accidentally substitutes "the wife's admirers" for the wife's "advisors" (12.767–69) at just the time that Molly is with Boylan, a question about Molly's concert: "who's getting it up?" leads Bloom to spontaneously recall the end (*"It grew bigger and bigger and bigger"*) to the limerick about the cannibal chief *"Who ate or something the somethings of the reverend Mr MacTrigger"* (8.748–49, 773–84).[35] Memory tells its own story, following its own rules.[36]

As a creative force, memory is linked both to narrative and to a particular nonlinear view of time, which we may again (though perhaps fancifully) compare to weaving. In contrast to Deasy's teleological sense of time, a comparison of time to weaving suggests an interlocking of past and future. Outer, public time pictures the relation of past, present, and future as linear.[37] As on a number line, the units, seconds, minutes, hours, proceed regularly and without distinction, directed by the second law of thermodynamics, which decrees that the line can proceed in only one direction. As a result, past and present appear similar: both are actual, in contrast to a future that is merely possibility.

When time is seen as inner and experienced, however, the picture changes. Here the present, as it is being experienced, differs from past or future, which exist only as they are imagined. Rather than proceeding in a linear fashion, past, present, and future are now interlinked at numerous points. To use the image of weaving, the present is simply the whole created by the interlocked perceptions of past and future. Thus, as Norbert Elias points out, the words, "past," "present," and "future," although in one sense opposed, also refer to a single idea: to think of the present as present is to think also of past and future; to think of the past as past implies a present from which it is distinguished.[38] Past, present, and future form a whole, or a web. As in Joyce's use of the *Dance of the Hours,* time does not march in a line; it dances: *"Arabesquing wearily [the night hours] weave a pattern on the floor, weaving, unweaving, curtseying, twirling, simply swirling"* (15.4091–92, 4053–84).

Awareness, which defines the present, and which in Augustine's view *is* the present, now includes past and future indiscriminately, as in "Proteus" or, as we have seen, "Penelope." In this way as well, the fluidity of "Penelope" eliminates any sequence of cause and effect as effectively as the episodic "vignette" approach of *Ulysses*'s second half. It also eliminates the reification of "past," "present" and "future," and makes it clear that the language of the number line (in which the past has happened, the present is happening, and the future will happen) only uses time to define time. Latin, and so English, makes this pretty explicit, since "*futurus*" is only the word "being" in the future tense.

Most of all, however, the association of memory and weaving brings out the contrast of Molly and Stephen. Stephen, the least flexible character in *Ulysses*, opens the novel thinking persistently in images of weaving. He also wants to keep things distinct: "I want his life still to be his, mine to be mine" (3.27–28). Molly, also associated with weaving, closes *Ulysses* with an episode notable for its fluidity and interconnections.[39] Like the daughters of Memory, the Muses, she re-creates "what is, what will be, and what was before" (Hesiod, *Theogony* 38, 32). For Stephen, weaving implies a trap and memory shuts it closed. Molly suggests rather an identity that comes through interconnection.[40] If time is a kind of weaving, we are the figures woven into the web, distinct, but not separate from the fabric or from each other. As in Bloom's wonderful, and tautological, reflection on the stopping of his watch: "Back of everything magnetism. Earth for instance pulling this and being pulled. That causes movement. And time, well that's the time the movement takes" (13.987–89), we are all both "pulling this and being pulled."[41]

MOLLY, PENELOPE, AND IDENTITY

The Rootedness of Marriage

The importance of Penelope and Molly appears in one of the clearest parallels between *Ulysses* and the *Odyssey*: the way Odysseus and Bloom feel about their wives. In both cases the theme is more surprising than one might think. Epic, like classical Greek literature generally, did not tend to take marriage as its subject, and while nineteenth-century novels certainly did, they were not marriages that had occurred sixteen years before.[42] Or, to take a different tack, it is not surprising that a man in a novel would focus on a woman. What is surprising is that a Dublin man would.[43]

The marriages of Odysseus and Bloom are set in contexts that emphasize

a tension between women and men. The *Odyssey*'s reminders of Clytemnestra's murder of Agamemnon and Helen's role in the Trojan War (recalled
in *Ulysses* by Mr Deasy, 2.390–94) introduce a theme of female duplicity
echoed in Odysseus's encounters with Circe and Calypso.[44] Moreover,
while both women and men can be bought and sold in this world (see Eurycleia and Eumaeus), women, generally captured rather than killed in war,
are most liable to this form of slavery (as appears in the simile at 8.523 ff.).
The reminders of Troy are thus also reminders of a world where women,
from Helen to Briseis, are prizes, and a skilled woman can be valued in
the same terms as (and as less than) a tripod (*Iliad* 23.704, 263).[45] Eurymachus's declaration that Antinous really desired not Penelope but the kingdom (22.49–53), reinforces a suspicion that she, too, may have been such a
prize.[46] It is essentially what Telemachus declares as he opens the contest
of the bow (21.106–10).

As examinations of Joyce and feminism have shown, the Dublin of 1904
was not far behind Homeric Greece in commodifying women. As in Gerty
MacDowell's equation of commodity culture and femininity, or in the ob-
jectifying view of Molly held by pretty much every male character who
mentions her, Deasy's view of women prevails: a woman is an object, and
one often bought too dear.[47] Stephen's description of the whore of the lane:
"She is a bad merchant. She buys dear and sells cheap" (16.738) clarifies the
reason for the novel's continual references to prostitution.

Nor, in either work, are the marriages we encounter encouraging. *Ulysses*'s portrayal of the dysfunctional marriages of Martin Cunningham, Simon Dedalus, the Breens, the Purefoys, Jack Power ("Nice fellow. Who
knows is that true about the woman he keeps? Not pleasant for the wife"
6.244–45) and the Dignams (10.1167 ff.) matches the *Odyssey*'s Helen and
Menelaus, Agamemnon and Clytemnestra, or Nestor and his invisible wife
(3.403), not to mention Hephaestus and Aphrodite, or, in the background,
Hera and Zeus.[48] In contrast to the *Iliad*'s moving depictions of Hector
and Andromache or Hecuba and Priam, the only positive marriage in the
Odyssey, aside from Odysseus and Penelope, is that of Arete and Alcinous,
despite (or perhaps because of) Arete's clear predominance (6.304 ff.; 7.66
ff.). In *Ulysses*, the best we can do is the relation that Molly wonders at, of
Bloom's parents: "his father must have been a bit queer to go and poison
himself after her still poor old man I suppose he felt lost" (18.1061; 6.364;
17.1880 ff.).

Odysseus and the Bed

It can be difficult to remember that, while Odysseus's was a traditional tale, for Homer's audience it was not a fixed text. That Odysseus would achieve *nostos* (return home), was a given, but where the focus of that return would lie could vary with the singer.[49] It seems unlikely that Homer's audience expected it to be marriage. Samuel Butler, even as a schoolboy, may have seen the *Odyssey* as the *Iliad*'s female counterpart, but the poem itself leads us to expect an emphasis on Odysseus's valor, not his wife.[50] Penelope, after a single hint from the narrator (1.13), does not at first seem all that central. She does not come up in the conversation between Athena and Zeus; Telemachus doubts her devotion, encouraged (as we will see) by Athena, while in his visits to Pylos and Sparta she is mentioned only incidentally, introduced by Nestor (3.212–13) and Menelaus (4.111, 321) and, as in Book 2, only as the object of the suitors' depredation.

Nor does Odysseus often discuss his wife. When Calypso (as she would) wonders why he would prefer his wife to her (5.209–12), Odysseus replies that Penelope, of course, cannot compare to a goddess, but still, he always desires, rather generally, "to return home and see the day of homecoming" (5.220).[51] The audience may find a hidden meaning in his encomium to Nausicaa on marriage (6.181–85), but primarily it simply (and skillfully) plays on her particular concerns (as 6.25–30, 66–67, 242–45, 276–89). A special interest in his wife may peek through Odysseus's questions to his mother in the Underworld (11.170–79), but since he has just let a year with Circe slip by (10.467), we could miss the hint. In general, his attitude (as usual) is hard to know. He relates Agamemnon's warnings about treacherous wives to the Phaeacians (11.441 ff.), listens to Athena's rather ambiguous account of Penelope (13.333–48, 375–81), agonizes over the lovemaking of the serving-women with the suitors (20.5–13), and makes sure that his wife does not know he has returned (16.300 ff.). He praises her effusively to her face when in disguise (19.107–14, 262–64), but then again, he would. We are told that he pities her (19.210), but not why he continues to deceive her. Even in the extraordinary scene that opens Book 20, when the two are in each other's thoughts and, unusually, we have access to Penelope's feelings, we learn that "evil dreams" made Penelope believe that Odysseus lay beside her "as he was when he went with the army. And then my heart / rejoiced" (20.89–90). For Odysseus, however, we learn only that "she seemed to him in his spirit / already knowing, standing by his head" (20.93–94).[52] We are told he is aware of her, not how he feels.

This silence builds into the unexpected climax of the poem. As we saw in chapter 4, the poem has led us to see the conquest of the suitors as the key to Odysseus's return. Penelope's welcome should follow hard upon. Eumaeus has implied that, if anything, she accepts strangers only too readily (15.122), and we have been teased with the possibility that she has already recognized Odysseus. As a result, Telemachus's shock when she holds off after the slaughter seems only natural. Nor could we expect that Odysseus, the master trickster and player with words, will be deceived by a simple misrepresentation.[53] In Menelaus's first account of the Trojan horse he described starting up when Helen imitated their wives' voices (4.280–89), a scene reinforced when Odysseus, in his version of the story, describes the unmarried Neoptolemus's restraint (11.523–32). In neither account is Odysseus himself moved.

In a not uncommon pattern in the poem's treatment of her, when Penelope orders that Odysseus's bed be placed outside their chamber (23.177–80), we have no idea what she is thinking.[54] In contrast to her earlier warning that she was testing the stranger (19.215), her words here are run of the mill. Knowing nothing of the bed, we have no reason to expect that Odysseus will react, as he does, with fury. The outburst is thus as much a surprise to the audience as it is to Odysseus, particularly as it is one of the very few places in the poem where he loses self-control. Once it has occurred, however, it recalls the pattern of repression and outbreak that we saw with the Cyclops and the suitors, when the stress of being "Noman" led finally to violent assertions of identity. There, however, the assertions were either disastrous or problematic. Here, exactly because he is tricked into the assertion, his identity is finally restored.

Odysseus's outburst stresses the importance of the secret that occasions it and that only Penelope and Odysseus know—that their bed is unmovable. The emphasis is quite deliberate. In the case of Odysseus's scar, for example, we learn the history of the scar (19.393–465) before we see Eurycleia's reaction to it (19.467–79), and so understand exactly why she responds as she does. In contrast, we only learn the reason for Odysseus's response in the course of his outburst, when Odysseus describes how he originally made the bed. The structure of the scene thus confirms the symbol. It is less that Odysseus knows the secret of the unmovable bed, rooted in the earth, than that he has finally, unequivocally, displayed how much it matters to him.[55] Odysseus has already shown us that he can manipulate the memory of the past as easily as he manipulates his appearance in the present (19.204 ff.). It is no surprise that Penelope weeps at his "recollection" of meeting

Odysseus and at the masterful description of the clothing and brooch that Penelope herself had given him (19.221–57). History, for Odysseus, seems to be simply raw material. The revelation that there is one place where he cannot accept change reveals, most importantly to Penelope, where his own rootedness lies.

The Way to Molly

In contrast to the *Odyssey, Ulysses* tells us from the first how Bloom feels about Molly, and finally also (in all its contradictions) how she feels about him. Again in contrast to the *Odyssey,* neither Bloom nor Molly hear any of this; only the reader is given access to their thoughts. But what the two works do have in common is that in neither is the way to the mother through the child, as Bloom hopefully imagines (17.943–44). As we have seen, Odysseus's relationships with his son and his wife develop independently. Bloom's crisis involves Rudy and Molly together, but his thoughts of his dead son divide him from his wife, rather than bringing them together. The two also think about Rudy quite differently, with Molly's memories being far less charged than Bloom's. As Luca Crispi has pointed out, Joyce regularly changed Molly's memories of Rudy into memories of Milly, and never has Molly use Rudy's name.[56] This is not because she is hard-hearted, any more than her realistic view of Milly means that she does not care about her daughter.[57] It implies instead a fundamentally different orientation than Bloom's.

Molly and Bloom will not reunite through Rudy, nor, as "Ithaca" points out, can they reunite through Milly (17.1963–67).[58] Bloom and Molly both regularly think of her, and of the mother repeated in the daughter ("I was just like that myself they darent order me about the place" 18.1077–78, 1036), but, unlike the usual pattern, in which they think of the same events but see them differently, they remember different events. They share no memory from Milly's childhood, as they do the memory of Rudy's wooly jacket (14.264–71; 15.4967; 18.1448–49).[59] Unlike Odysseus recalling the gift of the trees to his father, it is as if both saw Milly grow up, but in two different narratives.

Nor, finally, will Molly and Bloom reunite through Stephen. The tripartite structure of *Ulysses,* with the first section dedicated to Stephen and the final episode (and much of the final section) occupied by Molly, suggests a triad of Stephen, Bloom, and Molly. Accordingly, scholars have seen Bloom and Stephen, Joyce's Odysseus and Telemachus, as surrogate father and son, and a conclusion in which Molly's interest in Stephen leads her to leave

Boylan and reunite the "family."[60] The pattern, however, dissolves. Bloom and Molly both think of the time they saw the five-year-old Stephen with his mother, but Bloom's recollection does not include Molly, and Molly's does not include Bloom (14.1369–78; 18.1311–13, 1327–28; 6.693–701). Stephen is not looking for a father and has no intention of remaining with the Blooms.[61] Molly can be critical of Boylan (as of everyone), but she certainly intends the affair to continue. As the paradigms in "Ithaca" demonstrate, "the irreparability of the past" and "the imprevidibility of the future" are unavoidable: the clown was not Bloom's son, and the coin never returned (17.973–88).

Rudy is dead; Milly is gone; and Stephen Dedalus is not going to serve as a surrogate child to reunite Bloom and Molly. But this does not mean that there is no hope at all. The way to the mother may be simply through the mother.[62] Molly's thoughts of Stephen and of becoming Stephen's Muse do in fact surround her most forceful (though temporary) rejection of Boylan (18.1300–1315, 1368–77, 1442–94). They also lead her to thoughts of Rudy, but ones that reveal that she has not become trapped by his death. While she thinks of it as Bloom does: "I suppose I oughtnt to have buried him in that little woolly jacket I knitted crying as I was but give it to some poor child but I knew well Id never have another our 1st death too it was we were never the same since" (18.1448–50), the thought, in her usual way, is interwoven with present and future: "O Im not going to think myself into the glooms about that any more I wonder why he wouldnt stay the night I felt all the time it was somebody strange he brought in" (18.1450–52). In accord with her general tendency, Molly's "I knew we'd never have another" coexists perfectly easily with thoughts about having another child (18.166–68). It is a very different approach to the relation of past and future than Bloom's or Stephen's.

This difference is reflected in Molly's feeling about Rudy as well. With the one exception of the apparition in "Circe," Bloom's memories of Rudy are static. Molly's, in contrast, like all her thoughts, blend people, events, and tenses. In this regard, it is interesting to note how Joyce, in his usual technique of constantly adding to the text, expanded Molly's recollection of seeing Stephen while she was pregnant with Rudy (the additions are in brackets, with bold and italics added):

[*showing him my photo its not good of me* [[**I ought to have got it taken in drapery that never looks out of fashion**]] *still I look young* *in it I wonder he didnt make him a present of it altogether and me too after all why not]* I saw him driving down to the Kingsbridge station with his father and mother I was in mourning thats 11 years ago now yes hed be 11 though what was the good in going into mourning for what was neither one thing nor the other [*the first cry was enough for me I heard the deathwatch too ticking in the wall*] of course he insisted hed go into mourning for the cat I suppose hes a man now by this time [*he was an innocent boy then and a darling little fellow in his lord Fauntleroy suit and curly hair like a prince on the stage when I saw him at Mat Dillons he liked me too I remember they all do*] wait by God yes wait yes hold on he was on the cards this morning when I laid out the deck union with a young stranger neither dark nor fair you met before [*I thought it meant him but hes no chicken nor a stranger either besides my face was turned the other way*] (18.1302–17)

Joyce adds to the mourning for Rudy the photograph from "Eumaeus," the idea of drapery as timeless, Molly's prediction from Rudy's first cry (the "ticking deathwatch" is, significantly, not a clock but a kind of beetle), the recollection of Stephen at Mat Dillon's, and the application of the tarot cards to Boylan. All intertwine past, present, and future just as Molly's indeterminate "hims" blend Stephen and Rudy, Bloom and Boylan. In so doing, they also transform recollections of Rudy from the obsessive trap they are for Bloom into something with many more possibilities.

Molly, Penelope, and the Mystery of the Female

Although a current reader may anticipate Molly's monologue, *Ulysses* never suggests that it is coming, any more than we expect Penelope's test of the bed. Until we reach page 690 (in the 1922 version), the only view of Molly we have or expect is through the eyes of others. The unexpected move to Molly in "Penelope," and to Penelope in the last part of the *Odyssey*, suggests in itself that neither Bloom nor Odysseus can complete their search for identity on their own. But while we are given a chance to see the intertwining of time through Molly's eyes, and to see how the events that have formed Bloom's awareness have also formed hers (although far from identically), the case is different with Penelope. She proves key to Odysseus's sense of identity, but remains enigmatic herself. It is as if we can hold past, present, and future together only by also acknowledging an "other," an element we cannot comprehend.

Penelope's Non/Recognition

Joyce is not the only one to have "put in enough riddles and enigmas to keep the professors busy for centuries" (*JJ* 521). Despite her reputation as "a patient Griselda, a Penelope stay-at-home" (*U* 9.620), Homer's Penelope, like Stephen's Anne Hathaway (as explored in 9.214 ff.), is far more elusive than she appears.[63] For example, what seems at first a minor detail (or even oversight), the question of when exactly Penelope recognizes Odysseus, opens into a fundamental element of her portrayal.[64] The question also refuses to be resolved. In taking it up, however, we will need to allow for Homer's control of his material. We will have to assume that the sheer co-incidence of Penelope's deciding to marry again on the very day that Odysseus arrives home did not escape him.

The longstanding controversy over whether or not Penelope recognizes Odysseus in Book 19 suggests in itself that the poem does not mean us to answer the question. Even further, the narrative seems to deliberately undercut either possibility.[65] If Penelope recognizes the disguised Odysseus, we undermine the extraordinary simile of Book 23 in which she welcomes him "as when the land appears welcome to men who are swimming / when Poseidon has wrecked their strong-built ship on the open water" (23.233–34).[66] Moreover, if she knows who he is, her holding off is every bit as harsh, perverse, and incomprehensible as Telemachus declares it (23.97 ff.). Alternately, if she does not recognize Odysseus, the coincidence that she happens just now, with this particular stranger, to decide that the test of the bow will determine her future husband (19.571 ff.) implies a very sleepy (or lazy) Homer indeed. The poet could easily have had Eumaeus, for example, tell the stranger that Penelope has finally decided that she will have to remarry. The glaring improbability would then disappear or at least be muted. He does not.

Rather than trying to resolve the issue, it seems best to examine the enigma. Whatever the intentions of either speakers or poet, the language is certainly suggestive:

> But come, prudent Eurycleia, now, rising up
> bathe one the same age as your master. Somewhere Odysseus
> must already have such feet and hands,
> since mortal men grow old quickly among evils.
> (19.357–60)

So I shall bathe your feet, both for Penelope's sake
and for your own, since within me the spirit is stirred
by grief; but come now, attend the word I tell you.
Many strangers after traveling hard have come here,
but never, I declare, have I seen one as you are
in your shape, and voice and feet, like to Odysseus.
    (19.376–81)

To which Odysseus, in his inimitable fashion, replies that people are always telling him that (19.383–85).

Without venturing (too far) into the game of guessing at the "original" story, one can imagine a poet creating these lines to enhance the irony of Penelope's meeting with the stranger—or even to turn to account a coincidence needed for the plot. But however it came about, once the uncertainty was introduced, it brought up another and deeper issue: Penelope's feelings about her husband altogether.

The question has lain just below the surface from the beginning of the poem, augmented, of course, by the fact that what we know of Penelope we generally hear from others. As initially described by Telemachus, Penelope's resistance seems at best lukewarm: "she does not refuse the hateful marriage, nor is she able / to make an end to it" (1.249–50). The tone is particularly marked as it follows his comment that Penelope says Odysseus is his father, but he himself does not know (1.215–16). "Mentes" replies by suggesting exactly what the suitors also want, that Penelope should return to her father's house and be remarried from there (1.275–78; 2.111–14). Her intentions then come up again only in Book 15, when Athena tells Telemachus that his mother is about to marry Eurymachus and take off with the household goods:

For you know the spirit in the breast of a woman:
she wants to make rich the house of the one who marries her,
and of her children from before and her dear husband
she remembers nothing, once he is dead, nor inquires.
    (15.20–23; and see 16.31–35)[67]

Penelope, of course, declares that her only desire is for Odysseus, even as she wheedles gifts out of the suitors (18.251–73).[68] For what it is worth, Butler thought that she (and her poet) were being less than straightforward.[69] Penelope is, after all, every bit as adept with words as her husband, so that, as Bloom speculates about Kitty O'Shea, her protestations could be made "with tears in her eyes though possibly with her tongue in her fair cheek" (16.1541–42).[70] While we may feel certain that Penelope truly cares for Odysseus and only for Odysseus (and I admit to believing this), a close look reveals that the feeling stems more from our assumptions than from the evidence.

The scene in which we learn the backstory story of Odysseus's name further unsettles us about Penelope. We are shown Eurycleia's completely unambiguous recognition of Odysseus (in contrast to Penelope), and her response to that recognition. As Adolf Kohnken has demonstrated, the scene is carefully motivated.[71] Since Odysseus has just been abused by the young maids, he avoids the rudeness of refusing to be bathed by allowing that an older servant might do so, thinking presumably of Eurynome, to whom Penelope has just spoken (19.96–97). But since the conversation has brought Odysseus vividly to mind, Penelope asks his old nurse, Eurycleia, instead. She of course experienced the events surrounding the scar and so has it interwoven into her sense of Odysseus (19.401–4).[72] Penelope, in contrast, has no such history, sees nothing of the scar, and will be unmoved by it later on (23.73 ff.). In other words, she is not, as Eurycleia is (see 1.427–35), embedded in or determined by Odysseus's family history.

Eurycleia's explicit recognition of Odysseus is followed by even more ambiguity, as Penelope describes dreaming about an eagle killing her geese. That Penelope weeps in the dream for the death of the geese/suitors (19.541–43) can hardly fail to come as a shock.[73] Critics have explained that what Penelope mourns are the twenty years that Odysseus has been away, represented by the twenty geese. In contrast, we have Odysseus's explicit declaration—both within the dream and in their conversation (19.546 ff., 555 ff.)—that the dream represents Odysseus killing the suitors. But then has Penelope just revealed, in the presence of a sympathetic stranger, that on some level she does not want Odysseus to return? Or is she testing a man who may be Odysseus? Or is she testing, or warning, a man whom she *knows* to be Odysseus? Again, the question would be easily settled, say by a participial phrase ("and so, having / not having recognized her husband, Penelope spoke . . .").[74] The poet does not settle it.

The ambiguity adds a level of complexity much like that which surrounds Molly Bloom. Like Molly, Penelope holds the emotional center of the work and yet is seen primarily through the eyes of others. Even when she is center stage, as in her conversation with the stranger, the poet manipulates the audience through his reticence. When Penelope weeps over the stranger's lying story of entertaining Odysseus we know that the stranger is actually Odysseus, who "through deception hid his tears" (19.212). Like Odysseus, we seem to be in control, since we too understand what is actually happening. The ambiguity of Penelope's response changes all that. We know that Penelope wept. We are no longer certain what she was weeping for.

As we have seen, the test of the bow, which Penelope proposes just after describing her dream, is the critical lead-in to Odysseus's homecoming. Not only, in the absence of guns, does it give him a weapon that can hold off a multitude (while other weapons are being fetched), it is also an enormous psychological victory. The test is so perfectly designed, in fact, that the suitors assume it was planned between husband and wife (24.167–69).[75] The audience knows better, which again means that we, like Odysseus, do not know at all. The test asks if the middle-aged veteran can perform the feat of the young hero. In other words, it asks the critical question of the poem: whether the man who returned is the same as the man who left.[76] As far as the suitors, Telemachus, Eumaeus, Philoitius, Phemius, Eurycleia, and the maids (22.495–501; 23.1–9) are concerned, the answer, confirmed by the slaughter of the suitors, is unequivocally yes. Penelope is not so sure. She declines to believe that the person who drew the bow and killed the suitors was necessarily Odysseus. We never learn why.

The Female as Other: Molly as Non-Muse

In "Proteus," Stephen attempts to hold onto a stable identity in the most fluid of episodes. As the last moments of "Penelope" put the rocks of Howth and Gibraltar together with the sea, we realize that the "Gea-Tellus" (17.2313) that *Ulysses* is founded on is itself a wandering planet (17.2306–10).[77] The interplay also involves Molly's role as "other," a position that can suggest either a fixed stereotype, like the photo of Molly that Bloom carries with him, or a mysterious and teasing unknown, like Hesiod's Muses.

The importance of Molly's "otherness" comes out most directly in relation to Stephen. If Molly is the character most "other" to Joyce, Stephen is the one made to seem most the "same." As Nietzsche put it: "For to many a one is marriage promised and more than marriage—to many a one who is stranger to himself than man is to woman: and who has fully grasped *how strange* to each other man and woman are!"[78] The opposition between Stephen and Molly that runs throughout the novel extends to his keeping the roles that Molly weaves together, of virgin, mother, and whore, strictly separate.[79] As we have seen, Stephen's "nightmare of history" reflects his dream of his mother (his *mère*), and his terror of the sea (Latin *mare*). *Ulysses*'s final "night mother" will of course be Molly, linked to a "rock in the sea" that recalls both Howth Head and Martello Tower.[80]

* * *

Not only *Ulysses* as a whole, but also Molly herself, suggests one way in which the otherness of the female may become part of Stephen's world. This is in the role that Molly projects herself into, that of Muse:

> they all write about some woman in their poetry well I suppose he wont find many like me where softly sighs of love the light guitar where poetry is in the air the blue sea and the moon shining so beautifully (18.1333–36; 1364–67)

Joyce takes the idea even further by suggesting, as we saw in chapter 2, that "Bloomsday" is Joyce's first day with Nora, the day that transformed Stephen/Joyce from would-be author, to author in fact.[81] Molly is thus Nora, and so the Anne Hathaway, seductress and Muse, that Stephen both fears and longs for. As Joyce used his description of Nora's body in the *Dead*: "musical and strange and perfumed" (*SL* 163, *D* 215), so he immortalizes her (and her writing style) in *Ulysses*.[82]

Molly's role as Muse seems also to have the advantage of allowing for her otherness. As we have seen, the Muses are inherently ambiguous, both in inspiring truth and falsehood and in interweaving "that which is and will be and was before" (*Iliad* 70 = *Theogony* 38 and see *Odyssey* 24.450 etc.).[83] Like Pygmalion's Muse, Galatea, and as goddesses associated with Bloom's Nymph, they are also quite independent: "Suppose she did Pygmalion and Galatea what would she say first? Mortal! Put you in your proper place" (8.924–25; 15.3245–400).

The ambiguity of the role is also traditional. In poetry the female is both the subject of poetry and its originator, temptation and inspiration, threat and promise, the salvation of Dante's Beatrice and the lure of Petrarch's Laura, both Shakespeare's Dark Lady and his Venus, "the greyeyed goddess who bends over the boy Adonis" (9.258). Similarly, within epic, as Circe and Calypso serve as threats to Odysseus, and Athena and Penelope as guide and goal, so the *Aeneid* positions Dido as threat against Creusa and Lavinia, and *Paradise Lost* places Eve against Mary.[84] And Molly plays all these roles. She is both Calypso and Penelope, Circe and Siren (as she draws Boylan to her in "Sirens"), lure, seducer, cuckolder, scorner, danger, and salvation.[85] In epic terms, all par for the course, although, by collapsing all the female roles into one, Joyce does bring out the inherent contradiction in the idea of a "female role."

But while the role of Muse may seem to allow agency to the female, it also takes it away. For Hesiod and Homer the female Muse inspires song, but for Dante and Petrarch the female inspires by becoming song's subject. In this role, again like Pygmalion and Galatea, art can freeze the female form as well as bring it to life—as in the "museum" (or "museyroom," *Finnegans Wake* 8.9) to which the Muses give their name. Bloom thus keeps Molly with him in the form of a photograph ("He dwelt, being a bit of an artist in his spare time, on the female form in general developmentally" 16.1446–49), a frozen memory, reminding us that we see her through the gaze of others, and making her into an object, now even for him.[86] Stephen may worry about how much control, or "authority," the poet has over his work, but the issue seems far more pressing for Laura.[87]

The question comes up, for example, in the *Odyssey* just before Odysseus begins the great tale of his Wanderings, when Alcinous declares that the gods spin destruction for humans so that there will be song for those to come (8.579–80; 24.196–202). Herodotus saw his task as like the traditional task of the poet, preserving the *kleos* of great deeds (1.1).[88] In Alcinous's view, however, the deeds exist for the sake of the song, rather than the song for the deeds. Thus, also according to Herodotus, Homer knew that Helen was actually in Egypt, and never got to Troy—but saw that the *Iliad*'s version made a better story (Herodotus, 2.116–20).[89] The subject of song now depends on the singer, not the other way around. The poet, once subject to the whim of the Muses, has become master.

In all these lights, while Molly's notion of being a Muse may suit Stephen's Byronic "To E—C—." (*P* 70), it does not finally work for either Molly or Penelope. The issue crystalizes around Helen, who, like Antinous, declares that the gods cause destruction for the sake of song to come (*Iliad* 6.357–58). The difference is that she is herself song's quintessential subject. Her attempt in *Odyssey* 4 to reshape her presence in Troy through the story she tells is also an attempt to claim agency by becoming the singer rather than the subject of song. In Book 4 this only provokes Menelaus's counter-story and Telamachus's suggestion that they all retire for the night (4.290–95). She will not be defended again until Penelope, out of the blue, compares her own situation to Helen's, and just as she acknowledges Odysseus (23.218–24).[90] Given that she began the poem by objecting when Phemius made Odysseus into an object of song, this may be an implicit protest on her own account. Wisest to resist being the subject of song at all. Richard

Best, the Dublin librarian who appears in "Scylla and Charybdis," insisted afterward that he was not a character in *Ulysses* but a real living being (*JJ* 363–64).[91] Despite Molly's thoughts about playing Muse to Stephen, she does not, finally, like books with a Molly in them (18.657–58). Nora Joyce preferred not to read *Ulysses* (*JJ* 525).[92]

*   *   *

Rather than subsuming the female as Muse and subject of song, *Ulysses* emphasizes the otherness. One way Joyce does this is by adding to "Penelope" an element that is completely new: Molly's childhood in Gibraltar. Molly is accepted as Irish ("My Irish Molly, O" 11.512), but in many ways, such as her Jewish-Gypsy mother, "Lunita Laredo" (18.848), she is a good deal more foreign than Bloom, whose maternal grandmother was named Hegarty (17.536) and who was born at Clanbrassil St. and baptized (among other baptisms) in the same place and by the same priest as Stephen (17.545–46, 547).[93] This also gives Molly a set of experiences inaccessible to any of the other characters, including Joyce.[94] Most of Dublin simply ignores this, and even Bloom's curiosity goes largely unsatisfied, from his misapprehension about their bed (4.60; 18.1213–15) to D. B. Murphy's disinclination to recall "all them rocks in the sea" (16.622). Finally, Gibraltar remains as enigmatic to him as Molly does, or as Homer's Penelope is to us.

This consideration of the female as other does not unravel the knot of Joyce's relation to feminism. What I am suggesting is only that, however Joyce actually viewed women, what matters most in *Ulysses* is that he was not one. Any word in Joyce's earlier title, *A Portrait of the Artist as a Young Man*, can be stressed, not least the final one. As we have seen, the narrator's voice in *Ulysses* is distinctly masculine. In this light, Joyce may cast women in general, and Molly in particular, as "other" simply in order to include an element necessarily "other" to him.[95]

Which brings up the question of the "him." In many ways the author of *Ulysses*, living a foreign country, nearing forty, with a young son and daughter and in a deeply committed (if somewhat irregular) relationship, is more like Bloom than Stephen. *Ulysses* captures this dynamic as well. The novel is structured as a triptych, a central panel with smaller, parallel sections on either side. The first is Stephen's and the last is devoted largely to Molly.[96] This pairing, however, appears only if we view *Ulysses* as an object in space, like a painting, Stephen's *nebeneinander* (3.15). If we think of it rather as an object in time, like Stephen's *nacheinander* (3.17) or an oral poem, the pairing is more like that of youth and age, suggesting not opposition, but succession. Bloom's "Wanderings" are thus positioned between Stephen and Molly, as, for example, Aeneas is placed between father and son, Troy and Rome, and Creusa and Lavinia. As "Ithaca" puts it (in the episode's inimitable style) Bloom's "progressive extension of the field of individual development and experience was regressively accompanied by a restriction of the converse domain of interindividual relations" (17.63–65). In other words, Bloom is no longer a young man talking all night to Owen Goldberg and Cecil Turnbull and Percy Apjohn (17.48–53). He is with Molly. In a negative light, he is stuck with her, like the flies (8.896). But being stuck with an "other" may also be a way to see into the multiplicity that is the self. Or, as Bloom puts it: "Longest way round is the shortest way home" (13.1109–11). Time may be a web, but it has its linear aspect as well, even if progress is circular. The future may be intertwined with the past and present, but the only movement is forward.

PENELOPE, ATHENA, AND OPEN ENDINGS

A final aspect of Penelope's role in the *Odyssey* can also help us transition from the poem's human characters to the next chapter's consideration of the gods. This is the implicit competition that appears in Athena's regular tendency to undercut Penelope with both Telemachus and his father. As Nestor declares, Athena's fondness for Odysseus surpasses any other interrelation of god and man (3.218–24). Their intimacy, and playfulness, appears vividly in their meeting on Phaeacia (where, in Robert Fitzgerald's translation, she is "the awesome one in pigtails" 7.44), in Athena's making fun of his worries in Ithaca (20.30–53), and even during his battle with the suitors, when Athena—before finally cleaning things up (22.298 ff.)—appears as Mentor, reproaches Odysseus, and turns, as is her wont, into a bird (22.224 ff.).[97]

The closeness, however, is clearest at the opening of the *Odyssey*'s second half, when Athena (in disguise) makes herself the first to welcome Odysseus home. Just as Penelope uses a dual verb for herself and Odysseus during the recognition scene (23.110), here it is Athena and Odysseus who appear in the dual (13.372–73).[98] Odysseus graciously accepts his loss (or perhaps his apparent loss) in their trickery competition and tweaks her in turn by referring casually to the times when she (in disguise) was with him—and when she was not (13.311 ff.; 6.328–31). The scene, unparalleled in Greek literature, may be most telling not in Athena's stroking Odysseus, or in her famous remark that they are two of a kind (13.286 ff.), but in his direct challenge after he learns that Telemachus has gone to inquire about him: "whyever did you not tell him, you, who know all things?" (13.417). The question hints at the goddess's love of drama and resembles Penelope's response to Athena in her dream (4.831). Still, it is one thing to respond to a dream, and another to reproach a goddess (and a major one) face to face.[99]

As we will see in chapter 6, the divine in Homer serves as an essential foil to the human. This is certainly the case with Athena and Penelope. The goddess's relation to Odysseus sets off his relation to his wife, making Penelope's concern that she might be deceived by a god at least suggestive (23.62 ff.).[100] What emerges is, for once, unequivocal. As close as Odysseus and Athena are (and they are amazingly close), Odysseus's relation to Penelope is of a different order. Athena's jesting with Odysseus's concerns in Book 20 (20.30–55) has the playful and intimate tone of their first conversation in Book 13. Here, however, the jesting follows Odysseus and Penelope's encounter in Book 19, an encounter fraught with unspoken meaning, and is set against the extraordinary scene of the two of them, him in the forecourt and her in her upstairs chamber, half-consciously aware of one another and of what they may or may not wish (20.54–59, 79–90, 91–94).

As we would expect, Homer centers the contrast between Athena and Penelope in the themes that run throughout the *Odyssey*: time, change, and loss (20.66–83). As Odysseus's initial conversation with Calypso raised the question of why he would prefer his wife to an immortal goddess, the contrast between Athena and Penelope suggests, paradoxically, that it is not despite the fact that she is human and growing old (5.203 ff.), but rather because she is.

To a god, time is irrelevant. Unlike her transformations of Odysseus, which recall his young manhood and forecast his old age, Athena's transformations of herself are non-transformations, the sort of weaving and unweaving that Stephen aspires to, changes that bring no real change. For humans, in contrast, time is irreversible, as Penelope recalls upon reuniting with Odysseus. The reunion positions human time against the time of the gods, setting Penelope's words, which we finally quote, against Athena's solution to the problem of time. Penelope declares:

> Odysseus, do not be angry with me, since otherwise, most of all
> among humans, you have understanding. The gods gave us grief,
> begrudging us two that, remaining beside one another,

we should delight in our prime, and reach the threshold which is old
age.
(23.209–12)

Athena, in one of the extremely rare "magical" acts in the poem, has another approach: she stops the dawn from rising (23.241–6), quite literally
stopping time.[101]

Despite Athena, who will soon cheerfully re-become Mentor, even the
stopping of the dawn gives Odysseus and Penelope only a brief time. Here
Minna Skafte Jensen's view that the poet influenced the division of the
poem into books is tempting.[102] Book 23 does not end with Odysseus and
Penelope drifting off to sleep, as in the transition to Phaeacia at the end of
Book 5 or to Ithaca at the opening of Book 13. Although many scholars,
ancient and modern, have felt that this is where the poem ought to end, it
rather goes on, and in the same book, to their waking to an uncertain and
perilous future (23.344–60). In contrast to the fairy-tale "happily ever after"
ending that Athena gives the poem in Book 24, the last we see of Penelope
is Odysseus telling her, in the face of the coming trouble, to go "up to the
upper chamber with your attending women / sit still, and neither look
about nor make inquiries" (23.361–65). It would be an unsettling ending if
we did not know that this chamber is the only timelessness that Odysseus
seeks.

*   *   *

Both *Ulysses* and the *Odyssey* finally, and necessarily, base identity in remembering, the faculty that Circe, among others, threatened to obliterate
(10.235–36). As such both are grounded in a sense of the past. But since they
also explore identity as it is created and re-created in time, they are, not
surprisingly, open-ended as well.[103] In this way Odysseus and Penelope, like
Bloom and Molly, negotiate between fixity and indeterminacy. The depth
of their relation lies in an end both know is inevitable, which is death, but
it is negotiated in the openness that is ordinary time. *Ulysses* will take the
openness much further.

Despite the fairy-tale quality of *Odyssey* 24, Odysseus has returned and
found his place in ordinary time, if only for now. *Ulysses* has no such definition. Critics have seen the novel both as paralleling the *Odyssey* in leading
to a reunion of Bloom and Molly, and as inverting it in depicting a couple
deeply and irrevocably divided within a radically fragmented world. There
is evidence for both points of view.[104] Bloom and Molly end the novel in

the "limitation of activity, mental and corporal" that Bloom perceived in "Ithaca" (17.2284–85). They are both grounded in their common memory of his proposal on Howth Head, but only the narrator and the reader know that.

What the narrator and the reader know is also the critical place where *Ulysses* and the *Odyssey* diverge. "The reader," of course, is shorthand for a multiplicity. There are many readers, with many different viewpoints, just as Phemius's song "of the homecoming of the Achaeans / a bitter one, which from Troy Pallas Athena had accomplished" (1.326–27) sounds quite differently to Telemachus, the suitors, Penelope, and to Athena, had she bothered to listen. The difference is that in *Ulysses* the narrator is also a multiplicity. Every narrative voice, even Molly's, is only one of many. The ending is completely open, leaving it, in many ways, as the ultimate unknown in *Ulysses*.

Joyce does not determine where Bloom and Molly will go from here. We are uniquely privy to Molly's plans for the future, but those plans are protean and contradictory.[105] As "Ithaca" reminds us, the more we learn, the more conscious we are of the gaps that remain. And perhaps most importantly, as the narrative styles deny us any single interpretation of what is happening, they also force us to see that the characters are finally only creations of the written page. Just as there is no answer to the question of whether Bloom is really Poldy or Papli or Siopold or Herr Professor Luitpold Blumenduft (12.468) or Leopold the First (15.1473), there is no answer to the question of where Stephen Dedalus goes when he leaves Eccles St., or whether Bloom and Molly reunite.[106] Unlike Odysseus and Penelope, who have a tradition to inhabit, Bloom and Molly have no existence outside of *Ulysses,* and *Ulysses* ended on June 17, 1904, sometime before sunrise.

The Gods and Narrative Styles

No man is an island, entire of itself; every man is a piece of the continent, a part of the main; if a clod be washed away by the sea, Europe is the less, as well as if a promontory were, as well as if a manor of thy friend's or of thine own were; any man's death diminishes me, because I am involved in mankind.

John Donne, Meditation XVII

As we move from what might be termed the "novelistic" view of *Ulysses* (the approach of scholars interested in plot and character) to the "stylistic" approach (the approach more interested in the play of narrative styles) it is important to note that the two are in fact one. Although Joyce tempts us to see his characters as "real" figures obscured behind increasingly opaque screens of narrative, they are rather like figures woven in a web, composed of the words that seem to hide them.[1] This sheer textuality has its positive side. The characters are constituted by the narrative they are part of and so also, Joyce seems to suggest, are we.

Although Bloom and Molly do not reunite on the level of the narrative, they have been shaped by the same experiences. On a less naturalistic level, even while Bloom and Stephen are divided within the narrative, they also begin to fuse (Joyce's term in the Linati schema) as Stephen's thoughts and experiences are attributed to Bloom and vice versa. One result of *Ulysses*'s shift in narrative styles is to reveal the self as protean—not one and individual, but multiple, particularly in its relations to others. Another, as the distinction between inner and external time evaporates, will be to break down the separation between individual selves.

Both *Ulysses* and the *Odyssey* set their play with multiple kinds of time against a backdrop of the timeless. In the case of the *Odyssey*, this is the realm of the gods. In the case of *Ulysses*, the move outside of narrative time comes rather in the narrative styles, for example in the headers of "Aeolus" or the gigantisms of "Cyclops." The episodic quality of a chapter like "Oxen of the Sun," or the discontinuity of "Ithaca" further removes us from any narrative causality. In other words, the timelessness comes from the presence nicknamed "the Arranger." As I explained in the book's introduction, I have preferred (despite the clunkiness) to speak of "the varied styles of *Ulysses*'s second half" rather than "the Arranger" in order to emphasize the styles' multiplicity. Here, however, where we will explore the way in which the styles are one as well as many, I will be using the term more often.[2]

Just as there are many realities in *Ulysses* and the *Odyssey*, the self is also multiple. Stephen is both "I, I and I. I."; Penelope's bare "Odysseus" acknowledges the young husband, the epic warrior, the returned beggar, the coming old man, and even the boy she never knew who was wounded by a boar. But while we know, or are forced to acknowledge, that we are constantly changing (and always aging) we still experience a single self as well, what Dante called the soul. Bloom's question "Or was that I? Or am I now I?" (8.608), recognizes the inevitability of change, but also posits some "I" that is, then or now, himself. It is precisely these contradictory views of the self, external and internal, public and private, in time and outside of time, that are explored through the gods in the *Odyssey* and through the varying narrative styles of *Ulysses*.

∗   ∗   ∗

Although it may appear fanciful to associate the gods of Homer with the narrative voices of *Ulysses*, there are striking similarities. Both styles and gods enter and leave the level of the human narrative at will and are, at one and the same time, interior and exterior to the human characters. In addition, and determining the structure of this chapter, gods and styles are both one and many. Hayman's "Arranger" points to the way in which *Ulysses*'s numerous narrative styles are also one. This is also true of Homer's gods. As the Greek scholar Hugh Lloyd-Jones put it, early Greek religion was neither mono- nor polytheistic. There are many gods, but they also make up a pantheon, a whole, of which Zeus is (or can be) the epicenter and epitome.[3] Greek is thus perfectly happy with the singular, *theos* (god) for "the divine" (*Iliad* 1.178; *Odyssey* 2.372; 3.131; 8.170; 9.158; 11.292; 17.399; 18.265 etc.). But while the gods form a pantheon, they are also free to quarrel with one another. So too, one might argue, with the narrative voices of *Ulysses*.[4]

For the modern reader, Homer's gods also resemble Joyce's narrative voices in being something of an elephant in the room: obvious, but often neglected. In the case of Homer, this presumably stems from unfamiliarity. The Homeric gods do not settle into easily categorized roles. Having no slot for them, modern readers (other than scholars of Homeric religion) tend to focus on the humans and leave the gods to the epic scenery.[5] Similarly, although Joyce's narrative styles have been studied extensively, studies still tend to consider either the styles or the characters rather than both together.[6] But considering Stephen, Bloom, and Molly without the narrative styles is like considering Newton and his apple without the law of gravity— or imagining the *Odyssey* without the gods.

And finally, for all their importance, the gods of the *Odyssey* only share, not determine, the meaning of the poem: the human characters are foremost. A parallel would imply that on its deepest level, *Ulysses* is also, finally, about its human characters, and that the novel's extraordinary narrative strategy simply tells their story. Or the opposite: the point may be that the characters are not compatible with the narrative styles. The world of 1904 Dublin, unlike Homer's Archaic Greece, may be one in which contradictory forces that are only barely perceived dominate human reality. As we have seen throughout, the *Odyssey* does not provide a key that unlocks *Ulysses*. Rather, it points us to where the issues lie, as does *Ulysses* for the *Odyssey*.

THE MANY: GODS, STYLES, AND REALITIES

The Naturalistic Side of Polyrealism

What I am calling the "polyrealism" of both the *Odyssey* and *Ulysses* exists, in one respect, on a purely naturalistic level, as an example in *Ulysses* makes clear. Bloom, like Odysseus, is trying to return, in his case to his lost youth—a return rendered "irrational" by "An unsatisfactory equation between an exodus and return in time through reversible space and an exodus and return in space through irreversible time" (17.2025). For a moment, however, in "Oxen of the Sun," it seems that you can go home again:

> What is the age of the soul of man? As she hath the virtue of the chameleon to change her hue at every new approach, to be gay with the merry and mournful with the downcast, so too is her age

changeable as her mood. No longer is Leopold, as he sits there, rumi-
nating, chewing the cud of reminiscence, that staid agent of publicity and holder of a modest substance in the funds. A score of years
are blown away. He is young Leopold. There, as in a retrospective
arrangement, a mirror within a mirror (hey, presto!), he beholdeth
himself. (14.1038–45)

Through the power of memory, and by the grace of the narrative style of
Charles Lamb (author of *The Adventures of Ulysses*), Bloom can regain his
youth. In fact, the awareness of a single paragraph encompasses that youth,
his present companions (14.1060–62), a less pleasant past (14.1063–73),
an impossible future (14.1072–74), and the present he is fleeing, in which
"There is none now to be for Leopold, what Leopold was for Rudolph"
(14.1076–77). Bloom and his companions exist in multiple time frames, just
as they do within the multiple styles of the episode. The reverie reminds us
that we can all do the same, even with no Arranger to help us.

Bloom's daydream, although cast in Lambian style, recalls the nonlinear,
internal time of the initial style and "Penelope." Similarly, as we have seen,
although the narrative of the *Odyssey* occurs within forty-one carefully
charted days, and as such allows for no more change in character than the
eighteen hours of *Ulysses,* the poem also gives us, in a purely naturalistic
way, Odysseus as a child, a young man, a young hero, and (as Penelope
acknowledges him) the old man he will someday be.[7] The way in which
Homer achieves this reinforces both the multiplicity and the naturalism,
not despite, but because of what has been called the "uniform illumination"
of Homer's style.[8]

In Erich Auerbach's classic comparison of the *Odyssey* and Genesis, characters such as Abraham are always aware of the past, being "not so entirely
immersed in the present that they do not remain continually conscious of
what has happened to them earlier and elsewhere." In contrast, according
to Auerbach, Homeric heroes "wake every morning as if it were the first
day of their lives." While this view, which sees each Homeric scene as an
exclusive present, filling "both the stage and the reader's mind completely"
requires some qualification, it points to an important and often neglected
quality in Homer's approach to time, that it is as paratactic as anything else
in the poem.[9]

First, the qualification. Although Auerbach's description: "fully exter-
nalized description, uniform illumination, uninterrupted connection, free

expression, all events in the foreground, displaying unmistakable meanings, few elements of historical development and of psychological perspective" captures an essential feature of Homeric style, one must take the lack of "historical development" and "psychological perspective" in the right way.[10] As we saw in chapter 5, Adolf Kohnken, taking umbrage at Auerbach, demonstrates the deep psychological and temporal resonances in the episode Auerbach analyzes, Eurycleia's recognition of Odysseus's scar.[11] Moreover, as we have seen throughout, disjunctions in time and identity are thematic in the poem. Nonetheless, Auerbach's observation highlights the fact that the *Odyssey* works by juxtaposing, rather than subordinating, moments of time. One particularly important juxtaposition, that of mythic and ordinary time, was introduced in chapter 1. But there are others as well.

The effect appears vividly in the episode of Odysseus's scar. At first glance, Auerbach's choice seems paradoxical, since the scar, the focal point of the scene, implies exactly the persistence of the past into the present. Nor is this unusual, since, as we have seen, objects in Homer regularly carry their past histories along with them, so that a new element is often introduced through its past.[12] The scene of the scar is only a longer version of, for example, our learning the history of the bow or Penelope entering the store-chamber, whose threshold "the carpenter had once / planed expertly and made straight by the chalkline, / fitting the doorposts on it, and putting on the shining doors" (21.43–45).[13] Since Homeric narrative does not go backward, there are no flashbacks, only the histories of people and objects in time.[14]

In this regard, what stands out in the *Odyssey*'s treatment of the past is the absence of subordination. In a manner that closely resembles the structure, as well as the use of similes, Homer shifts completely from one scene to the other, employing the ring structure typical of oral composition. The effect appears in our first meeting with Eurycleia:

There [Telemachus] went for sleep, pondering much in his mind
and with him, carrying the flaming torches, went devoted
    Eurycleia. She was the daughter of Ops, Peisenor's son,
    whom Laertes once bought with his own possessions,
    and gave twenty oxen, while she was still in first youth,
    and favored her in the house equally with his own wife
    but never slept with her, for he shunned his wife's anger;

she now carried the flaming torches for him and more than any
of the servant-women, loved him, and had raised him when he was
small.

(1.427–34; offset to bring out the structure)

Here, as with the description of the scar, the precise details, the name of
Eurycleia's father and grandfather, the price Laertes gave for her, and the
tense relation of Laertes, his wife, and his new slave, create a momentary,
but complete, present. The effect is striking in another way as well. Eurycleia's experience as a young woman, presented in snapshot, may be relevant to her tending Telemachus, or it may not. Homer gives only a fore-
grounding that reveals (and here Auerbach quotes Friedrich Schiller) "the
quiet existence and operation of things in accordance with their natures."[15]
Any connection between the juxtaposed time frames of the young, attractive daughter of Peisenor, exchanged for twenty oxen, and "the shrewd old
woman" (1.438) who folds Telemachus's tunic, is left to the audience.

The multiplicity is supported by the uniform narrative style that is so
radically unlike *Ulysses*. Homer's formulaic language, the *Kunstsprache* of
Greek epic, is the same whether he is describing Ithaca, Olympus, the fairy-
tale world of Phaeacia, the swineherd's hut, or the Lestrygonians. Similarly,
within this poetic convention, all characters, whether gods, slaves, Greeks,
Trojans, or the dead, speak in the same mode.[16] What the uniformity allows
is not only a juxtaposition of mythic and ordinary time, but also a whole
series of layers of world-times, that of each character's past, of the similes,
and, of particular concern here, of the divine as opposed to the human.
Rather than panning up to a far-away Olympus or fading off to a distant
past, Homer foregrounds all worlds equally and in the same language. Zeus
and Athena's conversation on Olympus (1.44–95) exists on the same level as
that of "Mentes" and Telemachus (1.113–319) or as that of Telemachus and
Penelope (1.328–59). In much the same way Homer puts us into Odysseus's
naming as an infant, into his boar fight as a young man, and then, just
as directly, back into the Ithaca of his middle age. Just as when Odysseus
suddenly breaks off his story, and we realize that we are in Phaeacia, not
the Underworld (11.333), the effect is of multiple realities. In this way the
technique, for all its differences, forecasts *Ulysses*.

Polyrealism and the Gods

Just as the human characters of both the *Odyssey* and *Ulysses* appear from many perspectives, the *Odyssey*'s gods appear in many different roles. Here, however, the polyrealism goes well beyond mere perspective. The gods can manifest nature, as when Helios, the Sun, sees all (11.109), or when Poseidon occasions a storm at sea, or (although Homer steers away from this) they can act supernaturally, as when Athena stops the dawn.[17] As we saw in chapter 1, they provide, most emphatically with Calypso, the timeless backdrop against which humans seek identity. And finally, they both act in the human realm (as in Athena's little drama of competing with Penelope) and have their own separate existence. This last is the primary way in which they create multiple levels of reality.

The human and the divine can work in complement, like Odysseus and Athena, but the gods can also be chillingly distinct, and often at the same time. At the end of *Iliad* 1, for example, as Zeus's nod poises the human world on the edge of Armageddon (1.528–30), the gods laugh merrily at Hephaestus's bumbling (1.595–600). Similarly, if less ominously, the parallel assemblies of the gods that open *Odyssey* 1 and 5 prepare us for Athena's departure for Olympus in Book 6:

> So grey-eyed Athena spoke, and left [Nausicaa] for Olympus
> where the gods dwell firm and unmoving
> forever, as they say, and it is not shaken by wind nor drenched
> with rain, nor does snow ever mound up, but the shining bright air
> stretches cloudless away, and the white light glances upon it.
> There, all the days, the blessed gods take their pleasure
> and there the grey-eyed one went, when she had spoken to the young
> girl.
> (6.41–47)

The trip is not made for the sake of the plot, and hardly seems worth the time, since Athena will be back to help Odysseus at the opening of the next book (7.14 ff.). What it does do is to set the immutable divine world against the human one, where Odysseus is barely keeping the spark of life alive (5.465–93). As close as Athena is to Odysseus, on another level the gods are involved in the human action (in an anachronistic image) like the spectators at the gladiatorial games. They may be complicit, but they are not responsible for setting the games up. They may feel fiercely for or against one champion or another—and even so fiercely as to involve themselves in the battle—but for them, unlike for the participants, there will always be other games.[18]

Just as the gods are both outside and within the narrative, they are also both outside and within the world of human values.[19] One of the most vivid places in which this appears concerns the question of justice. In contrast to the *Iliad*, where the crucial disconnect between a divine and a mortal perspective underlies the tragedy, the *Odyssey* is often said to uphold a new, moral view of the gods. Thus the suitors tell Antinous, after his abuse of the stranger, "the gods, appearing as strangers from away, / taking on all manner of forms, wander at large through cities / watching over the *hubris* and the law-keeping of humans" (17.485–87).[20]

And in fact, the audience knows, as the suitors do not, that there is actually a god among them at that very moment, observing their hubris and stirring Odysseus up "to learn which of them are right-thinking and which lawless" (17.363). The distinction, however, proves moot, since Athena is resolved that, however the test comes out: "even so / she would not keep any of them from disaster" (17.364). The right-thinking and the lawless will be slaughtered together, although admittedly far the most of them are lawless. Homer nonetheless underlines the point by emphasizing the case of Amphinomus, whom Penelope thinks well of, Odysseus praises, and who intervenes to save Telemachus, but who dies nonetheless, and at Telemachus's hands (15.400–406; 16.394; 18.125–28,152–56; 22.89–94).

In fact, the *Odyssey*'s increased emphasis on divine justice occurs almost entirely among the human characters. It also sets up a divide between their views and the gods'.[21] Odysseus asserts that the gods have punished the suitors (22.411–18; and see 3.130–35). Eumaeus also says that the gods are just, although he adds that Zeus grants some plunder to the lawless and then that the suitors know somehow that Odysseus is dead, and so are not worried (14.83–88).[22] The gods' view is even more ambivalent. Zeus, who is not thinking about Odysseus at all, opens the poem in apparent sympathy with its poster boy for iniquity, Aegisthus, called here, "blameless Aegisthus" (1.29).[23] He protests that Aegisthus had been warned—not that the gods would punish his injustice, but that Orestes would avenge his father (1.32–43). Similarly, Aeolus's interpretation of Odysseus's return as a sign that the gods hate him (10.70–74) does not argue for particularly moral gods, while Odysseus's claim that the gods avenge wickedness like that of the Cyclops (9.266–71, 474–79) is somewhat ironic, given what follows.

The *Odyssey*, moreover, brings out this discrepancy at just the moment that punishment becomes a primary concern, as Odysseus lands on Ithaca.

The issue arises in a completely anomalous scene, that of Zeus approving Poseidon's punishment of the Phaeacians for bringing Odysseus home (13.140–45). The time we have spent in Phaeacia highlights the issue. Although, like human beings generally (and unlike most of the divine beings of the Wanderings), the Phaeacians are not simply good or bad, Alcinous's posturing, Arete's reserve, the rashness and amends of Laodamus and Euryalus, all build our ties to them. We've shared their role as Odysseus's audience in Books 9–12 and feel the unfairness of his complaint that they unjustly set him on an unknown shore (13.209–16).[24] We have a kind of personal relation. That Poseidon wants to bury the island therefore comes as rather a shock. It is hard to think that Nausicaa, engulfed by a mountain, may never marry at all.

The sudden violation of our sympathies is matched by other incongruities, all designed to engage our attention. The scene comes out of nowhere, intrudes the mythic side of the *Odyssey* into the Ithacan half, and, uniquely, is never concluded.[25] It also calls into question anything we thought we knew about the gods. Poseidon's freezing the ship is the opposite of his usual fluidity, and even the situation is strange. In the parallel scene between Zeus and Helios (12.374–88), the guilt of Odysseus's crew has been heavily stressed (even in the proem, 1.6–9), and the appeal to Zeus is natural, since Helios has no agency on the sea. In contrast, Poseidon controls both earthquakes and the ocean, so did, not, for example, need Zeus's help when he sank Odysseus's raft with a storm (5.282–318, 365–70). Moreover, Zeus, the god of *xenia* or hospitality (as 13.213 reminds us; and see 9.268–71; 11.338; 14.56–58), is being asked to punish precisely the virtue of which he is patron. And finally, Zeus's response is so odd that most translators have emended it, changing his reply, which in the manuscripts is identical to Poseidon's request, from "and hide their city under a great mountain" to:

Good brother, here is the way it seems to my mind best
to do. When all the people are watching [the ship] from the city
as she comes in, then turn her into a rock that looks like
a fast ship, close off shore, so that all people may wonder
at her. **But do not** hide their city under a mountain.
    (13.154–58; Lattimore translation; emphasis added)

The emendation redeems Zeus's moral status and gives some purpose to his presence in the scene. It is by no means clear, however, that this was Homer's intention.[26]

The scene of Zeus and Poseidon also reminds us that while we, Homer's audience, can see and hear the gods as the human characters cannot, we still share the general human condition of being unable to comprehend them.[27] The Greek gods are contradictory: Apollo is the god of both plague and healing; Artemis, the god of hunting, also protects the young of wild animals; Zeus, the god of order, is also the wolf-god. Although the eye of Zeus sees all, as Hesiod assures us (*Works and Days* 267–68), we do not always know from what point of view he is looking. Not unlike our situation regarding the Arranger.

The Many Realities of Joyce's Styles

Like the gods of the *Odyssey*, *Ulysses*'s narrative styles exist on a different level than the characters of the novel, and, like the gods, can transform them. The shapeshifting we looked at in chapter 4, particularly of Bloom and Odysseus, reflects who they are as people, often in relation to others. It also reflects the multiple reality of the narrative styles, particularly against the background that Joyce gives it, the actual facts of Dublin in 1904.

Ulysses's narrative styles can seem like the oculist's device, the phoropter, that alternates lenses through which we try to decipher the eye chart.[28] Joyce encourages the impression. "Aeolus," for example, seems like a simple narrative in the initial style with odd headings stuck into it—an effect Joyce created by doing just that.[29] In "Cyclops," it seems, what is really happening is recounted by the unnamed "I," while the "gigantisms" or "parodies" or "interjections" are Joyce's jeu d'esprit with the episode. The first half of "Nausicaa" appears through the gauzy film associated with Gerty MacDowell (with occasional "real" intrusions like "squinty Edy" or "their squalling baby ... and the little brats of twins" 13.128, 404–6), while the second, which returns to the initial style, gives it to us straight. "Circe" is admittedly more unsettling, but still Bloom's "Bloomusalem" or Stephen's vision of Father Dolan seem to occur just in their heads, while Bloom actually pays for the broken lampshade (15.4312–13) and Stephen in fact gets knocked down by Private Carr (15.4747–50). Corny Kelleher really does show up and save the day. Rudy is a hallucination.[30]

On second glance, however, we may wonder. "But he, the young chief of the O'Bergan's, could ill brook to be outdone in generous deeds but gave therefor with gracious gesture a testoon of costliest bronze" (12.290–93) seems to describe Alf Bergan "really" putting down a penny for his drink, and we know from both Bloom and Molly (6.381–82; 13.1144; 18.953; and see 14.1472–73) that the "dreadful dragon" (14.130) that wounded Bloom was in fact a bee. But things get more complicated. Bloom's button really pops off in "Circe" (15.3439–41) since it is still gone in "Eumaeus" (16.35–37), but was Edy Boardman really in Nighttown (15.89–96)? Were Tommy and Jacky Caffrey (15.131–34)? Was Cissey Caffrey really, coincidentally, out walking with Private Carr?[31] What were Bloom and Stephen actually saying during the long discourse on the Dublin water system in "Ithaca"? Is the scene that the anonymous narrator of "Cyclops" depicts the true one? His view of Bloom, for example—"Gob, he'd let you pour all manner of drink down his throat till the Lord would call him before you'd ever see the froth of his pint" (12.684–86)—says a good deal about himself, but has little to do with Bloom. Bloom's section in "Nausicaa" returns us to the narrative style we are used to, but his "met him pike hoses frillies for Raoul de perfume your wife black hair heave under embon" as he drifts to sleep (13.1280–82) is no more "real" than the "namby-pambyjammy marmalady drawersy" (*LI* 135) view of the episode's first half.[32]

The effect of the narrative styles is thus to force us to face the quotation marks around "really." This is underlined by the obsessive realism that characterizes *Ulysses*. Any story involves a distinction between what is told and the "reality" implied as a background—the distinction, narratologically, between *fabula* and *syuzhet*. *Ulysses* adds to this not only the varying narrative styles but also the painstaking attention to historical fact that has Joyce scholars searching actual maps and directories of 1904 Dublin for the novel's *syuzhet*. The conjuction goes well beyond Joyce's plotting the various journeys of "Wandering Rocks" or finding out if there was ivy on the Star of the Sea Church (*LI* 136).[33] As Dante knew, if art loves chance the feeling is mutual.[34] On June 16, 1904, the day (perhaps) that Joyce first walked out with Nora, a dark horse named Throwaway in fact won the Gold Cup (and over Sceptre and Zinfandel) at odds of twenty to one.

Joyce's multiple realities may also explain the otherwise surprising fact that *Ulysses*, like the *Odyssey*, is focused on time, and yet uninterested in history. Both works play with events happening at the same time in different places, as in *Ulysses*'s "matutinal cloud" (17.40–42) and the interpolations of "Wandering Rocks," or the *Odyssey*'s possibility that Telemachus and Odysseus's journeys happen at the same time.[35] They are not as interested in what happened in the same place at different historical times. Scholars have set themselves to untangle the various Mycenaean, Geometric, and Archaic elements in Homer, but the poem simply opposes the human to the mythic. Similarly, Joyce, who described Rome as like "a man who lives by exhibiting to travellers his grandmother's corpse" (*LII* 165), has little interest in the consecutive progress of Dublin's history. Ned Lambert may exhibit "the most historic spot in all Dublin" for his own motives (10.406–49), but Bloom passes the "Irish house of Parliament" (8.401), dissolved in 1800, "Trinity's surly front" (8.476), erected in 1759, and the Provost's House (8.496), built in 1799, and thinks of the Pyramids, Babylon, Round Towers, and the low-cost "Kerwan's mushroom houses built of breeze" (8.484–92) without distinguishing between them.[36] The various realities that Joyce includes in his work are ones that, like Homer's, resist subordination or ordering.

As in Joyce's well-known comment that he wanted: "to give a picture of Dublin so complete that if the city one day suddenly disappeared from the earth it could be reconstructed out of my book," *Ulysses* self-consciously remakes the "real" Dublin, including not only actual events and streets but also real Dubliners. A response such as Robert Martin Adams's, who complains when the novel does not correspond to real life, or the controversies about where, actually, on Clanbrassil Street the Blooms lived, is no more than Joyce himself seems to demand.[37] But what this also means is that the actual city of Dublin now shares a reality with Bloom and Stephen's conversation in "Ithaca." Eccles St., Throwaway, John Howard Parnell, Nelson's Pillar, and, despite his best efforts, Richard Best, all have, for the reader of *Ulysses,* the same reality as Molly Bloom, or as Elsinore, or as the conversations between Athena and Zeus.

THE DUALITY OF ATHENA AND POSEIDON

The Greek gods embodied many contradictions. We have every reason to believe that Athena was just as real to Homer as the Muse that inspired him, but both he and his audience knew that when he described Zeus's conversation with her, he made it up.[38] Phemius is inspired by the god, but also *autodidactos* (22.345–49). Herodotus declares that everything the Greeks know about the gods—gods crucial to his view of history—comes from Homer and Hesiod (2.53), but is unperturbed by Homer changing history to suit his poem (2.116). The Athenians, whose religious witch hunt disastrously sabotaged the Sicilian expedition, also ridiculed the gods in comedy, accepted contradictory versions of them, and periodically added new ones. As not only the gods but also the very existence of fiction demonstrates, we all live on multiple levels of reality.

It is the beauty of Greek to have not only a singular and a plural but also a dual, the grammatical number we saw in chapter 2 when Penelope told Telemachus of signs known only to herself and Odysseus, the two of them. As it happens, the gods of the *Odyssey* are not only both one and many, they are also, in the pairing and opposition of Athena and Poseidon, dual. The pairing informs the poles of flux and fixity built into the structure of the poem. Just as the importance of the gods overall appears in structural devices like the parallel conversations on Olympus in Books 1, 5, and 24, Athena and Poseidon organize the poem. In the first half of the poem we move from Athena, as she encounters and travels with Telemachus, through Phaeacia, which juxtaposes Poseidon and Athena, to the Wanderings, which are the realm of Poseidon alone. Then, in the second half, we move from Poseidon's reestablishing his authority in Book 13 back to Athena's occupancy of Ithaca. The transitions are well marked. Athena's success with Zeus in Book 1 is explicitly due to Poseidon's absence (1.22–26, 76–79). From here on, when Athena is present, Poseidon is not, and vice versa. The poem calls our attention to this, both comically, in citing Athena's not wanting to annoy her uncle (6.328–31) and by marking the moments of transition. Thus Poseidon's departure in Book 5 is set against Athena's arrival (5.380, 382; and see 5.427, 437, 446, 491–92; 6.328–31), and his conversation with Zeus about the Phaeacians is juxtaposed with Odysseus and Athena's conversation on Ithaca (13.125–58, 221–437).

Phaeacia proves to be a halfway house here as well. Dedicated to Poseidon, this is also the place where Athena, albeit disguised, rejoins Odysseus. The Phaeacians have weaving from Athena and ships from Poseidon, a grove to Athena, and a shrine to Poseidon (7.110, 6.267–72, 291). Book 6 opens with the surprising information that although the Phaeacians are related to the Cyclopes, they found their company so difficult that they settled elsewhere. This apparent distance from Poseidon, which sets the stage for Athena's exuberant interference, proves, however, to be complicated. Although Homer's audience has heard Poseidon say that Odysseus's arrival on Phaeacia marks the end of his suffering (meaning, presumably, his suffering at the hands of Poseidon, 5.288–90), Odysseus has not. What he has heard, from Athena, is that Alcinous is Poseidon's grandson and Arete the god's great-granddaughter (7.56–66; and see 6.267; 7.35–36; 8.564 ff.). As was suggested in chapter 3, this may motivate his disinclination to identify himself. It is also given a structural emphasis. In contrast to the *Iliad,* the *Odyssey* strikingly limits its pantheon to Zeus, Athena, and Poseidon and only seldom moves to Olympus.[39] It is thus notable that Athena's departure for Olympus (6.41–45) opens Odysseus's stay on Phaeacia and Poseidon's conversation with Zeus closes it.

Poseidon, god of the sea, and Athena, goddess of war and weaving, also divide the *Odyssey* between them in terms of flux and fixity. We might even see them as a pair of ontological filters, since in some ways reality is different in Athena's company than in Poseidon's. The opposition also takes advantage of most of the binary possibilities of the Greek pantheon: old against young, male against female, sexual against virgin, gods of nature against gods of culture and, most importantly here, the ever fluctuating sea against firm land (recalling that "land" in Greece most often means rock).[40] As we have seen, the opposition also sets the death of a hero in battle, and the fixed mound of earth that commemorates it, against death at sea and the anonymity and absorption such a death implies (see 1.234–43; 5.306–12; 14.367–71).[41] And it frames Odysseus's return between the account of his captivity that comes from Poseidon's ever-fluid servant, Proteus (4.386), and Athena's stopping of time (23.241–46).

The overall opposition is pervasive. Athena, a goddess of weaving, is associated with the stratagem through which Penelope has been preventing change, the weaving and unweaving of Laertes's funeral shroud. Poseidon is associated not only with the old man of the sea, Proteus, but also with Polyphemus, and so with a world without technology and textiles. Throughout the *Odyssey*, Athena has a close and even playful interaction with the human characters of the poem; Poseidon, in contrast, is a distant god, from his initial visit to the far-off Ethiopians to his far-off glimpse of Odysseus before Phaeacia (5.282–84). And while Athena acts through instantaneous transformations, the changes that Poseidon brings are more gradual and permanent, as Odysseus describes how the sea wears away one's strength (8.231–33) and Menelaus how he and his men wasted away as they were held by the gods (4.351–67). The description prepares us to meet an Odysseus worn down by the constant flux of the sea and facing the possibility of a return to loss, like Menelaus's to Agamemnon's murder.

But while Poseidon and Athena embody the opposition of flux to fixity, they also, like yin and yang or Giordano Bruno's contraries, reveal that neither opposite exists without the other. Athena's transformations may not have the intrinsic quality of Poseidon's, but they are transformations all the same, while Poseidon's son, the Cyclops, constrains Odysseus's mutable identity with one huge boulder that blocks the cave entrance and another that nearly destroys his ship (9.240–44, 481–86, 536–42). For all of Athena's affection for humans in the *Odyssey*, Phemius sings in the first book of the bitter homecoming she brought to the Achaeans (1.327). Above all, in a scene whose strangeness we have seen, the sea god's last action in the

Odyssey turns a ship into stone and threatens to cover an island with a mountain, hardly what is expected in a god of flux.

The last word in the *Odyssey*, like (nearly) the first, will belong to Athena. But this does not mean that she is victorious. Having absented herself for ten years, Athena rejoins Odysseus in Ithaca with a vengeance, in all senses of the word. She, and the order she represents, helps Odysseus regain his identity. Nonetheless, he must still perform a land odyssey to the god of the sea (11.121–34; 23.266–84), and render the oar, a tool of the element of flux, into a stable thing, as with Elpenor's funeral mound (11.78; 12.13–15). Finally, death will come to him gently from—or away from—the sea (11.134; 23.281). On Ithaca, Odysseus can leave Poseidon behind, but not quite.

*   *   *

While *Ulysses*, like the *Odyssey*, is structured around an opposition of flux and fixity, Joyce's play with Athena and Poseidon points primarily to the futility of seeking simple parallels. Each is named only once: both as "inspirational," both incidentally, and both completely embedded in the narrative. Poseidon, as Neptune, appears as a figure of Dan Dawson's not entirely limpid prose (7.245; and as a planet, see 17.1095), while Athena inspires Buck Mulligan's onanistic drama "Everyman His Own Wife" (9.876, 1171) as well as appearing, blended with Venus, as Stephen's Anne Hathaway, a "greyeyed goddess who bends over the boy Adonis" (9.258). *Ulysses* does not explore flux and fixity through Athena and Poseidon. Instead it incorporates them directly into the narrative styles.

As we saw earlier, *Ulysses*, like the *Odyssey*, has a distinct midway point. Unlike the *Odyssey*, however, where the first half is characterized by the flux of Poseidon's realm and the second by the increasing definition of Athena's, Joyce blurs the distinction. Although he described Harriet Weaver as preferring the initial style "much as the wanderer did who longed for the rock of Ithaca" (*JJ* 462; *SL* 241), the Arranger is not an agent of either flux or fixity simply, and begins his infiltration well before the midway point. The headings of "Aeolus," for example, give the episode a staccato quality, while also progressing from a staid Victorianism to the sensational. The asterisks that divide "Wandering Rocks," the gigantisms of "Cyclops" or, a fortiori, the question-and-answer approach of "Ithaca" are also staccato, while "Circe" is nothing but fluid transformations, as are "Proteus" and, above all, "Penelope." As Athena takes over from Poseidon once Odysseus has arrived home, Joyce's hyper-objective "Ithaca" fixes reality for us. But as Odysseus has one more journey to go to placate Poseidon, we also have "Penelope."

What finally stands out is not a neat pattern that matches Joyce's narrative styles to Athena and Poseidon, but rather the constant involvement of either extreme with the other. Just as Odysseus had to encounter both flux and fixity in his search for home and identity, so also does the reader of *Ulysses*. Still, as water wears away rock, and as "Circe" has a more critical role in *Ulysses* than "Hades," and as Joyce told Power that a character is an arc of emotion not a fixed page, it seems appropriate that the novel should end less with fixity than with flux, on a rock by the sea, but one that joins Molly and Bloom/Mulvey/Boylan in the flux that is Molly's memory.

UNITY

Where there is a many, there is also a one. *Ulysses*'s variations in style, for all their differences, have something pointedly in common: they are available to the reader, not to the characters in the novel. As such they are removed from the time of the narrative. Like Joyce's styles, the Homeric gods, particularly Athena and Poseidon, occupy multiple and often opposite positions within the human narrative. But they also define a reality beyond the human. In this sense the gods have a different language than humans (*Iliad* 1.403–4; *Odyssey* 10.304–6; 12.61), different food (5.195–99; *Theogony* 639–42), different oaths (5.185–86; *Theogony* 399–401, 793 ff.), and appear simply in the singular, as "the god."[42] They also exist independently of time, the sense in which (until Protagoras, and despite their dubious moral character) the divine gives the human its measure.

Homer's gods and Joyce's narrative styles unify in another way as well. In the *Odyssey*, just as the gods bridge the distinction between mythic and human time, they are also both inner and outer. The role is a crucial one, since the *Odyssey*'s concern with identity also involves the possibility of Penelope, Odysseus, or Telemachus escaping the isolation they are trapped into. This is true of *Ulysses* as well. As Fritz Senn has pointed out periodically, one of the things that the novel is about is loneliness. Although neither expresses it to another character, both Bloom and Stephen have a desperate need to connect.[43] That need seems to be frustrated as Joyce's initial style sets an internal, purely personal experience of time against a shared external clocktime that only intensifies the isolation. Each character occupies his own reality. *Ulysses*, it seems, has avoided the dogmatism of the absolute by falling headfirst into inescapable solipsism.

It is largely the Arranger who addresses the problem. Like the perspectivism of the first part, the narrative styles of the second thrust us into a set of mutually exclusive realities. In so doing, however, they also complete a merging of the inner and the outer that was only hinted at in the initial style.[44] As the distinction between inner and outer breaks down, there is also a shuffling: elements of the novel experienced by one character now appear willy-nilly in another's consciousness.[45] Partially, this becomes possible through multiplication: by the time we get to "Circe," pretty much every element of the novel, from the flier Bloom throws away, to the blind stripling's cane, to the Citizen's handkerchief, has been allowed its own reality—"Circe" only finalizing the move. It also comes about because, as this happens, the novel creates a mutually dependent dialectic between subject and object and observer and observed. As Bloom speculates as early as "Hades," we may all be somebody else (6.836).

Connecting Halves

The Gods and Theoclymenus

While Joyce's novel may fall into two parts (including, as Joyce boasted, eighteen different points of view, *LI* 167) it is also a single work, a unity he reinforces through the triptych structure, which has the "Wanderings" stretch over both halves. Similarly, Homer's gods unite mythic and ordinary time by existing in both. The Lestrygonian king is not going to appear on Eumaeus's threshold, but Athena can.

As noted in chapter 1, however, there are distinct sets of rules. In the mythic world, humans, particularly the older generation of heroes, such as Heracles and Theseus, are often the children of gods and encounter them directly, as apparently occurs in Phaeacia (7.199–206). Odysseus experiences this with the (admittedly lesser) divinities, Circe and Calypso, as Achilles does in his encounters with his mother, Thetis, in the *Iliad*. Or, even when the gods do not take on their own form explicitly, they can be quite clear about who they are, as Aphrodite with Helen (*Iliad* 3.390–420), or Athena with Achilles (*Iliad* 1.197–218, 2.169 ff.).

In ordinary time by contrast, the gods generally appear in disguise, the kind of visitation Antinous is warned about (17.485–87), or as Athena appears to Telemachus. The convention is so established that Homer can even poke fun at it, as when Phronius happens to see the real Mentor after the supposed one has left with Telemachus (4.653–56). Here the god's presence is known by its effects, as when Athena sheds sleep on Odysseus (5.491–93) or gives Penelope the idea of visiting the suitors (18.158–62), or when the Muse inspires the poet.[46] Accordingly, there are far more omens in the second half of the *Odyssey* than in the first, as the gods continue their attention, but at a distance.

Homer underlines the way in which the gods bridge mythic and ordinary time, and so the two halves of the poem, both with Athena and Poseidon, as above, and with Theoclymenus, a character otherwise so minor that even Joyce found no use for him. As the one person that Telemachus brings back from the world of Nestor and Menelaus (15.222–81), Theoclymenus belongs more to the old heroic world than to the ordinary time of Ithaca. A seer and a suppliant, he is introduced through a complicated Iliadic genealogy that reaches back to the Seven against Thebes, and has a backstory like that of Medon, Lycophron, or Patroclus in the *Iliad*.[47] His macabre vision of the palace streaming with blood (20.350) recalls the eerie lowing of Helios's slaughtered cattle (12.395–6), or Zeus's bloody tears in the *Iliad* (16.462), rather than regular day-to-day Ithaca.[48] It is thus not surprising that there is no place for him among the suitors (16.511 ff.), who mock his prophecies of doom (20.350 ff.).

Theoclymenus, however, whose name means "god-famed" or "god-called," is correct in his warnings, and is thus far more important than he seems. As a seer, he is located at the bridge between the mythic world, where gods speak face to face with heroes, and the ordinary where they remain hidden. He thus reminds us, as he does the suitors, that the gods, whatever their motivation, underlie both realms.

The Initial Style and the Arranger

Although *Ulysses* falls into two parts, structured around the Linati schema's "umbilicus," the two also intermingle, as in the headings Joyce introduced into "Aeolus" or the reminders of the initial style in "Penelope" and the second half of "Nausicaa."[49] While the Arranger's ability to erase the difference between internal and external appears most vividly in "Circe," an episode that gives an equal voice to the gramophone (15.2170–73), Stephen's dead mother (15.4157–242), Bloom's erotic connection to Josie Breen (15.385–577), and his trouser button (15.3440), the blend has already been prepared. On the most naturalistic level, while Stephen's Parable of the Plums seems to wrench the old women seen on the strand into his own reality, the story also reflects the talk in the newspaper office, the plum sellers in front of him, and his knowledge that Fumbally's Lane is off Blackpitts (7.923–26). All of these create the story, and Stephen, just as much as he creates them.

An example as simple as the brief scene in "Aeolus," where Bloom has left (7.436) and Stephen not yet arrived (7.506), already undermines our idea that *Ulysses* simply explores Stephen and Bloom's psyches. Moreover, the initial style itself, while it absorbs us in Stephen and Bloom's perspectives, also sets up the varied narrative styles to come. This happens through the increasingly intense interaction between the external and internal. In the simplest relation the two are linked directly; Stephen or Bloom sees or hears something, and then thinks about it. So, in characteristic passages:

Warm sunshine merrying over the sea. The nickel shavingbowl shone, forgotten, on the parapet. Why should I bring it down? Or leave it there all day, forgotten friendship?

He went over to it, held it in his hands awhile, feeling its coolness, smelling the clammy slaver of the lather in which the brush was stuck. So I carried the boat of incense then at Clongowes. (1.312 ff.)

He crossed under Tommy Moore's roguish finger. They did right to put him up over a urinal: meeting of the waters. Ought to be places for women. (8.414–16)

The distinction between external description and inner experience, however, is not always so clear-cut. As many critics have noticed, thoughts in *Ulysses* are colored by their surroundings in ways that the characters may or may not realize, as when Dlugacz's butcher-shop emerges in Bloom contemplating the next-door servant's "moving hams" (1.172) or Martha Clifford's flower appears in his thoughts about her period: "Has her roses probably" (5.285). Nor do internal and external remain distinct. A passage such as "Mr Bloom smiled O rocks at two windows of the ballastoffice" (8.114), blends external description with Bloom's thoughts. And even a simple "It rose" teeters between being description and being Bloom's thought:

Clay, brown, damp, began to be seen in the hole. It rose. Nearly over. A mound of damp clods rose more, rose, and the gravediggers rested their spades. All uncovered again for a few instants. (6.906 ff.)

Ulysses notoriously makes it difficult to know when description ends and interior monologue begins. Joyce's elaborate use of free indirect discourse, in which a character's point of view colors the third-person narration, necessarily blends the two, an effect intensified by the "Uncle Charles principle," in which the description is colored not only by the character's feelings but also by their idea of what constitutes good writing.[50] On the simplest level, Joyce's blending of "inner" and "outer" appears in his refusal to mark direct speech with quotation marks or thoughts with italics—often making it impossible to differentiate between heard speech, imagined speech, and thought, as in the ambiguous "I paid the rent" (1.631) discussed in chapter 2. Had Stephen's inner discourse been printed as follows, a great deal of confusion might have been avoided.

> He walked on, waiting to be spoken to, trailing his ashplant by his side. Its ferrule followed lightly on the path, squealing at his heels. *My familiar, after me, calling, "Steeeeeeeeeeeephen!" A wavering line along the path. They will walk on it tonight, coming here in the dark. He wants that key.* "It is mine. I paid the rent." *Now I eat his salt bread. Give him the key too. All. He will ask for it. That was in his eyes.*
> "After all," Haines began. (1.627–33)

The example, however, also shows why the ambiguity is important. Stephen's thoughts about borrowing from Mulligan: "my two feet in his boots are at the end of his legs" (3.16), "His boots are spoiling the shape of my feet" (9.47), alongside Mulligan's efforts to remake Stephen in his own image, make it clear that the real question is not who gets the key, but where Stephen stops and Mulligan begins.

*   *   *

Stephen's intense self-absorption—in which everything he sees, from Mulligan's cracked mirror to Sargent to the old women in "Proteus," is increasingly drawn into his own inner world—has suggested a reality that is not so much observed from a particular point of view, as created by it. As Joyce pushes that envelope, the "external" descriptions of "Scylla and Charybdis," just before the novel's midpoint, leave any ordinary idea of objective description behind:

> —Bosh! Stephen said rudely. A man of genius makes no mistakes. His errors are volitional and are the portals of discovery.
> Portals of discovery opened to let in the quaker librarian, softcreak-footed, bald, eared and assiduous. (9.228 ff.)

> —It is clear that there were two beds, a best and a secondbest, Mr Secondbest Best said finely.
> —*Separatio a mensa et a thalamo,* bettered Buck Mulligan and was smiled on.

> —Antiquity mentions famous beds, Second Eglinton puckered, bed-smiling. Let me think. (9.714 ff.)

In itself the narration simply extends what Karen Lawrence has termed the "narrative sympathy" characteristic of the initial style.[51] Here, however, it also moves into much more extreme cases, like the musical notation (9.499) or play format (9.894 ff) that recall the idiosyncrasies of "Circe" or "Ithaca." It is no longer possible to know if we are encountering Stephen's thought, which is coloring the external world, or something like the Arranger, that proceeds from a different world altogether.

Finally Joyce blurs the distinction between the initial style and the Arranger by his use of convention. Just as Homer's gods are a convention in epic, so many of the elements that the Arranger uses are not in themselves surprising. We do not expect the characters in *Ulysses* to notice the roman numerals that Joyce put between sections, just as we do not expect a character in any novel to notice the chapter titles. The asterisks that separate the sections of "Wandering Rocks" or the space between the questions and answers in "Ithaca" may fall into this category. But when we get to the sudden play format in "Scylla and Charybdis" or the dot that Joyce insisted should end "Ithaca," simple conventions of formatting have become part of the novel itself, and one as unavailable to Bloom, Stephen, or Molly as Olympus is to Telemachus or Penelope.

Nor has the distinction between clocktime and time as experienced entirely disappeared. "Nausicaa" ends with the "cuckoo" of the clock in the priest's house (13.1289–1306). Bloom's transformation into "young Leopold" in "Oxen of the Sun" (14.1043), may respond to the young men's meeting "at Westland Row station at ten past eleven" (14.1027). Molly's final soliloquy is punctuated by the same church bells, marking the time, that ended "Calypso." Similarly, alongside the animations of clock and cash register, Bloom's intense awareness of the hour in "Sirens" creates an interplay of inner and outer familiar from the initial style:

> Clock whirred. Miss Kennedy passed their way (flower, wonder who gave), bearing away teatray. Clock clacked.
> Miss Douce took Boylan's coin, struck boldly the cashregister. It clanged. Clock clacked. Fair one of Egypt teased and sorted in the till and hummed and handed coins in change. Look to the west. A clack. For me.
> —What time is that? asked Blazes Boylan. Four?
> O'clock.

> Lenehan, small eyes ahunger on her humming, bust ahumming, tugged Blazes Boylan's elbowsleeve.
> —Let's hear the time, he said. (11.380–89)

The difference is that the reader has heard the initial overture and so knows (theoretically, at least) the overall pattern of the piece, as Bloom cannot. It is, appropriately, a pattern that makes Bloom's intense sense of linear time into a circle:

> Where bronze from anear? Where gold from afar? Where hoofs?
> Rrrpr. Kraa. Kraandl.
> Then not till then. My eppripfftaph. Be pfrwritt.
> Done!
> Begin! (11.59–63)

Fate and Coincidence

Before we examine how characters in *Ulysses* and the *Odyssey* connect to each other, we need to consider a kind of timeless pattern that connects them to the background reality of their works. In the *Odyssey*, this is fate. In *Ulysses*, it is a plot device.[52] For while Bloom, in particular, is quite interested in fate, the novel enjoys pointing out that what he sees as fate, Joyce uses to set up the narrative:[53]

> Fifteen yesterday. Curious, fifteenth of the month too. Her first birthday away from home. Separation. Remember the summer morning she was born, running to knock up Mrs Thornton in Denzille street. (4.415–17)

> What am I following him for? Still, he's the best of that lot. If I hadn't heard about Mrs Beaufoy Purefoy I wouldn't have gone and wouldn't have met. Kismet. (15.639–41)

> First night when first I saw her at Mat Dillon's in Terenure. Yellow, black lace she wore. Musical chairs. We two the last. Fate. After her. Fate. Round and round slow. Quick round. We two. (11.725–27)

Joyce, however, has even more devious reasons for pointing out the interchangeability of fate, coincidence, and the arrangements of the author as deity. Although he regularly dwells on the idea of fate, the one truly remarkable occurrence in *Ulysses*—that Bloom's watch happens to stop just as Molly and Boylan are in bed together—suggests to Bloom only scientific explanations:[54]

> Funny my watch stopped at half past four. Dust. Shark liver oil they use to clean. Could do it myself. Save. Was that just when he, she? (13.846–48)

> Very strange about my watch. Wristwatches are always going wrong. Wonder is there any magnetic influence between the person because that was about the time he. Yes, I suppose, at once. Cat's away, the mice will play. I remember looking in Pill lane. Also that now is magnetism. Back of everything magnetism. (13.983–87)

Bloom's lack of imagination here is the more pointed since he is back to thinking of fate not long after: "See him [Dennis Breen] sometimes walking about trying to find out who played the trick. U. p: up. Fate that is. He, not me" (13.1238–9). Psychologically, however, it is perfectly understandable that Bloom sees Josie Powell's marriage to Breen as fated, but not Molly's affair with Boylan. As his ideas flow on, "it's all arranged" and "Woman and man that is. . . . Molly, he" appear intermixed with the greater whole we saw in chapter 5:

> Earth for instance pulling this and being pulled. That causes movement. And time, well that's the time the movement takes. Then if one thing stopped the whole ghesabo would stop bit by bit. Because it's all arranged. Magnetic needle tells you what's going on in the sun, the stars. Little piece of steel iron. When you hold out the fork. Come. Come. Tip. Woman and man that is. Fork and steel. Molly, he. (13.987–93)

Bloom does not see fate in the stopping of his watch for the same reason that he does not link it to Athena's holding back the dawn. For all his multiple perspectives, what Bloom sees depends on "the whole ghesabo" that he comprehends only imperfectly but that he is part of.[55] His continued connection to Molly is fundamental to that whole. To see Molly's affair with Boylan as fated would simply be too painful.

Joyce's fun with mixing up psychology, plot contrivances, and fate comments as well on the "coincidences" that lead to Bloom and Stephen's fusing. It is a handy coincidence that both Bloom and Stephen end up at the Holles Street Maternity Hospital at 10:00, and interesting that the Blooms should have lived at the City Arms Hotel where Mrs. Riordan (Stephen's "Dante") moved after leaving the Dedaluses (17.477–86).[56] As we have seen, Molly thinks remarkably often of the same things as Bloom, but then they have spent the past fifteen years together. Similarly, although Stephen and Bloom have met only a handful of times, they share the cultural ambience of Dublin, so the pianola might well suggest Professor Goodwin to them both (15.4018–20). The plum sellers that Bloom notices at the base of Nelson's pillar (having Plumtree's Potted Meat on his mind, 6.293) also suggest the "Parable of the Plums" (7.941) to Stephen when he is in the same location (as it happens, just before Bloom appears).[57] Bloom and Stephen happen to look over the same bookstall in "Wandering Rocks" so Bloom may have seen the same "Nebrekada" as Stephen (10.585–41, 835–80; 15.319).[58] That Rudy Bloom should happen to die at the age of eleven days, however, and Hamnet Shakespeare at eleven years, is on the level of Stephen and Bloom both happening to associate red jujubes with Edward VII (8.4; 15.4454, 4477). And to go even further, there are all the coincidences, like the victory of "Throwaway" over "Scepter" and "Zinfandel," that actually happened.[59]

Joyce's shading between multiple kinds of "coincidence" thus sets up a "fate" that both is and is not parodic. In contrast to Deasy's teleology, Joyce's composition, as many commentators have noticed, is *bricolage*. In this way it resembles the newspapers that Joyce pored over for material, not least because what the novel's various elements finally have in common is that they are all, somehow, related to a single day.[60] For Dante, fate is God, the binding that holds together the many pages of the universe (*Paradiso* 33.85–96). For Virgil, history, specifically the destiny of Rome, provides the meaning behind events, as it connects the apparently random experiences of Aeneas (*Aeneid* 1.254–96; 6.756–886; 8.626–728). Joyce just raises the question.[61]

It is no huge shock that Joyce would play games with the idea of destiny. *Ulysses* is a comic novel, and comedy loves to mock fate.[62] As we have seen in looking at Penelope, Homer also toys with coincidence. What may be more surprising is that the *Odyssey* treats fate with something of the same equivocation. The stately roll of Homer's prologue:

> But when the year had come with the revolving seasons
> in which for him the gods had spun return homeward
> to Ithaca . . .
>
> (1.16–18)

is echoed by Poseidon's reflection that once Odysseus reaches Phaeacia, he is fated to escape misery (5.288–89). It is also undermined, however, by the poem's using a chance visit to the "distant Ethiopians" (1.20–25; 5.286–87) to set this up.[63] The Greek word *moira* (portion, hence, one's portion in life), is far less determinate than the Latin "fate" (that which has been spoken), commonly used as a translation. When Penelope tells the disguised Odysseus that no one can go without sleep, it is because the immortals have put this *moira* upon mortals (19.592). *Moira* also, as Teiresias makes clear, allows for a number of permutations. Generally, that which is *huper moron* (beyond *moira*) never happens in Homer, but it is regularly brought up as a possibility (*Iliad* 2.155; 16.780; 17.321; 20.30, 336; 21.517; *Odyssey* 5.436), and the one instance of something that does happen "beyond fate" is also the one that opens the *Odyssey* (1.34–35).[64] There is an unquestioned absolute in Homer as there is not in *Ulysses*—but Homer still teases us into wondering about it.

The role of *moira* also brings out the way in which the Homeric gods operate inside and outside the human action, both in moving into and out of the human story, and in being both internal and external to the human actors. In both cases, the idea of "double determination" is crucial.[65] This principle, which sees the human will and the divine as acting together, means that there is no either/or to the question of whether a hero or the god who inspires him (or her) is acting. And as the human retains agency, there are no puppeteers and no clockwork necessity.[66] Agamemnon's choice to sacrifice his daughter in the *Oresteia*, or (in Herodotus) Xerxes's to invade Greece, is made both freely and as determined by the gods.[67]

The best approach may be in terms of the very different frames involved. We express ourselves as individuals in the world through human action, but that action is also an element within a much larger overarching complex of events (like Bloom's magnetism). As such it has both a purely human aspect and an existence *sub specie aeternitatis*. In a somewhat similar relation, E. E. Evans-Pritchard describes the Azande as seeing a single event as due to natural causation and also to witchcraft. In his example, the granary falls because termites have eaten away its wooden supports. It falls at the particular moment that a family was sitting under it because of witchcraft.[68] The first exists in the realm of nature, the second in that of human concerns. Similarly (although without any one-to-one correspondence), double determination posits a realm of action that concerns human experience, emotion, and understanding, and also a more universal realm of fate and the gods. The two are the same, but like Aristotle's example of the convex and concave (*Nicomachean Ethics* 1.13, 1102a30; *Physics* 222b) they may also be distinguished. Even more importantly for our purposes, the division speaks to the Homeric view of the self as both one and many.

Fusion: If We Were All Suddenly Somebody Else

Clocktime and Durée

Something like the *Odyssey*'s two levels of divine and human action appears also in *Ulysses*, and in an even more complex fashion. Bloom and Stephen do not "reunite" as father and son, nor, as Stephen's anti-Semitic ballad suggests (17.795–849), do they really connect at all on the narrative level. And while they do merge on the level of the narrative styles, this does not mean that they "really" connect and do not know it. However essential Stephen's "*Lui, c'est moi*" (3.182–83) may be for *Ulysses*, Stephen, at the end of the novel, wants simply what he wanted at its beginning: "his life still to be his, mine to be mine" (3.327–28). Similarly, Bloom's ability to see others' points of view does not bring him closer to them; if anything, his understanding of how others differ from himself only isolates him further. What the Arranger introduces into the novel does not undo these experiences. Rather it shows that the individual and the whole interact in a far more complex dynamic than we might have imagined.

The initial effect of Joyce's radical narrative styles is to render the distinction between internal and external time moot. In "Sirens" we may still (dimly) distinguish between imagined time, as when Bloom recalls first meeting Molly (11.725–34), and the actual narrative time in which Boylan travels toward 7 Eccles St and the "Tap. Tap." of the blind stripling's cane approaches the hotel (11.933, 951, 989 etc.). In "Cyclops," however, to ask if the gigantisms occur in internal or external time is simply to make a category error. The "external" time of "Oxen of the Sun" comprises both Mortimer Purefoy's birth and the formation of the English language, making a mockery of the idea of "real" time. If any distinction between the external and the internal remains, the fantasies in "Circe" dissolve it.

Ulysses also undermines the distinction between the internal and the external in both directions. Gerty's romantic idiom in "Nausicaa" subsumes the external world, as does Bloom's in "Eumaeus." The novel then goes to the opposite extreme in "Ithaca," where only the external exists, and Bloom's memories, daydreams, plans, and fears become of precisely the same importance as "The influence of gaslight or electric light on the growth of adjoining paraheliotropic trees" (17.44–45). The description of Rudolf Bloom's suicide in "Ithaca" is nothing if not complete:

> Rudolf Bloom (Rudolf Virag) died on the evening of the 27 June 1886, at some hour unstated, in consequence of an overdose of monkshood (aconite) selfadministered . . . after having, though not in consequence of having, purchased at 3.15 p.m. on the afternoon of 27 June 1886 a new boater straw hat, extra smart (after having, though not in consequence of having, purchased at the hour and in the place aforesaid, the toxin aforesaid), at the general drapery store of James Cullen, 4 Main street, Ennis (17.622–32)

It does not explain why someone about to commit suicide would buy a new hat. The narrative style of "Ithaca" has no place for such questions. The purchase of the poison and the purchase of the hat exist on precisely the same level.[69] The result parodies both causality and the notion that human experience can be rendered with pure external objectivity.

The narrative styles, however, have not so much negated the distinction between clocktime and *durée* as developed from a dialectic between them. Most Joycean oppositions, such as, in Cheryl Herr's analysis, the natural and cultural, turn out to be mutually productive.[70] So also here. Gerty's internal romantic haze, as the episode continually notes, derives from an extensive industry amongst whom "Madame Vera Verity" (13.109–10) is only the most amusing. Bloom's idiom in "Eumaeus" ("*My Experiences, let us say, in a Cabman's Shelter*" 16.1227–36; italics in the original) is just as carefully connected back to Mr Philip Beaufoy and *Titbits*. Similarly, the purely external gigantisms of "Cyclops" emerge from the emotions of a fraught situation, and while "Ithaca" adopts a purely objective, external, and universal approach, the material it works with is Bloom's memories, daydreams, plans, and fears.

So, too, with external and internal time in human experience. Stephen's awareness of himself does not stem from the milkwoman coming after 8:00, "Hockey at ten," or "The Ship. . . . Half twelve," but neither is that awareness purely the product of his internal musings. Rather, Stephen (like all of us) experiences his day as the interaction of external and internal time, the one bouncing against the other. In the same way, Molly's internalized reality in "Penelope" still includes the church bells striking the time, and while Bloom's internal time, time as he experiences it, speeds up and slows down throughout Bloomsday, it does so around the pivotal moment of clocktime: "At four, she said."

Inner and Outer

We are isolated individuals living our own realities, and we are also webs of interaction within a common and objective measure of time. By revealing the impossibility of either extreme on its own, *Ulysses* locates the "I" in the interaction between them.[71] The *Odyssey* does something similar with the gods. They may operate from completely outside the self, as when Zeus hurls a thunderbolt or Athena stops the dawn, or completely from inside, as when she casts sleep on Penelope or makes Odysseus unable to recognize his home (13.187–93).[72] And then there are cases between the two, as when Athena makes Odysseus more beautiful to Nausicaa, notably after he has bathed and put on new clothing (6.227–37; and see 23.153–64).[73] The gods are both inside and outside the human characters. As a result they can also bridge the space between them.

The gods' role in Homer is also involved with a very particular view of what it means to be a person. In a very influential approach that postdates Joyce, and which, I suspect, he would not have taken very seriously, Bruno Snell's *The Discovery of the Mind* (*Die Entdeckung des Geistes,* first published 1946) proposed that Homer had no sense of an individual self.[74] Pointing out that Homeric Greek has no word for "self," Snell saw Homeric characters as moved by the gods and by various internal elements such as their *thumos, noos, phrenes,* or *kardia* (loosely, spirit, mind, breast, heart) rather than as autonomous agents making deliberate and conscious choices.[75] Although few scholars would still agree, the view reminds us that if Homer does have a sense of the self, it is not necessarily the same as our own.

* * *

When Odysseus is described, programmatically, as "striving for his *psuche*" (1.5), the goal is primarily life, as *psuche,* often translated as "soul" means something more like "life-force."[76] It is, however, as we see in the individual *psuchae* in Hades, also a very individual life-force, compared by James Redfield to a person's particular appearance.[77] In this sense it implies an "identity," in contrast to Snell. The identity, however, is composed of many parts, as we see, for example, in the *Odyssey:*

> As a bitch, standing over her young pups,
> growls at an unknown man, and rages to fight,
> so [Odysseus's] heart (*kardia*) growled inside him, vexed at the evil
> deeds [of the maids and suitors].

And having struck his chest, he reproached his heart with a word:
"Bear up, heart. You have endured more outrage other times
as on that day that the Cyclops, irresistible, ate
my strong companions, but you endured it, until your cunning
led you out of the cave, though you thought to perish there."
So he spoke, addressing the dear spirit (*êtor*) in his chest
and his heart (*kardia*) endured in obedience and stood it,
without blenching, though he himself rolled side to side.

> (20.14–24)

This sense of the self as a composite being relates as well to double determination. In the *Iliad*, for example, when Aphrodite compels Helen to sleep
with Paris (3.390 ff.), the text emphasizes Helen's resistance, and so also the
conflict within her. Aphrodite is not simply a personification of sexual desire, as we can see in her snatching Paris from the battlefield (3.373–82), but
she is that as well, and Paris is quite aware that his powers of attraction are
those of the goddess (3.39–66). In short, Aphrodite is a force both internal
and external to Helen, just as Helen is herself a matrix of forces.[78] Like any
human individual in Homer, she is a self, not an island.

In this context, it is significant that Odysseus and Telemachus's encounters with Athena tend to occur at times of (what we would call) internal
conflict.[79] And, as Athena is absent during Odysseus's Wanderings, these
encounters occur largely in ordinary time, in which the gods are in disguise. Athena can act directly here, and even supernaturally, as when she
lights the way for Telemachus and Odysseus (19.31–44) or stops the dawn.
But more often her involvement reflects the characters' emotions, as when
Odysseus experiences the mistreatment of the suitors, Laertes wishes for
strength in the coming battle (24.513–24) or Telemachus, in Sparta, worries about how to speak to Nestor (3.21–28) or what is occurring at home
(15.1–8).

That humans tend to interact with the gods at times of internal conflict
does not mean that the gods are merely psychological symbols. First, the
gods do not "symbolize" anything; they simply are. Second, and more importantly, seeing the gods as forces that are really inside the person, but
portrayed as coming from outside, presupposes "internal" and "external"
as the critical categories. For Homer, the conflict—and the intensified sense
of self that accompanies it—is both "outside" and "inside." He feels no particular need to localize it.

In this way it is not difficult to see why divine action would be an aspect of, rather than an alternative to, human or natural causation. God's interventions in Exodus occur exactly to point out to the Egyptians and the Jews that they are God's. In contrast, neither Telemachus's steeling himself to speak to Nestor (3.21 ff., 76), nor Penelope's dreams about Telemachus and Odysseus (4.795–837; 20.87–90 ff.), nor Odysseus's idea of clinging to the cliff in Phaeacia (5.424–29) are surprising, although all are occasioned by Athena. Telemachus, in his astonishment, knows that a god must be involved in his father's transformation (16.178 ff.), just as a god must be involved in his return (3.225–31). Neither event is against nature; they only have particularly deep reverberations.

Just as Odysseus does under the hands of Athena (6.229; 23.156), Bloom regains his youth for that brief moment in "Oxen of the Sun." The experience is repeated early in the next episode when the enchantment of "Circe" transforms him again into a young man (15.268 ff.). In a comic version of Jimmy in "After the Race," young Bloom has come to grief by falling in with the wrong companions, accepting a challenge, and losing his money.[80] Here, however, Bloom's own wariness of pickpockets (15.244) triggers the parental disapproval that follows, and that he has internalized. In other words, for Joyce, as for Homer, the self is not monolithic. The point is not that Bloom can return to his past, but rather that it has never left him. The young Bloom is just one of the very many selves (as will be amply illustrated in "Circe") that make up our hero.[81]

And just as there is a quite ordinary sense in which we are each many selves, there is an ordinary way in which we are also other people.[82] When Stephen thinks "Smile Cranly's smile" (9.21) or "That is Kevin Egan's movement I made" (3.438–39) or, somewhat bitterly, of his father as "the man with my voice and my eyes" (3.45–46), we recognize the feeling, as we do Bloom's recognition that he increasingly resembles his father (17.1355–56). No one is surprised that Gerty MacDowell senses Bloom's admiration (13.411–13), or at the dancing partners: "Bloombella Kittylynch Florryzoe" (15.4122–23). When Bloom's absorption in Simon Dedalus's song about Lionel results in "Siopold" (11.752), the experience is as that described by Eliot: "music heard so deeply / That it is not heard at all, but you are the music / While the music lasts" (*Dry Salvages* 5.210–12). Stephen's split into "Philip Drunk" and "Philip Sober" (15.2512–39) is just as recognizable, if on the other side of the equation.[83]

Ulysses, however, builds from these quite ordinary experiences to a fusion of Bloom and Stephen on a very different level. When Lynch's cap comments "Jewgreek is greekjew. Extremes meet" (15.2097–98) or when "Ithaca" transforms our heroes into "Stoom" and "Blephen" (17.548–54), only the reader can hear it.[84] Joyce also makes sure that we notice this:

> BLOOM
> (points to his hand) That weal there is an accident. Fell and cut it twentytwo years ago. I was sixteen.

> ZOE
> I see, says the blind man. Tell us news.

> STEPHEN
> See? Moves to one great goal. I am twentytwo. Sixteen years ago he was twentytwo too. Sixteen years ago I twentytwo tumbled. Twentytwo years ago he sixteen fell off his hobbyhorse. (he winces) Hurt my hand somewhere. Must see a dentist. Money? (15.3713–21)

For the reader, who knows that the title of the book is *Ulysses,* there is a deep parallel here to the scar through which Odysseus is recognized. Like the mole on Stephen's right breast, which "is where it was when I was born, though all my body has been woven of new stuff time after time" (9.378–80), Odysseus's scar marks the continuation of the past into the future. As the scar gives Odysseus a recognition occasioned (literally) by vulnerability, this scene is also where we discover that Stephen has broken his glasses (as in the fall sixteen years before, *P* 49–50), and so has had particularly imperfect vision all day (15.3628–29).[85] And as that fall was a crucial one in *Portrait,* Stephen's past has just recurred to him with Zoe's "I see it in your face" (15.3663–76), connecting as well to his present and future: "Zoe: What day were you born? / Stephen: Thursday. Today. / Zoe: Thursday's child has far to go. (she traces lines on his hand) Line of fate. Influential friends. / Florry: (pointing) Imagination" (15.3683–90).

But while Stephen's hurt hand comes up again (16.1296, 1608–9; 17.2260–64), the coincidence of the scar does not, even though the conversation occurs completely on the level of the characters' consciousness. Nor is this particularly surprising. To someone who realizes that Bloom and Stephen are also Odysseus and Telemachus, and are in the process of fusing, the scene is a critical one. To Stephen and Bloom, although Stephen may parody Deasy: "Moves to one great goal" (15.3718), it is just a coincidence. As Stephen comments: "I never could read His handwriting except His criminal thumbprint on the haddock" (3680–81).

Like Joyce's play with coincidence and fate, the "Fusion of Bloom and Stephen" (*Fusione di Bloom e Stephen*), which Joyce's Linati schema places just before "Eumaeus," in fact builds up throughout the novel. The movement, from the purely naturalistic level of "Smile Cranly's smile" to "Stoom" and "Blephen" has infinite gradations, from their both knowing "Dante" Riordan, to their both thinking of Shakespeare in Fetter Lane (9.651–52; 11.905–8). The links, however, do not contain any simple key. Bloom and Stephen are both dressed in black (15.1295; 14.1575–77), but for Stephen this is fraught (and see 1.120–22), while for Bloom it is incidental. As "Ithaca" comments, both are keyless (17.80–81), a conscious choice for Stephen (1.631–33, 721–22), and perhaps a subconscious one for Bloom (4.72–73; 17.70–79).[86] Joyce also revels in the artifice. When Stephen and Bloom identically misquote Shakespeare, Joyce pokes us in the ribs by having the line be "Hamlet, I am thy father's spirit" (8.67; 9.170). The coincidence that "Ithaca" points out, of their observing the same "matutinal cloud" (17.40–42), already had the Arranger's fingerprints on it: "A cloud began to cover the sun slowly, wholly, shadowing the bay in deeper green. It lay beneath him, a bowl of bitter waters. Fergus' song" (1.248); "A cloud began to cover the sun slowly, wholly. Grey. Far. / No, not like that. A barren land, bare waste" (4.218). Stephen and Bloom both sense the menace; only the reader sees the repetition of "A cloud began to cover the sun slowly, wholly."[87]

It is when the fusion becomes clearest, however, in "Circe," that we best see what is happening. Of the thirty-two "anomalies" that John Gordon points out here, eighteen combine Stephen and Bloom, while the remainder concern matters common to Dublin or are derived from the narrative styles, such as the gigantisms in "Cyclops" (15.1234–35) or Gerty's half of "Nausicaa" (1595–98).[88] In other words, the fusion of Stephen and Bloom is not particular to them; it pervades the world of *Ulysses,* just as it will become central to *Finnegans Wake.*

Joyce thus seems to use the fusion to comment on how the various levels of *Ulysses* fit together. The clearest example is the scene most often used to illustrate. Here Bloom and Stephen, both gazing into a mirror at Bella Cohen's, see their reflections joined with that of "the reindeer antlered hatrack in the hall," which then becomes the face of Shakespeare with horns, that is, as a cuckold (15.3820–30). Like "Bloom's thoughts about Stephen's thoughts about Bloom and about Stephen's thoughts about Bloom's thoughts about Stephen" in "Ithaca" (17.527–29), the reflection blends the two. It also points out, in case we had not noticed, that Stephen's account of Shakespeare applies pretty closely to Bloom, from Molly/Anne Hathaway as adulterous wife to Rudy/Hamnet as sacrificed son.[89] The connection is made painfully emphatic by the scene that precedes the Shakespeare vision: the fantasy of Bloom watching Boylan have sex with his wife.

The dissolve thus points, simultaneously, to what Bloom and Stephen "actually" see in the mirror and to a fusion outside their awareness. The reflection is "beardless" because Hamlet, "the beardless undergraduate" (9.832) is, at thirty, exactly between Stephen's age, twenty-two, and Bloom's, thirty-eight.[90] And as the reflection begins to morph, it is also about Othello (15.3828), the purely fictional Zoe, Napoleon, the Dignams, and Martin Cunningham, whose face resembles Shakespeare's (6.345; 15.3854–63), who has difficulties with a drunken wife, and who this morning attended the funeral of his own historical counterpart.[91] For Lynch, this is "The mirror up to nature" (15.3820). Bloom asks: "When will I hear the joke?" (15.3831), perhaps reminding us that a joke, like a riddle or a pun, is often two different things that are also the same.[92] See the wheeze?

*　*　*

Sometimes we are aware of our overlaps and sometimes not. Just as neither Stephen nor Bloom know that the "auk's egg" from Stephen's discussion in the library occupies Bloom's thoughts as he drifts off to sleep (9.446; 17.2328), Bloom knows nothing of Hamnet Shakespeare, nor is it likely, given Stephen's self-absorption, that he recalls Bloom's dead son. Nonetheless, as we saw in chapter 4, when the ghost who has haunted Bloom for the past eleven years is filtered through Stephen's consciousness, he may bear the key to Bloom's escape from the past.[93] And so he is a "changeling," with glass shoes, like Cinderella, and a bronze helmet (and ivory cane) like Hermes (15.4957–58, 4966). It may really be a matter for the gods.[94]

This is not to say that the Arranger has solved the problem. Bloom and Stephen come together on the level of the narrator—but then the narrator has as many internal conflicts as the characters. Unlike Chekhov, whose revolvers always go off, or Dante, where everything signifies, *Ulysses* (like life) contains many clues that lead nowhere.[95] Just as we never find out what happened to the Phaeacians, we never learn who M'Intosh or Molly's mother really was (6.805–99; 17.2063–66).[96] The last clock that Bloom looks at in *Ulysses* is in his parlor in Eccles St. It has stopped at 4:46 (17.1335–36). Given the stopping of Bloom's watch, this should matter. In fact, however, as the omniscient narrator informs us, the clock "stopped at the hour of 4.46 a.m. on the 21 March 1896," a date of no particular significance, a fact that could not be discerned from the dial, and an event that it is unlikely that anyone other than the narrator observed, or cares about.

The fusion of Bloom and Stephen thus cuts both ways. On the one hand, we increasingly see that their coming together (like their resemblance to Odysseus and Telemachus) exists only on the level of the narrative styles, and those styles undercut one another. On the other, although Bloom and Stephen, or Bloom and Molly, come together only on the level of the novel's language, that is also the only level on which they exist. As Stephen realized with perplexity at school, language does not have a one-to-one relation to reality: one name may have several different objects ("And belt was also to give a fellow a belt" *P* 9), and one object may have several different names (Stephen, Stevie, Dedalus, Stephanoumenos, Kinch). Worst of all, one can only use words created by others (*P* 189). Stephen's resistance to this leads to his, rather surprisingly, including language along with religion and nationalism as one of the nets he must fly past (*P* 203). But the recycling has its positive side. It means that Bloom and Stephen cannot be the isolated and independent entities they see themselves as. The words they are made of, inevitably shared and with multiple references, also imply that they contain more selves than they can know.

*   *   *

Ulysses's increasing revelation that the characters are composed from the narrative may seem to have left Homer behind. The *Odyssey*, for all its metanarrative inclinations, does not pull Telemachus, Odysseus, or Penelope out of the normal reality of epic. That reality, however, already includes something rather like Joyce's fusion. Even more than in Joyce's novel, the characters of oral epic are creations of its language—a language that also exists for their sake. That Hector, Telemachus, and Alcinous should all claim, in identical words, that war, language, and conveyance is "a concern for men, / for all, but for me most of all" would in any other context be astounding (*Iliad* 6.492–93; *Odyssey* 1.358–59; 11.352–53; and see 21.352–53). Here, however, it is simply the normal formulaic language of epic. In this respect, if Joyce's characters, on a level beyond their awareness, have identical thoughts, experiences, and even epithets, they are only imitating their epic forbearers.

Of course, what is an extraordinary narrative innovation in *Ulysses* is simply convention in the *Odyssey*. But then Homer can take advantage of convention just as easily as Joyce. It is notable, for example, that all of Athena's lines to Zeus at the beginning of Book 5 also occur somewhere else, and particularly that her histrionic lament for Odysseus (5.8–12) follows hard upon the real Mentor's genuinely heartfelt reproach (2.230–34).[97] Even more significantly, and in a comparison that deserves further study, Homer's characters fuse like Joyce's in the great "reverse similes," which we have only been able to glance at. Thus Eumaeus, with Odysseus sitting beside him, greets Telemachus as a father welcomes an only son who has been long away (16.17–20). Thus also Penelope and Odysseus become one another, as she embraces her husband with the joy of a shipwrecked man embracing dry land (23.233–39), as he earlier wept like a woman mourning her husband, slain in war (8.521–32).[98] The characters do not know of the shifts that the similes have created for them and the shifts do not change their relation to each other. But the audience knows, and it changes our relation to them.

Homer's reverse similes point as well to the actual connection between the characters of epic. Whatever their origins (and it seems significant that the etymology of names like "Achilles" or "Agamemnon" is difficult to trace), the Odysseus we know has been developed through his opposition to Achilles, and vice versa, just as, in a different way, Achilles is who he is because of his opposition to Agamemnon. Telemachus is who he is because he is the son of the hero who successfully returns, just as Orestes is the son of the hero who does not. Penelope's identity is shaped in her relation to Clytemnestra and Helen, and even Athena is herself because of her place in the complex web of identities that exist among the gods. Epic heroes and heroines, unlike those in novels, have the advantage of centuries, and even millennia, over which to develop—but like Molly and Stephen and Bloom, and like ourselves, they still develop only in relation to each other.

CRE

Conclusion

The Comic and the Human

An Irishman walks into a bar in New York, orders three pints, lines them up, and drinks them. Next Friday he comes in and does the same. When he comes in the third Friday the bartender suggests he just order the beers one by one. "Well," says the man, "there are three of us brothers, and one is in Sydney and one is in London and here I am and who knows when we'll be together again. So with us all leaving we said every Friday we'd go into a pub and order three pints and it would be like we were together." It was a great story and all the regulars loved it.

So things went on that way, every Friday, until about four months passed and your man comes in and orders only two pints. Everyone went quiet, and then, when the bartender brought the drinks he said how sorry he was. "What?" says the man, then, "Oh, no, it's not like that, but thanks. It's just I've given up drinking for Lent."

ULYSSES, THE ODYSSEY, AND COMEDY

Many of the qualities we have observed in the *Odyssey* and *Ulysses* are summed up in a side of the two works that we have touched on, but not explored. This is that they are both comic. As such they have both a "meta" and a very human concern. The conjunction points to an idea I have argued for elsewhere, that comedy is funny not because it is insignificant, but because it tells us truths that our mere rational selves cannot comprehend.[1] This is the sort of comedy we find in the *Odyssey* and *Ulysses*—the comedy that reminds us, like the joke above, that we are ourselves paradoxical.

We are flux and fixity, immortal souls and the playthings of time, totally absorbed in our world and watching ourselves be so absorbed. We are the same, and yet continually other. Perhaps only comedy can deal with such a creature.

As Zack Bowen points out, one important aspect of *Ulysses*'s comedy is its concern with the human in the most ordinary sense.[2] In this way it also recalls the *Odyssey*. Bloom is no Odysseus, but, as I have tried to argue, neither is Odysseus. In fact, it is exactly the trap of being an epic hero that Odysseus needs to escape. Bloom is not a model husband, Molly is not a model wife, and Stephen, God knows, is not a model anything—but then neither are we, and since this is a comedy, neither do they, or we, need to be.

As generally in comedy, the absolute view of Homer's gods does not make their perspective (sub specie aeternitatis though it be) more meaningful than the flawed human vision. If anything, the human view can make the gods seem comic. Hermes's explanation to Calypso that he doesn't often visit because the trip is long and there's nothing to eat on the way (or, in his case, no sacrifices to enjoy, 5.100–103) is set against Odysseus staring out over the ocean as if he could see Ithaca from there (1.58). Penelope and Odysseus's unanswered questions about Telemachus and each other (4.830–37; 13.416–28) bring out Athena's reluctance to let them into the plot any more than necessary. This does not mean that we care more about her grand design than about the humans experiencing a world greater than themselves.

In this way also *Ulysses,* like the *Odyssey,* opposes itself to tragedy. While tragedy engages the injustice of the cosmos, comedy has other concerns. Like Candide, the comic hero tends his own garden, even though, like Bloom, he may have somewhat grandiose ideas about it (17.1499–1671). Bloom, unlike Stephen, does not fear "those big words . . . which make us so unhappy" (2.264)—and only partially because he often fails to understand them. More generally he sees the great claims of moral principle as just something else to be dealt with, and often as something curiously at odds with common sense. About the sin that so occupies "Oxen of the Sun," Bloom thinks: "That's in their theology or the priest won't give the poor woman the confession, the absolution. Increase and multiply. Did you ever hear such an idea? Eat you out of house and home" (8.31–33). About suicide, which Hamlet wrestles with so deeply: "They have no mercy on that here or infanticide. Refuse christian burial. They used to drive a stake of wood through his heart in the grave. As if it wasn't broken already" (6.345–48). Bloom's one great stand for social justice occurs as a distraction from thoughts of Molly and Boylan. For him nationalism means "the same people living in the same place" (12.1422–23). His main concern is not divine justice (as 7.210–15), but just living in the world—which again makes the novel resemble the *Odyssey*.[3]

*   *   *

But while the *Odyssey* and *Ulysses* are involved in the human comedy, they are also comic on a much more meta level. In *Ulysses* this is the realm of the Arranger, whose bizarre styles are almost always comic, as in the parodies of "Cyclops" or "Oxen of the Sun," or even in Molly and Bloom's inability to see the dot (perhaps the egg?) that locates them at the end of "Ithaca."[4] This is the same level of humor as the *Odyssey*'s "O divine swineherd" (14.3 etc.) or as Priam's journey for Hector's body becomes, in the *Odyssey*, Nausicaa taking out the laundry (*Iliad* 24.265–80; *Odyssey* 6.71–84). The gods are also often funny on this level. Zeus's puzzlement at his daughter's histrionics is more amusing for being formulaic (1.63–64 = 5.21–22; and see 5.23–27). Mentor's prayer to Poseidon is funny because the audience knows that "Mentor" is really Athena and "herself was accomplishing it all" (3.62). Even funnier is the umbrage she takes when Telemachus says that not even the gods could bring Odysseus back (3.225–35). But when Athena declares that the gods can do anything—except keep a mortal from death (3.236–38)—the deeper point begins to come clear.

This is also the comedy of being both in and out of time. The gods are comic because they are absolute, and yet act like humans. Humans are comic because we are, in the Greek phrase, mere "things of a day . . . the dream of a shadow" (Pindar, *Pythia* 8.95) and yet tend to regard ourselves as absolute.[5] Athena's jealousy of Penelope sets off Odysseus's relation to her, a relation whose intensity comes from the fact that it must be bounded by death.[6] This does not make either Odysseus or Penelope tragic. Nor, as is common in "romance," is the relationship comic because it is eternal in their children. Rather, it is comic exactly because it is so human, as the poem's "meta" side brings out. Just as Homer can portray Athena competing for Odysseus's attention, we can place ourselves on the level of the gods—and then catch ourselves doing that.

*   *   *

As it is inclined to resist definition, comedy tends to the open-ended. Aristotle pointed out that a narrative must have a beginning, a middle, and an end (*Poetics* 1450b25). He also said (in another context) that for humans the only final end is death (*Ethics* 1.10, 1100a10; Herodotus 1.32).[7] Under these circumstances, both *Ulysses* and the *Odyssey* seek an ending that is something less than definite.

But while comedy tends to the open-ended, it also inclines toward its opposite, the cyclical.[8] There is something profoundly human in this as well. The life of an individual, Hamlet, Achilles, Molly Bloom, or James Joyce, is linear, but also open-ended. We are born, we grow up to be something, and we die. As *Ulysses* pertinently remarks, "It is interesting because . . . we are all born in the same way but we all die in different ways" (14.1241–42). But the life of humankind, like the leaves on Glaucon's tree (*Iliad* 6.145–50), is cyclical and always the same: as one generation of leaves dies and is followed by another, so one generation of humans brings forth another—a reason that comedy so often focuses on marriage and children.

The cyclical is embedded in epic, from the epic cycle overall to the basic device of ring-composition, which both shapes the poems as a whole and marks every simile and reference to the past.[9] Joyce, who loved chiasmus from an early age, structured *Ulysses* through ring-composition as well, having the second half of the novel reflect the first, matching the first three episodes against the last three, and placing his overview of Dublin, "Wandering Rocks," in the center.[10] Just as the *Odyssey* opens and closes with an Assembly and a conversation between Zeus and Athena (2.6–59; 24.420–66; 1.44–98; 24.472–88), Molly's final "yes" (18.1609; and see 18.1) returns us to her first, ambiguous "Mn" (4.57). Bloom and Molly end the novel as they began it, in their bedroom.

And the cyclical works on the "meta" level as well. It is not only the gods that join the world of myth to the world of the poet and his audience: the poem does that as well. So also Odysseus breaks out of myth only to become the mythologized subject of song, where each of us (if we listen carefully) experience him, once more, breaking out of myth. Traditional stories are transformed as they become part of Odysseus's Wanderings and then, as part of Odysseus's Wanderings, become traditional. Even the author (like Odysseus telling his Wanderings) creates the work only in turn to be created by it. "Homer" is only the poet of the *Iliad* and *Odyssey*, and who, after all, is "James Joyce," other than the author of *Ulysses*?

Despite plans (17.960–72), Stephen does not return to 7 Eccles St., except as Joyce re-created the scene in *Ulysses*. Stephen creates nothing from his *Hamlet* piece—except the carefully crafted work that Joyce makes of it. Joyce thus creates himself attempting to make himself his own author. When Myles Crawford, under the heading "'YOU CAN DO IT,'" tells Stephen,

"Give them something with a bite in it. Put us all into it, damn its soul" (7.6614–21) the paradox is amusing, but amusing because it is true. Just as we exist only through the "dead breaths we living breathe," we are ourselves because we also stand outside ourselves. Odysseus becomes himself in the cycle of belonging and not belonging to myth. Stephen, as predicted, meets himself in the library (9.1044–46), but, unbeknownst to himself, he does so in encountering the dark back of Bloom (9.1214).

LANGUAGE AND THE HUMAN SIDE

The self in *Ulysses* turns out to be neither simply in nor simply outside of time, and above all, it relies on others. In one sense this is just part of being a creature of language. Bloom, Molly, and Stephen have escaped time. They came to be before I was born (that is, me now, as I type these words) and will (most likely) still be here after all of us are gone. But while in one sense their existence, which is in a book, is outside of time, in another they only exist while someone is reading it.[11] As Alcinous told Odysseus and Helen told Hector, these things happen so that there will be song for people to come. The song, however, only exists while people continue to sing it.

And as they exist only in the novel, Stephen, Molly, and Bloom only exist because of each other.[12] *Ulysses* would not be *Ulysses* without all three, and if *Ulysses* were not *Ulysses*, they would not be themselves. The *Odyssey*, similarly, shows us how Telemachus, Penelope, and Odysseus are who they are because of each other. Metapoetically we see this when Penelope embraces her husband with the joy of a shipwrecked man embracing dry land (23.233–39). On the level of the narrative we see it as Telemachus meets his father, and so can see for himself how he resembles him. And the depth of the connection appears in Odysseus's outburst at the thought that his and Penelope's bed has been moved. The narrative styles of *Ulysses* take the notion of our interconnectedness to much wilder places, and *Finnegans Wake*, of course, will go even further. In the end, however, *Ulysses*'s interdependence of selves appears in a much more ordinary way, in the book's final image, which Joyce found in Homer, of a man and a woman in bed, talking and sleeping, moved in different ways but in the same final direction (17.2302–18).

* * *

Here again, what is true of fiction is true of life. Just as Odysseus only exists while his song is sung, so any event may be timeless in memory, but only while it is remembered. Nor are our memories as individual as they may seem. We experience them internally, but the experience was shaped by the outer world. We experience them alone, but they shape our interactions with others. And the critical question is not really whether they are true or not. Memory, as we have seen, is no more stable, and just as creative, as any other experience of time.

Ulysses itself undermines Stephen's desire to keep things distinct. The characters blend into one another, and the novel explains why. Joyce creates the illusion that some "real" narrative has been obscured, for example, by the romantic filter of "Nausicaa" or the catechism of "Ithaca." Finally, however, the shifts themselves make us see that there is no independent reality.[13] Just as, in any ordinary fiction, the question of Lady Macbeth's children, of what Hamlet studied at Wittenberg, or, for that matter, the name that Achilles bore among women (9.249–51), has no answer, there are no conversations in "Ithaca" that we are unable to hear. The only words that "Bloom" and "Stephen" and "Molly" speak or think are those that Joyce put on the page.

And yet we worry about Bloom and Molly, and about Telemachus's dispossession, and are right to do so.[14] *Ulysses* does not draw attention to its own artificiality for the sake of cleverness, any more than the *Odyssey* brings Odysseus out of the world of myth in order to disparage epic. As Mulligan says: "We have grown out of Wilde and paradoxes" (1.554). If Bloom and Stephen and Molly, like Odysseus, Penelope, and Telemachus, are made up of other people's viewpoints, so are we all, not isolated figures stuck onto a background, but part of a dialectic of active and passive, creating and created by the world around us. The fact that we are moved by the characters on the page reveals how deeply interconnected we are—at the same time that each one of us sometimes relies upon, sometimes endures, and sometimes clings to our own individual self.

Ulysses implies that we are all many people, which may be why we like hearing their stories.[15] The image of weaving applies here as well. Language is a kind of weaving, and the characters of the novel are the figures woven through its web. And in a sense we are all creations of language, since it is through language, which is both inside and outside, both our own and inherently received from others, that we assign meaning.

Just like any matter of identity, the song is continually being reshaped. It is both itself and not itself precisely in being continually retold. The *Odyssey* divides mythic from ordinary time, but the time of the stories and of the audience were never completely distinct, just as the individuals of the poem were never completely separate. Odysseus's escape from the time of myth into ordinary time is itself timeless as it is the subject of song, but the song only exists as it is sung—just as, even in the world of writing and books, *Ulysses* is not really one of the square parcels of 1 kilo 550 grams shipped off by Joyce and Sylvia Beach in 1922, but the infinite possibilities that that single object entails.[16] So it is to have an identity.

Appendix

The Episodes of *Ulysses*

I.

1. "Telemachus," Martello Tower, 8 a.m.   (Stephen)
2. "Nestor," Mr. Deasy's School, 10 a.m.
3. "Proteus," Sandymount Strand, 11 a.m.

II.

4. "Calypso," Bloom's home, 7 Eccles St., 8 a.m.   (Bloom)
5. "Lotus Eaters," Dublin (Post Office, All Hallows Church), 10 a.m.
6. "Hades," Glasnevin Cemetery, 11 a.m.

7. "Aeolus," *Freeman's Journal* Newspaper Office, 12 noon   (Bloom/Stephen)
8. "Lestrygonians," Davy Byrne's Pub, 1 p.m.   (Bloom)
9. "Scylla and Charybdis," The National Library, 2 p.m.   (Stephen/Bloom)

10. "Wandering Rocks," Dublin Streets, 3 p.m.   (Dubliners)

11. "Sirens," Ormond Hotel, 4 p.m.   (Bloom)
12. "Cyclops," Barney Kiernan's Pub, 5 p.m.
13. "Nausicaa," Sandymount Strand, 8 p.m.

14. "Oxen of the Sun," Holles St. Maternity Hospital, 10 p.m.   (Stephen/Bloom)
15. "Circe," Nighttown (Dublin's Brothel District), 12 midnight

III.

16. "Eumaeus," Cabman's Shelter, between 12 and 2 a.m.   (Stephen/Bloom)
17. "Ithaca," 7 Eccles St., between 12 and 2 a.m.
18. "Penelope," The Blooms' bedroom, 2 a.m.   (Molly)

Notes

Introduction: Joyce and Homer

1. Except in the few cases indicated, translations from the Greek (or Latin) are my own, with text taken from the Oxford Classical Texts *Odyssey* (Allen, 1985) and *Iliad* (Monro and Allen, 1985). As line numbers differ in different translations, I have kept the numbering from the Greek text (these are often printed at the top of the page in translations). Lattimore's translations of the two poems (*Iliad* [1951]; *Odyssey* [1967]), which also tend to be more literal than most, conveniently keep the Greek line numbers, as does Wilson's translation of the *Odyssey* (2018). For those interested, the prose *Odyssey* by Butcher and Lang (1879; 1900), largely used by Joyce, is not at all bad, while Butler's more quirky translation (1900; 1968) is guaranteed to provide interesting insights.

2. See, for example, R. Ellmann, "Joyce and Homer"; Kenner, "Eye on Homer," in Frehner and Zeller, *Collideorscape of Joyce*, 115–19; de Almeida, *Byron and Joyce*; Zajko, "Homer and Ulysses," in Fowler, *Cambridge Companion to Homer*, 311–23, as well as the references made standard in Gilbert's *James Joyce's "Ulysses."* Among Senn's numerous articles on *Ulysses* and Homer see "Remodeling Homer," in O'Neill, *Inductive Scrutinies*, 111–32, and "Book of Many Turns," in *Joyce's Dislocutions*, 68–83.

For studies with a thematic focus see Ames, "Convergence"; "Rebirth of Heroism," in Jones and Beja, *Twenty-First Joyce*, 157–78; and "Joyce's Aesthetic," in Jaurretche, *Art of the Negative*, 15–45. With a focus on Modernism see Flack, *James Joyce* and *Modernism and Homer*, and 6–9 in particular for a summary of views.

3. As Samuel Beckett puts it in Beckett, *Our Exagmination:* "The danger is in the neatness of identifications" (3). See Kenner, "Joyce's *Ulysses*," 97, for Joyce's "ambivalent and sometimes twofold use of Homeric material"; Thwaites, *Joycean Temporalities*, 42–43, on the "multiple and insistent inconsistencies of the parallels." For valuable overall studies of Joyce's use of Classical models see Schork, *Greek and Hellenistic Culture* and *Latin and Roman Culture*.

4. Printed in many works on *Ulysses*, such as R. Ellmann, *Ulysses on the Liffey*; Killeen, *"Ulysses" Unbound*, or J. Johnson's edition of *Ulysses*.

5. See Senn, *Joycean Murmoirs*, 77, for the allusions as "marginal grace notes" and "peripheral sparkles." Hornbeck, "Greekly Imperfect," 90: "loose adaptations, coupled with the seeming red herring of minor verbal correspondences, have discouraged recent critics from examining individual episodes closely in the light of their Homeric origins"; and see Kenner, *Ulysses*, 27–29, for some of these often amusing "minor correspondences," which he also describes as "largely comic" (*Dublin's Joyce*, 182). As Groden, *"Ulysses" in*

Progress, 36, 52, and Crispi, *Becoming the Blooms,* 70–71, point out, many of the allusions were added at a late stage of the writing.

Joyce's recommendation to his Aunt Josephine that she read Lamb's *Adventures of Ulysses* (*LI* 193), implies that he wanted readers to notice the correspondences in broad terms rather than in detail. See also Curran, *James Joyce Remembered,* 85–86, for his reading of Butcher and Lang, and for a reconsidered rejection of the idea that Joyce saw Homer as scaffolding.

6. As exceptions, Kenner, *Dublin's Joyce,* 181, looks at the correspondence "between situation and situation," while Senn, who sees the search for Homeric "parallels" as misdirecting Joycean scholarship, points out that "Perhaps the most pervasive Homeric features in *Ulysses* are not the one-to-one relationships that Gilbert began to chart for us, but principles or motive forces—such as the Protean force of transformation in the third chapter" (*Joyce's Dislocutions,* 206, 127).

7. See Kershner, *Culture of Joyce's "Ulysses,"* 68–72, for Joyce's riddles and misdirections. Glassco, *Memoirs of Montparnasse,* 189, recalls Joyce saying that puns "were the highest form of humour and that Spoonerisms ran them a close second. In the Middle Ages, gatherings of learned men were great festivals of puns, anagrams, leonine verses and so forth."

8. Mercanton, "Hours of James Joyce," in Potts, *Portraits of the Artist,* 217; R. Ellmann, "Joyce and Homer," 569, describes Joyce as initially wanting to use the Homeric titles but changing his mind; and see Bush, "Joyce's Museum of Homers," 322–57.

9. Beach, *Shakespeare and Company,* 38, writes that "Languages apparently were Joyce's favorite sport"; see R. Ellmann, *James Joyce* (hereafter cited as *JJ*), 408, for Joyce lamenting his lack of Classical Greek; Giedion-Welcker, "Meetings with Joyce," in Potts, *Portraits of the Artist,* 279; *JJ* 573, plate XXXVII, for Joyce spontaneously writing the *Odyssey's* first line in Greek along with a caricature of Bloom.

10. Percy Bysshe Shelley, *Defense of Poetry,* sect. 7, p. 678, in Shelley, *The Major Works,* ed. Zachary Leader and Michael O'Neil, Oxford World Classics (Oxford: Oxford University Press, 2003); and see *Portrait* (hereafter cited as *P*), 213; *Ulysses* (hereafter cited as *U*), 9.381–82; *Occasional, Critical, and Political Writing* (hereafter cited as *OCPW*), 57, 133.

11. Senn, *Joycean Murmoirs,* 82, for *Ulysses* and the *Odyssey* interacting and transforming each other, and 75 on "how the two epics electrify each other"; also Flack, *James Joyce,* 76. For a similar relation to Virgil, see Pogorzelski, *Virgil and Joyce,* 139.

12. See Flack, *James Joyce,* 88, for approaches to Homer that "emphasize their totalized, finalized worldview" taken "as a relatively straightforward backdrop for comparatively complex modern narratives." As Mahaffey points out in "End of Gender," in van Boheemen-Saaf and Lamos, *Masculinities in Joyce,* 144: "Joyce implicitly challenges two of the most common assumptions about heroism: that the hero is fully aware of his motives for acting, and that those motives are simple, unconflicted, and completely endorsed by the society he epitomizes." As does Homer.

13. Butler, *Authoress of the Odyssey,* 216: "Homer was writing of a time that was to him much what the middle ages are to ourselves," and see Morris, "Use and Abuse," in Cairns, *Oxford Readings,* 57–91. For a good overview see Saïd, *Homer and the "Odyssey,"* 1–56; for dating Graham, "*Odyssey,* History, and Women," in Cohen, *Distaff Side,* 3–16, and for an

excellent summary of orality and its implications, see Fowler, "Homeric Question," in Fowler, *Cambridge Companion to Homer*, 220–34. See also Jensen on performance of oral epic, "Performance," in J. M. Foley, *Companion to Ancient Epic*, 45–54, itself an excellent source on all things epic.

14. For the language of oral composition see Haubold, "Homer after Parry," 27–46; Scodel, *Listening to Homer*; Scully, *Sacred City*, 81–95. See also Beckett, in Beckett et al., *Our Exagmination*, 18–19, comparing the language of *Finnegans Wake* to the synthetic languages of Dante and Homer.

15. See M. L. West, "Homeric Question Today," 383–93, and Saïd, *Homer and the "Odyssey,"* 7–45. For a reading that balances the two, see Clay, *Wrath of Athena*.

16. M. L. West, "Homeric Question Today," 384, citing Wolf in particular: "It is often supposed that the conception of Homer as an illiterate oral poet was an original insight of the American scholar Milman Parry, about eighty years ago; in fact it was commonplace in the eighteenth century."

17. Butler, *Authoress of the Odyssey*, 2–3, and passim. Joyce responds by having his "Nausicaa" authored in a lady novelist style. For Butler's influence on Joyce see Knowles, "The Substructure of 'Sirens,'" 447–63, esp. 447–48; Kenner, *Pound Era*, 45–50; Gilbert, *Ulysses*, 395–97. "Wolf's Theory of Homer" appears in Joyce's notebook VI.B.20.22, and see Martin Nilsson, *Homer and Mycenae*, 2–55, for a survey of the Homeric Question in terms Joyce would have been familiar with.

18. Bakhtin, *Dialogic Imagination*, 84–258.

19. As Joyce described it in R. Ellmann, *Selected Letters of James Joyce* (hereafter cited as *SL*), 242.

20. For the "Arranger" see Hayman, *Ulysses*, 70; Kenner, "The Arranger," in Attridge, *James Joyce's "Ulysses,"* 17–32; McGee, *Paperspace*, 72–75; Conley, *Joyce's Mistakes*, 51–57.

21. On what is commonly referred to as the Rosenbach manuscript. Kenner, *Ulysses*, 61–62, points out that if it ended at this point *Ulysses* would be a fairly standard ironic novel of normal length.

22. As Groden, *"Ulysses" in Progress*, points out, Joyce's idea for the novel changed (or "developed") as he wrote, not unlike the improvisational approach of an oral poet.

23. Gorman, *James Joyce*, 45. As overseen by Joyce, Gorman's biography is useful for telling us what Joyce wanted us to know.

24. See Scott, *Joyce and Feminism*, 43, and B. Maddox, *Nora*, 24.

25. See Hutton, "Development of *Ulysses*," 126 n. 7 and Taplin, *Homeric Soundings*, 14–22, for tripartite structures in Homer.

26. Despite the remark attributed to Robert Nicholson that "Bloomsday has as much to do with *Ulysses* as Christmas with Jesus," Joyce, who was never above an advertising opportunity, was fine with the idea. See *LI* 216, 281, and Banta and Silverman, *Letters to Sylvia Beach*, 127, for the phenomenon of celebrating June 16 as "Bloomsday."

27. For the well-publicized Kidd/Gabler tempest and its residential teapot see Mahaffey, "Intentional Error," in Attridge, *James Joyce's "Ulysses,"* 231–56. Among other editions, there are particularly good notes in J. Johnson's reprint of the original 1922 edition and Slote, Mamigonian, and Turner's reprint of the 1939 edition. Textually, as J. Johnson notes (842), the crucial change is Gabler's inclusion of Stephen's "Do you know what

you are talking about? Love, yes. Word known to all men" (9.429–30), responding to his earlier "What is that word known to all men?" (3.435). Otherwise, most readers will not notice any major differences between editions.

28. The standard references are Gifford and Seidman's *"Ulysses" Annotated* and R. Ellmann's biography, *JJ*, along with the various collections of Joyce's letters (vols. 1, 2, and 3 hereafter cited as *LI*, *LII*, and *LIII*, and the *Selected Letters*—*SL*—cited above, n19). Of the many "how to" books designed to serve as guides through the novel, I recommend Killeen's *"Ulysses" Unbound*, but any standard work, including numerous online aids such as The Joyce Project, will provide the basics.

29. See Ungar, *National Epic*, 12–13, on the hints in the National Library episode. Epic poetry is, of course, far from the only tradition explored in *Ulysses*, as, for example, Bowen, *Comic Novel*, 73–113, on the "long-standing comic tradition" Joyce participates in, as well as 115–21 on Dante's role in that tradition.

30. See Hall, *Return of Ulysses*, 5–15, and Hutton, "Development of *Ulysses*," 123, on questioning what it means to read a text "in the original." Cheng, *Joyce, Race, and Empire*, 3, perceptively describes Joyce's "attempts to resist and defy the authorized centrality of canons, empires (especially English), and totalizing structures" and Fairhall, *Question of History*, 62: "For Joyce, like Vico, sought freedom from tradition, from received history, and from linguistic convention." What needs to be added is that the epic tradition itself was one of overturning previous artistic models.

CHAPTER 1. TIME IN JOYCE AND HOMER

1. For works on Joyce and time see Thwaites, *Joycean Temporalities;* Wawrzycka, *Reading Joycean Temporalities;* Norris, "Philosophy of History," in Rabaté, *James Joyce Studies,* 203–26.

On time and literature see Ricoeur, *Time and Narrative,* for the necessary interrelation of time, identity, and narrative; Stephen Kern, *Culture of Time,* esp. 11–29; Kennedy, *Antiquity,* and more generally, Elias, *Time,* for time as a cultural construct, and Rovelli, *Order of Time,* 4, for time as not an independent entity but rather a "complex collection of structures, of layers."

2. Ferrucci, *Poetics of Disguise,* 37: "The *Odyssey* is assuredly one of the works in which the problem of identity is most acutely and profoundly perceived. A doubt is often voiced by its characters: And what if I am not what I am?"; Van Nortwick, *Unknown Odysseus,* 98: "The *Odyssey* begins with the question: where is Odysseus? As the story unfolds, a second, more difficult quandary surfaces: who is Odysseus?"; Katz, *Penelope's Renown,* 5: "The poem promotes but also questions its own fantasies and ideals, such as the idea that time and change can be undone, and the notion that there is such a thing as home, where people and relationships can stay forever the same."

3. Curran, *James Joyce Remembered,* 85–86, connects the importance of Homer to Joyce with his interest in time: "these [Homeric] and similar parallels and correspondences had begun to be of great importance to him. They lay at the foundation of Joyce's experimental and characteristic work where time is expanded or folded up like a concertina with the same overlapping of planes and with metamorphoses or liquefaction of

objects." For time and identity in Joyce see, in particular, Rickard, *Joyce's Book of Memory* and Pizarro, *Joyce's Vision of Time,* esp. 31–33.

4. Hartog, *Regimes of Historicity,* xvi (italics in the original).

5. Vidal-Naquet, "Land and Sacrifice," in Schein, *Reading the Odyssey,* 37: "In effect, as has often been recognized, the *Odyssey* contrasts a "real" world . . . with a mythical world that is roughly coterminous with that of the stories told in Alcinous' palace"; Grene, "The *Odyssey,*" 47–68; Beye, *Epic Tradition,* 58–63. Bakhtin's contrast of time in the epic and in the novel makes a similar distinction; see Bakhtin, *Dialogic Imagination,* 12–14: "absolute epic distance separates the epic world from contemporary reality," and 18–19: "This past is distanced, finished and closed like a circle"; Morson, *Narrative and Freedom.*

6. As Joyce would have seen, Butcher and Lang, *Odyssey,* xi ff., xxiv, describe the poem as juxtaposing the adventures, as fairy stories, with the ordinary. See Feeney, *Caesar's Calendar,* 70: "Homer's attitude to the past is grounded in a powerful feeling that the heroic action of the poems is taking place long ago, at a time from which the current audience . . . 'such as mortals are now,' is irrevocably cut off, a time to which the audience has access only when the past is revivified in the poet's song." As Hartog, *Regimes of Historicity,* 53, points out, this approach makes the *Odyssey* itself an "anachronistic epic, or at least one that questions its own mechanisms." For Joyce see Gifford, "James Joyce and Myth," 124, on the constant metamorphosis that keeps myth alive, creating a sense of myth as "outside of history."

7. Hartog, *Regimes of Historicity,* 53, 54.

8. For Odysseus's need to regain identity see Christensen, *Many-Minded Man;* Underwood, *Mythos and Voice.* See also Katz, *Penelope's Renown,* 174: "the indeterminacy that characterizes the *Odyssey* as a whole extends to all of the relationships of "identity" that constitute it, including that of self-identity."

9. Hartog, *Regimes of Historicity,* 55.

10. See Hagberg, "A Portrait of Consciousness," in Kitcher, *Joyce's "Ulysses,"* 84, for a "dialogical interaction between (what we too quickly call) the inner and the outer, the self and its relationally webbed or nested context"; Williams, "Dominant Ideologies," in Benstock, *Augmented Ninth,* 312–22, for the interpenetration of "external" and "internal" narrative; Rabaté, *Politics of Egoism,* overall 67: "in a typically Modernist fashion, it seems that the only way for Joycean egoism to go beyond its narcissistic shortcomings is to blend with language."

11. For both Joyce and Modernism more generally on objective and subjective time see Bazarnik and Kucula, *James Joyce and After.*

12. See Herr, "Difficulty," in Latham, *Cambridge Companion to "Ulysses,"* 158, on later episodes in *Ulysses* and "the rigorously controlled clock-time of Bloomsday breaking apart and overlapping so that competing nighttime chronologies seemingly distort the go-ahead daytime narrative."

13. *U* 6.149–50; 10.783–84; 11.797–98; 14.1044; 15.443; 16.1400–1401; 17.1906–7—all appropriate for a novel set in "doublin" (*Finnegans Wake* 1.8; hereafter cited as *FW*). See Riquelme, *Teller and Tale,* overall for Joyce's technique of return with a difference; Mahaffey, "Importance of Playing Ernest," in McCormick and Steinberg, *Approaches*

to *Teaching*, 145: "the second half of *Ulysses* is partly a playful revision, parody of, and supplement to the conventions and techniques of the first half"; Kain, *Fabulous Voyager*, 35: "Successive books are variations and elaborations of already chosen themes." See Knowles, *Dublin Helix*, 100–102, for "Sirens" recapitulating the novel and Joyce's letter (*SL* 252) on "Oxen" linking back to earlier episodes; Gabler, "Early Joycean Progressions," in Ebury and Fraser, *Joyce's Non-Fiction Writings*, 68: "In preparation for "Circe" (as well as "Oxen of the Sun") James Joyce, as we know, intently reread all preceding *Ulysses* text. In an important respect, therefore, all preceding chapters became the "perception text" out of which "Circe" was generated." See Kenner, *Ulysses*, 76–80, for the building up of scenes from numerous partial recalls; Senn, *Inductive Scrutinies*, 75, for postponed clarification "This is nothing new in fiction (in life too we often understand long afterwards or too late)" and Spoo, *Language of History*, 153–58, for a link to Eliade and the Myth of Eternal Return.

14. Nelson, "Calypso's Choice," in Breyfogle, *Literary Imagination*, 163-89; Segal, "*Kleos* and Its Ironies" in Schein, *Reading the "Odyssey,"* 201–22; Redfield, *Nature and Culture*, 101: a man "becomes a hero because he cannot become a god." See also Vernant, "A 'Beautiful Death,'" in Cairns, *Oxford Readings*, 319–20: "Heroic striving has its roots in the will to escape aging and death, however 'inevitable' they may be, and leave them both behind."

15. For this "continuity of time principle" see de Jong, *Narratological Commentary*, xii-xiii, 499–500; Nelson, "Telling Time," in Wawrzycka, *Reading Joycean Temporalities*, 125–26. For Joyce's similar use of time, see A. Goldman, *Joyce Paradox*, 79–80.

16. And see 4.791–94 for Penelope's lion simile.

17. On fairy-tale elements in the *Odyssey* see Heubeck's introduction, in Heubeck and Hoekstra, *A Commentary*, vol. 2, 3–11; Reinhardt, "Adventures in the *Odyssey*," in Schein, *Reading the "Odyssey,"* 63–132; Peradotto, *Middle Voice*, 32–93; Carpenter, *Folk Tale*. Stanford, *Ulysses Theme*, 9, points out that there are no fewer than 120 versions of the Cyclops story, ranging from India to Ireland.

18. Heubeck, introduction, in Heubeck, West, and Hainsworth, *A Commentary*, vol. 1, 20.

19. The placement of Helen within heroic time is reinforced by the emphasis on her being the daughter of Zeus himself (4.569–70).

20. See Dougherty, *Raft of Odysseus*, 81–101; Edwards, "Homer's Ethical Geography," 27–78; Garvie, *Homer*, 22–25.

21. Osborne, "Homer's Society," in Fowler, *Cambridge Companion to Homer*, 206–19, and see Kirk, *Homer and the Epic*, 74–82; P. Rose, "Class Ambivalence," in Doherty, *Homer's "Odyssey,"* 288–313; Morris, "Use and Abuse," in Cairns, *Oxford Readings*, 57–91; Finley, *World of Odysseus*, 48 and 27, for Homer as uninterested in history as such.

22. Homer also muddles the older and newer systems, straightforward in the *Iliad*, as 16.178, 190; 22.472. See S. West, "Commentary Books I–IV," in Heubeck, West, and Hainsworth, *A Commentary*, vol. 1, 59; Saïd, *Homer and the "Odyssey,"* 75–94, for "the distance, or rather the radical discontinuity, that the epics constantly establish between the mythical past and the present inhabited by the poet and his audience" (90).

23. See also 4.49, 8.454, as well as hesitations about bathing in Phaeacia (6.206–22).

In the Classical world men bathed themselves (S. West, "Commentary Books I–IV," in Heubeck, West, and Hainsworth, *A Commentary*, vol. 1, 189); Stanford (*Ulysses Theme*, 119) points out that the Alexandrians excised maidens washing heroes; and see Kevin Egan's reaction at *Ulysses* 3.234–38.

24. Even Odysseus's palace, although it has the great *megaron* of the Mycenaeans, is fairly limited, as P. Rose points out in "Class Ambivalence," in Doherty, *Homer's "Odyssey,"* 288–313; Redfield, "Economic Man," also in Doherty, 265–87.

25. S. West, "Commentary Books I–IV," in Heubeck, West, and Hainsworth, *A Commentary*, vol. 1, 77: "Homeric epic preserves an extremely ancient usage in its extensive employment of patronymics" and on the patronymics as much less common in the *Odyssey* than the *Iliad*. The greatest heroes can be referred to by patronymic alone, as "Atreides" or "Peliades" for Achilles, while Telemachus, of the "ordinary" world, is almost never given a patronymic.

26. Heubeck views the phrases as parody (in Heubeck and Hoekstra, *A Commentary*, vol. 2, 192); M. Parry as purely formulaic (*Making of Homeric Verse*, 151–52); and Stanford (*Homer*, vol. 2, 215), rather humorlessly, as acknowledging Eumaeus's royal birth.

27. De Jong, *Narratological Commentary*, 29, points out the prevalence of "eating" verbs describing the wasting of Telemachus's property.

28. In contrast, in Lamb's version, chap. 9, Ulysses's return is what the suitors most dread. See Cunliffe, *A Lexicon*, 76, on *geraie*, the vocative "old man," as respectful in the *Iliad*, without respect at *Odyssey* 14.131, 185, and used by Eurymachus to insult a prophet at 2.201.

29. See Heubeck's introduction in Heubeck, West, and Hainsworth, *A Commentary*, vol. 1, 21, on this as "an environment where the virtues of an aristocratic warrior reveal their fragility and lose their value, where heroic aims turn into empty posing and become ridiculous gestures"; and Pucci, "Song of the Sirens," in Schein, *Reading the "Odyssey"*: "A sort of self-destructive nostalgia compels these old heroes to dwell in the memory of their splendid and grievous past" (196). Joyce's remark about his father's friends, although made while requesting more information about them, strikes a similar note: "They all belong to a vanished world and most of them seem to have been very curious types" (*LI* 198).

30. Eliade, *Sacred and the Profane*, 68–115. Although no longer seen as universal, Eliade's distinction remains important. See Doniger's foreword in Eliade, *Shamanism*, xi–xv; similarly, Feeney, *Caesar's Calendar*, 69.

31. Hesiod, *Works and Days*, 174–76, 160. Hesiod thus ignores the nobility's claims to descent from heroes. The heroes also had an earlier generation to look back on—the generation of Heracles and Theseus as opposed to that of Achilles and Odysseus—but the fundamental break remains that between heroic time altogether and the time of ordinary life.

32. Herodotus, *Histories*, 2.142–43, on Hecataeus (*Herodoti Historiae*, ed. N. G. Wilson, Oxford Classical Texts, 2015); and see also Feeney, *Caesar's Calendar*, 72–77.

33. Thucydides 1.21 (*Thucydidis Historiae*, ed. H. S. Jones and J. E. Powell, Oxford Classical Texts, 1980).

34. Quotations are from Feeney, *Caesar's Calendar*, 109, 108–9, 117–18.

35. See Feeney, *Caesar's Calendar,* 115–18, on the Trojan War as the dividing point and below, on World War I, for Joyce's description of Odysseus as a postwar hero. Hartog, *Regimes of Historicity,* 45–46, also sees the Trojan War as axial. Homer, of course, fudges the issue by connecting Odysseus's technically postwar Wanderings with the heroic world.

36. And see *Iliad* 4.163–68, for the same formulaic expression spoken by Agamemnon.

37. Zweig, *World of Yesterday,* xiii.

38. As Lewis charged: "Mr. Joyce is very strictly of the school of Bergson-Einstein-Stein-Proust. He is of the great time-school they represent" (*Time and Western Man,* 89). For a particularly sensitive critique see Anyfanti, "Time, Space, and Consciousness."

For Bergson's concept of *durée* see Bergson, *Time and Free Will;* and for *durée* (psychological, internal, active living time) and external time (objective, chronological, historical), see Gillies, "Bergsonism," in *Concise Companion to Modernism,* 95–115, and *Henri Bergson,* 132–36; and in relation to Joyce, see Beplate, "Memory of Words," *Modern Language Review* 100 (2005): 298–312. Gell, *Anthropology of Time,* 314–28, gives a negative view of Bergson.

39. As Crispi has shown, *Becoming the Blooms,* 29, 53, etc., Joyce deliberately added and developed the precise hour of Molly's assignation with Boylan. Kain, *Fabulous Voyager,* 48–51, compares *Mrs Dalloway,* where Big Ben strikes the hour nine times in 296 pages.

40. Line counts are necessarily inexact, as in many places monologue, description, and even dialogue (deliberately not marked off by quotation marks, as *JJ* 353, *LI* 75) tend to blend.

41. Conley, "'Endlessnessnessness,'" in Wawrzycka, *Reading Joycean Temporalities,* 68–69; and O'Neill, "Some Temporal Aspects," 110–20, also in Wawrzycka. See, more generally, Ricoeur, *Time and Narrative,* esp. vol. 2; Kern, *Time and Space,* 33–35. As Proust puts it, "I had lived through so many hours in a few minutes" (*Remembrance of Things Past,* vol. 3, 117).

42. See Auerbach, *Mimesis,* 537: "the road taken by consciousness is sometimes traversed far more quickly than language is able to render it"; and Gaipa, Latham, and Scholes, *Little Review,* 357, 365, on Joyce's additions to the interior monologue slowing time down. Kenner, *Colder Eye,* 193, points to other time collapses.

43. See *U* 14.1181–82: "During the past four minutes or thereabouts he had been staring hard at a certain amount of number one Bass," Macaulay's view of the theosophists' "Any object, intensely regarded, may be a gate of access to the incorruptible eon of the gods" (*U* 14.1166–67). For a similar expansion/compression of time in Homer see Senn, *Inductive Scrutinies,* 114–15.

44. See B. Anderson, *Imagined Communities,* 27, for the more usual view of a progression from interior to exterior time confirming communal solidarity; and, on Joyce, Volpone, "Temporal Disharmonies," in Wawrzycka, *Reading Joycean Temporalities,* 138: "Joyce seems to suggest an inexorable progression towards the abandonment of an objective, and therefore shared, time, in favor of a subjective and individual one, as represented by the characters' consciousness. Such a peculiar temporal dimension cannot be shared, nor can it really be recounted: time becomes a solipsistic quantity of the mind, whose perception and effect on the subject can only be conveyed as a literary object and

verbalized through the interior monologue. Hence the only "perceptive sharing" is that between the character and the reader."

45. Elias, *Time*, 15: "What the clock communicates by the symbols on its clockface is what we call time. One looks at the clock and finds out that it is now such and such a time, not only for me but for the whole of the society to which I belong." Durkheim thus sees the concepts of time and space as originating in the social self, in *Elementary Forms*, 10–21; and see Gell, *Anthropology of Time* 3–14, for a critique.

46. Stevenson, *Reading the Times*, 9–17, 66–72, and 104, for Einstein working on new clocks in the patent office in Zurich; Rovelli, *Order of Time*, 57–63, for the uniformity of time coming from clocks rather than experience.

47. See Norris, *Joyce's Web*, with other views, 151–54.

48. Senn, *Joyce's Dislocutions*, 105–7.

49. Elias, *Time*, 73: "if they stop changing for good, watches cease to be watches and people cease to be people." In this light Conley's take is particularly interesting: "Joyce's texts are *not* 'what they are' but what they are *becoming*" (*Joyce's Mistakes*, 39); and see Booker, *Literary Tradition*, 127–28, on *Portrait* as created in the tension between being and becoming.

50. Bruno's philosophy as described by Joyce in *Critical Writings* (hereafter cited as *CW*), 34. See R. Ellmann, *Ulysses on the Liffey*, 53–56; Sabatini, "James Joyce," in Ferrer, Slote, and Topia, *Renascent Joyce*; Gose, *Transformation Process*, 14–16, 96. Groden, *"Ulysses" in Progress*, 52–53, points out that opposite episodes were written together: "Circe" and "Eumaeus" as well as "Ithaca" and the "human, all too human" (*LI* 160) "Penelope."

51. Bradford, *Ulysses Found*, 148, points out, from a nautical viewpoint, that while it seems natural to steer for the center between Scylla and Charybdis that course would be disastrous. Stanislaus Joyce records in his diary that "The golden mean is as abhorrent to me as to Jim" (*Complete Dublin Diary*, 53).

52. For Greek binaries generally see Lloyd, *Polarity and Analogy*, and Peradotto, *Middle Voice*, for a tension between the centripetal and centrifugal shaping the *Odyssey*.

53. Rickard, *Joyce's Book of Memory*, 22–29, and throughout. In *Finnegans Wake* the pairing of Howth Head and the river/sea is extended to tree and stone.

54. See Redfield, *Nature and Culture*, 30–39, for *kleos* as social identity, particularly associated with the gravestone, and 180–81 for the funeral mound as *empedon*, firmly fixed or unmovable.

55. Similarly at *Odyssey* 24.24–34. See Macleod, "Homer on Poetry," in Cairns, *Oxford Readings*, 295, on the resemblances between Achilles in *Odyssey* 11 and *Iliad* 24.

56. Or as Lamb, *Adventures of Ulysses*, chap. 2, puts it: "The dead delight in the occupations which pleased them in their time of living upon the earth."

57. Hence also Odysseus is to slaughter a barren cow for the dead (10.522). In contrast, in *The Divine Comedy*, as in the *Aeneid*, men and women pointedly appear together, as Dido and Sychaeus (*Aeneid* 6.472–74) or Paolo and Francesca (*Inferno*, Canto 5).

58. The anomalous *eidolon* has aroused suspicions that 602–4 are spurious, for which see Stanford, *Homer*, vol. 1, 403, and Heubeck in Heubeck and Hoekstra, *A Commentary*,

vol. 2, 114. While Heubeck suggests that Homer wanted the appearance of Heracles despite his immortality, I suspect the immortality is the reason his presence is so desirable.

59. Gorman, *James Joyce*, 95: "Aristotle still represented to him Dogma, a Rock set against the turbid tide of inchoate metaphysics. He was System, co-ordination, rationalization. He was the reverse of Plato and Plato's beautiful and ineffectual mysticism."

60. As also in Joyce's comments on *Finnegans Wake:* "Time and the river and the mountain are the real heroes of my book" (*JJ* 554), and "everything is inclined to flux and change nowadays and modern literature, to be valid, must express that flux" (A. Power, *Conversations with James Joyce*, 110). In *Ulysses* Mulligan's pointed identification of the sea as feminine is set against the phallic character of Martello Tower.

61. Or as Hamlet might have put it, between where one eats and where one is eaten (4.4.19).

62. Joyce's use of "Nighttown" rather than the more usual "Monto" reflects the darkness of Hades (*Odyssey* 11.11–19). See also Senn, *Portals of Recovery*, 99, on "the stiff walk" in "Circe" (15.207). For other connections see Pogorzelski, "Ghosts of Optimism," 443–66, and *Virgil and Joyce*, 91–109. The displacement of "Hades," *Ulysses's* first break with the sequence of episodes in the *Odyssey*, is also suggestive, and Joyce links the episodes structurally, as "Hades" ends the first and "Circe" the last three-episode sequence of the "Nostos."

63. "Lipoti" being Hungarian for "Leopold" (Raleigh, *Leopold and Molly Bloom*, 13), and see Reynolds, *Joyce and Dante*, 66–69.

64. Mamigonian, "Hunter and Gatherers," 13–31, points out that Joyce only definitely met Alfred Hunter, often taken as a model for Bloom, at Matthew Kane's funeral, the occasion behind "Hades" (as *U* 16.1255–60; 17.1253).

65. See Hogan, *Theory of Influence* and Tracy, *Story of the "Odyssey,"* 68, on Odysseus's narration as designed to put Hades in the center of the poem.

66. Adams's essay on "Hades," in Hart and Hayman, *Critical Essays*, 114, describes Bloom as "less alone physically, more alone spiritually."

67. Along with Stephen on Cranly (1.159) and his mother. The link to *Portrait*, however, is carefully made, as Stephen's thoughts of his mother picking lice at *U* 1.268–69 reflect *P* 174, 233–34.

68. Joyce decided on this approach early on, as in his description to Pound: "It is a continuation of *A Portrait of the Artist as a Young Man* after three years' interval blended with many of the persons of *Dubliners*" (*JJ* 383, and similarly to Mencken, *LI* 83).

69. Similarly, the flux of "Circe" will end with Stephen knocked cold.

70. See Gowing, *Empire and Memory*, 148, on memorials relieving rather than reinforcing the burden of memory.

71. See the contribution written by Colum, 64, in O'Connor, *Joyce We Knew* and O'Connor's piece, 11–12 and 13, for Joyce as "aware of the dangers of becoming the victim of his own image"; S. Joyce, *My Brother's Keeper*, 248–49; and see Gogarty quoted by Senn, "Book of Many Turns," in Attridge, *James Joyce's "Ulysses,"* 37–38.

72. As the first reader points out, Joyce was rumored to be working on a book on water after he finished *Finnegans Wake*.

73. See Raaflaub, "Epic and History," in J. M. Foley, *Companion to Ancient Epic*, 55–70;

J. M. Foley, "Epic as Genre," in Fowler, *Cambridge Companion to Homer,* 185: "For national identity, epic is a foundational genre." Gilbert, in Beckett, *Our Exagmination,* 51–52 (vetted by Joyce), quotes Vico: "The diversity of views as to Homer's birthplace forces us to the conclusion that, when the various races of Greece disputed among themselves the honour of claiming him as one of theirs, it was because *they themselves were Homer*" (italics in the original).

74. Weir, *"Ulysses" Explained,* 15, sees *Ulysses*'s title as a reference to Roman/British usurpation; but see Pogorzelski, *Virgil and Joyce,* arguing also against the position that the title shows a lack of reference to the *Odyssey.* Senn, *Joycean Murmoirs,* 78, points out that "Ulysses" is a hybrid of the Latin "Ulixes" and "Odysseus"; and see chap. 3 for more on Joyce and naming.

75. As Reynolds points out, Joyce liked to cast himself as Dante lost in the dark wood (*Joyce and Dante,* 3; *JJ* 393); and see Weir, *"Ulysses" Explained,* 3: "Dante and Joyce both write about an earlier stage of their lives from the perspective of maturity. They also write about their homelands from the perspective of exile."

76. Senn, *Joycean Murmoirs,* 78–79: "Moreover, as a highly ambitious artificer—if you take on Homer, Dante and Shakespeare you must be ambitious—he may have realized at an early stage that practically everything has happened before."

77. The single critical difference between Greek gods and humans is immortality, as Otto, *Homeric Gods,* 131: "The relationship between man and gods, then, is that they are akin to one another, and yet separated by an abyss"; and see 169–228.

78. As Feeney, *Gods in Epic,* 129–55; Kennedy, *Antiquity,* 44–74; Mack, *Patterns of Time;* and see Quint, *Epic and Empire,* 50–96 and overall, for Virgil's as a teleological epic. Bakhtin, *Dialogic Imagination,* 138, comments on the Romans adding historicity to the Greek view and see Pizarro, *Joyce's Vision of Time,* 28–30 and 44, on the "interplay of narrative and historical thinking and how historical narratives are constituted from the *interaction* of two perspectives, a 'human' one from 'within' time and the 'God's eye view' from 'outside' time."

79. See Reynolds, *Joyce and Dante,* 33: "Joyce's recovery of Dante resembles Dante's recovery of Virgil in being a combination of devoted attachment and radical difference." Dante makes his relation to Virgil explicit in following Virgil's mention of "my high tragedy" (*l'alta mia tragediu; Inferno* 20.113) with a mention, in passing, of "my comedy" (*la mia comedia; Inferno* 21.2). Interestingly, perhaps particularly to Joyce, Dante had no Greek, so gained his knowledge of Homer through Latin.

80. See Hartog, *Regimes of Historicity,* 60–61, on how Christ "broke time in two"; Eliade, *Sacred and the Profane,* 72 and 111, on the paradox of Christ being in time, although also "for the Christian, time begins anew with the birth of Christ." See also B. Anderson, *Imagined Communities,* 23–24, on the medieval view of God's eternal time encompassing past, present, and future in contrast to modern blank homogenous time.

81. See Reynolds, *Joyce and Dante,* 16, on how Joyce and Dante both "intend to set forth the universal in the particular," and Rickard, *Joyce's Book of Memory,* 139–40 and 132: "the careful reader of *Ulysses* can see a pattern behind the seemingly accidental or chance events of *Ulysses* that is not clearly visible to the characters themselves, a pattern

that reflects the cultural unconscious of *Ulysses* and helps to create a tension between frustration and fragmentation and meaning in the text."

82. This may be appropriate, as Milton, who reshapes Dante's epic of hell, the human world, and paradise, himself refers explicitly to Homer and Virgil (3.35; 9.14 ff.), but not Dante. Budgen, *Making of "Ulysses,"* 181, describes Joyce reciting *Lycidas* from memory.

83. See Bell, *Jocoserious Joyce*, 211, for Joyce's parody of a Miltonic fall as well as Joyce's claim that *Paradise Lost* is merely a "puritanical transcript" of Dante (*OCPW* 164).

84. A word Joyce calls attention to through its unlikely location in the soft-porn novel, *Ruby the Pride of the Ring* (4.324–41). See Feeney, *Gods in Epic*, 188: "From its first lines the [*Metamorphoses*] continually confronts us with the problem of the extent to which, and the ways in which, it is and is not epic"; and 190–93, on Minerva and Ariadne as "a lesson in perspective, with divine and human order and flux, fixity and instability." *Ruby* itself has metamorphosed in *Ulysses* from an anti-circus tract to a work of pornography, as M. Power, "Discovery of Ruby," 115–21 has shown.

85. Kenner, *Ulysses*, 166–68.

86. Budgen, *Making of "Ulysses,"* 323–24, comments on Einstein being in Zurich at the same time as Joyce; and see Beckett, "Dante . . . Bruno. Vico . . . Joyce," in Beckett, *Our Exagmination,* 22: "In what sense, then, is Mr. Joyce's work purgatorial? In the absolute absence of the Absolute."

87. Weygandt, *Irish Plays and Playwrights*, 121–22. Castle, "Ousted Possibilities," 306–28, points to Joyce's fundamental "resistance (sometimes fierce, sometimes playful) against the tendency of historical points of view to converge and dissolve in the absolute logic of a master discourse" (307).

88. Kain, *Fabulous Voyager*, 12, quotes Levin, *James Joyce*, 25: "Joyce lost his religion but kept his categories." See also Eco, *Aesthetics of Chaosmos*, 3: "speaking about Catholicism in connection with Joyce is a bit like speaking about filial love in connection with Oedipus and Jocasta," and 7: "If you take away the transcendent God from the symbolic world of the Middle Ages, you have the world of Joyce"; and Manganiello, "Pouring New Wine," 171–93, for Joyce's as an epic without God. On Joyce's rejection of religion see Lernout, *Help My Unbelief.*

89. As Senn, *Joycean Murmoirs*, 156, has noted, the two references were added at the same time: "Stephen responds with a tiny Latin tit for an earlier Greek tat."

90. I owe the phrase to Rich Young.

91. See Taplin, *Homeric Soundings*, esp. 144–78, for the *Iliad* in particular as structured around the sequence of day and night, as marked by the formulaic "rosy-fingered dawn." Gordon, *Joyce and Reality*, 122–37, points to the importance of sun, moon, and stars in *Ulysses*.

92. Proust, in contrast, remarks on "the sky that knew nothing of summer time and winter time and did not deign to recognize that half past eight had become half past nine" (*Remembrance of Things Past*, vol. 3, 785).

93. Although international time zones were generally established between 1884 and 1900, 1:00 in London was still only 12:35 in Dublin, which was on Dunsink rather than Greenwich time, as in Bloom's scheme at *U* 17.1672–78. See Gibbons, *Joyce's Ghosts*, 178–

83, 186; Bénéjam, "Dramatic Time and Timing," in Wawrzycka, *Reading Joycean Temporalities*, 13–30, esp. 20–22.

94. Although see Cohn, *Transparent Minds*, 219, on Molly's period and biological time.

95. Mrs Breen concludes as well from her husband's behavior that "There must be a new moon out . . . He's always bad then" (8.245). A new moon rose on June 13, 1904.

96. Mercanton, "Hours of James Joyce," in Potts, *Portraits of the Artist*, 237–38.

97. Noted in "Ithaca" as occurring on the 15th of September 1903, nine months and one day before the date of the novel (17.2287 ff.), so that June 16 is the first day on which Milly could have given birth to a full-term child.

98. Hoffmeister, "Portrait of Joyce," in Potts, *Portraits of the Artist*, 129–30. Joyce was also concerned about the year he finished *Ulysses*, since $1 + 9 + 2 + 1 = 13$ (*LI* 161).

99. See Rickard, *Joyce's Book of Memory*, 149–53. As Rickard points out (attributing the slip to Bloom), Rudy would actually have been 10½, but even Joyce cannot arrange everything.

100. Gifford and Seidman, *"Ulysses" Annotated*, 572; see also Hart's essay on "Wandering Rocks" in Hart and Hayman, *Critical Essays*, 183: "The amusing erroneous calculations about their relative ages in 'Ithaca' provide an ironic comment on the emptiness of any attempt at harmony. The search for unity is, it seems, a failure."

101. Kitcher, *Joyce's Kaleidoscope*.

102. In contrast, Sherry, *Great War*, 150, quotes Gertrude Stein: "only when the war was at its height did the generals understand that it was a war of the 20th c, and not a war of the 19th c."

103. See, for example, Fairhall, *Question of History*, 165–67; Winston, *Joyce and Militarism*, 111–54; Duffy, "Setting," in Latham, *Cambridge Companion to "Ulysses"*: "In *Ulysses*, this single day and these seven years it took to describe it face each other in magnificent tension, throwing open questions of time, of dating and of history itself in the text" (81).

104. For Joyce's political involvement see Gibson, *Joyce's Revenge*; McGee, *Joyce Beyond Marx*, esp. 153–91; Valente, "Joyce's Politics," 73–96, in Rabaté, *James Joyce Studies*; Cheng, *Joyce, Race, and Empire*; Manganiello, *Joyce's Politics*; Nolan, *Joyce and Nationalism* and Groden, "Writing *Ulysses*," in Latham, *Cambridge Companion to "Ulysses,"* 14, for Joyce as less sublimely indifferent to World War I than Gorman implies in his biography. For the role of the war in *Ulysses* see Gaipa, Latham, and Scholes, *Little Review*, 397–99; Rise, "*Ulysses* in Tempore Belli," in Armand, *joyceMedia*, 144–51. See also Pogorzelski, *Virgil and Joyce*, 22: "Ultimately, *Ulysses* refuses to valorize an idealized and unified Irish culture as a basis for building an anti-colonial nation-state"; and see 25–26 for recent scholarship on the complexity of Joyce's relation to nationalism.

105. Budgen, *Making of "Ulysses,"* 32; and see Bowker, *James Joyce*, 219.

106. Winston, *Joyce and Militarism*, 23.

107. Spoo, *Language of History*, 89–112; and see Devlin and Reizbaum, *"Ulysses"—EnGendered Perspectives*, 20–29.

108. Parandowski, "Meeting with Joyce," in Potts, *Portraits of the Artist*, 158. Parandowski also reports Joyce saying that, like Dante, he rose daily at 5 a.m. to write. Consid-

ering Joyce's drinking habits, this seems unlikely. See also S. Joyce, *My Brother's Keeper*, 103, on Joyce's late rising.

109. A. Power, *Conversations with James Joyce*, 95; Bowker, *James Joyce*, 322. Joyce's letter to Harriet Weaver on *Finnegans Wake* is also worth noting: "this stands for the title but I do not wish to say it yet until the book has written more of itself" (*LI* 213; Conley, *Joyce's Mistakes*, 51).

110. Crispi, *Becoming the Blooms*, 4–5, points out that the bulk of *Ulysses* was written between 1917 and 1921; and see Beach, *Shakespeare and Company*, 58, for Joyce himself saying that he wrote a third of *Ulysses* on proofs.

111. Tony Tanner's description of *Pride and Prejudice*: "during a decade in which Napoleon was effectively engaging, if not transforming, Europe, Jane Austen composed a novel in which the most important events are the fact that a man changes his manners and a young lady changes her mind" is relevant to *Ulysses* as well. See Tanner, introduction to *Pride and Prejudice*, by Jane Austen (London: Penguin, 2003).

112. Alan Clark, *The Donkeys* (London: Pimlico, 1996), 20; Fussell, *Great War*, 161: "The Great War was perhaps the last to be conceived as taking place within a seamless purposeful 'history' involving a coherent stream of time running from past through present to future." Fairhall, *Question of History*, 198, sees Joyce as "working in a period of wars and revolutions which pushed the Dublin of 1904 further and further into a naïve doomed past"; and see Rodstein, "Rule of the Waves," in Frehner and Zeller, *Collideorscape of Joyce*, 193, on "the way in which 1904 itself would seem to be on the other side of an enormous temporal divide after 1914."

113. Proust, *Remembrance of Things Past*, vol. 3, 748: "one of the ideas most in vogue was that the pre-war days were separated from the war by something as profound, something of apparently as long a duration, as a geological period."

114. However, see also Foster, *Modern Ireland 1600–1972*, 433 and 448, for the "galvanic effect of the Boer War" on Irish nationalism; and S. Joyce, *My Brother's Keeper*, 97, reporting that his father "like all Irish Nationalists, was loquaciously pro-Boer." Bloom also thinks of the Spanish-American War of April 23 to August 12, 1898, as "the war" (16.1128).

115. World War 1, at least immediately, called up far more references to the *Iliad* than the *Odyssey*, as Vandiver points out in *Stand in the Trench*, 228–80; G. Steiner, "Homer in English Translation," in Fowler, *Cambridge Companion to Homer*, 372.

116. Kiberd, review of *Irish Identity*, by Watson, in *Review of English Studies*, 97–99; R. Ellmann reports Joyce saying to Djuna Barnes "A writer should never write about the extraordinary. That is for the journalist" (*JJ* 457). See also Leonard, "Popular Culture," in Rabaté, *James Joyce Studies*, 39–51, esp. 47: "Such apparently trivial, ephemeral, and arbitrary moments are often presented in Joyce's fiction as fundamentally more authentic than 'historical events' not despite their insignificance but *because* they are insignificant"; Fairhall, *Question of History*, xii: "Joyce, in his fiction, attempted to subvert history, which he saw as both a chronicle of violence and oppression, and as a fixed past that had ousted other possible pasts and thus delimited the present."

117. See also Budgen, *Making of "Ulysses,"* 16–17; *JJ* 435–36; and R. Ellmann, "Backgrounds of *Ulysses,*" 342. For Homer see Pache, "University War Games," 15: "many of

[Odysseus's] words and deeds reflect a stance of ambivalence towards the war and his role in it. Just as his words and deeds are often incongruous, the very role Odysseus performs in the *Iliad* is an ambiguous one"; Schein's introduction, in Schein, *Reading the "Odyssey,"* 8: "By contrast, the central fact of life in the *Odyssey* is not mortality and the effort to transcend it by dying young in battle and achieving 'imperishable glory.' Rather, it is the need to survive in a postwar world, where options are more numerous and complex than in the *Iliad*." For sources in the epic cycle on Odysseus avoiding war, see Felson and Slatkin, "Gender and Homeric Epic," in Fowler, *Cambridge Companion to Homer*, 91–114. And to indulge in a digression: Joyce's remark also reveals how closely he identified the twenty-two-year-old Stephen with Telemachus, so that he missed the fact that any ordinary two-year old, when about to be run down by a plow, would run away. In the epic cycle, Telemachus is an infant when he is placed in the furrow.

118. In contrast see Kershner, *Culture of Joyce's "Ulysses,"* 96: "It is in part this historical slippage in *Ulysses* that gives us the impression of an Edwardian life-world being dragged rapidly, if reluctantly, into full-scale modernity."

119. See Pogorzelski, *Virgil and Joyce*, 3–17, particularly for the contrast between *Ulysses* and the *Aeneid* in this respect.

120. Butler, *Authoress of the Odyssey*, 130. See also Butler, *Humour of Homer*, which Joyce read, and the collection's editor, R. A. Streatfeild, on Butler's academic critics: "They did not so much resent the suggestion that the author of the *Odyssey* was a woman; they could not endure that he should be treated as a human being"; and quoting Butler: "If a person would understand either the *Odyssey* or any other ancient work, he must never look at the dead without seeing the living in them, nor at the living without thinking of the dead. We are too fond of thinking of the ancients as one thing and the moderns as another."

121. In this way Homer anticipates Booker's description of Joyce: "suggesting that epic heroes were never so grand as we might like to believe, that perhaps Ulysses, like Leopold Bloom, had his human flaws" and "call[ing] the authority of the epic into question, exposing the cracks and fissures in a genre that would seek to pass itself off as a seamless whole" (*Literary Tradition*, 18–19, 25).

Chapter 2. Stephen and Telemachus: The Case of the Displaced Son

1. Pierce, "Titles, Translation and Orientation," in Bosinelli and Torresi, *Joyce and/in Translation*, 25.

2. Butler, *Authoress of the "Odyssey,"* 122: "the writer makes Telemachus take no pains to hide the fact that his grievance is not so much the alleged ill-treatment of his mother, nor yet the death of his father, as the hole which the extravagance of the suitors is making in his own pocket."

3. In contrast, for a deliberately subversive view of Odysseus as bourgeois, see Redfield, "Economic Man," in Doherty, *Homer's "Odyssey,"* 265–87, as well as Dougherty, *Raft of Odysseus*, 38–60, for the economic side of the *Odyssey* altogether. As Kitto, "Exclusion of Surprise," in Bloom, *Homer's the "Odyssey,"* 9, points out, the assembly in *Odyssey* 2, which accomplishes nothing practically, underlines Telemachus's concern with the wasting of valuables.

4. See Versenyi, *Man's Measure*, 16, for *timē* as visible honor; Finley, *World of Odysseus*, 122–23.

5. While the concern with the weapons being spoiled is a ploy on Odysseus's part, Eurycleia, for one, readily agrees (19.21–23).

6. In this regard it is important that epithets apply to things as well as people: there are "well-greaved Achaeans," "well-walled cities," and "ruddy-cheeked ships," etc., just as there is "swift-footed Achilles" and "rosy-fingered Dawn." Bell, *Jocoserious Joyce*, 193, contrasts *Ulysses* to the *Odyssey*, "where the reiterated epithets suggest a persistent, apprehensible continuity beneath the flux of experience."

7. Stephen can also, however, see his dispossession as that of the prodigal son, as in "Circe": "Play with your eyes shut. Imitate pa. Filling my belly with husks of swine. Too much of this. I will arise and go to my" (15.2495–96).

8. Soul, which has the capacity of memory, is not only form, as the essence of the person, but also the "form of forms," as enabling us to grasp the essences of things.

9. French, *Book as World*, 67–68, points out that as a borrower, Stephen is another kind of usurper. As Osteen has shown in *Economy of "Ulysses,"* 2–29, the pairing of Stephen and Bloom reflects Joyce's own poles of profligacy/debt and husbandry/order—poles linked to the extremes of flux and fixity. See also S. Joyce, *Complete Dublin Diary*, 38: "Both Jim and Pappie seem to be a little proud of having spendthrift blood in them. This is a little ridiculous in Jim at present, as he has nothing to spend."

10. Although the movement from periods to commas, present from the *Little Review* version on, suggests a certain anxiety.

11. See Kenner, *Ulysses*, 55–56 n; Sultan, *Eliot, Joyce and Company*, 274–75; Osteen, *Economy of "Ulysses,"* 39–44.

12. The Caliban remark appears in Wilde's preface to *The Picture of Dorian Gray*, and the cracked looking glass in his *The Decay of Lying*, both quoted in Gifford and Seidman, *"Ulysses" Annotated*, 16, and discussed in Riquelme, *Teller and Tale*, 136–37.

13. P. W. Joyce, *English as We Speak It*, 187; Douglas Hyde, "My Grief on the Sea," quoted in Gifford and Seidman, *"Ulysses" Annotated*, 33, 62; Killeen, *"Ulysses" Unbound*, 90.

14. See also Brandes, *William Shakespeare*, 150–52: "preoccupied with the ideas of acquisition, property, money-making, wealth . . . [Shakespeare] longed for land and houses, meadows and gardens, money that yielded sound yearly interest, and, finally, a corresponding advancement in rank and position" (151).

15. Or, to shift to *The Winter's Tale* (4.3.25), Stephen's process of composition (like Joyce's) involves a good bit of snatching up of unconsidered trifles. (See the 1998 edition by Barnet.)

16. Similarly, "From force of habit he had written at the top of the first page the initial letters of the jesuit motto: A.M.D.G." (*P* 70)—an even more insidious influence, as now unconscious.

17. Letter to Louise Colet, December 9, 1852; Bush, "Joyce's Modernisms," in Rabaté, *James Joyce Studies*, 17. As Joyce wrote Larbaud, since the reader "will know early in the book that S.D.'s mind is full like everyone else's of borrowed words," the fewer quotation marks the better (*LI* 263). For Stephen's borrowings see Deane's introduction, in *Portrait*,

xxi; Bell, *Jocoserious Joyce*, 25: "To call Stephen 'derivative' would be too kind; almost nothing he says or thinks all day long is original, which may be why he is always 'feeling one behind'" (9.1197).

18. For Joyce's own borrowings see Kershner, "Intertextuality," in Latham, *Cambridge Companion to "Ulysses*," 174: "the longer scholars study Joyce's writing, the more passages that were thought to have originated with Joyce turn out to be adapted quotations"; and Thrane, "Joyce's Sermon on Hell," in Gillespie, *Foundational Essays*, 104, on *Portrait*: "the fact remains that much of the famous sermon on hell (recently elevated to textbook rank) was cribbed." Joyce also recycled his own clever phrases, for example, "those big words which make us so unhappy" (*OCPW* 62; *U* 2.264), the "horrible example of free thought" (*LI* 218; *U* 1.625–26), or the Hamlet theory, as Brown, "Joyce's 'Single Act' Shakespeare," in Pelaschiar, *Joyce/Shakespeare*, 123–26.

19. Like Odysseus, who exists both in the world of the *Iliad* and, simultaneously, in the later world of the *Odyssey*, as Brandon Jones points out to me.

20. For Stephen as author see also *U* 14.1110–22, 17.642–56, and 17.800 ff., where Stephen's ballad is written out in Joyce's hand. For Stephen as future author see Brivic, *Joyce the Creator*, 69; Culleton, *Names and Naming*, 98–99; Nelson, "Bullockbefriending Bards," 37–51. See chap. 1 for *Ulysses* as a continuation of *Portrait* and Hoffmeister, "Portrait of Joyce," in Potts, *Portraits of the Artist*, 129, quoting Joyce: "My work is a whole and cannot be divided by book titles"; R. Ellmann, *Ulysses on the Liffey*, 6, on Joyce using leftover *Portrait* material in *Ulysses*; Litz, "Early Vestiges," in Gillespie, *Foundational Essays*, 160: "There is a sense in which one can say James Joyce wrote only one book." Gaipa, Latham, and Scholes, *Little Review*, 350, also point out that "Nestor" was composed while Joyce was also working on *Portrait*.

21. "See this. Remember" is added to the manuscript. For Joyce's own conversation in the National Library see *JJ* 118. Levin, *James Joyce*, 53, points to *Portrait*'s "he'll remember all this when he grows up" (*P* 33) as well as the parallel of Shakespeare (in Stephen's theory) using his life as material for his art (117).

22. In 1904 Joyce signed a letter as "Stephen Daedalus" (*LI* 54) and published *The Sisters* under that name (*JJ* 164).

23. See Meisel, *Myth of the Modern*, 139, on Modernism as "largely a defensive response to the increasingly intolerable burdens of coming late in a tradition." See also Nash, *Act of Reception*, esp. 171, on "this time-honored disguise and this borrowed language"; Joyce in Zweig, *World of Yesterday*, 298: "I'd like a language which is above all languages, a language to which all will do service. I cannot express myself in English without enclosing myself in a tradition."

24. See Flack, *Modernism and Homer*, 34–43, on the question of "what's left for me to do?"; Conley, *Useless Joyce*, 46: "the finitude of expression, bearing down upon every user of words, makes plagiarism inevitable and individual expression perhaps impossible."

25. See Meisel, *Myth of the Modern*, 139.

26. Slote, *Joyce's Nietzschean Ethics*, 32, and 43–47, 52–61, describes Stephen as paralleling Satan's desire to be his own creator and so take the place of God. Lack of repentance, perhaps ironically, brings in Claudius as well (*Hamlet* 3.3.64–72, 97–98).

27. See also Budgen, *Making of "Ulysses*," 107.

28. Joyce's indebtedness thus becomes "intertextuality," as Baron, *Strandentwining Cable*, 105–6, on Stephen's quotation/plagiarism as constituting "a recognition that the voices of the dead permeate all creative endeavors" (106).

29. See R. Ellmann's introduction in S. Joyce, *My Brother's Keeper*, xv: "Inspired cribbing was always part of James' talent; his gift was for transforming material, not for originating it . . . As he remarked in later life to Frank Budgen, 'Have you ever noticed, when you get an idea, how much *I* can make of it?'" and Lawrence, *Odyssey of Style*, 145, on "Oxen of the Sun": "Eliot also said that bad poets borrow and good poets steal—Joyce was an expert thief who could create something new out of old materials. To borrow a phrase from *Finnegans Wake*, 'Oxen of the Sun' is 'the last word in stolentelling,' a chapter fashioned out of the signature styles of other writers."

30. For their temperamental similarities see de Fénelon's *Adventures of Telemachus* (which Joyce knew; see Kershner, *Culture of Joyce's "Ulysses,"* 45): "His mother Penelope, in spite of Mentor, had cherished in him a haughtiness and pride that tarnished all his good qualities. He looked upon himself as of a superior nature to the rest of mankind, who seemed to him to have been sent into the world by the gods for no other purpose but to minister to his pleasure; to serve him, to prevent [i.e., provide for] all his wishes, and to regard him as a sort of divinity" and "Whoever had observed this temper and behavior of his would have thought that he was incapable of loving any besides himself" (Bk. 13, p. 214).

31. See Felson, *Regarding Penelope*, 67–92; D. Steiner, *Odyssey Books XVII–XVIII*, 28–30, notes glances "towards the 'Oedipal' path not taken (see 1.215–20, 350–55, 21.125–89)." Rabaté, *Politics of Egoism*, 134–37, points out that Stephen, like the younger Joyce and unlike Mulligan, is whiskerless.

32. See Rutherford, "*Iliad* to the *Odyssey*," in Cairns, *Oxford Readings*, 141: Penelope's "submission forms part of the subtle presentation of tension and unease between mother and son which is sustained throughout the Ithacan books"; Wilson, *Odyssey*, 49–52.

33. After Telemachus's earlier refusal to discuss his journey (17.57), some needling ("you could not endure to tell me, / before the proud suitors arrive at our home, / of your father's homecoming" 17.104–6) finally brings it out. Stanford, *Homer*, vol. 1, 284, comments: "The tone, as Merry observes, may be one of lonely resignation or pettish annoyance, the former being more like a traditional heroine, the latter more human. In any case she extorts what she wants, a statement from Telemachus. The strained relations between a just grown-up son and an anxious mother are well depicted."

34. Hector and Priam are a notable exception, but Hector is also unique in many ways, not least in his focus on family. See D. Miller, *Epic Hero*, 68–92, 280–81, 316–17, on the inherent tension between heroic father and son; Scully, *Sacred City*, 62–63; and Redfield, *Nature and Culture*, 110–13, on Priam and Hector.

35. This was Joyce's response to his question, posed about his photo of the statue pictured on the cover here: what was Penelope thinking about? Joyce's answer was that she was trying to remember what Odysseus looked like since they had no photographs. In contrast see *Ulysses*'s interest in photographs, as Bloom's of Molly (16.1425–44; 18.1004–6) or Milly's new occupation (1.684–85; 4.400–404, etc.). See also Brann, *Homeric Mo-*

ments 163, on Helen saying not that Telemachus looks like Odysseus, but that he looks like Odysseus's son, i.e., like himself.

36. For the parallel, see Reece, "Cretan Odyssey," 157–73; Fenik, *Studies in the "Odyssey,"* 5–70; and Minerva's first words in Fénelon, *Adventures of Telemachus*, 6: "Are these, then O Telemachus! the thoughts which ought to possess the heart of the son of Ulysses? Rather revolve [resolve] the means of supporting your father's reputation." For a similar view of Stephen see Baron, "Beginnings," in Latham, *Cambridge Companion to "Ulysses,"* 55, and Kenner, *Joyce's Voices*, 59–60: *Ulysses* "begins with a second-hand character wearing second-hand clothes in a second-hand epic which begins like a second *Portrait*."

37. Deane's introduction in Joyce, *Portrait*, xxi, points as well to Simon Dedalus's response to "'Then he's not his father's son,'" "'I don't know, I'm sure, said Mr Dedalus smiling complacently'"; and see Crispi, *Becoming the Blooms*, 236, on the original version of "Cyclops": "Bit of a sharper that fellow son of Si Dedalus, He was in Paris in the quartier latin and he came back an atheist. He'll never be as good a man as his father anyhow" (*James Joyce Archive* 13:134d).

38. Agamemnon, in his talk with Odysseus in the Underworld, also compares Orestes and Telemachus (11.447–53), although neither knows how close the parallel is.

39. In his 1927 lecture Italo Svevo etymologizes as "far from the struggle" (see Svevo, *James Joyce*, n.p.). See also Schork, *Greek and Hellenistic Culture*, 87; S. West, "Commentary Books I–IV, in Heubeck, West, and Hainsworth, *A Commentary*, vol. 1, 51, 91–92. Pisistratus's name, "Persuading the host," thus reflects Nestor's rhetorical skill.

40. Butler, *Authoress of the "Odyssey,"* 122: "what [Telemachus] really wants is evidence of [Odysseus's] death, not of his being alive, though this may only be because he despairs of the second alternative." For the importance of age-mates, see also Telemachus's fellow sailors, at 3.364; Athena likening herself to Nausicaa's companion at 6.23; and Odysseus's speech to "Mentor" at 22.209.

41. Significantly, the *Odyssey's* greatest use of patronymics (as of similes) is in Bk. 22, in the temporary return to the heroic that marks the battle with the suitors (as appears in lines 22.212, 241, 242, 287, etc.; see also 23.117–22).

42. See Brivic, *Joyce the Creator*, 116, on the male spiritual and female material principles; Theoharis, *Anatomy of the Soul*, 12; Kenner, *Dublin's Joyce*, 138–41, and also 246. See Bowker, *James Joyce*, 79, for Joyce, "steeled in the school of old Aquinas," as also attracted to theosophy, and 378, for Connolly on Joyce as temperamentally "a medievalist in revolt."

43. From *brotos* (liable to death), cognate with Latin *mors*, *mortis* (mortal). As Apollo says to Poseidon, ephemeral creatures that live by grain are hardly worth fighting over (*Iliad* 21.461–67). See Watkins, *How to Kill a Dragon*, 391–97, on "nectar" as similarly "that which overcomes death."

44. Here in contrast to Bloom's healthy interest in food, apparent from his introductory "ate with relish" (4.1) onward. Stephen's claim not to have eaten all day (16.1572–77) ignores what seems to have been a substantial breakfast (1.349–74). See Conley, *Useless Joyce*, 127–32, for what Stephen eats and for his refusal to eat as rebellion, like Telemachus's refusal to dine with the suitors. Joyce, as Beach describes him (*Shakespeare and Company*, 98), fussed over food for others, but had little interest in it himself.

45. See J. Johnson, "'Beyond the Veil,'" in van Boheemen, *Joyce, Modernity, and Its Mediation,* 212; Hill, "'Amor Matris,'" 329–43. Slote, *Joyce's Nietzschean Ethics,* 151, quotes Margot Norris as well on the link between *mère* (mother) and *mer* (sea).

46. See van Boheemen-Saaf, "Postcolonial Masculinity and Gender Trauma," in Boheemen-Saaf and Lamos, 234–36, on both "Mother Ireland" and Stephen's mother as the "green crab" of 15.4220, along with the connections of mother tongue and mother church to mother Ireland.

47. The reference to Clongowes also recalls the "cold and slimy" water of the school's cesspool, leading to the dream/vision blending waves, Brother Michael, the death of Parnell, and "Dante" (*P* 27).

48. With a bow as well to *Hamlet* 4.3.18–31; 5.1.205–18 (see the 1998 edition by Barnet). For Stephen's fear of water/drowning/absorption and the maternal, as well as the link to a transformation of identity through baptism, see, among others, Leonard, "Transubstantiation of Masculinity," in Devlin and Reizbaum, *"Ulysses"—En-Gendered Perspectives,* 1: "Stephen's well-noted hydrophobia is both a fear of personal annihilation and a suspicion that the very psychological 'barriers' which permit interiority, in fact offer no permanent or absolute protection from the exterior world they appear to exclude"; Kenner, *Dublin's Joyce,* 211–13; and for Joyce's metaphor of "drowning" in debt, Osteen, *Economy of "Ulysses,"* 168–73.

49. In "Wandering Rocks" they are on opposite sides of the river and in contiguous episodes.

50. Haines mistakes the "he himself" for Stephen rather than Hamlet, which Mulligan happily picks up on. *Japhet in Search of a Father* (a novel by Capt. Frederick Marryat) also brings in the biblical Japhet's brother, Ham, cursed with servitude for showing his father's nakedness (Genesis 8.18–28; *U* 15.1901, 3867).

51. See Osteen, *Economy of "Ulysses,"* 211, for Stephen "replicating his consubstantial father" as both depart the newspaper office for drinks, separately, but in sequence.

52. As in Stephen on "Elsinore's tempting flood" (3.278), it is a temptation. His back-and-forth performance with Mulligan (1.364 ff.) shows that he is good at the game, and knows it. As he (alone) appreciates his witticism on Kingstown pier as "a disappointed bridge" he thinks "For Haines's chapbook" and then, characteristically, despises himself for the thought: "A jester at the court of his master, indulged and disesteemed" (2.39–47).

53. R. Ellmann, "Joyce and Homer," sees Joyce adopting Bacon's view of the Homeric scene as illustrating the rocks of distinctions and the whirlpool of universals.

54. Weir, *"Ulysses" Explained,* 74, points out that Bloom replaces walking "the night" with walking "the earth," recalling Deasy's wandering Jew (2.362). For the "Circe" scene see chap. 6.

55. Kenner, *Dublin's Joyce,* 194.

56. Both of Joyce's early essays on the Irish poet, James Clarence Mangan, cite Mangan referring to his father as a boa constrictor (*OCPW* 55, 131). The second time, and while he was turning *Stephen Hero* into *Portrait,* Joyce goes Mangan one better and turns the boa constrictor into a rattlesnake.

57. Dilly is short for Delia (17.146), recalling Cordelia, another child made "food of

thy abused father's wrath," as Gloucester says of his son Edgar (*King Lear* 4.1.22; and see 9.314).

58. Cixous, *Exile of James Joyce*, 701; Mahaffey, *States of Desire*, 28, on the Shakespeare theory as implying "that we *create* or father the ghostly selves that haunt us. If *we* construct the self through the act of self-representation and its corollary, exclusion and repression, we can truly say that the child is himself his own father (*and* mother)"; Meisel, *Myth of the Modern*, 149: "Like Shakespeare, Joyce becomes his own father as a function of, rather than despite, the belatedness that otherwise makes him a disciple"; and Slote, "Loving the Alien," in Pelaschiar, *Joyce/Shakespeare*, 134–37.

59. The warnings of both Agamemnon (11.441–56) and Athena (13.333–37) prepare us for Odysseus's insistence that Penelope not be told (16.300–304).

60. In contrast Felson, *Regarding Penelope*, 91, sees this as a way to "catalyze his further development."

61. Telemachus's failure in the Assembly is underlined by the parallel to Achilles (*Iliad* 1.113), whose oath, essentially, kicks off a holocaust.

62. Budgen, *Making of "Ulysses,"* 262, describes Telemachus here as "a sickeningly sadistic young prig."

63. See Felson, *Regarding Penelope*, 89–91, for Telemachus's restraint as a sign of his maturity and connection with his father.

64. See M. Ellmann, "Ghosts of *Ulysses*," in Attridge, *James Joyce's "Ulysses,"* 83–102.

65. That is, the "love of the mother" both by the child and for the child.

66. He is significantly called a "hero" three times in Bk. 4 (4.21, 303, 321), as shown by Tracy, *Story of the "Odyssey,"* 63.

67. In contrast to *Stephen Hero* as well as *Portrait,* as discussed in Gordon, *Joyce and Reality,* 44. See Ames, "Rebirth of Heroism," in Jones and Beja, *Twenty-First Joyce,* 157–78; Aubert, "Prudent Grammartist," in Frehner and Zeller, *Collideorscape of Joyce,* 83–90.

68. Stephen's walk along the shore also recalls Telemachus's at *Odyssey* 2.260–66, which calls forth Athena, while his isolation is also suggested, more comically, by his pier as a "disappointed bridge" (2.39). What Hart, *James Joyce's "Ulysses,"* 12, says of Joyce is even more true of Stephen: "Being aware of the invalidity of any community of belief, he was equally aware of man's inevitable loneliness."

69. An allusion also made by Eliot in "Little Gidding," lines 78–149.

70. In the Gilbert schema the "technics" of the first three episodes: Narrative (young), Catechism (personal), and Monologue (male) parallel the last three: Narrative (old), Catechism (impersonal), and Monologue (female).

71. An isolation predicted in *Portrait,* 247, and see Kain, *Fabulous Voyager,* 72: "*Ulysses* is one of the loneliest of books"; Bersani, "Against *Ulysses*," in Attridge, *James Joyce's "Ulysses,"* 227: "The anxiety which *Ulysses* massively, encyclopedically struggles to transcend—however we choose to understand its origins—is that of disconnectedness."

72. In good "Ithacan" fashion, this comes down to "Stephen disliked water because of its wateriness." See S. Joyce, *Complete Dublin Diary,* 23, on Joyce adopting the word from a classmate who "applied it to obvious statements and to platitudes"; Mahaffey, "Sidereal Writing," in Devlin and Reizbaum, *"Ulysses"—En-Gendered Perspectives,"* 260: "Stephen's hatred of water, glass, and women is an extension—perhaps a projection—of

his fear of being fractured: he fears not only the fragility of glass and the power of water to overwhelm and inundate, but also the division (and multiplication) of the self through mirrored reflections."

73. Senn, *Joycean Murmoirs*, 164; R. Ellmann, *Ulysses on the Liffey*, xiv; *JJ* 155–56. According to Ellmann's account, Nora assumed this was the significance of June 16. Joyce's letters to Nora describe himself as "a strange lonely boy, walking about by myself at night and thinking that someday a girl would love me" (*SL* 161) when Nora "took me so easily into her arms and made me a man" (*SL* 159); and see *SL* 165 (with Joyce speaking of himself in the third person): "It is you who have opened a deep chasm in his life." See Theoharis, *Anatomy of the Soul*, 104–7, and Reynolds, *Joyce and Dante*, 183, 190, for a comparison to Dante and Beatrice. Weir, *"Ulysses" Explained*, 92, sees Molly's given name, Marion, as an anagram for "I'm Nora," which seems a bit much, although Joyce would have appreciated the wordplay.

74. See Bloom's misinterpretation of Stephen's muttered "Fergus' Song": "Ferguson, I think I caught. A girl. Some girl. Best thing could happen him" (15.4949 ff.) and Gordon, *Joyce and Reality*, 230–36, on Stephen leaving home to seek "Miss Fortune" (16.252–53). For Joyce distancing Stephen see Kenner, "The *Portrait* in Perspective," 361–81; Latham, "Portrait of the Snob," 774–99.

75. William Blake, *The Marriage of Heaven and Hell*, ed. Geoffrey Keynes (Oxford: Oxford Paperbacks, 1975), 6.

76. Adams, *Surface and Symbol*, 71, points out the connection in regard to Bloom.

77. See Groden, "Genetic Joyce," in Rabaté, *James Joyce Studies*, 228, 230.

78. Kitcher, *Joyce's Kaleidoscope*, xix–xxi. The stress in *Portrait* thus falls (as Joyce complained it too seldom did) on the *young* man (Budgen, *Making of "Ulysses,"* 61). Beach, *Shakespeare and Company*, 43, describes Joyce as more interested in Bloom than Stephen "who had come between them. After all, there was a good deal of Bloom in Joyce"; see also *JJ* 373–74 for Joyce transforming his experience into Bloom's.

79. J. M. Fraser, *Rite of Passage*, 2: "Joyce seems to battle against an anxiety of origin rather than an anxiety of influence; rather than expressing distress about powerful literary ancestors, Joyce strives to create out of the void an intertextual self that integrates and celebrates influence." And see Osteen, *Economy of "Ulysses,"* 209, on Taylor's speech as embodying "the condition of history as verbal debtorship" and reflecting *Ulysses*, itself, "a revision of an epic borrowed from a group of folktales and collected by 'Homer,' who placed some of the tales in the mouth of Odysseus, within a larger frame tale told by a third-person narrator."

Chapter 3. Odysseus and Bloom: Names and Stories

1. Dimock, "Name of Odysseus," in Taylor, *Essays on the "Odyssey,"* 54–72.

2. For the *Odyssey* see Christensen, *Many-Minded Man*, 6, 23–53, and for *Ulysses*, Spoo, *Language of History*, 162, on the impossibility of escape or transcendence through language "because language is where the enthrallment to history begins."

3. Forster, *Aspects of the Novel*, 86. See also Kermode, *Sense of an Ending*, 164, on the human need to connect beginning and end: "We give ourselves meaning by inventing critical time."

4. *Iliad* 9.413 and see 2.325 etc., for "*kleos* which never perishes"; Nagy, *Best of the Achaeans*, 174–210.

5. Senn, *Inductive Scrutinies*, 10–14.

6. See *Gulliver's Travels*, Bk. 3, chap. 5, where the Laputans try to abolish words on the grounds "that since words are only names for things, it would be more convenient for all men to carry about them such things as were necessary to express a particular business they are to discourse on." Sadly, the attempt is thwarted by their wives.

7. Joyce's birth certificate in fact registered him as "James Augustine" (*JJ* 21) rather than "Augustus," an inadvertence that "Leopold Paula Bloom" (17.1855) inherits; see Gabler, "Early Joycean Progressions," in Ebury and Fraser, *Joyce's Non-Fiction Writings*, 55–56.

8. As Alcinous comments to the stranger: "No one among people is without a name altogether, / whether a poor man or a noble, when once he is born / but parents put one upon all when they engender them" (*Odyssey* 8.552–54).

9. See Freud, *Totem and Taboo*, translated by James Strachey (New York: W. W. Norton, 1990), 139, on early societies where "A man's name is a principal component of his personality, perhaps even a portion of his soul"; and in the Greek context, Redfield, *Nature and Culture*, 178: "A proper name is the concept of a particular person."

10. Nagy, *Best of the Achaeans*, 297–300. See also Giedion-Welcker, "Meetings with Joyce," in Potts, *Portraits of the Artist*, 268–69, for Joyce on "nomen est omen" (the name is the omen) and *JJ* 490 for his interest in the similar meanings of "Joyce" and "Freud."

11. See de Jong, *Narratological Commentary*, 203, for Odysseus's many *polu-* epithets; Saïd, *Homer and the "Odyssey,"* 46–74; A. Parry, *Language of Achilles*, 70, for formulae as unifying, 301–26, for fixed epithets, and 309–10 for *polutropos* in particular.

12. See Christensen, *Many-Minded Man*, 126, 144, on the various names.

13. For a survey of the recognition scenes, detailing their common elements, see Emlyn-Jones, "Reunion of Odysseus," 6–7.

14. See de Jong, *Narratological Commentary*, 6–7, 127, for the motif of suppressing Odysseus's name and for "*andra*" opening a line as a reference to Odysseus; for the delayed naming of Odysseus see Higbie, *Heroes' Names, Homeric Identities*, 170–75. As Tracy, *Story of the "Odyssey,"* 10, points out, Telemachus first names his father in saying that he was not the only one to lose his homecoming (1.354) and this after "Mentes"'s declaration that his race will not be "nameless" (1.222).

15. See Clay, "Odysseus: Name and Helmet," in Bloom, *Homer's "The Odyssey,"* 103-12; Austin, "Name Magic in the *Odyssey,*" in Doherty, *Homer's "Odyssey,"* 91–110. For Joyce taking "Odysseus" as a combination of *outis* and Zeus see Flack, *James Joyce*, 121.

16. Van Nortwick, *Unknown Odysseus*, vii, 118–19, and see de Jong, *Narratological Commentary*, 72, for Telemachus's reluctance to give his name to Nestor or Menelaus.

17. "Zeus-sprung" (*diogenes*), used of numerous heroes in the *Iliad*, is used in the *Odyssey* only of Odysseus (15 times altogether: 5.203; 10.401, 456, 488; 11.60, 92; 14.486; 16.167; 22.164; 24.542). As with *dion genos* (of divine stock), for Hesiod's distinctly not divine brother (*Works and Days* 299), it is not literal, and if anything, contrasts Odysseus's to a heroic descent like that of *dios Achilleus* (*Iliad* 1.7).

18. Even the narrator moves from the opening "man" to "godlike Odysseus" (1.21).

Athena as Mentor (22.226), and Leodes and Phemius, when they are supplicating Odysseus (22.312 = 344), also call him by his unadorned name.

19. Stephen's mention of "Murphy" also calls forth D. B. Murphy's version of "Simon Dedalus," in a reciprocal sort of arrangement.

20. "John Eglinton" was the pseudonym of William Magee (Gifford and Seidman, *"Ulysses" Annotated,* 194) as "AE" was for George Russell. Joyce had already come up with "Mr Goodbetterbest" in a letter to Stanislaus in 1905 (*LII* 110). Killeen, *Ulysses Unbound,* 85, notes that the Italian dancing master Maginni transformed himself from a plain Dublin Maginnis (or Maginn, as reported in Igoe, *Real People,* 197). See Culleton, *Names and Naming,* 95–103, on Stephen using naming as a means of revenge in the Library scene. And see also S. Joyce, *Complete Dublin Diary,* 12–14, and *My Brother's Keeper,* 154, on Gogarty and his father's satirical renamings.

21. Or even the "lapwing," Perdix (*Metamorphoses* 8.236–59), who, thrown from a cliff by Daedalus for being too inventive, never flies at all, "remembering that ancient fall and fearing heights" (8.259). See Spoo, *Language of History,* 168, for the Dedalus name as a prophecy and Levin, *James Joyce,* 61, for the labyrinth implications. Sultan, *Eliot, Joyce and Company,* 62, points to the lapwing in Blake that flies on the heath and cannot see the nets beneath.

22. See also his concern with names such as "Athy" (*P* 25) or "Dolan" (*P* 55). Bloom, who reflects that there are "more languages to start with than were absolutely necessary" (16.352–53), has a more straightforward approach.

23. See Raleigh, *Leopold and Molly Bloom,* 1–4, 13, 16, on Karoly/Higgins and the confusion surrounding Hungarian names.

24. Of the many possibilities, I prefer I AM A stick in the mud (Bloom having just thrown a stick that stuck), as in Molly's "O Poldy, Poldy, you are a poor old stick in the mud!" (15.329–30). See, however, Knowles, *Dublin Helix,* 9; Bell, *Jocoserious Joyce,* 43.

25. See Crispi, *Becoming the Blooms,* 37, for Joyce reinforcing "Mrs Marion" and Osteen, *Economy of "Ulysses,"* 81, for this as the proper inscription if Bloom were dead. Molly also goes, professionally (and with Bloom's support), by "Madam Marion Tweedy," as shown in 6.693; 16.798, 1437, 1745 (and, for other versions, 6.224; 11.496; 15.3767; 16.525).

26. Joyce resisted first names even with such close associates as "Budgen" or "Miss Beach," whom everyone else called Sylvia. See Culleton, *Names and Naming,* 5–7; Beach, *Shakespeare and Company,* 41; Budgen, *Making of "Ulysses,"* 344; Gilbert in *LI,* 28–29. See also the remark in *Stephen Hero* (hereafter cited as *SH*), 44, on a house where "it was the custom to call a young visitor by his Christian name a little too soon" and Joyce commenting that among his friends only Clancy (Davin in *Portrait*) ever called him by his Christian name (*LI* 357).

27. See Crispi, *Becoming the Blooms,* 30–34; Norris, "Boylan's Narrative Caricature," 229–49.

28. Also prepared by the "Bloom" of Circe's play format.

29. See A. Parry, *Language of Achilles,* 310–25, and chap. 1.

30. As noted in Budgen, *Making of "Ulysses,"* 118.

31. Although see the Arranger at 11.519; 12.1006; 14.1041–77; 15.3444 as well as the

Kisses in "Circe": "Leopopold! *(twittering)* Leeolee! *(warbling)* O Leo!" (15.1274). For the importance to Odysseus of being recognized by his father see chap. 4.

32. Interestingly, the question of truth arises most often in a meta context, as in Alcinous's distinction between liars and poets (11.363–69) or Stephen arguing about Shakespeare in the Library (9.671 ff.). Odyssean narrators generally point to the truth of their stories when they are lying (de Jong, *Narratological Commentary*, 27). Similarly, Joyce tempts us to see *Ulysses* as his retelling his own story to himself, leading Joyceans to some compulsive fact-checking.

33. Segal, "*Kleos* and Its Ironies in the *Odyssey*," in Schein, *Reading the "Odyssey*," 213–18, on the Sirens and Demodocus, showing: "heroic adventure as something frozen and crystallized into lifeless, static form, something dead and past, a subject for song and nothing more" (214).

34. Ames, *Convergence*, 131 ff.; Senn, *Inductive Scrutinies*, 121: "By this negation, the *Odyssey* acknowledges its own narrative principle, the parallactic doubling already referred to."

35. Ezra Pound, *Make It New* (London: Faber, 1934) and see Sherry, *Great War*, 84.

36. See de Jong, *Narratological Commentary*, 38, for the "newest song" as metanarrative. Scodel, *Listening to Homer*, 82, argues that Odysseus's fictions in Bk. 14 "reveal how the poet works when his freedom to invent is greatest and when he is least likely to rely on an audience's familiarity with the stories."

37. On the Greek epic cycle see M. L. West, *Epic Cycle*, and, for a source consulted by Joyce, Butler, *Authoress of the "Odyssey*," 249. See also Stanford, *Ulysses Theme*, overall, for Odysseus's extensive *nachleben*.

38. See Biles, "Perils of Song," 191–208; M. Ellmann, "Ghosts of *Ulysses*," in Attridge, *James Joyce's "Ulysses*," 85, for Odysseus hearing his story "from the mouths of strangers, thus learning that his legend had already usurped his life and reduced him to the phantom of his name" or Tennyson's "Ulysses": "I am become a name."

39. See Walcott, "Art of Lying" in Doherty, *Homer's "Odyssey*," 135–54; Christensen, *Many-Minded Man*, 120–23.

40. Morrison, "Shipwreck Narratives," 239: "it is difficult not to notice the echoes of Odysseus's own life in the tale he tells of the Cretan wanderer"; Christensen, *Many-Minded Man*, 118: "The lying tales, I suggest, offer a continuing although coded probing of the relationship between the self, internal motivation, external action, and an evaluation of consequences." De Jong, *Narratological Commentary*, 326–27, summarizes the mixture of fact and fiction, and see 596–97 for the tales' recurrent elements.

41. See Kenner, *Dublin's Joyce*, 190, on Rouse's translation of *Odyssey* 24.304–6: "I come from Wonderland . . . and I am the son of my lord Neverstint Griefanpain; my name is Battledown."

42. This is the Odysseus Tennyson saw, for whom experience was "an arch wherethro' / Gleams that untravell'd world whose margin fades / Forever and forever when I move" ("Ulysses"). For *psuche* as "identity" see chap. 6.

43. Achilles's singing the *klea andron* (famous deeds of men) at *Iliad* 9.185–90 is itself a sign that he is beginning to move beyond the heroic code, for which see Beck, "Odysseus: Narrator, Storyteller, Poet?" 213–27.

44. The poet vouches for the cattle of Helios (1.8), the Cyclops (2.19; 1.68–75), and Circe (8.448) as well as Calypso. See H. Parry, "*Apologus* of Odysseus," 1–20.

45. Similarly, Kenner, *Dublin's Joyce*, 44: "It is a worthwhile guess that the writing-out of *Stephen Hero* was the cathartic labour of [Joyce's] life" and Riquelme, *Teller and Tale*, 105, on first-person narration as the encounter of the teller with himself.

46. Slatkin, *Power of Thetis*, 139–49, and in Schein, *Reading the "Odyssey,"* 223–24; W. S. Anderson, "Calypso and Elysium," in Taylor, *Essays on the "Odyssey,"* 81–85; and see Otto, *Homeric Gods*, 140–48, for the dead as utterly separate from both the living and the gods.

47. See Haubold, "Homer after Parry," in Graziosi and Greenwood, *Homer in the Twentieth Century*, 30–31, for oral poetry as entirely located in the present and Nagy, *Poetry as Performance*, 1, for performance and composition "as two aspects of one process in oral poetics."

48. Taplin, *Homeric Soundings*, 30–31. Taplin also suggests that Homer's songs went through the night like Odysseus's in Phaeacia, so that "tomorrow" in narrative time and "tomorrow" in performance time were the same (26). How often the poem was performed as a whole rather than in selections is impossible to know.

49. For Poseidon and Phaeacia see 6.267; 7.34–36, 56–62; 8.564–69; 9.412, 517–36; and 8.564–72 for his threat to punish their conveyance of travelers. Homer seeds this by connecting the Phaeacians and Cyclopes long before we hear the story of Polyphemus (6.4–6). In contrast, de Jong, *Narratological Commentary*, 171, sees no explanation for Odysseus's reticence in naming himself in Phaeacia.

50. See Tracy, *Story of the "Odyssey,"* 129, on how the singer might act out the simile.

51. Lamb's preface to his *Adventures of Ulysses* describes Odysseus as challenged by life's "twofold danger": "things which denote external force or inner temptations"; and see Gilbert, *James Joyce's "Ulysses,"* 43; Feeney, *Gods in Epic*, 378, with sources. G. de F. Lord, "*Odyssey* and the Western World," in Taylor, *Essays on the "Odyssey,"* 39, sees allegorical and realistic readings as the two main ways of viewing the poem.

52. Macleod, "Homer on Poetry," in Cairns, *Oxford Readings*, 305: "Odysseus can feel what he does because the passage of time allows him to look afresh at his own heroic achievements"; Christensen, *Many-Minded Man*, 98–131, on "Odysseus using his tale of travels in order to revise his own past among the Phaeacians, ultimately re-authoring his tale and creating a sense of identity that prepares him to act in the future" (22) and see Kennedy, *Antiquity*, 5, for the narrating self looking back on the narrated self.

53. Levin, *James Joyce*, 96: "As an advertising man he is a man of letters in a small way."

54. See *JJ* 362–63 for the disparity.

55. Gabriel in *The Dead*, may be an exception, for a moment at any rate. See Kitcher's introduction to *Joyce's "Ulysses,"* 20, and Goldberg, "Artist's Fingernails," in Gillespie, *Foundational Essays*, 133, on Bloom's "utter lack of either self-importance or self-pity [which] is subtly played off against the attitudes of his companions and his society." See also Senn, "Bloom among the Orators," 168–90, for Bloom, unusually, not having a characteristic spoken idiom.

56. See J. Maddox, "Mockery in *Ulysses*" in Reynolds, *James Joyce*, 141, on Bloom's "readiness to identify with his enemies and his mockers" and Berrone, *James Joyce in*

Padua, 23, for Joyce on the modern world as best "in creating in ourselves and in our art the sense of compassion for each thing that lives and hopes and dies and deludes itself. In this at least we surpass the ancients: in this the ordinary journalist is greater than the theologian."

57. Notably, Bloom rejects narrative in advertising in favor of instantaneous effect: "a poster novelty, with all extraneous accretions excluded, reduced to its simplest and most efficient terms not exceeding the span of casual vision and congruous with the velocity of modern life" (17.1771–73, 581–91; 8.130–42). See Alonso, "Advertising in *Ulysses*," in Brockman, Mecsnóber, and Alonso, *Publishing in Joyce's "Ulysses*," 107–29, for the appeal to emotion and the unconscious that this implies.

58. See also 8.661–63: "Bitten off more than he can chew. Am I like that? See ourselves as others see us. Hungry man is an angry man" and "People could put up with being bitten by a wolf but what properly riled them was a bite from a sheep" (16.1639), which amusingly reflects the Citizen's view of Bloom as "A wolf in sheep's clothing" (12.1666). See, however, 15.660 for Bloom's idea that Garryowen took a liking to him. No one is perfect.

59. Rutherford, *The Odyssey*, 63, makes a similar point about Odysseus and Calypso (7.261).

60. As Hamlet's "Seems, madam? Nay, it is. I know not 'seems'" rejects mere "actions that a man might play" (1.2.76–86). Similarly, Stephen, as he looks into his "symbol of Irish art" (1.146), thinks, with dislike, "as he and others see me" (1.136).

61. Gilbert, *James Joyce's "Ulysses*," 206: "The comedy is played to himself, not for the benefit of possible onlookers."

62. Spoo, *Language of History*, 75–78.

63. "One morning you would open the paper, the cabman affirmed, and read: *Return of Parnell*," is preceded by Bloom's even more unexpected: "There was every indication they would arrive at that, he, Bloom, said" (16.1296–98). This is also, significantly, where "Mr Bloom" becomes "Bloom," as above.

64. Brann, *Homeric Moments*, 117: "It appears that Coming Home, Return, is not so simple as surviving the sea and retaking a palace; you may come home but not be there, you may return but not be you."

65. Parnell becomes increasingly gracious as Bloom recalls the story, adding a "Sir" to his thanks the second time around (16.1336, 1523), as noted by Senn, *Joycean Murmoirs*, 3.

66. See Senn, "Active Silences," in Wawrzycka and Zanotti, *James Joyce's Silences*, 27, and Crispi, *Becoming the Blooms*, 174–75, for Joyce changing Molly's final "yes I would" to "yes I will." See chap. 2 for the application to Stephen's *non serviam*.

67. Bowen, *Bloom's Old Sweet Song*, 127. Even more creatively in "Circe" Bloom becomes Mrs Miriam Dandrade, about to be violated by "signor Laci Daremo, the robust tenor" (15.3002-3), while the motif also links Bloom to Shakespeare's "assumed dongiovanism" (9.458); and see Hodgart and Bauerle, *Joyce's Grand Operoar*, 3–23. In regard to creative retelling, Spoo's point (*Language of History*, 30), that Joyce always talked of Odysseus in terms of Bloom rather than the other way around, is worth noting.

68. Moreover, any moralistic reading is undercut by Hermes's remark that he would

sleep with Aphrodite with three times as many chains and all of Olympus watching (8.339–42).

69. Washington Irving, "*The Legend of Sleepy Hollow" and Other Stories from "The Sketch Book"* (New York: Signet Classics, 2006), 18.

70. Ben Bolt and Caoc O'Leary both return after twenty years, Bolt to find his beloved Alice dead and O'Leary to promptly die himself. Enoch Arden returns to find his wife married to another (Gifford and Seidman, *"Ulysses" Annotated*, 539–40). For the "man who disappeared" theme and the *Odyssey* see Carpenter, *Folk Tale*, 136–67; and for the Tichbourne case of *U* 16.1341–49, Knowles, *Dublin Helix*, 115–27.

71. See 16.1238–39 for a similar close call. In another case of the present influencing the past, Joyce added the Boland reference to the printer's typescript in 1921.

72. For the confusion over whether Bloom and Molly first met at Mat Dillon's in Roundtown playing musical chairs (11.725–28) or at Luke Doyle's in Dolphin's Barn playing charades see Crispi, *Becoming the Blooms*, 140–44, and for the circularity and musical chairs, 142–43: "almost all of Leopold and Molly's memories of their early courtship revolve around the theme of the repeating cycles of time in life" (145).

73. See A. Goldman, *Joyce Paradox*, 118–37, on the cyclical in *Ulysses* more generally.

74. De Jong, *Narratology and Classics*, 73, and see chap. 1. Thus, for example, Bk. 5 significantly opens with Dawn rising from the bed of Tithonus, an ill-omened conjunction of goddess and mortal.

75. Notice also how often Athena "casts sleep which is sweet" upon Penelope's eyelids, as 1.363–64; 16.449–51; 18.188–89; 19.603–5; 21.356–58 etc. Joyce's declaration that *Finnegans Wake* was a book about the night, paired with *Ulysses*, a book about the day, makes the importance of the day-night, wake-sleep cycle all the clearer (*JJ* 695; and see Potts, *Portraits of the Artist*, 149, 209).

76. As Penelope says, "it makes one forget all / both good and evil, when it has covered over the eyelids" (20.85–86). On the sleep motif see de Jong, *Narratological Commentary*, 148; Van Nortwick, *Unknown Odysseus*, 79; Brann, *Homeric Moments*, 173, on Odysseus's "opportunistic passivity" and Penelope as an "opportunistic sleeper."

77. Clive Hart, "Gaps and Cracks," 427–37; Kenner, *Ulysses*, 47–49, and see his "Rhetoric of Silence," 382–94, for the gap surrounding "at 4:00 she said." See also Mahaffey, "Intentional Error," in Attridge, *James Joyce's "Ulysses*," 247, on meaning in *Dubliners* occurring "between the acts"; Lawrence, *Odyssey of Style*, 126–27, and Bowen, *Comic Novel*, 29: "The basic absurdity of U lies in its representation of B's life from the time he gets up on June sixteenth to the time he goes to bed on the early morning of the seventeenth as a complete action."

78. *Tristram Shandy*, 4.13; see Fludernik, *Introduction to Narratology*, 33.

79. See A. Goldman, *Joyce Paradox*, 83, on Joyce making his chapters into self-contained units.

80. See chap. 1 and de Jong, *Narratology and Classics*, esp. 73–104; de Jong and Nünlist's epilogue to *Time in Ancient Greek Literature*, 505–22, for more on narrative time in Homer.

Chapter 4. Odysseus and Bloom: Ambiguity and Doing the Deed

1. Goldman, *Joyce Paradox*, 112, refers to Erik Erikson for Stephen's identity crisis and Bloom's middle-aged "integrity crisis."

2. Similarly, see Tracy, *Story of the "Odyssey,"* 30–31, for Odysseus's passivity in the second half of Book 5, including the extraordinary accumulation of five extended similes in the last 200 lines.

3. See Nooter, "Wooden Horse," in King and Doherty, *Thinking the Greeks*, 38–53, for the Trojan horse compared to both the revelation of the bed and Penelope's weaving. See also chap. 5 for the weaving story.

4. *U* 12.1556–66; 14.1131–33; 16.1242–44. See Andersen, "Odysseus and the Wooden Horse," 5–18; and for *Ulysses* on horses, Cheng, "White Horse, Dark Horse," 101–28, and in his *Joyce, Race, and Empire*, 251–77.

5. See Scott, *James Joyce*, 47–54, on Simon passing on his male discourse to Stephen.

6. See Seidel, *Epic Geography*, 141, on Pyrrhus losing by winning.

7. Cook, "'Active' and 'Passive' Heroics," in Doherty, *Homer's "Odyssey,"* 111–34, and see Saïd, *Homer and the "Odyssey,"* 313; Stanford, *Ulysses Theme*, 44–47.

8. Nagy, *Best of the Achaeans*, 42–58, and see Beye, *Epic Tradition*, 177–78 and 180, for Odysseus's opposition to Achilles; Silk, "*Odyssey* and Its Explorations," in Fowler, *Cambridge Companion to Homer*, 41, for Odysseus's guile as a female quality, although Odysseus "in the end proves himself, as he evidently must, by a man's physical prowess."

9. Klein, "Odysseus as 'New Womanly Man,'" 617–19, and see Kitcher, "Something Rich and Strange," in Kitcher, *Joyce's "Ulysses,"* 222–24, and Mahaffey, "End of Gender," in van Boheemen-Saaf and Lamos, *Masculinities in Joyce*, 145–47, for Bloom's unique ability to see a woman's perspective. D. Miller, *Epic Hero*, 93–94, points out, in regard to the Irish hero, Tristan, that "To have seductive and winning ways with women is not a typical or desirable heroic trait" (94).

10. Butler, *Humour of Homer*, 29, and also his *Authoress of the "Odyssey,"* 34: "My father will be sitting close by her; never mind about him, but go and embrace my mother's knees, for if she looks favorably on your suit you will probably get what you want." See also Doherty, "Gender and Internal Audiences," in Doherty, *Homer's "Odyssey,"* 247–64. Arete's importance appears as well in her name, which, with its long e, Arēte, means "prayed to/for" but resembles arête "virtue" or (particularly male) "excellence." See also Garvie, *Homer*, 12, on worries that Arete doesn't live up to the role; and in contrast Saïd, *Homer and the "Odyssey,"* 264–66.

11. Austin, "Power of the Word," in Bloom, *Homer's "The Odyssey,"* 78–85; de Jong, *Narratological Commentary*, 282.

12. See Stanford, *Ulysses Theme*, 10–13, for Odysseus's two sides, as heroic and as trickster; D. Miller, *Epic Hero*, esp. 242–60, for the usual opposition of the two.

13. See R. Ellmann, *Ulysses*, 308–13, *JJ* 463, on Otto Weininger's *Sex and Character*, viewing Jews as by nature womanly men, as well as Deasy on "the darkness in their eyes" (2.362).

14. Homer says that Circe's drug transformed the heads, voices, and shapes of Odysseus's men "but the mind (*noos*) was steady, as before" (10.338–40). Virgil translates almost directly, but does not include the last line (*Aeneid* 7.19–20).

15. See Senn, "Book of Many Turns," in Attridge, *James Joyce's "Ulysses,"* 33–54; Bell, *Jocoserious Joyce,* 11–20, 247.

16. See Stanford, *Ulysses Theme,* 10–11, on Autolycus; Finley, *World of Odysseus,* 69: "There was something equivocal about Odysseus as a hero precisely because of his most famed quality, his craftiness."

17. Similarly, while the fantastical first half of the *Odyssey* stems from the narrator, the romantic stories of the second half (other than Eumaeus's account of his childhood kidnapping) are the creations of Odysseus.

18. See Fairhall, *Question of History,* 252, for "Circe's" "various versions of Bloom, each of them no less "true" and no more fictional than the other."

19. See Eliade, *Sacred and the Profane,* 156–57, 180, on the moon as a symbol of change, particularly death and rebirth.

20. French, *Book as World,* 66; Attridge, "Molly's Flow," 560 for Henry "Flower" as one who flows; Flack, *James Joyce,* 67: "The movements of Bloom's mind reveal his genuine engagement with himself and the world in terms of dynamic potentiality. History is not a nightmare for Bloom because it is continually in flux and is open to his inner reshaping of it, moment by moment."

21. See Murnaghan, *Disguise and Recognition,* and, in contrast, P. V. Jones, "Past in Homer's *Odyssey,*" 78, for the more general tendency that "young heroes—Telemachus, Neoptolemus, Orestes—remain young, Odysseus, Achilles, and Diomedes remain in their prime, and Nestor stays old. It is easy to phrase an appropriately pithy canon: 'In myth, apart from genealogy and rites de passage, the age of any hero is deemed to remain constant.'"

22. See also Senn, "History as Text," in Wollaeger, Luftig, and Spoo, *Subject of History,* 55, for Bloom as Childe Leopold, Sir Leopold, Master Bloom, Calmer, and Pubb. Canv. etc.

23. As in Sophocles's *Ajax* and *Philoctetes* or Euripides's *Hecuba* or *Iphigeneia at Aulis.*

24. A quality that emerges in the *Odyssey.* Hector's relation to Andromache brings out the tension between a role as epic hero and a role as husband and father (*Iliad* 6.405–93), just as it brings out the contrast between Hector and the supreme epic hero, Achilles, as discussed in Redfield, *Nature and Culture,* 28, and passim.

25. Stanford, *Ulysses Theme,* 66–69, points out also that no Iliadic hero or heroine as much as mentions the "belly"; and on sleep in the *Odyssey,* see de Jong, *Narratological Commentary,* 147–48. As Achilles returns to the human realm, he, significantly, insists that Priam eat and then goes off to sleep with Briseis (24.600–620, 675–76).

26. They are paired again at 11.310–400. See Pache, "University War Games," 15: "Often alone, often aloof, Odysseus stands apart from his companions, and does not fully share in either their glory or their sufferings." In contrast, see Dante's treatment of Odysseus and Diomedes, paired in *Inferno* 26.55–63. For *Iliad* 10 as spurious see Hainsworth, *The Iliad: A Commentary,* vol. 3, 151–54.

27. The absence of names is brought out, for example, in the contrast between "I chose out twelve men" and the wine "which Maron, son of Euanthes, had given me, the priest of Apollo, the god that watched over Ismarus" (9.195–97). Virgil, in contrast, amply names

Aeneas's men, not only "faithful Achates." For the importance see Nelson, "Bullockbefriending Bards," 37–60.

28. Gibson, *Joyce's Revenge,* 56, quotes Joyce's comment to Mercanton: "Only a foreigner would do. The Jews were foreigners at that time in Dublin"; and see McCourt, *Years of Bloom,* 217–38, for Joyce and Jews in Trieste.

29. Budgen, *Making of "Ulysses,"* 280–82. In contrast, Bloom, "chapfallen" at John Henry Menton's rudeness (6.1027; 7.171–73), associated with Molly (6.1010–14), retaliates with his Parnell memory (16.1513–28).

30. As Joyce told Budgen, Jews are "better husbands than we are, better fathers and better sons" (*JJ* 373; 9.783–91).

31. Just as Aeneas, iconically, is positioned between Anchises and Ascanius, as shown by Charles Brian Rose, *The Archaeology of Greek and Roman Troy* (Cambridge: Cambridge University Press, 2014), 239–40.

32. And as Stephen says (neglecting the possibility of a daughter), "the father who has not a son [is] not a father" (9.864). See also Bradford, *Ulysses Found,* 175, on the tradition of Odysseus having only sons, including those by Circe and Calypso.

33. See Crispi, *Becoming the Blooms,* 198–99, 201–2, for Joyce putting Milly and Molly's cycles in rhythm (17.2284; 18.1104–7).

34. Knowles, *Dublin Helix,* 111: "Stephen is haunted by his mother, and Bloom is torn apart by the twin vultures of his present and his past"; "All of *Ulysses* is trying to put Rudy behind it." Joyce wrote to Stanislaus after Nora's miscarriage in Rome: "I am probably the only one to regret" (*JJ* 268–69). See Karen McCarthy, "Present-Tense Narration and Representing Trauma in Anne Enright's *The Gathering*" (*Kronoscope* 19 [2019]: 212–27) for trauma being "always of the present, and never successfully relegated to the past."

35. Senn, *Joycean Murmoirs,* 91; McMichael, *Ulysses and Justice,* 172–94. See, however, Crispi, *Becoming the Blooms,* 223, for Joyce's note suggesting that what Bloom could never like was Lombard St. West and 219–30 for Rudy overall. The ten years since Bloom and Molly have had intercourse reflects the ten years of Odysseus's wanderings, as well as the ten years between Beatrice's death and the narrative date of *The Divine Comedy.*

36. See Rickard, *Joyce's Book of Memory,* 34–41, and generally for Bloom's need to get past memories of Rudy.

37. Crispi, *Becoming the Blooms,* 221, points out that Joyce added the Eton suit to match the vision of Rudy in "Circe."

38. See S. Joyce, *My Brother's Keeper,* 21, for both his father and grandfather as the only child of an only child. Bloom, of course, is further separated from relatives by his father's wanderings. The surprising dearth of information on Bloom's mother or her family reinforces this sense.

39. Hence also, for Joyce, the number of Armistice Day: "Why was the Armistice of the Great War trumpeted forth on the eleventh minute of the eleventh hour of the eleventh day of the eleventh month?" (Hoffmeister, "James Joyce," in Potts, *Portraits of the Artist,* 130) and see chap. 1.

40. Pogorzelski, *Virgil and Joyce,* 91–92, 109.

41. R. Ellmann, *Ulysses on the Liffey,* 147; Reynolds, *Joyce and Dante,* 36–37.

42. See James Stephens to Joyce on Ibsen (*LIII* 390): "If a character of his sneezes in the first-act he will have a cold in the second-act, and will die of pneumonia in the third."

43. Crispi, *Becoming the Blooms*, 121–22 and 262: "As has long been recognized, the information and sentiments in this episode ["Ithaca"] are not to be taken at face value"; Conley, *Useless Joyce*, 171n4, on the budget of Ithaca "as a kind of fictional genre of its own."

44. See Quint's distinction between teleological epics, such as the *Aeneid*, and episodic ones, as discussed in *Epic and Empire*, 9: "the narrative romances that we are most familiar with, including the *Odyssey* itself, contain seemingly aimless episodes of wandering and digression—*adventures*—"; Redfield, *Nature and Culture*, 60: "The incidents of Odysseus's narration are not connected to one another by probability or necessity—there is no inner logic which determines that they should occur in just this order but the narrative is formed and unified in other ways."

45. As in his thought that Mulligan "fears the lancet of my art as I fear that of his" (1.152) or his "Usurper" (1.744). Bloom has a similar idea with "All ousted" (11.728), but note that Molly in fact wins the game. See Redfield, *Nature and Culture*, 210, on *timē*.

46. Katz, *Penelope's Renown*, 7–8.

47. As in Stephen Phillips's popular verse play, *Ulysses*, which Joyce read (Kershner, "Stephen Phillips' *Ulysses*," 194–201, and also his *Culture of Joyce's "Ulysses*," 41–49). As Nagy points out (*Poetry as Performance*, 152) in oral poetry there is no "right" version of the poem.

48. Stanford, *Ulysses Theme*, 14–16.

49. Stephen thus proposes to express himself "using for my defence the only arms I allow myself to use—silence, exile and cunning" (*P* 247).

50. The ram is a particularly nice example since Odysseus ties his companions under the other sheep, but has no one to tie him—although it is not clear why he has to cling to the ram all night.

51. See chap. 6 and Russo's commentary on Books XVII–XX in Russo, Fernandez-Galiano, and Heubeck, *A Commentary*, vol. 3, 108–10. In all other instances when a Homeric character "addresses his heart" in formulaic decision-making, action follows (as *Iliad* 22.98–130 etc.).

52. See Valente, "Perils of Masculinity," in Devlin and Reizbaum, *"Ulysses"—En-Gendered Perspectives*, 115, and Joyce coming to see the slaughter as in character for Odysseus (*SL* 274); Groden, *"Ulysses" in Progress*, 186.

53. In contrast see de Jong, *Narratological Commentary*, 11, 21, 545–46; Redfield, *Nature and Culture*, 90, who views the level of satisfaction achieved as finally superficial. For the ethical problems, see D. Steiner, *Odyssey*, 17–20.

54. Ajax declares that even one who has lost a brother or son finally gives up his anger and accepts compensation (*Iliad* 9.632–36), later echoed by Apollo and confirmed by Zeus (24.46–76).

55. See J. M. Foley, "Penelope as Moral Agent," in Bloom, *Homer's "The Odyssey*," 87–103; Rutherford, "*Iliad* to the *Odyssey*," in Cairns, *Oxford Readings*, 143: "Heroic combat in the *Odyssey*, I should argue, is seen as tragic in the past, but often grotesque in the present: in both lights its value is questioned"; Lamb, *Adventures of Ulysses*, 52, where

Demodocus "made Ulysses even pity his own slaughterous deeds, and feel touches of remorse."

56. Brann, *Homeric Moments*, 16, compares to a Beethoven symphony's concluding climax on concluding climax; Lamb's version has more of a Count of Monte Cristo flavor: "he that had been so long absent was returned to wreak the evil upon the heads of the doers; in the place where they had done the evil, there wreaked he his vengeance upon them" (*Adventures of Ulysses*, 88). S. West, "Commentary Books I–IV," in Heubeck, West, and Hainsworth, *A Commentary*, vol. 1, 56, sees "indications that the poet was not altogether happy about the ethical implications of the hero's savage vengeance, but felt unable to modify a traditional element in the story."

57. As described by Goldman, *Joyce Paradox*, 81–83.

58. See McMichael, *Ulysses and Justice*, 186–87; Crispi, *Becoming the Blooms*, 269–79, on Joyce adding ties between Bloom and Boylan, and 42 on the exchange at 4.526–36 that "frames the scene in a conspiratorial manner between wife and husband." See also J. King, "Trapping the Fox," 300, on Nora complaining "that Jim wanted her to 'go with other men so that he would have something to write about,'" and Goldman, *Joyce Paradox*, 166–67, on *Exiles* and Richard's desire that Bertha be unfaithful.

59. In general Bloom keeps his mildly nationalistic views to himself, as in "Eumaeus" (16.1029–55).

60. Kenner, *Ulysses*, 142, and *Joyce's Voices*, 87–89; R. Ellmann, *Ulysses on the Liffey*, 8; Sultan, *Eliot, Joyce and Company*, 289–93.

61. John Henry Menton: "his boiled eyes of all the big stupoes I ever met and thats called a solicitor" (18.43); Val Dillon: "looking at me with his dirty eyes Val Dillon that big heathen" (18.429); Pisser Burke: "spying around as usual on the slip always where he wasnt wanted if there was a row on youd vomit a better face" (18.965); and, at times, Boylan: "has he no manners nor no refinement nor no nothing in his nature" (18.1368 ff.); and see Gifford and Seidman, *"Ulysses" Annotated*, 603–4.

62. On the *Odyssey*, see Schein's introduction in Schein, *Reading the "Odyssey*," 31: "the poem itself is correspondingly open-ended, interpretively ambivalent or indeterminate, and irreducible to a single, straightforward, one-dimensional reading"; Silk, "*Odyssey* and Its Explorations," in Fowler, *Cambridge Companion to Homer*, 44, on the epic's "restless, exploratory character," where "ends are opened, questions raised, alternative voices let loose"; Wilson, *Odyssey*, 73: "The poem refuses to offer us a definitive moment at which home and peace are achieved, once and for all." In contrast see Norris, "Character, Plot, and Myth," in Latham, *Cambridge Companion to "Ulysses*," 79: "Unlike the *Odyssey*, which appears to offer a general and satisfactory resolution to all the conflicts of its protagonists, *Ulysses* remains open ended and suspenseful even at the novel's close"; Bakhtin, *Dialogic Imagination*, 11 and 3–40, on epic's absolute, closed past compared to the novel as open.

63. See D. Miller, *Epic Hero*, 39; Redfield, *Nature and Culture*, 99–103 and x: "in Hector's ethic—the ethic of the Iliad—there is no complete manhood without war."

64. Quint, *Epic and Empire*, 50–51.

65. See Christensen, *Many-Minded Man*, 2, 96, and Hall, *Return of Ulysses*, 184–86, for Jonathan Shay's work with veterans. Flack, *Modernism and Homer*, 43, on World War

I, where "Homer enabled modernist writers to raise questions about the possibilities for homecoming and recovery" (and see 196–97).

66. On the opinion, expressed from Aristarchus on, that the poem proper ends at 23.295 see Rutherford, *Odyssey*, 14–15; Saïd, *Homer and the "Odyssey,"* 27, 217–20. For features that mark Bk. 24 as an "accretion to the *Odyssey*'s Homeric Core," see Marks, *Zeus in the Odyssey*, 64; for a defense, Moulton, "End of the Odyssey," 153–69.

67. Butcher and Lang, *Odyssey*, 409, point out that no Greek poet could leave this out. And see Loney, *Ethics of Revenge*.

68. See de Jong, *Narratological Commentary*, 586, for this as the prototype for tragedy's deus ex machina endings.

69. Butler, *Authoress of the "Odyssey,"* 103: "Jove told her that she had had everything her own way so far, and might continue to do as she pleased."

70. For various views see Christensen, *Many-Minded Man*, 124; Wender, *Last Scenes*, 45, 57–59; Fenik, *Studies in the "Odyssey,"* 47–50; Purves, *Space and Time*, 225–26.

71. Ames, "Convergence," 148; Nagler, "Entretiens Avec Tirésias," 90–95; Katz, *Penelope's Renown*, 11.

72. 24.548 = 2.268, 481; 22.206; 24.503. On the scene as disappointing, Minta, "Homer and Joyce," in Graziosi and Greenwood, *Homer in the Twentieth Century*, 92–93; Van Nortwick, *Unknown Odysseus*, 42: "We want closure because we want things to make sense, to add up. To find meaning, as interpreters of literature or observers of the world around us, requires the discerning of patterns in the flux of experience. But, as we have seen, things in the *Odyssey* do not quite add up."

73. As Joyce wrote to Budgen "A point about Ulysses (Bloom). He romances about Ithaca . . . and when he gets back it gives him the pip" (*LI* 152; *JJ* 470).

74. See Bespaloff, *On the Iliad*, 44, for force in the *Iliad* "as both the supreme reality and the supreme illusion of life."

75. See Budgen, *Making of "Ulysses,"* 263, on Joyce as "a great hater of bloodshed."

76. Flack, *Modernism and Homer*, 95–123.

77. Zionism would make Bloom's return "home," like Aeneas's, historical rather than personal. For the contrast of wandering and being a citizen see Montiglio, *Wandering in Ancient Greek Culture*, 34; Dougherty, *Raft of Odysseus*, 7. As a "Wandering Jew" Bloom also pairs with Stephen as "Wandering Aengus" (9.1193, 1206; 10.1066).

78. Raleigh, *Leopold and Molly Bloom*, 48–49. Notably, however, the description of his early radical politics is followed by the question: "How much and how did he propose to pay for this country residence?" (17.1667).

79. Not founded by Griffith until 1905. *The Resurrection of Hungary* was serialized in the *United Irishman* from January to June 1904 (Gifford and Seidman, *"Ulysses" Annotated*, 367). See Gibson, *Joyce's Revenge*, 119–23; Pogorzelski, *Virgil and Joyce*, 105, on the names.

80. *U* 8.184–85; 12.775–79; 17.1808; 18.1224, and see 15.1576. For an actual "Privileged Royal Hungarian Lottery" scheme, reported in the Dublin *Weekly Independent and Nation* on June 16, 1904, see Gifford and Seidman, *"Ulysses" Annotated*, 162. For Bloom's finances, Osteen, *Economy of "Ulysses,"* 92, and Kenner, *Ulysses*, 44, on Bloom's ability to "buy and sell most of the people he deals with on Bloomsday."

81. Ungar, *National Epic*, 49–66.

82. Kenner, *Colder Eye*, 195, and also his *Ulysses*, 31–42.

83. Fairhall, *Question of History*, 169, contrasts the younger generation's view with that of Field Marshall Haig: "We were fighting, not only for ourselves and for our own Empire, but for a world ideal in which God was with us." See Sherry, *Great War*, 66, but also Vandiver, *Stand in the Trench*, 8–9, for "the old paradigm" of World War I cynicism as not quite so simple.

84. Molly's comment also casts an ironic light on Mr Deasy's view that war, from Troy onward, is the fault of women (2.390 ff.); and see Flack, *James Joyce*, 63–64.

85. See Schneider, "Rollicking Rattling Song," in Bauerle, *Picking Up Airs*, 84, for the popularity of the song in music halls.

86. See Wollaeger, "Seduction and Estrangement." The protest occurred on December 18, 1899.

87. Crispi, *Becoming the Blooms*, 113–16; Raleigh, *Leopold and Molly Bloom*, 33–34; Senn, *Inductive Scrutinies*, 92–93.

88. Like the Blooms' bed, brought from Gibraltar (1.58–65; 18.1212–15) and linked to the solved and unsolved mysteries of Odysseus's and Shakespeare's beds (9.682–719).

89. *Ulysses*, edited by Slote, Mamigonian, and Turner, 771. See Crispi, *Becoming the Blooms*, 258, for Bloemfontein added along with Gardner's death.

90. For Tweedy and the Citizen as interchangeable see Cheng, *Joyce, Race, and Empire*, 233. Joyce's revenge on the actual Henry Carr over an Irishman's English play (Wilde's *The Importance of Being Earnest*) and a pair of trousers (*JJ* 425–59) may have seemed to him a fitting version of World War I.

91. From Stoppard's *Travesties*, a play written in 1974.

CHAPTER 5. MOLLY AND PENELOPE, WEAVERS OF THE WIND

1. See Pelaschiar, "Joyce's Art of Silence," in Wawrzycka and Zanotti, *James Joyce's Silences*, 33–49; Knowles, *Dublin Helix*, 104: "Molly throws her shadow from beginning to end of *Ulysses*"; Christensen, *Many-Minded Man*, 202–33, for Penelope's "subordinated agency."

2. Winkler points out (*Constraints of Desire*, 158–59) that the bed-trick makes us realize that we have seen Odysseus's perspective throughout; see also Katz, *Penelope's Renown*, 148; Felson, *Regarding Penelope*, ix–xv.

3. See also Brivic, "Consciousness as Conflict," in McCormick and Steinberg, *Approaches to Teaching*, 59–66, for the Laconian "other" in *Ulysses*, particularly in relation to Stephen and Bloom.

4. See also *love's bitter mystery* (1.239–53; 15.4190) and the opening of "Nausicaa": "The summer evening had begun to fold the world in its mysterious embrace" (13.1–2). It is reassuring, however, that the eyes of witchery are promoted by Madame Vera Verity, truthfulness herself.

5. Nora described Dublin as a place where "the women spend their days in church and the men in pubs" (*JJ* 220). Pogorzelski, *Virgil and Joyce*, 69: "the pub is a site of community in *Ulysses*"; and see Lin, "Standing the Empire," in van Boheemen-Saaf and Lamos, *Masculinities in Joyce*, 33–58 on "Counterparts." For Dublin's gendering of public

and private space see Mahaffey, *Reauthorizing Joyce*, 202–6; Scott, *James Joyce*, 46–47, and in "Diversions from Mastery," in Devlin and Reizbaum, *"Ulysses"—En-Gendered Perspectives*, 136–49, where she describes the women in the 1982 reenactment of "Wandering Rocks" as all inside, peering out (139–40).

6. See Mahaffey, "End of Gender," in van Boheemen-Saaf and Lamos, *Masculinities in Joyce*, 154: "Molly was never designed to represent Joyce's idea of womanhood, which would indeed make her a problematic character"; and see also van Boheemen, "Molly's Heavenly Body," in Devlin and Reizbaum, *"Ulysses"—En-Gendered Perspectives*, 267–82. Scott, *Joyce and Feminism*, 111, quotes Djuna Barnes on her conversations with Joyce: "about women he seems a bit disinterested. Were I vain I should say he is afraid of them, but I am certain he is only a little skeptical of their existence."

7. See Felson, *Regarding Penelope*, 15–42; Buitron-Oliver and Cohen, "Between Skylla and Penelope," and Murnaghan, "Plan of Athena," both in Cohen, *Distaff Side*; Slatkin, "Composition by Theme," in Schein, *Reading the "Odyssey*," 234–37.

8. As Joyce told Eugene Jolas: "I have discovered that I can do anything with language I want" (de Almeida, *Byron and Joyce*, 129).

9. Hamlet responds to Ophelia's "Nay, 'tis twice two months, my lord" with a similar recalculation: "O heavens! Die two months ago, and not forgotten yet?" (3.2.128–32).

10. For Homer see Nagy, *Poetry as Performance*, 64, 75; Kirk, *Homer and the Epic*, 215. And for Joyce, see Mahaffey, *Reauthorizing Joyce*, 133–91, 206; Norris, *Joyce's Web*. Joyce also wrote Harriet Weaver: "I am stitching away like a cobbler" (de Almeida, *Byron and Joyce*, 140).

11. Dougherty, *Raft of Odysseus*, 177–84, compares the structures of bed and raft, as well as their combination of the fluid and the fixed.

12. Budgen, *Making of "Ulysses*," 57, and see Hall, *Return of Ulysses*, 115–29, and Christopoulos, "Strange Instances," in Bierl, Christopoulos, and Papachrysostomou, *Time and Space*, 5–6, on *histos* as both loom and mast.

13. See Mahaffey, *Reauthorizing Joyce*, 97, as well as 129–30, 133–91, for the play with "text"; Spoo, *Language of History*, 38–65.

14. Ames, "Convergence," 182. Even Homeric messengers, despite appearances, do not in fact repeat their orders verbatim, as shown by Hutchinson's dissertation "Messengers and the Art of Reported Speech in the *Iliad*."

15. For Penelope as holding back time, see Van Nortwick, *Unknown Odysseus*, 108. P. V. Jones, "Past in Homer's *Odyssey*," 85, points out that Penelope refers more frequently to the past than any other character.

16. *Nostos*, the Greek term that Joyce used, does not imply repetition, as do English "return" (Latin *re-tornare*, turn back) or Stephen's "*agenbite*" (remorse) or "*agenbuyer*" (redeemer) (1.490; 9.200, 494, 825; 10.879; 14.295). See Frame, *Myth of Return*, for the etymology and application to the *Odyssey*.

17. Hall, *Return of Ulysses*, 115: "Penelope's making and unmaking of the same shroud for her father-in-law is also the primary image of the oral poet's endless re-creation of his song." On the retelling of the story see Christensen, *Many-Minded Man*, 262–65, and Lowenstam, "Shroud of Laertes," 333–48, for differences in the accounts.

18. See Cohn, *Transparent Minds*, 65, for Molly's blending tenses; Kern, *Culture of*

Time, 28, on Molly's as not a "stream" of consciousness, since it does not go in just one direction; and Scott, *Joyce and Feminism,* 179–80, for Molly associated with space as Bloom is with time. Volpone, "Temporal Disharmonies," in Wawrzycka, *Reading Joycean Temporalities,* 139, sees bedroom scenes as places where "time no longer follows the natural circadian cycle: past, present and future are interwoven in a continuum, which echoes, at least in the macrostructure, Bergson's *durée*"; Raleigh, *Leopold and Molly Bloom,* 9, notes that more than 50 percent of *Ulysses's* backstory comes from this episode.

19. See Cohn, *Transparent Minds,* 220–32, on "Penelope" and the "profusion and referential instability of its pronouns" (230–31).

20. Ames, "Convergence," 98; Cohn, *Transparent Minds,* 129.

21. See also the list of Molly's "lovers," discussed in chap. 4.

22. In "Penelope" "either" generally appears as an intensive, as in "half the girls in Gibraltar never wore them either" (18.440–41). The exceptions, interestingly, are "either its one of those night women . . . or else if its not that its some little bitch or other" (18.34–46) and Mary Driscoll: "I gave it to him anyhow either she or me leaves the house" (18.72–73).

23. Song lyrics from Gifford and Seidman, *"Ulysses" Annotated,* 77, and note also: "Softly it wove itself into our dream."

24. Molly also once considered (wonderfully) setting the clock ahead to speed up the time (18.768–69) and recalls Boylan's stylish "clocks" as "silk socks with the skyblue silk things on them" (18.421).

25. See S. Joyce, *My Brother's Keeper,* 147, on Joyce, like Mulligan/Stephen (1.517–18) quoting Whitman's "do I contradict myself?"; Scott, *James Joyce,* 13, on a feminist questioning of male-centered binary logic. On memory as creative see Shaw, *Memory Illusion;* Svevo, *James Joyce* (n.p.): "When an artist remembers, he creates at the same time." Meyenhoff, *Time in Literature,* 21: "Wishes and fantasies may not only be remembered as facts, but the facts remembered are constantly modified, reinterpreted, and relived in the light of present exigencies, past facts and future hopes." Or, as Bergson puts it: "states of consciousness are processes and not things . . . they are alive and therefore constantly changing" (*Time and Free Will,* 196).

26. In the Gilbert schema "Hour: none." See Lernout, *Help My Unbelief,* for a somewhat doctrinaire rejection of the infinity.

27. See Rickard, *Joyce's Book of Memory,* 13, for *Ulysses* as "an 'odyssey' through memory, a novel in which characters and readers struggle to come to terms with the past in order to move toward the resolution of the desire for closure—for Ithaca." Christensen, *Many-Minded Man,* 29, quotes Austin (*Archery,* 139): "remembering comes close to making a plan for the future. Since memory is so much part of what a man is for Homer, the properties of the lotus and Kirkê's drug, which cause forgetfulness of home or of the return home, are really statements on the dissolution of identity"; Stevenson, *Reading the Times,* 80–81, points out that Proust reset early scenes to places destroyed by the war, making them available only through memory.

28. "All this I do inside me, in the huge court of my memory. There I have by me the sky, the earth, the sea, and all things in them which I have been able to perceive—apart from what I have forgotten. There too I encounter myself . . . From the same store too

I can take out pictures of things which have either happened to me or are believed on the basis of experience; I can myself weave them into the context of the past, and from them I can infer future actions, events, hopes, and then I can contemplate all these as though they were in the present" (Augustine, *Confessions*, Bk. 10, chap. 8, 218–19). See also Aristotle, *Physics* 218a, on the nonexistence of past and future.

29. See Feeney, *Gods in Epic*, 3, on the importance of the gods to the truth-value of poetry; Porter, "Homer," in Fowler, *Cambridge Companion to Homer*, 327: "It is ironic, or simply telling, that the Greek sense of identity formed itself around a possible fiction"; Proust, *Remembrance of Things Past*, vol. 3, 31, on memory changing as we do; and Adams, *Surface and Symbol*, 173–74, on Bloom's struggle to remember.

30. Thornton, *Allusions in "Ulysses,"* 27–28, and see Joyce, *OCPW*, 59: "Poetry . . . makes no account of history, which is fabled by the daughters of memory." There may also be a reference to Isaiah 19:9 "and they that weave networks shall be confounded" and John Webster: "Vain the ambition of kings / Who seek by trophies and dead things / To leave a living name behind, / And weave but nets to catch the wind" (*The Devil's Law Case*).

31. As Polonius's "springes to catch woodcocks" (1.3.115), Claudius's address to his: "limèd soul, that, struggling to be free / Art more engaged!" (3.3.68–69), Hamlet's "benetted round with villains" (5.2.29), or Laertes's "as a woodcock to mine own springe" (5.2.307).

32. Rickard, *Joyce's Book of Memory*, 31–34; Senn, *Inductive Scrutinies*, 112: "If anyone, Joyce was always altering, remodeling times, including his own past."

33. For gramophones, 6.962–68; 15.605, 2115, 2168–73, 2210–12; for photographs 1.684–85; 4.369–70, 400–401; 8.171–74, 209–10; 18.20–22, 562–54, 655–56. See also the note of "Lafayette and Son, of Westmoreland street, Dublin's premier photographic artist, being responsible for the esthetic execution" (16.1435–36) and Molly's reflection below, that "I ought to have got it taken in drapery that never looks out of fashion" (18.1303–4).

34. See Rickard, *Joyce's Book of Memory*, 14, and Baron, *Strandentwining Cable*, 147–50, for the "instantaneous irruption of memory" in "Circe"; Joyce, incidentally, objected to "madeleine" being used for Molly's seedcake in the French translation (Banta and Silverman, *James Joyce's Letters*, 41).

35. For Joyce's awareness of Freud see Rickard, *Joyce's Book of Memory*, 35; Kimball, "Jung's 'Dual Mother,'" 477–90.

36. Senn, *Joycean Murmoirs*, 3: Joyce "demonstrates how the mind selects, assimilates, changes and adapts, according to impulses we are not aware of," and 5 on memory as a process rather than "a body of fixed items, or a set of files that can be consulted." See also R. Ellmann, "Limits of Joyce's Naturalism," 575: "In all his books up to *Finnegans Wake* Joyce sought to reveal the coincidence of the present with the past."

37. See Borg, *Measureless Time*, 52; J. T. Fraser, *Of Time, Passion and Knowledge*, 44–46 and 256: "For the agent, future and past are asymmetrical; for the observer they are symmetrical."

38. Elias, *Time*, 77, and see Rovelli, *Order of Time*, 111–15.

39. See Gose, *Transformation Process*, xv–xvi, on Stephen as immutable, Bloom as Becoming, and the flow of "Penelope." See also Joyce's 1904 "Portrait of an Artist" (in *P*

257–58; *JJ* 145) on the past as not an "iron memorial aspect" but "a fluid succession of presents," and on personality as a river, not a statue or fixed character but "individuating rhythm."

40. Stephen's "ghoststory" (*U* 2.55) is thus *Hamlet*, where the past Hamlet returns to entrap and destroy the present one. Molly's surprise appearance suggests *The Winter's Tale* instead, another tale "of sprights and goblins" (*Winter's Tale* 2.1.37; *U* 9.936, 406, 421–22, 651, 726–27, 790, 995–96), with a (literally) central role for Time (4.11–34). Here, as in *Hamlet*, vengeance for a wife's supposed adultery causes the death of the son, but in this case memory becomes wonder (5.1.7–12; 5.3.21–95) and so liberates and recovers a lost wife and daughter.

41. As Augustine points out (*Confessions* 11.14), one knows exactly what time is, until you think about it.

42. On epic see D. Miller, *Epic Hero*, 109–10 and 115. And for Joyce spoofing the novel's usual dependence on marriage, Spoo, *Language of History*, 11–12, 66–88. Martin, "*Ulysses* as a Whole," in Frehner and Zeller, *Collideorscape of Joyce*, 212, points out that everything is jammed into Bloomsday, except, interestingly, a wedding.

43. S. Joyce, *My Brother's Keeper*, 158: "In Ireland more than elsewhere the hen-pecked husband is a rarity and a laughing-stock. For the most part, women do not interest Irishmen except as streetwalkers or housekeepers"; "The indifference or concealed hostility of Irishmen to women is reflected in the character of the women."

44. Katz, *Penelope's Renown*, 28–29; Murnaghan, *Disguise and Recognition*, 124. Stephen picks up Deasy and McHugh's views of Helen, as "Prix de Paris" (3.483) and "the wooden mare of Troy in whom a score of heroes slept" (9.622–23), and see 7.536–37, 1032–39; 12.1271.

45. See Felson and Slatkin, "Gender and Homeric Epic," in Fowler, *Cambridge Companion to Homer*, 91–114; Taplin, *Homeric Soundings*, 212–18; Weil, "Poem of Force," 6, on the *Iliad* overall: "To define force—it is that x that turns anybody who is subjected to it into a thing."

46. Felson, *Regarding Penelope*, 8; D. Steiner, *Odyssey*, 25–28.

47. See Joyce in A. Power, *Conversations with James Joyce*, 44, on the "revolt of women against the idea that they are the mere instruments of men"; Reizbaum, "Re-Deeming 'Cyclops,'" in Devlin and Reizbaum, *"Ulysses"—En-Gendered Perspectives*, 178, on the irony of Deasy and the Citizen agreeing here; Hayward, "Advertising Language of 'Nausicaa,'" in Brockman, Mecsnóber, and Alonso, *Publishing in Joyce's "Ulysses,"* 89–106, on the masculine control of Gerty's "feminine" language.

48. Particularly in the formulaic invocation of "Zeus, husband of Hera," used most notably by Odysseus to Nausicaa (8.465 = 15.111 = 15.180); one might include Aeolus's marrying his daughters to his sons. See Scott, *Joyce and Feminism*, 62–63, for the dismal marriages of *Dubliners*, and 64 for Joyce describing his mother to Nora as a "victim" (*LII* 48).

49. Slatkin, "Composition by Theme," in Schein, *Reading the "Odyssey,"* 226: "The oral poem, therefore, continually repositions itself with respect to a tradition made up of alternative narrative possibilities."

50. Butler, *Authoress of the "Odyssey,"* 106.

51. See de Jong, *Narratological Commentary,* 136, on Odysseus's desire to return to his wife as Calypso's interpretation.

52. See Rutherford, *Odyssey,* 214; Russo, "Interview and Aftermath," 1–21.

53. On the test of the bed see Schein, "Female Representations," 17–28, and Zeitlin, "Figuring Fidelity," 117–54, both in Cohen, *Distaff Side,* 117–54; Felson, *Regarding Penelope,* 38, as reversing the usual chastity test. Lamb's *Adventures of "Ulysses,"* 87, does not include the test; Penelope is instead convinced by Telemachus's reproach.

54. See de Jong, *Narratological Commentary,* 41 and 449–50, on this "emancipation of speech" in the *Odyssey,* in contrast to the *Iliad,* where speeches are prepared by the narrator.

55. See Nagler, "Dread Goddess Revisited," in Schein, *Reading the "Odyssey,"* 152–62, on the tree image, and Senn, *Joycean Murmoirs,* 99, for the corresponding centrality of Molly's bed.

56. Crispi, *Becoming the Blooms,* 228 and 207, for Molly's transferring her attention as a way of coping with loss.

57. As "only I oughtnt to have stitched it and it on her it brings a parting and the last plumpudding too split in 2 halves see it comes out no matter what they say her tongue is a bit too long for my taste" (18.1031–33).

58. As Crispi, *Becoming the Blooms,* 200, points out, Milly has no individual presence, speaking only through her letter.

59. Crispi, *Becoming the Blooms,* 199. For Bloom on Molly and Milly's resemblance ("same thing watered down" 6.87; and compare Telemachus's resemblance to Odysseus) see chap. 4.

60. Hodgart, "Aeolus," in Hart and Hayman, *Critical Essays,* 115–30, and as Bloom's plan, Kenner, *Colder Eye,* 197–98.

61. See Rabaté, "Discussion," 195-203, in Benstock, *Augmented Ninth,* 219–25; Lawrence, "Paternity as Legal Fiction," also in Benstock, 236: "Fathers are most useful in their absence; the death of the father initiates the action of the son"; Kenner, *Ulysses,* 17: "Stephen in *Ulysses* is no longer in search of a father, as he was in the *Portrait.* He is obsessed by a dead mother. And as for fathers, living or mythic, elected or adoptive, his present instinct is to get clear of them."

62. For Joyce telling Nora that their children should not come between them see *SL* 165.

63. See H. Foley, "Penelope as Moral Agent," in Cohen, *Distaff Side,* 97, for Penelope as opaque, with sources; Austin, *Archery,* 228–29; Zeitlin, "Figuring Fidelity," also in Cohen, 138–42, and Amory, "The Reunion," in Taylor, *Essays on the "Odyssey,"* 100–121, on the involvement of a subconscious level.

64. For the recognition see Harsh, "Penelope and Odysseus," 1–21; C. Emlyn-Jones, "Reunion of Odysseus," 1–18; Saïd, *Homer and the "Odyssey,"* 63–64; Rutherford, *Odyssey,* 33–38, for further sources. Tracy, *Story of the "Odyssey,"* 98–139, argues in detail that Penelope gradually comes to believe that Odysseus is alive and returning.

65. See Murnaghan, "Penelope's *Agnoia,*" in Doherty, *Homer's "Odyssey,"* 231–46; Katz, *Penelope's Renown,* 93–113, for a summary of views, and 115–20 for Bks. 18–21 structured by Penelope's uncertainty. Penelope's deciding on the contest and Athena's putting it in

her mind (21.1–4) are, however, perfectly compatible, as discussed by Lesky, "Divine and Human Causation," in Cairns, *Oxford Readings*, 190; de Jong, *Narratological Commentary*, 505, and chap. 6 on double determination.

66. See Felson and Slatkin, "Gender and Homeric Epic," in Fowler, *Cambridge Companion to Homer*, 112, and chap. 6 for more on reverse similes.

67. Stanford, *Homer*, vol. 2, 239: "the ancient gods were not essentially truthful."

68. For the difficulty in explaining Penelope's behavior here see Hölscher, "Penelope and the Suitors," in Schein, *Reading the "Odyssey,"* 133–40, and Silk, "*Odyssey* and Its Explorations," in Fowler, *Cambridge Companion to Homer*, 31–44.

69. Butler, *Authoress of the "Odyssey,"* 122–29; for Joyce's awareness of stories in which Penelope was not faithful see Herring, "Bedsteadfastnes of Molly Bloom," 49–61.

70. Butler, *Authoress of the "Odyssey,"* 135: "Penelope indeed seems to have been such an adept at lying that it is very difficult to know when to believe her," and Buitron-Oliver and Cohen, "Between Skylla and Penelope," in Cohen, *Distaff Side*, 46–47, for representations of both Odysseus and Penelope (as on the cover of this volume) with head in hand, reflecting. See M. L. West, *Epic Cycle*, for traditions in which Penelope was not faithful and for further sources.

71. Kohnken, "Odysseus' Scar," in Doherty, *Homer's "Odyssey,"* 44–61, and see chap. 6 for Auerbach on this scene.

72. See de Jong, *Narratological Commentary*, 130, for Eurycleia as Eurynome's doublet.

73. See Katz, *Penelope's Renown*, 145–53; Wilson, *Odyssey*, 47–48. Dodds, *Greeks and the Irrational*, 106, 123, dismisses the discrepancy as the "inversion of affect" of dreams— but this is not how dreams work in narrative.

74. See de Jong, "Between Word and Deed," in Doherty, *Homer's "Odyssey,"* 62–90.

75. See Kirk, *Homer and the Epic*, 176–77, for a (logical) version of the story where Odysseus and Penelope decide on the contest together.

76. As Butler, *Authoress of the "Odyssey,"* 88, points out, the test is equally of strength and accuracy.

77. See Scott, *Joyce and Feminism*, 158–59; Osteen, *Economy of "Ulysses,"* 422: "Molly both repeats and contradicts herself, her turns and returns becoming verbal analogies of the earth's rotation."

78. Nietzsche, *Thus Spoke Zarathustra*, trans. Graham Parkes (Oxford: Oxford World Classics, 2008), 3.10.

79. Hence for Stephen the former prostitute: "Georgina Johnson is dead and married" (15.3620). Joyce himself, as *LII* 243, liked to mix the categories up. For Bell, *Jocoserious Joyce*, 20, Stephen "suffers from hardening of the categories." And see Burns, *Gestural Politics*, 29, on Stephen's inclination and Bloom's resistance to labels. See also *LI* 170; R. Ellmann, *Ulysses on the Liffey*, 8, for Joyce describing Molly as "the flesh that always affirms" ("*Ich bin der* [sic] *Fleisch der stets bejaht*") and for Mulligan as Mephistopheles, the spirit that denies (Goethe, *Faust* I, 1338). Mahaffey, *Reauthorizing Joyce*, notes the opposition overall between Stephen and Molly and casts Stephen, the great refuser, in this role (15–19, 140–42).

80. Like Gibraltar, the tower was a British defense against Napoleon (1.543).

81. See chap. 2 and McMichael, *"Ulysses" and Justice,* 115–16, 135–37; Theoharis, *Anatomy of the Soul,* 124–41.

82. Similarly, Joyce reused his "there is no word tender enough to be your [Nora's] name" in *The Dead* (*JJ* 246, *LII* 56; *D* 214). See Attridge, "Molly's Flow," as well as Joyce's: "Do you notice how women when they write disregard stops and capital letters?" (*LII* 173).

83. As the daughters of Memory, the Muses know the future because they recall the past (*Iliad* 2.485–86). See M. L. West, *Theogony,* 166, for "the close connection between poetry and prophecy which is widespread in early literature"; Gartziou-Tatti, "Prophecy and Time," 11–28; and Joyce's poet as "priest of the eternal imagination" (*P* 221). See also Saint-Amour, "Imprevidibility of the Future," in Ferrer, Slote, and Topia, *Renascent Joyce;* Scott, *Joyce and Feminism,* 181–82, on the traditional link between prophecy and the feminine, as in Molly's Tarot cards (5.154–56; 18.1313–21).

84. See also Reynolds, *Joyce and Dante,* 289, comparing Dante's Siren and Bloom's Nymph, and Bowen, *Comic Novel,* 122, for Harriet Weaver, Sylvia Beach, and Edith McCormick as Joyce's Mary, Lucia, and Beatrice (*Inferno* 2.94–117).

85. Senn, *Joycean Murmoirs,* 130, and, on the *Odyssey,* Zeitlin, "Figuring Fidelity," in Cohen, *Distaff Side,* 139: "Furthermore, as often noted, every female figure in the poem, including Kalypso, Kirke, Arete, and even Nausikaa, contributes some element to the complex and composite portrait of Penelope."

86. The flip side of Joyce's comment on his picture of Penelope, that she was wondering what Odysseus looked like, since they had no photographs in those days (*JJ* 430; Budgen, *Making of "Ulysses,"* 188–89, and 149 on Joyce saying that Bloom carries the photo to show his bond with other men). See also Lawrence, "Pocketed Objects as Props," in van Boheemen-Saaf and Lamos, *Masculinities in Joyce,* 169, 173–74, for the photo as a commodity and fetish.

87. For modern takes on this question see Atwood, *The Penelopiad;* Le Guin, *Lavinia;* M. Miller, *Circe* (who stresses the rivalry between Athena and Penelope). For Ovid asking a similar question, *Metamorphoses,* Bk. 5, and P. Johnson, *Ovid Before Exile,* 41–73.

88. Accordingly, Herodotus writes in Ionic, the prevalent dialect of Homer, rather than Doric, his native dialect.

89. This appears in Joyce's notes (Weir, *"Ulysses" Explained,* 23), hence *"Prix de Paris:* beware of imitations" (3.483).

90. The lines are athetized in the scholia. For various views see Fredricksmeyer, "Penelope *Polutropos,*" 487–97, with a further bibliography; Murnaghan, *Disguise and Recognition,* 104; Zeitlin, "Figuring Fidelity," in Cohen, *Distaff Side,* 143–44. For Helen's complexity overall see Taplin, *Homeric Soundings,* 96–103, and for condemnations of Helen as the cause of the war, 11.438; 14.68; 17.118–19; 22.227.

91. Kenner, *Colder Eye,* 188, and see Senn, *Joycean Murmoirs,* 263, on Reuben J. Dodd Jr. suing the BBC for broadcasting Joyce's *Ulysses.*

92. M. Ellmann, "Endings," in Latham, *Cambridge Companion to "Ulysses,"* 105. See also Gorman, *James Joyce,* 282–83; *JJ* 549 for Joyce's dream in which Molly told him "And I have done with you too, Mr. Joyce." Ellmann reports that when asked if she was Molly, Nora said: "I'm not—she was much fatter" (*JJ* 743).

93. Since Judaism comes through the mother's line, Bloom is technically not Jewish; while, if Molly's mother was Jewish, she is.

94. Raleigh, *Leopold and Molly Bloom*, 62, points out inaccuracies in Joyce's Gibraltar geography, and see Slote, "All the Way from Gibraltar," 81–92, for his sources. Hall, *Return of Ulysses*, 195, points out that Calypso's home was traditionally Gibraltar.

95. See French, "Women in Joyce's Dublin," in Benstock, *Augmented Ninth*, 267: "For Joyce, women were the surround. . . . Women frame men's lives, as if they existed before men and shall exist after them, like some eternal silent presence" and Joyce to Budgen: "my wife's personality is utterly proof against any influence of mine" (*JJ* 434).

96. The full-page S, M, and P (possibly Stephen, Molly, Poldy?) that open "Telemachus," "Calypso," and "Eumaeus" in the Random House edition bring out the structure, for which see Knowles, *Dublin Helix*, 1–4. For other aspects of the pattern see Kenner, *Joyce's Voices*, 35–36; Weir, *"Ulysses" Explained*, 58–59, 72.

97. See Fitzgerald's translation of the *Odyssey*, 112. For Athena's penchant for turning into a bird see Buxton, "Similes and Other Likenesses," in Fowler, *Cambridge Companion to Homer*, 142–43.

98. See chap. 2 and De Jong, *Narratological Commentary*, 335, who describes these as "significant duals."

99. Significantly, the only equivalent is Helen's far less comfortable challenge of Aphrodite at *Iliad* 3.380–420.

100. See Murnaghan, "Plan of Athena," in Cohen, *Distaff Side*, 71–73.

101. See Otto, *Homeric Gods*, 3–8, on Homer's disinclination to magic; Griffin, "Epic Cycle," in Cairns, *Oxford Readings*, 365–84; Saïd, *Homer and the "Odyssey,"* 322–24.

102. See Jensen, "In What Sense," in Doherty, *Homer's "Odyssey,"* 18–28, and Heiden, "Placement of 'Book Divisions,'" 247–59.

103. Cohn, *Transparent Minds*, 218; Bell, *Jocoserious Joyce*, 94 ff.; Groden, *"Ulysses" in Progress*, 63 and 202, on Joyce's "refusal to confine the contents of *Ulysses* to a closed fictional world."

104. R. Ellmann, *Ulysses on the Liffey*, 159–62; Rabaté, *Politics of Egoism*, 118–19; Sultan, *Eliot, Joyce and Company*, 289–98. Rickard, *Joyce's Book of Memory*, 189: "these two opposing poles—closure and the impossibility of closure—can easily become the Scylla and Charybdis of *Ulysses* criticism."

105. See Kershner, *Culture of Joyce's "Ulysses,"* 69, on Bloom and Molly: "each seems tacitly to blame the other, and our access to the consciousness of each, amazingly, does not resolve the question" as well as Joyce to Budgen: "Why all this fuss and bother about the mystery of the unconscious? What about the mystery of the conscious?" (*JJ* 436). See also Lawrence, *Odyssey of Style*, 206: "the idea of a natural resolution is precisely what is undermined in the book as a whole. Because my own reading of the book depends upon the notion that *Ulysses* presents possibilities instead of conclusions, the "Penelope" chapter seems to me to be regressive, to present something denied by the rest of the book. If Molly's monologue contains the truth or resolution, hasn't the book implicitly suggested that we cannot trust messages or any version of the truth?"

106. As in L. C. Knight's observation that it is meaningless to ask about Lady Macbeth's children (*How Many Children Had Lady Macbeth?: An Essay in the Theory and*

Practice of Shakespeare Criticism, Cambridge: Minority Press, 1933) and see Goldman, *The Joyce Paradox*, 79–117, for the tension in *Ulysses* between an initial humanism and the subsequent impression of filters.

CHAPTER 6. THE GODS AND NARRATIVE STYLES

1. See Kershner, *Culture of Joyce's "Ulysses,"* 70, for "Joyce's use of stylistic 'filters,' beyond which we can often dimly discern the virtual existence of realistic passages in something like the book's initial style." Like Goldman, *Joyce Paradox*, Groden, *"Ulysses" in Progress*, balances the two views: the story "now proceeds through a series of semi-transparent screens" (44), but this "does not mean that the style represents an impediment to our understanding of some real action, an intrusion we should get around or beneath" (45). As Atherton puts it in his essay on "Oxen of the Sun," in Hart and Hayman, *Critical Essays*, 337, Joyce "is using the medium as his message"; or see Hart, *James Joyce's Ulysses*, 86: "To attempt to get below the surface of Joyce's verbiage is like trying to reconstruct the real face behind a cubist portrait: it is an irrelevant exercise."

2. See Fairhall, *Question of History*, 205, for the Arranger as a collective, not individual, consciousness; Thwaites, *Joycean Temporalities*, 94–96, on the Arranger as a multiplicity. On Homer see Nagy, *Poetry as Performance*, 66: "The paradox of the metaphor [of "stitching together" the song] is that the many and the various become the single and the uniform—and yet there is supposedly no loss in the multiplicity and variety of the constituent parts."

3. Lloyd-Jones, *Justice of Zeus*, 160; Otto, *Homeric Gods*, 42, 127, 170–73; Saïd, *Homer and the "Odyssey,"* 315–55. With the proviso that Otto's study may apply only to Homer's treatment of the gods, it is well worth consulting.

4. See Martin, *"Ulysses* as a Whole," in Frehner and Zeller, *Collideorscape of Joyce*, 202–14, for the unity of *Ulysses*; Senn, *Joyce's Dislocutions*, 188–98, for the multiplicity: "There cannot be many other novels that allow us to treat their various chapters or sections separately, almost as individuals" (188).

5. Feeney, *Gods in Epic*, 53: "The modern slant originates, I imagine, in the unexamined first principle that the humans are 'really' the only characters in the story."

6. As Groden pointed out early on, in *"Ulysses" in Progress*, 4, 18–22, few works are able to unite considerations of the "human drama" and of the "symbolic structure" (as he does himself); and see Litz, "Genre of Ulysses," in Reynolds, *James Joyce*.

7. See de Jong, *Narratological Commentary*, 587–88, for the timeline. Including these references to the past, some scholars have seen Odysseus as developing, as discussed in Christensen, *Many-Minded Man*, and see G. de F. Lord, "The *Odyssey*," in Taylor, *Essays on the "Odyssey,"* 36–53; de Jong, 20, on Telemachus.

8. See Auerbach, *Mimesis*, 23.

9. Auerbach, *Mimesis*, 12 and 4–5.

10. Auerbach, *Mimesis*, 10. See also Bakhtin, *Dialogic Imagination*, 134, for the Greek hero having the complete exteriority of the public man.

11. Kohnken, "Odysseus' Scar," in Doherty, *Homer's "Odyssey,"* 44–61.

12. See Brann, *Homeric Moments*, 292–98, for these "time chasms"; Grethlein, "Mem-

ory and Material Objects," 27–51. See also Lessing, *Laocoön,* 80–81, on Homer preferring development over time to objects in space, as in the harnessing of a chariot or arming.

13. The description also echoes Odysseus's seat on the threshold, with 22.43–44 = 17.340–41.

14. The interruption at 11.330 ff. reminds us, for example, that the Wanderings are part of the ongoing narrative. Heubeck's introduction in Heubeck, West, and Hainsworth, *A Commentary,* vol. 1, 17–18, sees a poet who "still accepts the rules of epic narrative which forbid him to break out of the chronological sequence, to stop at a certain point and return to a moment his narrative has already passed" but who stretches it.

15. Auerbach, *Mimesis,* 5.

16. A convention that continues into Greek tragedy, although, interestingly, not Greek comedy. See A. Parry, *Language of Achilles,* 1–7; Friedrich and Redfield, "Case of Achilles," *Language* 54 (1978): 263–88, for differences in individual registers.

17. Though note 12.374–45, where Lampetia tells Helios about his oxen. Unlike the transcendent divinity of the Judeo-Christian tradition, the Greek gods, who are descended from Earth, are immanent within nature, as discussed by Feeney, *Gods in Epic,* 152.

18. Quint, *Epic and Empire,* 3: "What is life and death for the human warriors is a spectator sport for the gods."

19. See Redfield, *Nature and Culture,* 220, on the gods as "both part of the action and detached from it."

20. Similarly, M. L. West, *Works and Days by Hesiod,* 124–26, 222–24.

21. Even for Hesiod the gods enforce justice, rather than being necessarily just themselves, as discussed by Lloyd-Jones, "Zeus in Aeschylus," 55–67; Nelson, *God and the Land,* 125–38. For differences between the epics, see Allan, "Divine Justice and Cosmic Order," 1–35; P. Rose, *Class in Archaic Greece,* 147–51. Butler, *Humour of Homer,* 19, saw Homer as advising readers not to take the gods seriously. Observations on their immorality stretch from Xenophanes to Aristophanes (see, e.g., *Clouds* 1081–82) to Plato (see *Republic* 377d–386a etc.). De Jong points out that the first lie of the *Odyssey* is told by "Mentes" (*Narratological Commentary,* 26).

22. Similarly, Agamemnon insists in the *Iliad* that the gods will avenge Trojan injustice, not knowing that they caused that injustice (*Iliad* 4.64 ff., 158 ff.).

23. See 19.332–34 for the epithet, *amumon,* as "blameless"; Stanford, *Odyssey,* 210; S. West, "Commentary Books I–IV," in Heubeck, West, and Hainsworth, *A Commentary,* vol. 1, 77, for other explanations.

24. See de Jong, *Narratological Commentary,* 323–24. Ironically, Odysseus asks Zeus to punish this violation of *xenia* (13.213–14) just after the scene with Poseidon and Zeus concerning the Phaeacians (13.125–83).

25. Dougherty, *Raft of Odysseus,* 156–57; de Jong, *Narratological Commentary,* 319–21. The only other intrusion is the opening scene in the Underworld in Bk. 24.

26. See Hoekstra, "Commentary Book XIII," in Heubeck and Hoekstra, *A Commentary,* vol. 2, 174; Stanford, *Odyssey,* vol. 2, 205, on Aristarchus as the first to emend the line; Butcher and Lang do not emend, translating Zeus's reply as "and do thou overshadow their city with a great mountain" (200).

27. Even Hesiod says that he doesn't *think* Zeus will make injustice more profitable than justice (*Works and Days* 273).

28. The phoropter was invented in the early 1900s (though in the United States), so that Joyce, with his many eye troubles, may have had the experience.

29. For Joyce's introduction of the headings in "Aeolus" see Groden, "Genetic Joyce," in Rabaté, *James Joyce Studies*, 241–43, and also his *"Ulysses" in Progress*, 64–114. For the gigantisms of "Cyclops" written first and the characters fitted into the dialogue only later see *"Ulysses" in Progress*, 115–65, particularly 117, 124.

30. Kenner, "Circe," in Hart and Hayman, *Critical Essays*, 352, points out that "hallucinations" would be purely internal and solipsistic, as these are not.

31. See Kershner, *Culture of Joyce's "Ulysses*," 205, for the twins' sailor suits as middle-class, making Cissy's visit to Nighttown improbable. See also Gunn, Hart, and Beck, *James Joyce's Dublin*, 66, on the gradation in "Circe" from the real to the imaginary.

32. Senn, *Inductive Scrutinies*, 105: "The early, more realistic style is practically discontinued after 'Wandering Rocks' and 'Sirens,' when other, more parodistic modes take over and 'realism' is shown to be one judiciously confected illusion among others."

33. On "Wandering Rocks" see Budgen, *Making of "Ulysses*," 123–25; Curran, *James Joyce Remembered*, 92; and *LI* 175 for Joyce's famous inquiry about the area railings at 7 Eccles St.

34. See Budgen, *Making of "Ulysses*," 176, on Joyce's belief in luck, particularly in regard to *Ulysses*.

35. So that, for example, Telemachus and Odysseus may weep at a feast at the same time, but in very different places, as shown in 4.113–19; 8.83–95, 521–23. On the cloud see Rickard, *Joyce's Book of Memory*, 90, and below; Killeen, *Ulysses Unbound*, 104 ff., for a useful list of "Wandering Rocks" interpolations; Gordon, *Joyce and Reality*, 63–67, for Molly and Boylan's synchronicity in "Sirens"; Senn, "Tales Told," in Wawrzycka, *Reading Joycean Temporalities*, 31–50, for simultaneity more generally.

36. For other, rather cynical takes see Father Conmee on Old Malahide (10.155–78) and Tom Kernan missing the cavalcade as he considers the place where Emmet was hanged (10.764–91).

37. Adams, *Surface and Symbol*, and for Dubliners disputing where on Clanbrassil Street the Blooms lived see Reynolds's introduction to *James Joyce*, 1; Senn, *Joycean Murmoirs*, 286.

38. See also Aphrodite's different origins in Homer and Hesiod (*Theogony* 173–200; *Iliad* 5.370–72) or Hephaestus's different wives in the *Iliad* and *Odyssey* (*Iliad* 18.380–84; *Odyssey* 8.266–70).

39. In contrast to the *Iliad*, the *Odyssey* sets only five scenes on Olympus (1.22–96; 5.1–42; 12.376–90; 13.125–58; 24.472–86), as discussed in de Jong, *Narratological Commentary*, 10.

40. See Otto, *Homeric Gods*, 26–30, for Poseidon as a primal, archaic god, and 43–60 for Athena; Murnaghan, "Plan of Athena," in Cohen, *Distaff Side*, 61–80. Similarly see Gilgamesh's position between Shamash and Enlil, or (with Homer in mind) Aeneas's between Juno and Venus.

41. See chap. 1; S. West, "Commentary Books I–IV," in Heubeck, West, and Hain-

sworth, *A Commentary*, vol. 1, 105, for further references, and chap. 2 for Stephen's fear of water and being absorbed. For the additional absorption of being eaten by fish see *Iliad* 21.122–27, 203–5; *Odyssey* 14.135; 24.291; *U* 3.476–79; and Alonso on his son in *The Tempest*: "what strange fish / Hath made his meal on thee?" (1.2.113). A late eighth century vase from Pithekoussai depicts men flung overboard and sea creatures about to swallow them, as described in Susan Langdon, *Art and Identity in Dark Age Greece 1100–700 B.C.E* (Cambridge: Cambridge University Press, 2008), 8–10.

42. For further divine/human names see *Iliad* 2.813–14; 14.290–91; 20.74; *Odyssey* 10.306; 12.61.

43. See Senn, *Joyce's Dislocutions*, ix. Knowles, *Dublin Helix*, xi, quotes Forster's "only connect." Proust, *Remembrance of Things Past*, vol.3, 459: "Man is the creature who cannot escape from himself, who knows other people only in himself, and when he asserts the contrary he is lying."

44. See Kain, *Fabulous Voyager*, 131: "one of the striking features of J's style is the unusual fluidity with which it turns from the outer to the inner world"; and illustrating this, Friedman, "Lestrygonians," in Hart and Hayman, *Critical Essays*, 136–39.

45. Gordon, *Joyce and Reality*, 171–95, cites thirty-two examples, which he explains as naturalistic. In contrast, Adams, "Hades," in Hart and Hayman, *Critical Essays*, 110: "When other people's words turn up in Bloom's monologues, or his in theirs, it isn't a 'dropping out of character' but a deliberate dropping of character into some other continuum"; Joyce in A. Power, *Conversations with James Joyce*, 85–86: "Our object is to create a new fusion between the exterior world and our contemporary selves." Similarly, see Austin, "Nausikaa and the Word," 11: "One of the great gifts of the Homeric imagination is how inner and outer, or, if we prefer, objective and subjective, are fused together"; and for Homer and extended mind theory, Christensen, *Many-Minded Man*, 272. As Butler puts it (*Humour of Homer*, 105): "Everyone is both himself and all his direct ancestors and descendants as well. . . . This is practically making him one with all living things," "And all this has come of admitting that a man may be the same person for two days running!"

46. As Lamb, *Adventures of Ulysses*, 41: "Minerva (who is wisdom herself) put it into his thoughts."

47. *Iliad* 9.445 ff.; 13.695; 23.85 and in Odysseus's lies, *Odyssey* 13.259; 14.380. Odysseus sees Theoclymenus's relation, Eriphyle, in Hades (11.326).

48. See Guidorizzi, "Laughter of the Suitors," in Edmunds and Wallace, *Poet, Public, and Performance*, 1–7; Kirk, *Homer and the Epic*, 173–74; Nilsson, *Homer and Mycenae*, 273–74.

49. Joyce connected earlier episodes to later ones by adding corresponding references, as Crispi, *Becoming the Blooms*. Bowen, *Comic Novel*, 60, points to the "first of many times that the initial perspective will be reclaimed throughout the rest of the novel," and see 71 on "Penelope"; in contrast Killeen, *Ulysses Unbound*, 151, on "Nausicaa": "So we are not really back to the tone of the opening episodes: Bloom's own inner worlds and the world of the book have moved too far apart for that."

50. Kenner, *Joyce's Voices*, 15–38; on "Eumaeus" see Gibbons, *Joyce's Ghosts*, 100 (quoting J. Johnson, *Portrait of the Artist*, xxiii): "character here exists at the intersection between interiority and exteriority"; Hills, "Doing Dublin," in Kitcher, *Joyce's "Ulysses*," 158–206; Donoghue, "Styles of 'Nausicaa,'" in Frehner and Zeller, *Collideorscape of Joyce*,

131, on "Nausicaa" as "not what Gerty would say of herself but what she yearns to have someone say of her"; Slote, *Joyce's Nietzschean Ethics,* 59: "Simply put, Joyce's use of free indirect discourse in *Ulysses* is multipolar, which is to say that it is not strictly delimited by the consciousness of any one individual."

51. Lawrence, *Odyssey of Style,* 50–54.

52. See Mackey, *Chaos Theory,* 6, quoting Anatole France: "Chance is the pseudonym of God when he did not want to sign"; Sultan, *Eliot, Joyce and Company,* 49–87.

53. Senn, *Inductive Scrutinies,* 119: *Ulysses* "more and more denounces itself as narrative scheming"; Bell, *Jocoserious Joyce,* 181: "What looks like Accident is actually Comic Fortune." In contrast, Sherry, *Great War,* 42, quotes the *New Statesman* of August 1, 1914: "The chain of events that we have to fear . . . seems to have all the inevitableness of ancient tragedy, where persons and events are controlled not by reason, but by the spell of an ironic fate."

54. See R. Ellmann, *Ulysses on the Liffey,* 125: "Pathetic fallacy can go no further." Kenner, *Joyce's Voices,* 78, points out that the watch would stop in the kind of novel that the style of "Nausicaa" proposes.

55. See Gordon, *Joyce and Reality,* 58–60, 71–72, for magnetism and its implications.

56. See Crispi, *Becoming the Blooms,* 239–42, for Joyce connecting the dates.

57. And see Bloom's "I am a fool perhaps. He gets the plums, and I the plumstones" (13.1098). Similarly, Bloom and Boylan, it turns out, both have hats from Plasto's and employ the same tailor.

58. See Gunn, Hart, and Beck, *James Joyce's Dublin,* 27, on "Nebrekada"; and, for coincidence slipping into fusion, Conley, *Useless Joyce,* 49: "is this [the Rose of Castille] one of those slippery instances in which Bloom's consciousness is, as it were, quietly upstaged by the novel's own metaconsciousness?"; Crispi, *Becoming the Blooms,* 148–49, on Bloom and Menton's identical expressions; Rickard, *Joyce's Book of Memory,* 97–99, 186, on Bloom and Stephen's similar dreams, both recalled on Sandymount Strand.

59. Mercanton, "Hours of James Joyce," in Potts, *Portraits of the Artist,* 213, describes Joyce telling him: "Chance furnishes me what I need. I am like a man who stumbles along; my foot strikes something, I bend over, and it is exactly what I want."

60. See Kershner, *Culture of Joyce's "Ulysses,"* 106, for newspapers as the "very definition of dailiness" (79) and "a series of apparently random items united only by their dateline" (106); French, *Book as World,* 148, for "Cyclops" as like a newspaper. See Staten, "Decomposing Form," in Attridge, *James Joyce's "Ulysses,"* 173–200, and Eco, *Aesthetics of Chaosmos,* 8–10, on Joyce's bricolage; Joyce, *LI* 172; and Baron, "Joyce's Art of Mosaic," 21–34, for his work as "mosaic."

61. See Lawrence, "'Beggaring Description,'" in Frehner and Zeller, *Collideorscape of Joyce,* 151, on *Ulysses*'s "breakdown of the boundary between accident and purpose"; Sherry, *Great War,* 270–71, on the same in Woolf, *Jacob's Room;* and more generally Morson, *Narrative and Freedom,* 8, 86–96, on literary closure as a falsification of reality.

62. Nelson, *Aristophanes and His Tragic Muse,* 1–5, 31–38; Quint, *Epic and Empire,* 134–35, sees Lucan as similarly replacing the gods with Fortune, which "denies any meaningful historical teleology to either winners or losers."

63. See Christensen, *Many-Minded Man,* 26–29, on fate and agency and for further

sources; Redfield, *Nature and Culture*, 131–36; de Jong, *Narratological Commentary*, 9: "In a sense, Homeric fate is the tradition, the elements of the 'Odysseus' story which are given"; and Slatkin, "Plot of the *Iliad*," in King and Doherty, *Thinking the Greeks*, 12–23, for other links between *moira* and genre.

64. Saïd, *Homer and the "Odyssey*," 354n97; and for a moral reading S. West, "Commentary Books I–IV," in Heubeck, West, and Hainsworth, *A Commentary*, vol. 1, 78. On fate and the gods generally see Janko, *A Commentary*, vol. 4, 3–7; Otto, *Homeric Gods*, 263–86. See also the looser sense of speaking or acting not "according to *moira*" or what is right, as *Odyssey* 2.251; 8.393; 9.352.

65. See Taplin, *Homeric Soundings*, 99–103; Dodds, *Greeks and the Irrational*, 1–27; Lesky, "Divine and Human Causation," in Cairns, *Oxford Readings*, 170–202; Feeney, *Gods in Epic*, 53 ff.

66. Otto, *Homeric Gods*, 184, on there being "no alternative between the independent action of a human and the influence or injunction of a deity. What a man wills and does is himself and is the deity. Both are true, and in the last analysis the same"; Feeney, *Gods in Epic*, 2, on the gods as not "a more or less lame shorthand which the poets must perforce employ in order to achieve effects more satisfyingly achieved by novelistic naturalism."

67. Gaskin, "Homeric Heroes," in Cairns, *Oxford Readings*, 154–55: "the intervention of a god in a decision-making process does not derogate from the individual's autonomy or responsibility for his action"; Taplin, *Homeric Soundings*, 104–5, on *Iliad* 4.50–104: "It is important, however, that Athena does not coerce him, she does not manipulate his muscles or interfere with his nervous system. She simply says the right kind of thing to the right kind of man."

68. E. E. Evans-Pritchard, *Witchcraft, Oracles and Magic among the Azande* (Oxford: Oxford University Press, 1976), 22–23.

69. See the criticism of Stephen's paper in *SH*: "If this was drama he did not see why some Dublin Shakespeare should not pen an immortal work dealing with the new Main Drainage Scheme of the Dublin Corporation" (102). As, of course, the "Water Hymn" in "Ithaca" does.

70. Herr, "Art and Life," in Attridge, *James Joyce's "Ulysses*," and for the relation to fusion see 72: "one lives within a stream of consciousness that is finally not distinct from other discursive streams."

71. Booker, *Literary Tradition*, 191, compares Dostoevsky, for whom identity "is, in fact, consistently a narrative construct, something that happens in the course of events rather than something that preexists and then participates in those events." See also Winant, "Empathy and Other Minds," 374, locating this fusion in the philosophic "no man's land" between empathy and intersubjectivity.

72. Similarly, de Romilly, *Time in Greek Tragedy*, 43, "Time is no longer felt as being outside, but it is not really inside either" and 47, "all psychological forces were easily represented as having, outside us, a life which is ultimately ours."

73. And see 8.18–23. One might even point out that with Nausicaa at least, the beautification would have been more useful if it had occurred before Odysseus had won her over.

74. See also Versenyi, *Man's Measure*, 10 ff.: "Having no depth, the self is not so much the cause and ground of a man's acts as it is their sum" (12); Redfield, *Nature and Culture*, 21: "Such a man is not an enclosed identity; he is rather a kind of open field of forces"; and, against Snell, Gaskin, "Homeric Heroes," in Cairns, *Oxford Readings*, 147–69.

75. And see Sullivan, *Psychological Activity in Homer*; Zieliński, "Homeric Psychology," 15–45, and Zaborowski, "Tadeusz Zieliński," 291–300. For a similar effect consider "listening lips and eyes" in "Sirens" (11.266); "Miss voice of Kennedy answered" (11.237); "Miss gaze of Kennedy, heard, not seen, read on" (11.240) etc.

76. In Homer, the only thing the *psuche* does is to leave when a person dies, hence Redfield, "Proem of the *Iliad*," in Cairns, *Oxford Readings*, 466: "The dead bodies are spoken of [in *Iliad* 1.3–4] as the heroes themselves, the *psychai* as mere accessories."

77. Dimock, "Name of Odysseus," in Taylor, *Essays on the "Odyssey*," 57, describes Odysseus's striving for *psuche* as "in other words, something very like identity."

78. Taplin, *Homeric Soundings*, 101; Feeney, *Gods in Epic*, 80 ff., and see Amory, "Reunion of Odysseus and Penelope," in Taylor, *Essays on the "Odyssey"*; Cairns, "Affronts and Quarrels," in Cairns, *Oxford Readings*, 203–19, for the complex psychology implied by Homer's view of the gods.

79. Similarly, see Athena preventing Achilles from killing Agamemnon (*Iliad* 1.188–222) or luring Hector into confronting Achilles (22.225–52).

80. See also Odysseus's failed footrace at *Iliad* 23.740–84.

81. See Anyfanti, "Time, Space, and Consciousness," 23–24: "For Wyndham Lewis such understanding of the self [as Joyce's] is very dangerous. He claims that our self is our 'terra firma' in such a world of locomotive ataxia, and he perceives in the Bergsonian notion of duration a violation of the sense of self as the stable ground upon which experience is based."

82. See Knowles, *Dublin Helix*, 92–93, for Bloom's "I. He. Old. Young" (11.583) as blending himself and Boylan; J. T. Fraser, *Time, Conflict, and Human Values*, 9–10, on the self as having meaning only in regard to others.

83. On "Siopold" see Mahaffey and Truran, "Feeling *Ulysses*," in Kitcher, *Joyce's "Ulysses*," 109–10; Kenner, *Dublin's Joyce*, 25.

84. For opposite views see Osteen, *Economy of "Ulysses*," 399: "But the careers listed merely replicate the very different ones that Bloom and Stephen have already experienced: despite the blended names, their differences remain"; and J. Fraser, *Rite of Passage*, 159: "The two figures met at a threshold, an initiatory liminal zone in which they blend and then separate, and one may assume they are both changed by the experience."

85. Kitcher, "Something Rich and Strange," in Kitcher, *Joyce's "Ulysses*," 216 n16.

86. See Brivic, *Joyce the Creator*, 68, for over a hundred such "synchronicities." To reverse Stephen's repeated "no reconciliation without first a sundering" (9.334–35, 397–98) there is also no sundering without a joining first.

87. Thanks to John Paul Riquelme for pointing out that neither the 1922 nor the 1939 edition include the "wholly" in "Telemachus." Also, as only the reader can appreciate, "matutinal" suggests "maternal" as well as "in the morning."

88. That Gordon, *Joyce and Reality*, 171–204, is able to explain all of the "anomalies" in

purely realistic terms argues that Joyce has linked the naturalistic and stylistic elements of the novel very closely indeed.

89. See Slote, *Joyce's Nietzschean Ethics*, 53, who adds that Hamnet Shakespeare (and his twin, Judith) were born on February 2, Joyce's birthday.

90. Gordon, *Joyce and Reality*, 182, and see 181–83 for the effect overall as parallax.

91. See 17.1253 and Bowker, *James Joyce*, 125, for Matthew Kane's funeral; Mamigonian, "Hunter and Gatherers," 13, and for Kane as Cunningham.

92. For example, Lenehan's *Rose of Castile*: "See the wheeze? Rows of cast steel. Gee!" (7.591; 14.1510–11), and see *Finnegans Wake's* penchant for words that embody opposites, such as the "funferall."

93. For Hamnet's death on August 11 at age 11½ see Brandes, *William Shakespeare*, 140, also quoted in Gifford and Seidman, *"Ulysses" Annotated*, 205. Gordon, *Joyce and Reality*, 190–93, does not see Hamnet contributing here, as Rudy would also be eleven had he lived. See Osteen, *Economy of "Ulysses*," 353–55, on Rudy as "both Bloom's fantasy of return and Stephen's fantasy of departure" (354); Mahaffey, "Joyce and Gender," in Rabaté, *James Joyce Studies*, 121–43, on the "Rudy principle," in which Bloom and Stephen are "psychically interlocked" (125); and Spoo, *Language of History*, 156–57, for the apparition as a union of Stephen and Rudy.

94. See Gifford and Seidman, *"Ulysses" Annotated*, 529, particularly for the link to Hermes. Although Gordon sees no contribution from Stephen, at 289n11, he does note that the attributes reflect Stephen's hat, waistcoat, ashplant and handkerchief (Rudy's "white lambkin," 15.4967).

95. See Adams, *Surface and Symbol*, 234, for *Ulysses* "reproduc[ing] the untidiness of everyday life, through which we make our way, surrounded by thousands of names, familiar and unfamiliar, meaningful and meaningless, mythic and actual, fanciful and literal. Thus the surface of the novel is seen to be deliberately cluttered, even booby-trapped; in many particulars, it is a series of riddles with illogical answers or none at all."

96. Although see Gordon, "M'Intosh Mystery," 671–79, and "M'Intosh Mystery: II," 214–25; Gordon, *Joyce and Reality*, 237–49, and Knowles, *Dublin Helix* 6, 136–37.

97. As shown in de Jong, *Narratological Commentary*, 125, and see Zeus's somewhat sardonic reply.

98. See H. Foley, "'Reverse Similes,'" in Doherty, *Homer's "Odyssey*," for the seminal article on reverse similes; and 5.394–99 on Odysseus reaching dry land as like children welcoming the recovery of a dying father.

CONCLUSION: THE COMIC AND THE HUMAN

1. Nelson, *Aristophanes*, 7–14, and passim.

2. Bowen, *Comic Novel*, 31, and overall.

3. Bowen, *Comic Novel*, 11: "while his own misfit role is a source of anguish for Stephen, Bloom comfortably looks at the church's power, money and ludicrousness from a healthy sense of commonplace agnosticism," and xii: "*Ulysses*, by embracing a more realistic comic philosophy, eschews the pretenses of the high moral dilemmas of tragedy for the normal never-ending problems of everyday life"; or as Woody Allen put it: "Not

only is there no God, but try getting a plumber on weekends" (*Getting Even* [New York: Random House, 1978]).

4. See Bowen, *Comic Novel,* 46, and ff.

5. See Reinhardt, "Judgement of Paris," in Wright and Jones, *Homer,* 180, for "the sublime unseriousness" of the gods, and O'Neill, "Some Temporal Aspects," in Wawrzycka, *Reading Joycean Temporalities,* 112n4: "Eternity is a very long time, especially toward the end."

6. In Lamb, *Adventures of Ulysses,* chap. 4, Odysseus's excuse to Calypso is his "desire to see and converse again with a wife that is mortal: human objects are best fitted to human infirmities."

7. Or as Kermode puts it in *Sense of an Ending,* 138: "No novel can avoid being in some sense what Aristotle calls 'a completed action.'"

8. For time itself as both linear and cyclical see Gould, *Time's Arrow, Time's Cycle.*

9. See Douglas, *Thinking in Circles;* Whitman, *Homer and the Heroic Tradition.*

10. Like the "Doublends Jined" (20.16) of *Finnegans Wake* or *Ulysses*'s "making both ends meet" (16.308; 6.760).

11. Nagy, *Poetry as Performance,* 224–25, quotes Hardy's "The Selfsame Song," which remains the same although both singers and hearers are dead. Witen, *James Joyce and Absolute Music,* 7, cites R. Ellmann, *JJ* 702: "One day a visiting English-woman listened to him reading a passage from the book [*Finnegans Wake*] and sternly remarked, 'That isn't literature.' 'It was,' Joyce replied, meaning that it was while she was listening to it."

12. See Proust, *Remembrance of Things Past,* vol. 1, 22, for our "social personality" as "created by the thoughts of other people."

13. Adams, *Surface and Symbol,* 251: "Joyce, by writing from eighteen angles, shocks us into awareness of the act of authorial choice, seventeen times more than the average novel"; and see Mihálycsa, "Writing of Finitude in *Ulysses,*" in Wawrzycka, *Reading Joycean Temporalities,* 51–66; Mahaffey, *Reauthorizing Joyce,* 61: *Ulysses*'s "willful opacity compels the reader to look *at* language, as well as trying to peer through it."

14. See Senn, *Portals of Recovery,* 69–71, on the reader feeling the "characters as characters and not merely textual configurations," even as Joyce also reveals how character can dissolve.

15. Proust, *Remembrance of Things Past,* vol. 3, 949: "In reality every reader is, while he is reading, the reader of his own self."

16. Beach, *Shakespeare and Company,* 86.

Bibliography

Adams, Robert Martin. "Hades." In Hart and Hayman, *Critical Essays,* 91–114.

———. *Surface and Symbol: The Consistency of James Joyce's "Ulysses."* Oxford: Oxford University Press, 1967.

Ahrensdorf, Peter. *Homer on the Gods and Human Virtue: Creating the Foundations of Classical Civilization.* Cambridge: Cambridge University Press, 2014.

Allan, William. "Divine Justice and Cosmic Order in Early Greek Epic." *Journal of Hellenic Studies* 126 (2006): 1–35.

de Almeida, Hermione. *Byron and Joyce through Homer: Don Juan and Ulysses.* New York: Columbia University Press, 1981.

Alonso, Sabrina. "Advertising in Ulysses." In Brockman, Mecsnóber, and Alonso, *Publishing in Joyce's "Ulysses,"* 107–29.

Ames, Keri Elizabeth. "The Convergence of Homer's *Odyssey* and Joyce's *Ulysses.*" Dissertation, University of Chicago, Committee on Social Thought, 2003.

———. "Joyce's Aesthetic of the Double Negative and His Encounters with Homer's *Odyssey.*" In Jaurretche, *Art of the Negative,* 15–45.

———. "The Rebirth of Heroism in Homer's *Odyssey* and Joyce's *Ulysses.*" In Jones and Beja, *Twenty-First Joyce,* 157–80.

Amory, Anne. "The Reunion of Odysseus and Penelope." In Taylor, *Essays on the "Odyssey,"* 100–121.

Andersen, Øivind. "Odysseus and the Wooden Horse." *Symbolae Osloenses* 52 (1977): 5–18.

Anderson, Benedict. *Imagined Communities.* 1983. New ed. London: Verso, 2006.

Anderson, William S. "Calypso and Elysium." In Taylor, *Essays on the "Odyssey,"* 73–86.

Andersson, Theodore. *Early Epic Scenery: Homer, Virgil, and the Medieval Legacy.* Ithaca, NY: Cornell University Press, 1976.

Anyfanti, Alexandra. "Time, Space, and Consciousness in James Joyce's *Ulysses.*" *Hypermedia Joyce Studies* 4 (2003–2004), http://hjs.ff.cuni.cz/archives/v3/anyfanti.html.

Armand, Louis, ed. *joyceMedia: James Joyce, Hypermedia & Textual Genetics.* Prague: Litteraria Pragensia, 2006.

Atherton, J. S. "The Oxen of the Sun." In Hart and Hayman, *Critical Essays,* 313–39.

Attridge, Derek, ed. *James Joyce's "Ulysses": A Casebook.* Oxford: Oxford University Press, 2004.

———. "Molly's Flow: The Writing of 'Penelope' and the Question of Women's Language." *Modern Fiction Studies* 35 (1989): 543–65.

Atwood, Margaret. *Penelopeiad.* Edinburgh: Canongate Books, 2005.

Aubert, Jacques. "Of Heroes, Monsters, and the Prudent Grammartist." In Frehner and Zeller, *Collideorscape of Joyce*, 83–90.

Auerbach, Erich. *Mimesis*. 1953. Translated by Willard Trask. Princeton, NJ: Princeton University Press, 2003.

Augustine. *The Confessions of St. Augustine*. Translated by Rex Warner. New York: New American Library, 1963.

Austin, Norman. *Archery at the Dark of the Moon: Poetic Problems in Homer's "Odyssey."* Berkeley: University of California Press, 1975.

———. "Name Magic in the *Odyssey*." In Doherty, *Homer's "Odyssey,"* 91–110.

———. "Nausikaa and the Word That Must Not Be Spoken: A Reading of Homer's *Odyssey*, Book 6." *Arion* 25 (2017): 5–36.

———. "The Power of the Word." In Bloom, *Homer's "The Odyssey,"* 69–86.

Bakhtin, M. M. *The Dialogic Imagination*. Edited by Michael Holquist. Translated by Caryl Emerson and Michael Holquist. Austin: University of Texas Press, 1981.

Bakker, Egbert. *The Meaning of Meat and the Structure of the Odyssey*. Cambridge: Cambridge University Press, 2013.

Banta, Melissa, and Oscar Silverman, eds. *James Joyce's Letters to Sylvia Beach: 1921–1940*. Bloomington: Indiana University Press, 1987.

Baron, Scarlett. "Beginnings." In Latham, *Cambridge Companion to "Ulysses,"* 51–68.

———. "Joyce's Art of Mosaic." *James Joyce Quarterly* 57 (2019–20): 21–34.

———. *Strandentwining Cable: Joyce, Flaubert, and Intertextuality*. Oxford: Oxford University Press, 2012.

Bate, Walter Jackson. *The Burden of the Past and the English Poet*. 1970. Reprint, Cambridge, MA: Harvard University Press, 2013.

Bauerle, Ruth. *Picking Up Airs: Hearing the Music in Joyce's Texts*. Urbana: University of Illinois Press, 1993.

Bazarnik, Katarzyna, and Bożena Kucuła, eds. *James Joyce and After: Writer and Time*. Newcastle upon Tyne: Cambridge Scholars Publishing, 2010.

Beach, Sylvia. *Shakespeare and Company*. 1959. New ed. Lincoln: University of Nebraska Press, 1991.

Beck, Deborah. "Odysseus: Narrator, Storyteller, Poet?" *Classical Philology* 100, no. 4 (July 2005): 213–27.

Beckett, Samuel. "Dante . . . Bruno. Vico . . . Joyce." In Beckett et al., *Our Exagmination*, 5–13.

———, et al. *James Joyce/"Finnegans Wake": Our Exagmination Round His Factification for Incamination of "Work in Progress."* 1929. New York: New Directions, 1972.

Bell, Robert. *Jocoserious Joyce: The Fate of Folly in Ulysses*. Gainesville: University Press of Florida, 1996.

Benardete, Seth. *The Bow and the Lyre: A Platonic Reading of the Odyssey*. Lanham, MD: Rowman and Littlefield, 1997.

Bénéjam, Valerie. "A Writer 'dans le temps': Dramatic Time and Timing in Joyce's Aesthetics." In Wawrzycka, *Reading Joycean Temporalities*, 13–30.

Benstock, Bernard, ed. *James Joyce: The Augmented Ninth*. Syracuse: Syracuse University Press, 1988.

———. *The Seventh of Joyce*. Bloomington: Indiana University Press, 1982.

Beplate, Justin. "Joyce, Bergson, and the Memory of Words." *Modern Language Review* 100 (2005): 298–312.

Bergson, Henri. *Time and Free Will: An Essay on the Immediate Data of Consciousness.* Translated by F. L. Pogson. London: George Allen and Unwin, 1956.

Berrone, Louis, ed. and trans. *James Joyce in Padua.* New York: Random House, 1977.

Bersani, Leo. "Against *Ulysses.*" In Attridge, *James Joyce's "Ulysses,"* 201–29.

Bespaloff, Rachel. *On the Iliad.* Translated by Mary McCarthy. New York: Harper Torchbooks, 1947.

Beye, Charles Rowan. *The "Iliad," the "Odyssey," and the Epic Tradition.* Gloucester, MA: Peter Smith, 1972.

Bierl, Anton, Menelaos Christopoulos, and Athina Papachrysostomou, eds. *Time and Space in Ancient Myth, Religion and Culture.* Berlin: De Gruyter, 2017.

Biles, Zachary. "Perils of Song in Homer's *Odyssey.*" *Phoenix* 57 (2003): 191–208.

Bloom, Harold. *The Anxiety of Influence: A Theory of Poetry.* New York: Oxford University Press, 1973.

———, ed. *Homer's "The Odyssey": Modern Critical Interpretations.* New York: Chelsea House, 1988.

van Boheemen, Christine, ed. *Joyce, Modernity, and Its Mediation.* Amsterdam: Rodopi, 1989.

———. "Molly's Heavenly Body and the Economy of the Sign: The Invention of Gender in 'Penelope.'" In Devlin and Reizbaum, *"Ulysses"—En-Gendered Perspectives,* 267–81.

———. "Postcolonial Masculinity and Gender Trauma." In van Boheemen-Saaf and Lamos, *Masculinities in Joyce,* 219–59.

van Boheemen-Saaf, Christine, and Colleen Lamos, eds. *Masculinities in Joyce: Postcolonial Constructions.* European Joyce Studies 10. Amsterdam: Rodopi, 2001.

Booker, M. Keith. *Joyce, Bakhtin, and the Literary Tradition.* Ann Arbor: University of Michigan Press, 1997.

Borg, Ruben. *The Measureless Time of Joyce, Deleuze and Derrida.* London: Continuum, 2007.

Bosinelli, Rosa Maria Bollettieri, and Ira Torresi, eds. *Joyce and/in Translation.* Joyce Studies in Italy 10. Roma: Bulzoni Editore, 2007.

Bowen, Zack. *Bloom's Old Sweet Song: Essays on Joyce and Music.* Gainesville: University Press of Florida, 1995.

———. *"Ulysses" as a Comic Novel.* Syracuse: Syracuse University Press, 1989.

Bowker, Gordon. *James Joyce: A New Biography.* New York: Farrar, Straus and Giroux, 2011.

Bradford, Ernle. *Ulysses Found.* London: Sphere Books, 1963.

Bradley, Bruce, S.J. *James Joyce's Schooldays.* New York: St. Martin's Press, 1982.

Brandes, George. *William Shakespeare: A Critical Study.* New York: MacMillan, 1911.

Brann, Eva. *Homeric Moments: Clues to Delight in Reading the "Odyssey" and the "Iliad."* Philadelphia: Paul Dry Books, 2002.

Breyfogle, Todd, ed. *Literary Imagination, Ancient and Modern.* Chicago: University of Chicago Press, 1999.

Brivic, Sheldon. "Consciousness as Conflict: A Psychoanalytic Approach to *Ulysses.*" In McCormick and Steinberg, *Approaches to Teaching* Joyce's *"Ulysses,"* 59–66.

248 · Bibliography

———. *Joyce between Freud and Jung.* Port Washington, NY: Kennikat Press, 1980.

———. *Joyce the Creator.* Madison: University of Wisconsin Press, 1985.

Brockman, William, Tekla Mecsnóber, and Sabrina Alonso, eds. *Publishing in Joyce's "Ulysses": Newspapers, Advertising and Printing.* European Joyce Studies 26. Leiden: Brill Rodopi, 2018.

Brown, Richard. "Joyce's 'Single Act' Shakespeare." In Pelaschiar, *Joyce/Shakespeare,* 107–27.

Budgen, Frank. *James Joyce and the Making of "Ulysses."* Oxford: Oxford University Press, 1986.

Buitron-Oliver, Diana, and Beth Cohen. "Between Skylla and Penelope: Female Characters of the *Odyssey* in Archaic and Classical Greek Art." In Cohen, *Distaff Side,* 29–58.

Burns, Christy. *Gestural Politics: Stereotype and Parody in Joyce.* Albany: State University of New York Press, 2000.

Bush, Ronald. "Joyce's Modernisms." In Rabaté, *James Joyce Studies,* 10–38.

———. "Joyce's Museum of Homers." In Haynes, *Oxford History of Classical Reception,* 322–57.

Bushrui, Suheil Badi, and Bernard Benstock, eds. *James Joyce: An International Perspective.* Totowa, NY: Barnes and Noble, 1982.

Butcher, S. H., and A. Lang, trans. *The Odyssey of Homer done into English Prose.* By Homer. 1879. London: Macmillan, 1900.

Butler, Samuel. *The Authoress of the "Odyssey."* 1897. Edited by David Grene. Chicago: University of Chicago Press, 1967.

———. *The Humour of Homer and Other Essays.* Introduction by R. A. Streatfeild. Reprint, Great Britain: n.p., 1913.

Buxton, Richard. "Similes and Other Likenesses." In Fowler, *Cambridge Companion to Homer,* 139–55.

Cairns, Douglas. "Affronts and Quarrels in the *Iliad.*" In *Oxford Readings in Homer's "Iliad."* 203–19.

———, ed. *Oxford Readings in Homer's "Iliad."* Oxford Readings in Classical Studies. Oxford: Oxford University Press, 2001.

Card, James Van Dyck. *An Anatomy of Penelope.* Rutherford, NJ: Farleigh Dickinson University Press, 1984.

Carpenter, Rhys. *Folk Tale, Fiction and Saga in the Homeric Epics.* Berkeley: University of California Press, 1946.

Castle, Gregory. "Ousted Possibilities: Critical Histories in James Joyce's *Ulysses.*" *Twentieth Century Literature* 39 (1993): 306–28.

Cheng, Vincent. *Joyce, Race, and Empire.* Cambridge: Cambridge University Press, 1995.

———. "White Horse, Dark Horse: Joyce's Allhorse of Another Color." *Joyce Studies Annual* (1991): 101–28.

Childs, Peter. *Modernism.* New York: Routledge, 2000.

Christensen, Joel. *The Many-Minded Man: The Odyssey, Psychology and the Therapy of Epic.* Ithaca, NY: Cornell University Press, 2020.

Christopoulos, Menelaos. "Strange Instances of Time and Space in Odysseus' Return." In Bierl, Christopoulos, and Papachrysostomou, *Time and Space,* 3–8.

Cixous, Hélène. *The Exile of James Joyce.* Translated by Sally Purcell. London: Calder, 1972.

Clay, Jenny Strauss. "Odysseus: Name and Helmet." In Bloom, *Homer's "The Odyssey,"* 103–26.

———. *The Wrath of Athena: Gods and Men in the Odyssey.* Princeton, NJ: Princeton University Press, 1983.

Cohen, Beth, ed. *The Distaff Side: Representing the Female in Homer's "Odyssey."* New York: Oxford University Press, 1995.

Cohn, Dorrit. *Transparent Minds: Narrative Modes for Presenting Consciousness in Fiction.* Princeton, NJ: Princeton University Press, 1978.

Colum, Padraic. Contribution to Memoir. In O'Connor, *The Joyce We Knew,* 63–91.

Conley, Tim. "'Endlessnessnessness': Joyce and Time without Measure." In Wawrzycka, *Reading Joycean Temporalities,* 68–69.

———. *Joyce's Mistakes: Problems of Intention, Irony, and Interpretation.* Toronto: University of Toronto Press, 2003.

———. *Useless Joyce: Textual Functions, Cultural Appropriations.* Toronto: University of Toronto Press, 2017.

Cook, Erwin. "'Active' and 'Passive' Heroics in the *Odyssey*." In Doherty, *Homer's "Odyssey,"* 111–34.

Costello, Peter. *James Joyce.* 1980. Reprint, Dublin: Gill and Macmillan, 1988.

Cox, Fiona, and Elena Theodorakopoulos, eds. *Homer's Daughters: Women's Responses to Homer in the Twentieth Century and Beyond.* Oxford: Oxford University Press, 2019.

Crispi, Luca. "Joyce at Work on *Ulysses*: 1917–22." *Genetic Joyce Studies* 13 (2013), http://www.geneticjoycestudies.org.

———. *Joyce's Creative Process and the Construction of Characters in "Ulysses": Becoming the Blooms.* Oxford: Oxford University Press, 2015.

Culleton, Claire. *Names and Naming in Joyce.* Madison: University of Wisconsin Press, 1994.

Cunliffe, Richard. *A Lexicon of the Homeric Dialect.* Norman, OK: University of Oklahoma Press: 1963.

Curran, Constantine. *James Joyce Remembered.* New York: Oxford University Press, 1968.

D'Arcy, Anne Marie. "Dindsenchas, Mr Deasy, and the Nightmare of Partition in *Ulysses*." *Proceedings of the Royal Irish Academy: Archaeology, Culture, History, Literature* 114 (2014): 295–325.

Devlin, Kimberly, and Marilyn Reizbaum, eds. *"Ulysses"—En-Gendered Perspectives: Eighteen New Essays on the Episodes.* Columbia: University of South Carolina Press, 1999.

Dimock, George. "The Name of Odysseus." In Taylor, *Essays on the "Odyssey,"* 54–72.

Dodds, E. R. *The Greeks and the Irrational.* Berkeley: University of California Press, 1951.

Doherty, Lillian. "Gender and Internal Audiences in the *Odyssey*." In Doherty, *Homer's "Odyssey,"* 247–64.

———, ed. *Homer's "Odyssey."* Oxford Readings in Classical Studies. Oxford: Oxford University Press, 2009.

Doniger, Wendy. Foreword to *Shamanism* by Eliade, xi–xv.

Donoghue, "The Styles of 'Nausicaa.'" In Frehner and Zeller, *Collideorscape of Joyce*, 127–36.

Dougherty, Carol. *The Raft of Odysseus: The Ethnographic Imagination of Homer's Odyssey*. Oxford: Oxford University Press, 2001.

Douglas, Mary. *Thinking in Circles: An Essay on Ring Composition*. New Haven: Yale University Press, 2007.

Duffy, Enda. "Setting: Dublin 1904/1922." In Latham, *Cambridge Companion to "Ulysses,"* 81–94.

Durkheim, Emile. *Elementary Forms of Religious Experience*. Translated by Carol Cosman. Oxford: Oxford World Classics, 2008.

Ebury, Katherine, and James Alexander Fraser, eds. *Joyce's Non-Fiction Writings: Outside His Jurisfiction*. Cham, Switzerland: Palgrave Macmillan, 2018.

Eco, Umberto. *The Aesthetics of Chaosmos: The Middle Ages of James Joyce*. Translated by Ellen Esrock. Tulsa: University of Oklahoma Press, 1989.

Edmunds, Lowell, and Robert Wallace, eds. *Poet, Public, and Performance in Ancient Greece*. Baltimore: Johns Hopkins University Press, 1997.

Edwards, Anthony. "Homer's Ethical Geography: Country and City in the *Odyssey*." *Transactions of the American Philological Association* 47 (1993): 27–78.

Eliade, Mircea. *The Sacred and the Profane: The Nature of Religion*. Translated by Willard Trask. New York: Harcourt, 1987.

———. *Shamanism: Archaic Techniques of Ecstasy*. Translated by Willard R. Trask. Foreword by Wendy Doniger. Bollingen Series LXXVI. Princeton and Oxford: Princeton University Press, 2004.

Elias, Norbert. *Time: An Essay*. Translated by Edmund Jephcott. Oxford: Blackwell, 1992.

Eliot, T. S. *The Complete Prose of T.S. Eliot: The Critical Edition. Volume 2, The Perfect Critic, 1919–1926*. Edited by Ronald Schuchard and Anthony Cuda. Baltimore: Johns Hopkins University Press and Faber and Faber, 2014.

Ellmann, Maud. "Endings." In Latham, *Cambridge Companion to "Ulysses,"* 95–110.

———. "The Ghosts of *Ulysses*." In Attridge, *James Joyce's "Ulysses,"* 83–101.

Ellmann, Richard. "The Backgrounds of *Ulysses*." *Kenyon Review* 16 (1954): 337–86.

———. *The Consciousness of Joyce*. London: Faber and Faber, 1977.

———. [*JJ*] *James Joyce*. New ed. New York: Oxford University Press, 1982.

———. "Joyce and Homer." *Critical Inquiry* 3 (1977): 567–82.

———. "The Limits of Joyce's Naturalism." *Sewanee Review* 63 (1955): 567–75.

———, ed. *My Brother's Keeper: James Joyce's Early Years*. By Stanislaus Joyce. New York: Viking, 1958.

———. *Ulysses on the Liffey*. Oxford: Oxford University Press, 1972.

Emlyn-Jones, Chris. "The Reunion of Odysseus and Penelope." *Greece and Rome* 31 (1984): 1–18.

Eysteinsson, A., and Vivian Liska, eds. *Modernism*. 2 vols. Amsterdam and Philadelphia: John Benjamins, 2007.

Fairhall, James. *James Joyce and the Question of History*. Cambridge: Cambridge University Press, 1993.

Feeney, Denis. *Caesar's Calendar: Ancient Time and the Beginnings of History*. Berkeley: University of California Press, 2007.

————. *The Gods in Epic: Poets and Critics of the Classical Tradition.* Oxford: Clarendon Press, 1991.

Felson, Nancy. *Regarding Penelope: From Character to Poetics.* Norman: University of Oklahoma Press, 1994.

Felson, Nancy, and Laura Slatkin. "Gender and Homeric Epic." In Fowler, *Cambridge Companion to Homer,* 91–114.

de Fénelon, François. *The Adventures of Telemachus, the Son of Ulysses.* Edited and translated by Patrick Riley. Cambridge: Cambridge University Press, 1994.

————. *The Adventures of Telemachus, the Son of Ulysses.* 1776. Translated by Tobias Smollett. Edited by Leslie Chilton. Athens: University of Georgia Press, 1997.

Fenik, Bernard. *Studies in the "Odyssey."* Wiesbaden: Franz Steiner Verlag, 1974.

Ferrer, Daniel, Sam Slote, and Andre Topia, eds. *Renascent Joyce.* Gainesville: University Press of Florida, 2013.

Ferrucci, Franco. *The Poetics of Disguise: The Autobiography of the Work in Homer, Dante, and Shakespeare.* Translated by Ann Dunnigan. Ithaca, NY: Cornell University Press, 1980.

Finley, Moses. *The World of Odysseus.* 1954. Revised ed. New York: Viking, 1978.

Flack, Leah. *James Joyce and Classical Modernism.* London: Bloomsbury, 2020.

————. *Modernism and Homer: The Odysseys of H.D., James Joyce, Osip Mandelstam, and Ezra Pound.* Cambridge: Cambridge University Press, 2015.

————. "The News in the *Odyssey* Is Still News": Ezra Pound, W.H.D. Rouse, and a Modern Odyssey." *Modernism/modernity* 22 (2015): 105–24.

Fludernik, Monika. *An Introduction to Narratology.* New York: Routledge, 2009.

Foley, Helene. "Penelope as Moral Agent." In Cohen, *Distaff Side,* 93–115.

————. "'Reverse Similes' and Sex Roles in the *Odyssey.*" In Doherty, *Homer's "Odyssey,"* 189–207.

Foley, John Miles, ed. *A Companion to Ancient Epic.* Oxford: Wiley-Blackwell, 2009.

————. "Epic as Genre." In Fowler, *Cambridge Companion to Homer,* 171–87.

————. "Penelope as Moral Agent." In Bloom, *Homer's "The Odyssey,"* 87–108.

Forster, E. M. *Aspects of the Novel.* New York: Vintage, 1927.

Foster, R. F. *Modern Ireland 1600–1972.* London: Penguin, 1988.

Fowler, Robert, ed. *Cambridge Companion to Homer.* Cambridge: Cambridge University Press, 2004.

————. "The Homeric Question." In Fowler, *Cambridge Companion to Homer,* 220–34.

Frame, Douglas. *The Myth of Return in Early Greek Epic.* Washington, DC: Center for Hellenic Studies, 1978.

Fraser, J. T. *Of Time, Passion and Knowledge: Reflections on the Strategy of Existence.* New York: George Braziller, 1975.

————. *Time, Conflict, and Human Values.* Urbana: University of Illinois Press, 1999.

Fraser, Jennifer Margaret. *Rite of Passage in The Narratives of Joyce and Dante.* Gainesville: University Press of Florida, 2002.

Fredricksmeyer, Hardy. "Penelope *Polutropos*: The Crux at *Odyssey* 23.218–24." *American Journal of Philology* 118 (1997): 487–97.

Frehner, Ruth, and Ursula Zeller, eds. *A Collideorscape of Joyce: Festschrift for Fritz Senn.* Dublin: Lilliput Press, 1998.

French, Marilyn. *The Book as World: James Joyce's "Ulysses."* Cambridge, MA: Harvard University Press, 1976.

———. "Women in Joyce's Dublin." In Benstock, *Augmented Ninth,* 267–72.

Friedman, Melvin J. "Lestrygonians." In Hart and Hayman, *Critical Essays,* 131–46.

Friedrich, Paul, and James Redfield. "Speech as a Personality Symbol: The Case of Achilles." *Language* 54 (1978): 263–88.

Fussell, Paul. *The Great War and Modern Memory.* Oxford: Oxford University Press, 2013.

Gabler, Hans. "'He chronicled with patience': Early Joycean Progressions between Non-Fiction and Fiction." In Ebury and Fraser, *Joyce's Non-Fiction Writings,* 55–75.

Gaipa, Mark, Sean Latham, and Robert Scholes, eds. *The Little Review "Ulysses."* New Haven: Yale University Press, 2015.

Gardner, Hunter, and Sheila Murnaghan, eds. *Odyssean Identities in Modern Cultures: The Journey Home.* Columbus: Ohio University Press, 2014.

Gartziou-Tatti, Ariadni. "Prophecy and Time in the *Odyssey.*" *Quaderni Urbinati di Cultura Classica* 96 (2010): 11–28.

Garvie, A. E., ed. *Homer: Odyssey Books VI–VIII.* Cambridge: Cambridge University Press, 1994.

Gaskin, Richard. "Do Homeric Heroes Make Real Decisions?" In Cairns, *Oxford Readings,* 147–69.

Gell, Alfred. *The Anthropology of Time: Cultural Construction of Temporal Maps and Images.* Oxford: Berg Publishers, 1992.

Genet, Jacqueline, and Elisabeth Hellegouarch, eds. *Studies on Joyce's "Ulysses."* Caen: Université de Caen, 1991.

Gibbons, Luke. *Joyce's Ghosts: Ireland, Modernism, and Memory.* Chicago: University of Chicago Press, 2015.

Gibson, Andrew. *Joyce's Revenge.* Oxford: Oxford University Press, 2002.

———. *The Strong Spirit: History, Politics and Aesthetics in the Writings of James Joyce 1898–1915.* Oxford: Oxford University Press, 2013.

Giedion-Welcker, Carola. "Meetings with Joyce." In Potts, *Portraits of the Artist,* 256–80.

Giesecke, Annette Lucia. "Mapping Utopia: Homer's Politics and the Birth of the Polis." In *Reading Homer in the 21st Century. College Literature* 34 (2007): 194–214.

Gifford, Don. "James Joyce and Myth." *Hungarian Journal of English and American Studies* 8 (2002): 123–29.

Gifford, Don, with Robert Seidman. *"Ulysses" Annotated: Notes for James Joyce's "Ulysses."* Berkeley: University of California Press, 1988.

Gilbert, Stuart. *James Joyce's "Ulysses."* 1930. Reprint, New York: Vintage, 1958.

———. "Prolegomena to Work in Progress." In Beckett, *Our Exagmination,* 25–38.

Gillespie, Michael Patrick, ed. *Foundational Essays in James Joyce Studies.* Gainesville: University Press of Florida, 2011.

Gillies, Mary Ann. "Bergsonism: 'Time Out of Mind.'" In *A Concise Companion to Modernism,* edited by David Bradshaw, 95–115. Malden, MA: Blackwell Publishing, 2003.

———. *Henri Bergson and British Modernism.* Montreal and Kingston: McGill-Queen's University Press, 1966.

Glassco, John. *Memoirs of Montparnasse.* 1970. Reprint, New York: Review Books, 2007.

Goldberg, S. L. "Joyce and the Artist's Fingernails." In Gillespie, *Foundational Essays,* 125–38.

Goldman, Arnold. *The Joyce Paradox: Form and Freedom in His Fiction*. Evanston, IL: Northwestern University Press, 1966.

Goldman, Jonathan. "Joyce, the Propheteer." *NOVEL: A Forum on Fiction* 38 (2004): 84–102.

Gordon, John. *Joyce and Reality: The Empirical Strikes Back*. Syracuse: Syracuse University Press, 2004.

———. "The M'Intosh Mystery." *Modern Fiction Studies* 29 (1983): 671–79.

———. "The M'Intosh Mystery: II." *Twentieth Century Literature* 38 (1992): 214–25.

Gorman, Herbert. *James Joyce*. New York: Farrar and Rinehart, 1939.

Gose, Elliott. *The Transformation Process in Joyce's "Ulysses."* Toronto: University of Toronto Press, 1980.

Gould, Stephen Jay. *Time's Arrow, Time's Cycle: Myth and Metaphor in the Discovery of Geological Time*. Cambridge, MA: Harvard University Press, 1987.

Gowing, Alain. *Empire and Memory: The Representation of the Roman Republic in Imperial Culture*. Cambridge: Cambridge University Press, 2005.

Graham, A. J. "The *Odyssey*, History, and Women." In Cohen, *Distaff Side*, 3–16.

Graziosi, Barbara, and Emily Greenwood, eds. *Homer in the Twentieth Century: Between World Literature and the Western Canon*. Oxford: Oxford University Press, 2007.

Grene, David. "The *Odyssey*: An Approach." *Midway* 9 (1969): 47–68.

Grethlein, Jonas. "Memory and Material Objects in the *Iliad* and the *Odyssey*." *Journal of Hellenic Studies* 128 (2008): 27–51.

Griffin, Jasper. "The Epic Cycle and the Uniqueness of Homer." In Cairns, *Oxford Readings*, 365–84.

Groden, Michael. "Genetic Joyce: Textual Studies and the Reader." In Rabaté, *James Joyce Studies*, 227–50.

——— et al., eds. *The James Joyce Archive*. New York: Garland, 1978.

———. *"Ulysses" in Progress*. Princeton, NJ: Princeton University Press, 1977.

———. "Writing *Ulysses*." In Latham, *Cambridge Companion to "Ulysses,"* 3–18.

Guidorizzi, Giulio. "The Laughter of the Suitors: A Case of Collective Madness in the *Odyssey*." Translated by Edmunds. In Edmunds and Wallace, *Poet, Public, and Performance*, 1–7.

Gunn, Ian, and Clive Hart, with Harold Beck. *James Joyce's Dublin: A Topographical Guide to the Dublin of Ulysses*. New York: Thames and Hudson, 2004.

Hagberg, Garry. "A Portrait of Consciousness: Joyce's *Ulysses* as Philosophical Psychology." In Kitcher, *Joyce's "Ulysses,"* 63–99.

Hainsworth, Bryan. *The Iliad: A Commentary*. Vol. 3. Cambridge: Cambridge University Press, 1993.

Hall, Edith. *The Return of Ulysses: A Cultural History of Homer's "Odyssey."* London: I. B. Tauris, 2008.

Harsh, P. W. "Penelope and Odysseus in *Odyssey* XIX." *American Journal of Philology* 71 (1950): 1–21.

Hart, Clive. "Gaps and Cracks in *Ulysses*." *James Joyce Quarterly* 30 (1993): 427–37.

———. *James Joyce's Ulysses*. Sydney: Sydney University Press, 1968.

———. "Wandering Rocks." In Hart and Hayman, *Critical Essays*, 181–216.

Hart, Clive, and David Hayman, eds. *James Joyce's Ulysses: Critical Essays.* Berkeley: University of California Press, 1974.

Hartog, François. *Regimes of Historicity: Presentism and Experiences of Time.* New York: Columbia University Press, 2015.

Haubold, Johannes. "Homer after Parry: Tradition, Reception, and the Timeless Text." In Graziosi and Greenwood, *Homer in the Twentieth Century,* 27–46.

Hayman, David. *Ulysses: The Mechanics of Meaning.* 1970. Reprint, Madison: University of Wisconsin Press, 1982.

Haynes, Kenneth, ed. *The Oxford History of Classical Reception in English Literature.* Vol. 5. After 1880. Oxford: Oxford University Press, 2019.

Hayward, Matthew. "'But who was Gerty?': Intertextuality and the Advertising Language of 'Nausicaa.'" In Brockman, Mecsnóber, and Alonso, *Publishing in Joyce's "Ulysses,"* 89–106.

Heiden, B. "The Placement of 'Book Divisions' in the *Odyssey.*" *Classical Philology* 94 (2000): 247–59.

Herr, Cheryl. "Difficulty: 'Oxen of the Sun' and 'Circe.'" In Latham, *Cambridge Companion to "Ulysses,"* 154–68.

———. *Joyce's Anatomy of Culture.* Urbana: University of Illinois Press, 1986.

Herring, Phillip. "The Bedsteadfastnes of Molly Bloom." *Modern Fiction Studies* 15 (1969): 49–61.

———. *Joyce's Uncertainty Principle.* Princeton, NJ: Princeton University Press, 1987.

Heubeck, Alfred. General introduction to *A Commentary,* vol. 1. In Heubeck, West, and Hainsworth, 3–23.

———. Introduction to *A Commentary,* vol. 2. In Heubeck and Hoekstra, 3–11.

Heubeck, Alfred, and Arie Hoekstra, eds. *A Commentary on Homer's Odyssey.* Vol 2. Books IX–XVI. Oxford: Clarendon Press, 1989.

Heubeck, Alfred, Stephanie West, and J. B. Hainsworth. *A Commentary on Homer's Odyssey.* Vol 1. Books I–VIII. Oxford: Clarendon Press, 1988.

Higbie, Carolyn. *Heroes' Names, Homeric Identities.* Ann Arbor: University of Michigan Press, 1995.

Hill, Marylu. "'Amor Matris': Mother and Self in the Telemachiad Episode of *Ulysses.*" *Twentieth Century Literature* 39 (1993): 329–43.

Hills, David. "Doing Dublin in Different Voices." In Kitcher, *Joyce's "Ulysses,"* 158–206.

Hodgart, Matthew. "Aeolus." In Hart and Hayman, *Critical Essays,* 115–30.

Hodgart, Matthew, and Ruth Bauerle. *Joyce's Grand Operoar: Opera in "Finnegans Wake."* Urbana: University of Illinois Press, 1997.

Hoffmeister, Adolf. "James Joyce" and "Portrait of Joyce." In Potts, *Portraits of the Artist,* 121–36.

Hogan, Patrick. *Joyce, Milton, and the Theory of Influence.* Gainesville: University Press of Florida, 1995.

Hölscher, Uvo. "Penelope and the Suitors." In Schein, *Reading the "Odyssey,"* 133–40.

Homer. *Homeri Opera: Iliad.* Edited by David Munro and Thomas Allen. 2 vols. Oxford Classical Texts. Oxford: Oxford University Press, 1985.

———. *Homeri Opera: Odyssey.* Edited by Thomas Allen. 2 vols. Oxford Classical Texts. Oxford: Oxford University Press, 1985.

———. *The Iliad.* Translated by Richmond Lattimore. Chicago: University of Chicago Press, 1951.

———. *The Iliad: A Commentary.* Vol. 3. Edited by Bryan Hainsworth. Cambridge: Cambridge University Press, 1993.

———. *The Iliad: A Commentary.* Vol. 4. Edited by Richard Janko. Cambridge: Cambridge University Press, 1992.

———. *The Odyssey.* Edited by Alfred Heubeck and Arie Hoekstra. *A Commentary on Homer's "Odyssey."* Vol 2. Oxford: Clarendon Press, 1989.

———. *The Odyssey.* Edited by Alfred Heubeck, Stephanie West, and J. B. Hainsworth. *A Commentary on Homer's Odyssey.* Vol. 1. Oxford: Clarendon Press, 1988.

———. *The Odyssey.* Edited by Joseph Russo, Manuel Fernandez-Galiano, and Alfred Heubeck. *A Commentary on Homer's Odyssey.* Vol 3. Oxford: Clarendon Press, 1992.

———. *The Odyssey.* Edited by W. B. Stanford. 2 vols. London: Bristol Classical Press, 1996.

———. *The Odyssey.* Translated by Emily Wilson. New York: W. W. Norton, 2018.

———. *The Odyssey.* Translated by Richmond Lattimore. New York: HarperCollins, 1967.

———. *The Odyssey.* Translated by Robert Fitzgerald. New York: Vintage Classics, Random House, 1990.

———. *The Odyssey: Books VI–VIII.* Edited by A. F. Garvie. Cambridge: Cambridge University Press, 1994.

———. *The Odyssey: Books XIX and XX.* Edited by R. B. Rutherford. Cambridge: Cambridge University Press, 1992.

———. *Odyssey Books XVII–XVIII.* Edited by Deborah Steiner. Cambridge: Cambridge University Press, 2010.

———. *The Odyssey of Homer Done into English Prose.* Translated by S. H. Butcher and A. Lang. 1879. London: Macmillan, 1900.

———. *The Odyssey of Homer: Newly Translated into English Prose.* Translated by T. E. Lawrence. New York: Oxford University Press, 1991. First published 1932 under the name of T. E. Shaw.

———. *The Odyssey: Rendered into English Prose.* Translated by Samuel Butler. 1900. New York: AMS Press, 1968.

Hornbeck, Cynthia. "Greekly Imperfect: The Homeric Origins of Joyce's 'Nausicaa.'" *Joyce Studies Annual* (2009): 89–108.

Hutchins, Patricia. *James Joyce's Dublin.* Great Britain: Grey Walls Press, 1950.

Hutchinson, Laurie Glenn. "Messengers and the Art of Reported Speech in the Iliad." Dissertation, Boston University, 2018.

Hutton, Clare. "The Development of *Ulysses* in Print, 1918–22." *Dublin James Joyce Journal* 6–7 (2013–14): 109–31.

———. *Serial Encounters: Ulysses and the "Little Review."* Oxford: Oxford University Press, 2019.

Igoe, Vivien. *The Real People of Joyce's "Ulysses": A Biographical Guide.* Dublin: University College Dublin Press, 2016.

Janko, Richard, ed. *The Iliad: A Commentary.* Vol. 4. Cambridge: Cambridge University Press, 1992.

Jaurretche, Colleen, ed. *Beckett, Joyce and the Art of the Negative.* European Joyce Studies 16. New York: Rodopi, 2005.

Jensen, Minna Skafte. "In What Sense Can the *Iliad* and the *Odyssey* Be Considered Oral Texts?" In Doherty, Homer's *"Odyssey,"* 18–28.

———. "Performance." In Foley, *Companion to Ancient Epic,* 45–54.

Johnson, Jeri. "'Beyond the Veil': Ulysses, Feminism, and the Figure of Women." In van Boheemen, *Joyce, Modernity, and Its Mediation,* 201–28.

———, ed. *A Portrait of the Artist as a Young Man.* Oxford: Oxford University Press, 2000.

Johnson, Patricia. *Ovid Before Exile: Art and Punishment in the Metamorphoses.* Madison: University of Wisconsin Press, 2008.

Jones, Ellen Carol, and Morris Beja, eds. *Twenty-First Joyce.* Gainesville: University Press of Florida, 2004.

Jones, P. V. "The Past in Homer's *Odyssey.*" *Journal of Hellenic Studies* 112 (1992): 74–90.

de Jong, Irene. "Between Word and Deed: Hidden Thoughts in the *Odyssey.*" In Doherty, Homer's *"Odyssey,"* 62–90.

———. *A Narratological Commentary on the Odyssey.* Cambridge: Cambridge University Press, 2001.

———. *Narratology and Classics: A Practical Guide.* Oxford: Oxford University Press, 2014.

de Jong, Irene, and René Nünlist. *Time in Ancient Greek Literature.* Leiden: Brill, 2007.

Joyce, James. [CW] *Critical Writings.* Edited by Ellsworth Mason and Richard Ellmann. Ithaca, NY: Cornell University Press, 1989.

———. *Dubliners.* Edited by Robert Scholes and A. Walton Litz. New York: Penguin, 1996.

———. [FW] *Finnegans Wake.* New York: Penguin, 1999.

———. [LI, LII, LIII] *The Letters of James Joyce.* Edited by Stuart Gilbert (vol. 1) and Richard Ellmann (vols. 2–3). 3 vols. New York: Viking, 1957–66.

———. [OCPW] *Occasional, Critical, and Political Writing.* Edited by Kevin Barry. Oxford: Oxford World's Classics, 2000.

———. [P] *A Portrait of the Artist as a Young Man.* Edited by Chester Anderson. New York: Viking, 1968.

———. *A Portrait of the Artist as a Young Man.* Edited by Seamus Deane. New York: Penguin, 2003.

———. *A Portrait of the Artist as a Young Man.* Edited by John Paul Riquelme. New York: W. W. Norton, 2007.

———. [SL] *Selected Letters of James Joyce.* Edited by Richard Ellmann. London: Faber and Faber, 1975.

———. [SH] *Stephen Hero.* Edited by Theodore Spencer. Revised with foreword by John J. Slocum and Herbert Cahoon. Expanded ed. New York: New Directions, 1963.

———. [U] *Ulysses.* Edited by Hans Walter Gabler et al. New York: Random House, 1986.

———. *Ulysses.* Edited by Sam Slote, Marc Mamigonian, and John Turner. London: Alma Classics, 2017.

———. *Ulysses: The 1922 Text.* Edited by Jeri Johnson. Oxford: Oxford World Classics, 2008.

Joyce, P. W. *English as We Speak It in Ireland.* London: Longmans, Green, 1910.

Joyce, Stanislaus. *The Complete Dublin Diary of Stanislaus Joyce.* Edited by George Healey. Ithaca, NY: Cornell University Press, 1962.

———. *My Brother's Keeper: James Joyce's Early Years.* Edited by Richard Ellmann. New York: Viking, 1958.

———. *Recollections of James Joyce by His Brother Stanislaus Joyce.* New York: James Joyce Society, 1950.

Kain, Richard. *Fabulous Voyager: A Study of James Joyce's "Ulysses."* New York: Viking, 1947.

Katz, Marylin. *Penelope's Renown: Meaning and Indeterminacy in the "Odyssey."* Princeton, NJ: Princeton University Press, 1991.

Kennedy, Duncan. *Antiquity and the Meaning of Time: A Philosophy of Ancient and Modern Literature.* London: I. B. Tauris, 2013.

Kenner, Hugh. "The Arranger." In Attridge, *James Joyce's "Ulysses,"* 17–32.

———. "Circe." In Hart and Hayman, *Critical Essays,* 341–62.

———. *A Colder Eye: The Modern Irish Writers.* New York: Alfred A. Knopf, 1983.

———. *Dublin's Joyce.* 1956. Reprint, New York: Columbia University Press, 1987.

———. "Joyce's *Ulysses*: Homer and Hamlet." *Essays in Criticism* 2 (1952): 85–104.

———. *Joyce's Voices.* Berkeley: University of California Press, 1979.

———. "Keeping an Eye on Homer." In Frehner and Zeller, *Collideorscape of Joyce,* 115–19.

———. "The *Portrait* in Perspective." *Kenyon Review* 10 (1948): 361–81.

———. *The Pound Era.* Berkeley: University of California Press, 1971.

———. "Rhetoric of Silence." *James Joyce Quarterly* 14 (1977): 382–94.

———. *Ulysses.* London: George Allen and Unwin, 1980.

Kermode, Frank. *The Sense of an Ending: Studies in the Theory of Fiction with a New Epilogue.* 1966. Reprint, Oxford: Oxford University Press, 2000.

Kern, Stephen. *The Culture of Time and Space 1880–1919.* 1983. Reprint, Cambridge, MA: Harvard University Press, 2003.

Kershner, R. Brandon. *The Culture of Joyce's "Ulysses."* New York: Palgrave Macmillan, 2010.

———. "Intertextuality." In Latham, *Cambridge Companion to "Ulysses,"* 171–83.

———. "Joyce and Stephen Phillips' *Ulysses.*" *James Joyce Quarterly* 13 (1976): 194–201.

Kiberd, Declan. Review of *Irish Identity and the Literary Revival: Synge, Yeats, Joyce, and O'Casey; John Millington Synge: A Reference Guide,* by G. J. Watson. *Review of English Studies* 32 (1981): 97–99.

Killeen, Terence. *Ulysses Unbound: A Reader's Companion to James Joyce's "Ulysses."* Gainesville: University Press of Florida, 2018.

Kimball, Jean. "Jung's 'Dual Mother' in Joyce's *Ulysses*: An Illustrated Psychoanalytic Intertext." *Journal of Modern Literature* 17 (1991): 477–90.

King, Bruce, and Lillian Doherty, eds. *Thinking the Greeks: A Volume in Honour of James M. Redfield.* New York: Routledge, 2019.

King, John. "Trapping the Fox You Are(N't) with a Riddle: The Autobiographical Crisis of Stephen Dedalus in *Ulysses.*" *Twentieth Century Literature* 45 (1999): 299–316.

Kirk, G. S. *Homer and the Epic.* Cambridge: Cambridge University Press, 1965.

Kitcher, Philip. *Joyce's Kaleidoscope: An Invitation to "Finnegans Wake."* Oxford: Oxford University Press, 2007.

———, ed. *Joyce's "Ulysses": Philosophical Perspectives.* Oxford: Oxford University Press, 2020.

———. "Something Rich and Strange: Joyce's Perspectivism." In Kitcher, *Joyce's "Ulysses,"* 207–51.

Kitto, H.D.F. "'The Odyssey': The Exclusion of Surprise." In Bloom, *Homer's "The Odyssey,"* 5–33.

Klein, Scott. "Odysseus as 'New Womanly Man.'" *James Joyce Quarterly* 26 (1989): 617–19.

Knowles, Sebastian. *The Dublin Helix: The Life of Language in Joyce's "Ulysses."* Gainesville: University Press of Florida, 2001.

———. "The Substructure of 'Sirens': Molly as 'Nexus Omnia Ligans.'" *James Joyce Quarterly* 23 (1986): 447–63.

Kohnken, Adolf. "Odysseus' Scar: An Essay on Homeric Epic Narrative Technique." In Doherty, *Homer's "Odyssey,"* 44–61.

Lamb, Charles. *The Adventures of Ulysses: The Tale of Homer's Odyssey for Children.* 1808. Lexington, KY: Bravo Ebooks, 2017.

Latham, Sean, ed. *The Cambridge Companion to "Ulysses."* Cambridge: Cambridge University Press, 2014.

———. "A Portrait of the Snob: James Joyce and the Anxieties of Cultural Capital." *Modern Fiction Studies* (2001): 774–99.

Lawrence, Karen. "'Beggaring Description': Politics and Style in Joyce's 'Eumaeus.'" In Frehner and Zeller, *Collideorscape of Joyce,* 138–55.

———. *The Odyssey of Style in "Ulysses."* Princeton, NJ: Princeton University Press, 1982.

———. "Paternity as Legal Fiction in *Ulysses.*" In Benstock, *The Augmented Ninth,* 233–43.

———. "'Twenty Pockets Arent Enough for Their Lies': Pocketed Objects as Props of Bloom's Masculinity in *Ulysses.*" In van Boheemen-Saaf and Lamos, *Masculinities in Joyce,* 163–75.

Le Guin, Ursula. *Lavinia.* New York: Houghton Mifflin, 2009.

Leonard, Garry. "James Joyce and Popular Culture." In Rabaté, *James Joyce Studies,* 39–51.

———. "'A Little Trouble about Those White Corpuscles': Mockery, Heresy, and the Transubstantiation of Masculinity in 'Telemachus.'" In Devlin and Reizbaum, *"Ulysses"—En-Gendered Perspectives,* 1–19.

Lernout, Geert. *Help My Unbelief: James Joyce and Religion.* London: Continuum, 2010.

Lesky, Albin. "Divine and Human Causation in Homeric Epic." In Cairns, *Oxford Readings,* 170–202.

Lessing, Gotthold Ephraim. *Laocoön: An Essay on the Limits of Painting and Poetry.* 1766. Translated by Edward McCormick. Baltimore: Johns Hopkins University Press, 1984.

Levaniouk, Olga. *Eve of the Festival, Making Myth in Odyssey 19.* Washington, DC: Center for Hellenic Studies, 2011.

Levin, Harry. *James Joyce: A Critical Introduction.* Norfolk, CT: New Direction Books, 1941.

Lewis, Wyndham. *Time and Western Man.* Los Angeles: Black Sparrow Press, 1993.

Lin, Paul. "Standing the Empire: Drinking, Masculinity, and Modernity in Counterparts." In van Boheemen-Saaf and Lamos, *Masculinities in Joyce*, 33–58.

Litz, A. Walton. *The Art of James Joyce: Method and Design in "Ulysses" and "Finnegans Wake."* Oxford: Oxford University Press, 1968.

———. "Early Vestiges of Joyce's 'Ulysses.'" In Gillespie, *Foundational Essays*, 160–71.

———. "The Genre of *Ulysses*." In Reynolds, *James Joyce*, 109–17.

Lloyd, G.E.R. *Polarity and Analogy: Two Types of Argumentation in Early Greek Thought.* Cambridge: Cambridge University Press, 1966.

Lloyd-Jones, Hugh. *The Justice of Zeus.* Berkeley: University of California Press, 1983.

———. "Zeus in Aeschylus." *Journal of Hellenic Studies* 76 (1956): 55–67.

Loney, Alexander. *The Ethics of Revenge and the Meanings of the "Odyssey."* Oxford: Oxford University Press, 2019.

Lord, Albert. *The Singer of Tales.* Cambridge: Cambridge University Press, 1960.

Lord, George de F. "The *Odyssey* and the Western World." In Taylor, *Essays on the "Odyssey,"* 36–53.

Lowenstam, Steven. "The Shroud of Laertes and Penelope's Guile." *Classical Journal* 95 (2000): 333–48.

Mack, Sara. *Patterns of Time in Virgil.* Hamden, CT: Archon, 1978.

MacKay, Anne, ed. *Signs of Orality: The Oral Tradition and Its Influence in the Greek and Roman World.* Leiden: Brill, 1998.

Mackey, Peter Francis. *Chaos Theory and James Joyce's Everyman.* Gainesville: University Press of Florida, 1999.

Macleod, C. W. "Homer on Poetry and the Poetry of Homer." In Cairns, *Oxford Readings*, 294–310.

Maddox, Brenda. *Nora: The Real Life of Molly Bloom.* Boston and New York: Houghton Mifflin, 1988.

Maddox, James Jr. *Joyce's Ulysses and the Assault upon Character.* New Brunswick, NJ: Rutgers University Press, 1978.

———. "Mockery in *Ulysses*." In Reynolds, *James Joyce*, 130–44.

Mahaffey, Vicki. "The Importance of Playing Ernest: The Stakes of Reading *Ulysses*." In McCormick and Steinberg, *Approaches to Teaching Joyce's "Ulysses,"* 139–48.

———. "Intentional Error: The Paradox of Editing Joyce's *Ulysses*." In Attridge, *James Joyce's "Ulysses,"* 231–55.

———. "Joyce and Gender." In Rabaté, *James Joyce Studies*, 121–43.

———. *Reauthorizing Joyce.* Gainesville: University Press of Florida, 1995.

———. "Sidereal Writing: Male Refractions and Malefactions in 'Ithaca.'" In Devlin and Reizbaum, *"Ulysses"—En-Gendered Perspectives*, 254–66.

———. *States of Desire: Wilde, Yeats, Joyce, and the Irish Experiment.* New York: Oxford University Press, 1998.

———. "*Ulysses* and the End of Gender." In van Boheemen-Saaf and Lamos, *Masculinities in Joyce*, 137–62.

Mahaffey, Vicki, and Wendy Truran. "Feeling *Ulysses*: An Address to the Cyclopean Reader." In Kitcher, *Joyce's "Ulysses,"* 100–131.

Mamigonian, Marc. "Hunter and Gatherers: On the Trail of the *Dubliners* "Ulysses" and Its Mysterious Hero." *James Joyce Quarterly* 54 (2016): 13–31.

Manganiello, Dominic. *Joyce's Politics*. London: Routledge, 1980.

———. "Pouring New Wine into Old Bottles: Tolkien, Joyce, and the Modern Epic." In *Tolkien Among the Moderns*, edited by Ralph Wood, 171–93. Notre Dame, IN: University of Notre Dame Press, 2015.

Marks, J. *Zeus in the Odyssey*. Washington, DC: Center for Hellenic Studies, 2008.

Martin, Timothy. "*Ulysses* as a Whole." In Frehner and Zeller, *Collideorscape of Joyce*, 202–14.

McCormick, Kathleen, and Erwin Steinberg, eds. *Approaches to Teaching Joyce's "Ulysses."* New York: Modern Language Association of America, 1993.

McCourt, John. *The Years of Bloom: James Joyce in Trieste 1904–1920*. Dublin: Lilliput Press, 2000.

McGee, Patrick. *Joyce Beyond Marx: History and Desire in "Ulysses" and "Finnegans Wake."* Gainesville: University Press of Florida, 2001.

———. *Paperspace: Style as Ideology in Joyce's "Ulysses."* Lincoln: University of Nebraska Press, 1988.

McMichael, James. *"Ulysses" and Justice*. Princeton, NJ: Princeton University Press, 1991.

Meisel, Perry. *The Myth of the Modern: A Study in British Literature and Criticism after 1850*. New Haven: Yale University Press, 1987.

Mercanton, Jacques. "The Hours of James Joyce." In Potts, *Portraits of the Artist*, 206–52.

Meyenhoff, Hans. *Time in Literature*. Berkeley: University of California Press, 1974.

Mihálycsa, Erika. "'Weighing the Point': A Few Points on the Writing of Finitude in *Ulysses*." In Wawrzycka, *Reading Joycean Temporalities*, 51–66.

Miller, Dean. *The Epic Hero*. Baltimore: Johns Hopkins University Press, 2000.

Miller, Madeline. *Circe*. New York: Hachette Books, 2018.

Minta, Stephen. "Homer and Joyce: The Case of Nausicaa." In Graziosi and Greenwood, *Homer in the Twentieth Century*, 92–119.

Montiglio, Silvia. *Wandering in Ancient Greek Culture*. Chicago: University of Chicago Press, 2005.

Morris, Ian. "The Use and Abuse of Homer." In Cairns, *Homer's "Iliad,"* 57–91.

Morrison, James. "Shipwreck Narratives in Homer's *Odyssey* and Coetzee's *Foe*." In *Kinesis: The Ancient Depiction of Gesture, Motion, and Emotion*, edited by Christina Clark, Edith Foster, and Judith P. Hallett, 235–47. Ann Arbor: University of Michigan Press, 2015.

Morson, Gary Saul. *Narrative and Freedom: The Shadows of Time*. New Haven: Yale University Press, 1994.

Moulton, Carroll. "The End of the Odyssey." *Greek, Roman and Byzantine Studies* 15 (1974): 153–69.

Murnaghan, Sheila. *Disguise and Recognition in the Odyssey*. Princeton, NJ: Princeton University Press: 1987.

———. "Penelope's *Agnoia*: Knowledge, Power, and Gender in the *Odyssey*." In Doherty, *Homer's "Odyssey,"* 231–46.

———. "The Plan of Athena." In Cohen, *Distaff Side*, 61–80.

Nagler, Michael. "Dread Goddess Revisited." In Schein, *Reading the "Odyssey,"* 1–62.

———. "Entretiens Avec Tirésias." *Classical World* 74 (1980): 89–106.

Nagy, Gregory. *The Best of the Achaeans: Concepts of the Hero in Archaic Greek Poetry.* Baltimore: Johns Hopkins University Press, 1979.

———. *Poetry as Performance: Homer and Beyond.* Cambridge: Cambridge University Press, 1996.

Nash, John. *James Joyce and the Act of Reception: Reading, Ireland, and Modernism.* Cambridge: Cambridge University Press, 2006.

Nelson, Stephanie. *Aristophanes and His Tragic Muse: Comedy, Tragedy and the Polis in 5th Century Athens.* Leiden: Brill, 2016.

———. "Bullockbefriending Bards: The Ambivalent Role of Cattle in the *Odyssey* and *Ulysses.*" In Witen and Ebury, "Joyce, Animals and the Nonhuman," 37–60.

———. "Calypso's Choice: Immortality and Heroic Striving in the *Odyssey* and *Ulysses.*" In Breyfogle, *Literary Imagination,* 63–89.

———. *God and the Land: The Metaphysics of Farming in Hesiod and Vergil.* Oxford: Oxford University Press, 1998.

———. "Telling Time: Techniques of Narrative Time in *Ulysses* and the *Odyssey.*" In Wawrzycka, *Reading Joycean Temporalities,* 123–36.

Nilsson, Martin. *Homer and Mycenae.* Philadelphia: University of Pennsylvania Press, 1933.

Nolan, Emer. *Joyce and Nationalism.* New York: Routledge, 1995.

Nooter, Sarah. "The Wooden Horse and the Unmaking of the *Odyssey.*" In King and Doherty, *Thinking the Greeks,* 38–53.

Norris, Margot. "Character, Plot, and Myth." In Latham, *Cambridge Companion to "Ulysses,"* 69–80.

———. "Don't Call Him 'Blazes': Hugh E. Boylan's Narrative Caricature." *James Joyce Quarterly* 48 (2011): 229–49.

———. "Joyce, History, and the Philosophy of History." In Rabaté, *James Joyce Studies,* 203–26 .

———. *Joyce's Web: The Social Unravelling of Modernism.* Austin: University of Texas Press, 1992.

O'Connor, Ulick, ed. *The Joyce We Knew: Memoirs of Joyce.* Dingle, County Kerry: Brandon, 2004.

Oded, Brenda. "The Maternal Ghost in Joyce." *Modern Language Studies* 15 (1985): 40–47.

O'Neill, Christine. "'But time shall be no more': Some Temporal Aspects of *A Portrait of the Artist as a Young Man.*" In Wawrzycka, *Reading Joycean Temporalities,* 110–20.

———, ed. *Inductive Scrutinies: Focus on Joyce.* Dublin: Lilliput Press, 1995.

———, ed. *Joycean Murmoirs: Fritz Senn on James Joyce.* Dublin: Lilliput Press, 2007.

Osborne, Robin. "Homer's Society." In Fowler, *Cambridge Companion to Homer,* 206–19.

Osteen, Mark. *The Economy of "Ulysses": Making Both Ends Meet.* Syracuse: Syracuse University Press, 1995.

Otto, Walter. *The Homeric Gods: The Spiritual Significance of Greek Religion.* 1954. Translated by Moses Hadad. New York: Thames and Hudson, 1979.

Ovid. *Metamorphoses.* Translated by David Raeburn. Introduction by Denis Feeney. London: Penguin Books, 2004.

Pache, Corinne Ondine. "University War Games: Odysseus at Troy." *Harvard Studies in Classical Philology* 100 (2000): 15–23.

Page, Denys. *The Homeric Odyssey.* Oxford: Oxford University Press, 1955.

Palumbo, Donald. "Death and Rebirth, Sexuality, and Fantasy in Homer and Joyce." *Colby Quarterly* 20 (1984): 90–99.

Parandowski, Jan. "Meeting with Joyce." In Potts, *Portraits of the Artist,* 154–62.

Parry, Adam. *The Language of Achilles and Other Papers.* Oxford: Clarendon Press, 1989.

Parry, Hugh. "The *Apologus* of Odysseus: Lies all Lies?" *Phoenix* 48, no. 1 (1994): 1–20.

Parry, Milman. *The Making of Homeric Verse: The Collected Papers of Milman Parry.* Edited by Adam Parry. Oxford: Oxford University Press, 1987.

Pelaschiar, Laura. "Joyce's Art of Silence in *Dubliners* and *A Portrait of the Artist as a Young Man.*" In Wawrzycka and Zanotti, *James Joyce's Silences,* 33–49.

———, ed. *Joyce/Shakespeare.* Syracuse: Syracuse University Press, 2015.

Peradotto, John. *Man in the Middle Voice: Name and Narration in the "Odyssey."* Princeton, NJ: Princeton University Press, 1990.

Pierce, David. "Titles, Translation and Orientation: The Case of *A Portrait of the Artist as a Young Man.*" In Bosinelli and Torresi, *Joyce and/in Translation,* 17–28.

Pizarro, Charito. *Joyce's Vision of Time in "Ulysses": A Juxtaposition of James Joyce's "Ulysses" and Paul Ricoeur's "Time and Narrative."* Hamburg: Verlag Dr. Kovac, 2001.

Pogorzelski, Randall J. "Ghosts of Optimism: Virgil's Parade of Heroes in Joyce's "Circe." *International Journal of the Classical Tradition* 16 (2009): 443–66

———. *Virgil and Joyce: Nationalism and Imperialism in the Aeneid and Ulysses.* Madison: University of Wisconsin Press, 2016.

Porter, James. "Homer: The History of an Idea." In Fowler, *Cambridge Companion to Homer,* 324–43.

Potts, Willard, ed. *Portraits of the Artist in Exile: Recollections of James Joyce by Europeans.* Seattle: University of Washington Press, 1979.

Power, Arthur. *Conversations with James Joyce.* 1974. Reprint, Dublin: Lilliput Press, 1999.

Power, Mary. "The Discovery of Ruby." *James Joyce Quarterly* 18 (1981): 115–21.

Proust, Marcel. *Remembrance of Things Past.* Translated by C. K. Scott Moncrieff, Terence Kilmartin, and Andreas Mayor. 3 vols. New York: Vintage Books, 1982.

Pucci, Pietro. "The Song of the Sirens." In Schein, *Reading the "Odyssey,"* 191–200.

———. *The Song of the Sirens: Essays on Homer.* Lanham, MD: Rowman and Littlefield, 1998.

Purves, A. C. *Space and Time in Ancient Greek Narrative.* Cambridge: Cambridge University Press, 2010.

Quint, David. *Epic and Empire: Politics and Generic Form from Virgil to Milton.* Princeton, NJ: Princeton University Press, 1993.

Raaflaub, Kurt. "Epic and History." In Foley, *Companion to Ancient Epic,* 55–70.

Rabaté, Jean-Michel. "Discussion." In Benstock, *Augmented Ninth,* 204–6.

———. *James Joyce and the Politics of Egoism.* Cambridge: Cambridge University Press, 2001.

———, ed. *James Joyce Studies.* New York: Palgrave Macmillan, 2004.

———. "Paternity, Thy Name is Joy." In Benstock, *Augmented Ninth,* 219–25.

———. "A Portrait of the Artist as a Bogeyman." In Benstock, *Augmented Ninth,* 103–34.

Raleigh, John Henry. *The Chronicle of Leopold and Molly Bloom: "Ulysses" as Narrative.* Berkeley: University of California Press, 1977.

Redfield, James. *Nature and Culture in the Iliad: The Tragedy of Hector.* Chicago: University of Chicago Press, 1975.

———. "The Economic Man." In Doherty, *Homer's "Odyssey,"* 265–87.

Reece, Steve. "The Cretan Odyssey: A Lie Truer than Truth." *American Journal of Philology* 11 (1994): 157–73.

———. "The Proem of the *Iliad:* Homer's Art." In Cairns, *Oxford Readings,* 456–77.

———. *The Stranger's Welcome: Oral Theory and the Aesthetics of the Homeric Hospitality Scene.* Ann Arbor: University of Michigan Press, 1993.

Reinhardt, Karl. "The Adventures in the *Odyssey.*" In Schein, *Reading the "Odyssey,"* 63–132.

———. "The Judgement of Paris." In Wright and Jones, *Homer,* 170–91.

Reizbaum, Marilyn. "When the Saints Come Marching In: Re-Deeming 'Cyclops.'" In Devlin and Reizbaum, *"Ulysses"—En-Gendered Perspectives,* 167–84.

Reynolds, Mary, ed. *James Joyce: A Collection of Critical Essays.* Upper Saddle River, NJ: Prentice-Hall, 1993.

———. *Joyce and Dante.* Princeton, NJ: Princeton University Press, 1981.

Rickard, John. *Joyce's Book of Memory: The Mnemotechnic of Ulysses.* Durham: Duke University Press, 1998.

Ricoeur, Paul. *Time and Narrative.* Translated by Kathleen McLaughlin and David Pellauer. 3 vols. Chicago: University of Chicago Press, 1990.

Riquelme, John Paul. *Teller and Tale in Joyce's Fiction: Oscillating Perspectives.* Baltimore: Johns Hopkins University Press, 1983.

Rodstein, Susan de Sola. "The Rule of the Waves in *Ulysses.*" In Frehner and Zeller, *Collideorscape of Joyce,* 180–200.

de Romilly, Irene. *Time in Greek Tragedy.* Ithaca, NY: Cornell University Press, 1968.

Rise, Thomas Jackson. "'I Do Mince Words Don't I?': *Ulysses* in Tempore Belli." In Armand, *joyceMedia,* 144–51.

Rose, Gilbert. "The Quest of Telemachus," *Transactions of the American Philological Association* 98 (1967): 391–98.

Rose, Peter. "Class Ambivalence in the *Odyssey.*" In Doherty, *Homer's "Odyssey,"* 288–313.

———. *Class in Archaic Greece.* Cambridge: Cambridge University Press, 2012.

Rovelli, Carlo. *The Order of Time.* Translated by Erica Segre and Simon Carnell. New York: Riverhead, 2018.

Russo, Joseph. "Interview and Aftermath: Dream, Fantasy, and Intuition in *Odyssey* 19 and 20." *American Journal of Philology* 103 (1982): 1–21.

Russo, Joseph, Manuel Fernandez-Galiano, and Alfred Heubeck. *A Commentary on Homer's Odyssey.* Vol 3. Books XVII–XXIV. Oxford: Clarendon Press, 1992.

Rutherford, R. B. "From the *Iliad* to the *Odyssey.*" In Cairns, *Oxford Readings,* 117–46.

———, ed. *The Odyssey: Books XIX and XX.* By Homer. Cambridge: Cambridge University Press, 1992.

———. "Tragic Form and Feeling in the *Iliad.*" In Cairns, *Oxford Readings,* 260–93.

Sabatini, Federico. "James Joyce and Giordano Bruno." In Ferrer, Slote, and Topia, *Renascent Joyce.*

Saïd, Suzanne. *Homer and the "Odyssey."* Oxford: Oxford University Press, 2011.

Saint-Amour, Paul. "'The Imprevidibility of the Future': On Joycean Prophecy." In Ferrer, Slote, and Topia, *Renascent Joyce,* 90–104.

Schein, Seth. "Female Representations and Interpreting the *Odyssey.*" In Cohen, *Distaff Side,* 17–27.

———. *The Mortal Hero: An Introduction to Homer's "Iliad."* Berkeley: University of California Press, 1984.

———, ed. *Reading the "Odyssey": Selected Interpretive Essays.* Princeton, NJ: Princeton University Press, 1996.

Schneider, Ulrich. "'A Rollicking Rattling Song of the Halls': Joyce and the Music Hall." In Bauerle, *Picking Up Airs,* 67–104.

Schork, R. J. *Greek and Hellenistic Culture in Joyce.* Gainesville: University Press of Florida, 1998.

———. *Latin and Roman Culture in Joyce.* Gainesville: University Press of Florida, 1997.

Scodel, Ruth. *Listening to Homer: Tradition, Narrative, and Audience.* Ann Arbor: University of Michigan Press, 2002.

Scott, Bonnie Kime. "Diversions from Mastery in 'Wandering Rocks.'" In Devlin and Reizbaum, *"Ulysses"—En-Gendered Perspectives,* 136–49.

———. *James Joyce.* Atlantic Highlands, NJ: Humanities Press International, 1987.

———. *Joyce and Feminism.* Bloomington: Indiana University Press, 1984.

Scully, Stephen. *Homer and the Sacred City.* Ithaca, NY: Cornell University Press, 1990.

Segal, Charles. "*Kleos* and Its Ironies in *The Odyssey.*" *L'Antiquité Classique* 52 (1983): 22–47. Also in Schein, *Reading the "Odyssey,"* 201–22.

———. "The Phaeacians and the Symbolism of Odysseus' Return." *Arion: A Journal of Humanities and the Classics* 1 (1962): 17–64.

Seidel, Michael. *Epic Geography: James Joyce's Ulysses.* Princeton, NJ: Princeton University Press, 1976.

Senn, Fritz. "Active Silences." In Wawrzycka and Zanotti, *James Joyce's Silences,* 13–31.

———. "Bloom among the Orators: The Why and Wherefore and All the Codology." *Irish Renaissance Annual* 1 (1989): 168–90.

———. "Book of Many Turns." In Attridge, *James Joyce's "Ulysses,"* 33–54.

———. "History as Text in Reverse." In Wollaeger, Luftig, and Spoo, *Subject of History,* 47–58.

———. *Inductive Scrutinies: Focus on Joyce.* Edited by Christine O'Neill. Dublin: Lilliput Press, 1995.

———. *Joyce's Dislocutions: Essays on Reading as Translation.* Edited by John Paul Riquelme. Baltimore: Johns Hopkins University Press, 1984.

———. *Joycean Murmoirs: Fritz Senn on James Joyce.* Edited by Christine O'Neill. Dublin: Lilliput Press, 2007.

———. *Portals of Recovery.* Edited by Erika Mihálycsa and Jolanta Wawrzycka. Roma: Bulzoni Editore, 2017.

———. "Remodeling Homer." In *Inductive Scrutinies: Focus on Joyce,* edited by Christine O'Neill, 111–32. Dublin: Lilliput Press, 1995.

———. "Seemaultaneously sysentangled" (*FW* 161.12): Tales Told of Nebeneinander and Nacheinander." In Wawrzycka, *Reading Joycean Temporalities,* 31–50.

Shakespeare, William. *Hamlet.* Edited by Sylvan Barnet. New York: Signet Classics, 1998.

———. *The Winter's Tale*. Edited by Sylvan Barnet. New York: Signet Classics, 1998.

Shaw, Julia. *The Memory Illusion*. London: Random House, 2016.

Sherry, Vincent. *The Great War and the Language of Modernism*. Oxford: Oxford University Press, 2003.

Shloss, Carol Loeb. *Lucia Joyce: To Dance in the Wake*. New York: Bloomsbury, 2004.

Silk, Michael. "The *Odyssey* and Its Explorations." In Fowler, *Cambridge Companion to Homer*, 31–44.

Slatkin, Laura. "Composition by Theme and the Mētis of the *Odyssey*." In Schein, *Reading the "Odyssey,"* 223–37.

———. *The Power of Thetis and Selected Essays*. Washington, DC: Center for Hellenic Studies, 2011.

Slote, Sam. "All the Way from Gibraltar." *James Joyce Quarterly* 57 (2019–20): 81–92.

———. *Joyce's Nietzschean Ethics*. New York: Palgrave Macmillan, 2013.

———. "Loving the Alien: Egoism, Empathy, Alterity, and Shakespeare Bloom in Stephen's Aesthetics." In Pelaschiar, *Joyce/Shakespeare*, 128–39.

Somer, John. "The Self-Reflexive Arranger in the Initial Style of Joyce's "Ulysses." *James Joyce Quarterly* 31 (1994): 65–79.

Snell, Bruno. *The Discovery of the Mind*. Translated by T. G. Rosenmeyer. Oxford: Oxford University Press, 1953

Spoo, Robert. *James Joyce and the Language of History: Dedalus's Nightmare*. Oxford: Oxford University Press, 1994.

Stanford, W. B., ed. *Homer: Odyssey I–XII*. Vol. 1. London: Bristol Classical Press, 1996.

———, ed. *Homer: Odyssey XIII–XXIV*. Vol. 2. London: Bristol Classical Press, 1996.

———. *The Ulysses Theme: A Study in the Adaptability of a Traditional Hero*. Basil Blackwell: Oxford, 1954.

Staten, Henry. "The Decomposing Form of Joyce's *Ulysses*." In Attridge, *James Joyce's "Ulysses,"* 173–200.

Steiner, Deborah, ed. *Odyssey Books XVII–XVIII*. By Homer. Cambridge: Cambridge University Press, 2010.

Steiner, George. "Homer in English Translation." In Fowler, *Cambridge Companion to Homer*, 363–75.

Stevenson, Randall. *Reading the Times: Temporality and History in Twentieth-Century Fiction*. Edinburgh: Edinburgh University Press, 2019.

Sullivan, Shirley. *Psychological Activity in Homer: A Study of Phrên*. Ottawa: McGill-Queen's University Press, 1998.

Sultan, Stanley. *The Argument of Ulysses*. Columbus: Ohio State University Press, 1964.

———. *Eliot, Joyce and Company*. Oxford: Oxford University Press. 1987.

Suzuki, Mihoko. *Metamorphoses of Helen: Authority, Difference and the Epic*. Ithaca, NY: Cornell University Press, 1989.

———. "Rewriting the "Odyssey" in the Twenty-First Century: Mary Zimmerman's "Odyssey" and Margaret Atwood's "Penelopiad."" In *Reading Homer in the 21st Century. College Literature* 34 (2007): 263–78.

Svevo, Italo. *James Joyce*. Translated by Stanislaus Joyce. San Francisco: City Lights Books, 1969.

Taplin, Oliver. *Homeric Soundings: The Shaping of the Iliad.* Oxford: Oxford University Press, 1992.

Taylor, Charles, Jr., ed. *Essays on the "Odyssey": Selected Modern Criticism.* Bloomington: Indiana University Press, 1969.

Thacker, Andrew. *Moving through Modernity: Space and Geography in Modernism.* Manchester: Manchester University Press, 2009.

Theoharis, Theoharis Constantine. *Joyce's "Ulysses": An Anatomy of the Soul.* Chapel Hill: University of North Carolina Press, 1988.

Thornton, Weldon. *Allusions in "Ulysses": An Annotated List.* Chapel Hill: University of North Carolina Press, 1968.

———. *The Antimodernism of Joyce's Portrait of the Artist as a Young Man.* Syracuse, NY: Syracuse University Press, 1994.

Thrane, James R. "Joyce's Sermon on Hell: Its Source and Its Backgrounds. In Gillespie, *Foundational Essays,* 85–124.

Thwaites, Tony. *Joycean Temporalities: Debts, Promises, and Countersignatures.* Gainesville: University Press of Florida, 2001.

Tracy, Stephen. *The Story of the "Odyssey."* Princeton, NJ: Princeton University Press, 1990.

Underwood, Charles. *Mythos and Voice: Displacement, Learning, and Agency in Odysseus' World.* Lanham, MD: Lexington Books, 2018.

Ungar, Andras. *Joyce's Ulysses as National Epic.* Gainesville: University Press of Florida, 2002.

Valente, Joseph. "Joyce's Politics: Race, Nation, and Transnationalism." In Rabaté, *James Joyce Studies,* 73–96.

———. "The Perils of Masculinity in 'Scylla and Charybdis.'" In Devlin and Reizbaum, *"Ulysses"—En-Gendered Perspectives,* 111–35.

Vandiver, Elizabeth. *Stand in the Trench, Achilles: Classical Receptions in British Poetry of the Great War.* Oxford: Oxford University Press, 2010.

Van Nortwick, Thomas. *The Unknown Odysseus: Alternate Worlds in Homer's "Odyssey."* Ann Arbor: University of Michigan Press, 2008.

van Velze, Jan. "Noticeably Longsighted from Green Youth": Ocular Proof of James Joyce's True Refractive Error." *James Joyce Quarterly* 54 (2017): 45–65.

Vernant, Jean-Pierre. "A 'Beautiful Death' and the Disfigured Corpse in Homeric Epic." In Cairns, *Oxford Readings in Homer's "Iliad,"* 311–41.

Versenyi, Laszlo. *Man's Measure: A Study of the Greek Image of Man from Homer to Sophocles.* Albany: State University of New York Press, 1972.

Veyne, Paul. *Did the Greeks Believe in Their Myths?* Translated by Paula Wissing. Chicago: University of Chicago Press, 1988.

Vidal-Naquet, Pierre. "Land and Sacrifice in the *Odyssey:* A Study of Religious and Mythical Meanings." In Schein, *Reading the "Odyssey,"* 33–53.

Volpone, Annalisa. "'Come, hours be ours!': Temporal Disharmonies in Joyce's Sense of Time." In Wawrzycka, *Reading Joycean Temporalities,* 137–52.

Walcott, Peter. "Odysseus and the Art of Lying." In Doherty, *Homer's "Odyssey,"* 135–54.

Watkins, Calvert. *How to Kill a Dragon: Aspects of Indo-European Poetics.* Oxford: Oxford University Press, 1995.

Wawrzycka, Jolanta, ed. *Reading Joycean Temporalities*. Leiden: Brill, 2018.

Wawrzycka, Jolanta, and Serenella Zanotti, eds. *James Joyce's Silences*. London: Bloomsbury, 2018.

Weil, Simone, "The *Iliad*, or the Poem of Force." Translated by Mary McCarthy. *Chicago Review* 18 (1965): 5–30.

Weir, David. *"Ulysses" Explained: How Homer, Dante, and Shakespeare Inform Joyce's Modernist Vision*. New York: Palgrave Macmillan, 2015.

Wender, Dorothea. *The Last Scenes of the Odyssey*. Leiden: Brill, 1978.

West, M. L. *The Epic Cycle: A Commentary on the Lost Troy Epics*. Oxford: Oxford University Press, 2013.

———. "The Homeric Question Today." *Proceedings of the American Philosophical Society* 155 (2011): 383–93.

West, Stephanie. "Commentary Books I–IV." In Heubeck, West, and Hainsworth, *A Commentary*, vol. 1, 51–245.

Weygandt, Cornelius. *Irish Plays and Playwrights*. Boston: Houghton Mifflin, 1913.

Whitman, Cedric. *Homer and the Heroic Tradition*. Cambridge, MA: Harvard University Press, 1958.

Williams, Trevor. "Dominant Ideologies: The Production of Stephen Dedalus." In Benstock, *Augmented Ninth*, 312–22 .

Wilson, Emily, trans. *The Odyssey*. By Homer. New York: W. W. Norton, 2018.

Winant, Johanna. "Empathy and Other Minds in *Ulysses*." *James Joyce Quarterly* 55 (2018): 371–90.

Winkler, John. *The Constraints of Desire: The Anthropology of Sex and Gender in Ancient Greece*. New York: Routledge, 1991.

Winston, Greg. *Joyce and Militarism*. Gainesville: University Press of Florida, 2012.

Witen, Michelle. *James Joyce and Absolute Music*. London: Bloomsbury Academic, 2019.

Witen, Michelle, and Katherine Ebury, eds. "Joyce, Animals and the Nonhuman." Special issue, *James Joyce Quarterly* 58, nos. 1–2 (2020–21).

Wohl, Victoria. "Standing by the Stathmos: The Creation of Sexual Ideology in the *Odyssey*." *Arethusa* 26 (1993): 19–50.

Wollaeger, Mark. "Seduction and Estrangement: World War I Recruiting Posters and the Politics of *Ulysses*." *Hypermedia Joyce Studies*, no. 2 (1999), http://hjs.ff.cuni.cz/ archives/v2/wollaeger/index.html.

Wollaeger, Mark, Victor Luftig, and Robert Spoo, eds. *Joyce and the Subject of History*. Ann Arbor: University of Michigan Press, 1996.

Wright, G. M., and P. V. Jones, eds. *Homer: German Scholarship in Translation*. Oxford: Oxford University Press, 1997.

Zaborowski, Robert. "Tadeusz Zieliński and the Homeric Psychology." *Eos* 90 (2003): 291–300.

Zajko, Vanda. "Homer and *Ulysses*." In Fowler, *Cambridge Companion to Homer*, 311–23.

Zeitlin, Froma. "Figuring Fidelity in Homer's *Odyssey*." In Cohen, *Distaff Side*, 117–52.

Zieliński, Tadeusz. "Homeric Psychology." 1922. *Organon* 3 (2002): 15–45.

Zweig, Stefan. *The World of Yesterday*. 1942. Translated by Anthea Bell. Lincoln: University of Nebraska Press, 2013.

Index

STEPHANIE NELSON is professor of classical studies at Boston University. She has written on subjects ranging from narrative time to translation and the relation of philosophy and literature. Her work includes *God and the Land: The Metaphysics of Farming in Hesiod and Vergil* and *Aristophanes and His Tragic Muse: Comedy, Tragedy and the Polis in 5th Century Athens*, along with numerous talks and articles on the relation of Joyce's *Ulysses* and the *Odyssey*.

THE FLORIDA JAMES JOYCE SERIES

Edited by Sebastian D. G. Knowles

Joyce in Trieste: An Album of Risky Readings, edited by Sebastian D. G. Knowles, Geert Lernout, and John McCourt (2007)

Joyce's Rare View: The Nature of Things in "Finnegans Wake," by Richard Beckman (2007)

Joyce's Misbelief, by Roy Gottfried (2008)

James Joyce's Painful Case, by Cóilín Owens (2008; first paperback edition, 2017)

Cannibal Joyce, by Thomas Jackson Rice (2008)

Manuscript Genetics, Joyce's Know-How, Beckett's Nohow, by Dirk Van Hulle (2008)

Catholic Nostalgia in Joyce and Company, by Mary Lowe-Evans (2008)

A Guide through "Finnegans Wake," by Edmund Lloyd Epstein (2009)

Bloomsday 100: Essays on "Ulysses," edited by Morris Beja and Anne Fogarty (2009)

Joyce, Medicine, and Modernity, by Vike Martina Plock (2010; first paperback edition, 2012)

Who's Afraid of James Joyce?, by Karen R. Lawrence (2010; first paperback edition, 2012)

"Ulysses" in Focus: Genetic, Textual, and Personal Views, by Michael Groden (2010; first paperback edition, 2012)

Foundational Essays in James Joyce Studies, edited by Michael Patrick Gillespie (2011; first paperback edition, 2017)

Empire and Pilgrimage in Conrad and Joyce, by Agata Szczeszak-Brewer (2011; first paperback edition, 2017)

The Poetry of James Joyce Reconsidered, edited by Marc C. Conner (2012; first paperback edition, 2015)

The German Joyce, by Robert K. Weninger (2012; first paperback edition, 2016)

Joyce and Militarism, by Greg Winston (2012; first paperback edition, 2015)

Renascent Joyce, edited by Daniel Ferrer, Sam Slote, and André Topia (2013; first paperback edition, 2014)

Before Daybreak: "After the Race" and the Origins of Joyce's Art, by Cóilín Owens (2013; first paperback edition, 2015)

Modernists at Odds: Reconsidering Joyce and Lawrence, edited by Matthew J. Kochis and Heather L. Lusty (2015; first paperback edition, 2020)

James Joyce and the Exilic Imagination, by Michael Patrick Gillespie (2015)

The Ecology of "Finnegans Wake," by Alison Lacivita (2015; first paperback edition, 2021)

Joyce's Allmaziful Pluralities: Polyvocal Explorations of "Finnegans Wake," edited by Kimberly J. Devlin and Christine Smedley (2015; first paperback edition, 2018)

Exiles: A Critical Edition, by James Joyce, edited by A. Nicholas Fargnoli and Michael Patrick Gillespie (2016; first paperback edition, 2019)

Up to Maughty London: Joyce's Cultural Capital in the Imperial Metropolis, by Eleni Loukopoulou (2017)

Joyce and the Law, edited by Jonathan Goldman (2017; first paperback edition, 2020)

At Fault: Joyce and the Crisis of the Modern University, by Sebastian D. G. Knowles (2018; first paperback edition, 2021)

"Ulysses" Unbound: A Reader's Companion to James Joyce's "Ulysses," Third Edition, by Terence Killeen (2018)

Joyce and Geometry, by Ciaran McMorran (2020)

Panepiphanal World: James Joyce's Epiphanies, by Sangam MacDuff (2020)

Language as Prayer in "Finnegans Wake," by Colleen Jaurretche (2020)

Rewriting Joyce's Europe: The Politics of Language and Visual Design, by Tekla Mecsnóber (2021)

Joyce Writing Disability, edited by Jeremy Colangelo (2022)

Joyce, Aristotle, and Aquinas, by Fran O'Rourke (2022)

Time and Identity in "Ulysses" and the "Odyssey," by Stephanie Nelson (2022)

Printed in the USA
CPSIA information can be obtained
at www.ICGtesting.com
LVHW041120270823
756430LV00003B/14